DOES
WHO GOVERNS
MATTER?

INTERNATIONAL YEARBOOK FOR STUDIES OF LEADERS AND LEADERSHIP

A Northern Illinois University Series

DOES
WHO GOVERNS
MATTER?

Elite Circulation in Contemporary Societies

Edited by

Moshe M. Czudnowski

Northern Illinois University Press

Library of Congress Cataloging in Publication Data

Main entry under title:

Does who governs matter?

(International yearbook for studies of leaders and
leadership)
Papers presented at the International Mosca
Centennial Conference, held Sept. 1981, at Northern
Illinois University.
1. Elite (Social sciences)—Congresses. 2. Power
(Social sciences)—Congresses. 3. Comparative govern-
ment—Congresses. I. Czudnowski, Moshe M., 1924–
II. International Mosca Centennial Conference (1981 :
Northern Illinois University) III. Series.
JC330.D63 1982   305.5'2   82-22495
ISBN 0-87580-085-8
ISBN 0-87580-529-9 (pbk.)

Copyright © 1982 by Northern Illinois University Press
Published by the Northern Illinois University Press, DeKalb, Illinois 60115

Design by Leslie Wildrick

CONTENTS

CONTRIBUTORS

Volumes 1 and 2

Juan J. Baldrich is assistant professor of sociology at the University of Puerto Rico, where he has taught since 1978. From 1973 to 1977, he was a predoctoral fellow in the Yale University Comparative Sociology Training Program, doing research for a period in Jamaica. In 1981 he received his Ph.D. degree from Yale. He is the author of *Class and State: The Origins of Populism in Puerto Rico, 1934–1952.*

Wendell Bell has been professor of sociology at Yale University since 1963, serving as chairman of the department during 1965–1969 and directing the Comparative Sociology Training Program during 1969–1977. He has also served on the faculties of UCLA, Northwestern University, and Stanford University, after receiving his Ph.D. degree in 1952 from UCLA. His publications include *Social Area Analysis* (1965), *Public Leadership* (1961), *Jamaican Leaders* (1964), *Decisions of Nationhood* (1964), *The Democratic Revolution in the West Indies* (1967), *The Sociology of the Future* (1971), and *Ethnicity and Nation-Building* (1974). He is continuing his research in the Commonwealth Caribbean and his comparative studies of England and the United States, focusing primarily on inequality and social justice, race and class, and social change and futuristics.

Roland Cayrol is a member of the Fondation Nationale des Sciences Politiques, where his work focuses on the study of political elites and political personnel and also on the mass media in politics. He is professor at the Institut d'Etudes Politiques of Paris and serves as an advisor to the polling organization Louis Harris France. He is the author of the book *François Mitterrand 1945–1967* (Presses de la FNSP, 1967) and the coauthor (with Jean-Luc Parodi and Colette Ysmal) of *Le Député Français* (A. Colin, 1973). He has published many articles about French militants, mostly in *Revue Française de Science Politique* and *Projet*. He directs, with Karlheinz Reif, a cross-national survey of party congress delegates among 50 parties in Western Europe.

Harold D. Clarke is professor of political science and department head, Virginia Polytechnic Institute and State University. He is coauthor of *Political Choice in Canada, Citizen Politicians—Canada,* and *Representative Democracy in the Canadian Provinces,* and coeditor of *Parlia-*

ment, *Policy and Representation* and *Political Support in Canada: The Crisis Years.* His articles have appeared in journals such as the *American Journal of Political Science,* the *British Journal of Political Science,* the *Canadian Journal of Political Science, Comparative Politics,* and *Comparative Political Studies.*

Maurizio Cotta is associate professor of political science at the University of Siena. He has studied political science at the University of Florence with Giovanni Sartori and has recently spent a year as visiting fellow at Yale University. His major research interests have been in the field of legislative institutions and parliamentary elites. On these subjects he is author of the book *Classe politica e parlamento in Italia, 1946–1976.* He is currently engaged in comparative research on party system change in postauthoritarian democracies.

Moshe M. Czudnowski received his doctoral degree from the Sorbonne, Paris. Between 1959 and 1971, he was a member of the political science department at the Hebrew University in Jerusalem and held various visiting appointments in the United States, England, and West Germany. Since 1971 he has been professor of political science at Northern Illinois University. His works include books, book chapters, and journal articles on political recruitment, the social psychology of elites, and the methodology of comparative political analysis. He is cosponsor and managing editor of the International Yearbook for Studies of Leaders and Leadership.

Hans Daalder has been professor of political science at Leiden University since 1963. He received his doctorate from the University of Amsterdam in 1960, which was later published as *Cabinet Reform in Britain, 1914–1963* (Stanford University Press, 1963). From 1976 to 1979, he was head of the department of political and social sciences of the European University Institute, Florence, Italy. His major research interests are comparative European politics, elite analysis, legislative behavior, and party systems. At present he is one of the directors of a comparative study of changes in European party systems since 1945, sponsored by the European Consortium for Political Research. He is a founding member of this organization and served as its chairman from 1976 to 1979.

Salustiano del Campo is professor of sociology and head of the department of social structure at the University of Madrid. His books include *El ciclo vital de la familia espanola* (1980), *La cuestión regional española* (with Manuel Navarro y José Félix Tezanos) (1977), *Análisis de la población de España* (second edition, 1975), and *Cambios sociales y formas de vida* (second edition, 1973). He has edited *La Sociedad* (published in 1972 and currently out of print) and *Diccionario de Ciencias Sociales* in two volumes, sponsored by UNESCO and published in 1975–1976.

Samuel J. Eldersveld has been professor at the University of Michigan since 1946, specializing in American and comparative political parties, and elites and mass behavior. In 1964 he published *Political Parties: A Behavioral Analysis*, and more recently he has published *Citizens and Politics: Mass Political Behavior in India* (1978) (with Bashir Ahmed), and *Elite Images of Dutch Politics: Accommodation and Conflict* (1981) (with Jan Kooiman and Theo van der Tak).

Heinz Eulau is William Bennet Munro Professor and chair of the department of political science at Stanford University. A former president of the American Political Science Association, he now chairs the Board of Overseers, National Election Studies, Center for Political Studies at the University of Michigan; and he serves as an associate director of the Inter-University Consortium for Political and Social Research. A member of the American Academy of Arts and Sciences, he is the author or coauthor of many books and articles, including *The Legislative System* (1962), *The Behavioral Persuasion in Politics* (1963), *Micro-Macro Political Analysis* (1969), *Labyrinths of Democracy* (1973), *Technology and Civility* (1977), and *The Politics of Representation* (1978). Since 1980 he has been editor of the journal *Political Behavior*.

Bohdan Harasymiw, associate professor of political science at the University of Calgary, has published a number of articles on leadership and recruitment in the USSR. Among these have been his seminal explorations of the unique Soviet political patronage system, the *nomenklatura*, which appeared in the *Canadian Journal of Political Science* (1969) and *Osteuropa* (1977). He is a former secretary-treasurer and president of the Canadian Association of Slavists.

Suzanne Keller is professor of sociology at Princeton University. She received her Ph.D. degree from Columbia University in 1955. Dr. Keller has worked as a survey analyst and translator in Paris, Munich, Vienna, and Athens. She has received both a Fulbright and a Guggenheim award. Her interests include the planning of new communities, futurism, and the study of social hierarchies and elites. Her many publications include a 1981 study, *Building for Women*, for which she was the editor; a forthcoming publication, "Social Differentiation and Social Stratification: The Special Case of Gender"; and the pioneering study of elites, *Beyond the Ruling Class* (Random House, 1963). Dr. Keller was the first woman to be awarded tenure at Princeton University.

Michael Keren has been a lecturer at Tel Aviv University since 1975, at which time he received his Ph.D. in political science from the University of Minnesota. His major field of interest is "knowledge and power" in the context of societal policy making. Recent articles in this field have been published in *Policy Sciences, Behavioral Science,* and

Knowledge. Between 1978 and 1980, Keren was a research fellow at the Ben Gurion Research Institute and Archives at Sde Boker, Israel, where he was granted first access to Ben Gurion's private papers. His book, *Ben Gurion and the Intellectuals: Power, Knowledge, and Charisma* is forthcoming from Northern Illinois University Press.

Chong Lim Kim is professor of political science and associate director of the Comparative Legislative Research Center of the University of Iowa. His recent publications include *Legislative Connection: The Politics of Representation in Kenya, Korea, and Turkey* (Duke University Press, forthcoming); *Legislative Systems in Developing Countries* (Duke University Press, 1975); and *Political Participation in Korea* (ABC-Clio Press, 1980). He has also published articles in *American Political Science Review*, *American Journal of Political Science*, *American Politics Quarterly*, *Comparative Political Studies*, *Comparative Politics*, and *Legislative Studies Quarterly*.

Allan Kornberg is professor of political science at Duke University. He is author of *Canadian Legislative Behavior, Influence in Parliament: Canada* (with William Mishler), and *Citizen Politicians—Canada* (with Joel Smith and Harold Clarke). He also is coauthor and editor of *Legislatures in Developmental Perspective*, *Legislatures in Comparative Perspective*, and *Political Support in Canada: The Crisis Years*. He has contributed numerous articles to journals such as the *American Political Science Review*, the *British Journal of Political Science*, *Canadian Journal of Political Science*, and *The Journal of Politics*.

J. A. Laponce is professor of political science at the University of British Columbia, Vancouver, Canada. His main interests are the study of political perceptions, ethnic conflicts, and experimentation on small groups. His main works include *The Protection of Minorities* (1961), *The Government of France under the Fifth Republic* (1962), *People vs. Politics* (1970), and *Left and Right: The Topology of Political Perceptions* (1981).

Keith Legg (Ph.D., University of California, Berkeley) is professor of political science at the University of Florida. He has written extensively on Greek politics, including *Politics in Modern Greece* (Stanford University Press, 1969) and on political clientelism.

Peter McDonough is senior study director at the center for political studies, Institute for Social Research, University of Michigan. He is author of *Power and Ideology in Brazil*, *The Politics of Population in Brazil*, and of articles on Spain, Portugal, India, and Pakistan.

Dwaine Marvick is professor of political science at the University of California, Los Angeles. He is the author of *Career Perspectives in a*

Bureaucratic Setting, Competitive Pressure and Democratic Consent (with Morris Janowitz), and editor of *Political Decision Makers: Recruitment and Performance* and *Harold D. Lasswell on Political Sociology.* His writings on political recruitment and party activists have appeared in a wide range of journals and symposia. He is secretary of the Research Committee on Political Elites of the International Political Science Association.

Samuel C. Patterson, professor of political science at the University of Iowa, has been interested primarily in legislative elites. His books include: *The Legislative Process in the United States* (3rd ed., 1977, with M. E. Jewell); *Comparative Legislative Behavior: Frontiers of Research* (1972, coedited with J. C. Wahlke); *Representatives and Represented* (1975, with R. D. Hedlund and G. R. Boynton); and *Comparing Legislatures* (1979, with G. Loewenberg). His current work focuses on comparative analysis of legislator selection, focusing on state legislative elections in the United States. He has served as editor of the *American Journal of Political Science* and currently serves as coeditor of the *Legislative Studies Quarterly.* In 1980–1981, he was president of the Midwest Political Science Association.

Pascal Perrineau is doing research at the Centre d'Etude de la Vie Politique Française contemporaine (Fondation Nationale des Sciences Politiques, Paris) and is Maître de Conférence at the Institut d'Etudes Politiques de Paris. His main interests are the French Socialist party and voting behavior. He received his Doctorat d'Etat de Science Politique for a study of the electoral consequences of urban change in France under the Fifth Republic. He has contributed to several joint works devoted to democratic socialism, the most recent, *Eurocommunism and Transition in Western Europe: A Comparative Analysis*, published in London in 1982.

Thomas Rochon is an assistant professor in the department of politics at Princeton University. He is the author of articles on Dutch and Japanese political behavior and a forthcoming book on political activists in the Netherlands. He is currently working on a study of governmental response to citizens' movements in Western Europe.

Walter Santin is assistant professor of sociology at the University of Madrid and is working on his Ph.D. dissertation.

John R. Schmidhauser received his Ph.D. degree from the University of Virginia in 1954. He taught constitutional law and judicial process, as well as American government, at the University of Iowa from 1954 to 1973. He was a senior fellow in law and behavioral sciences at the University of Chicago Law School in the academic year 1959–1960.

Since 1973, he has been professor of political science (chairman of the department in 1973–1975 and 1977–1980) at the University of Southern California. Schmidhauser served as a member of the U.S. House of Representatives representing the 1st District of Iowa in 1965–1967 (89th Congress). His publications include *Constitutional Law in the Political Process* (Rand McNally, 1963), *Judges and Justices: The Federal Appellate Judiciary* (Little, Brown and Company, 1979), and numerous articles in political science and legal journals.

Edward Shils is Distinguished Service Professor in the Committee on Social Thought and in the department of sociology at the University of Chicago and Honorary Fellow of Peterhouse, Cambridge, England. His most recent major works include a collection of his selected papers, *Intellectuals and the Powers* (vol. 1, 1972), *Center and Periphery* (vol. 2, 1975), and *The Calling of Sociology* (vol. 3, 1980); and *Tradition* (1981) and *The Constitution of Society* (1982).

José Félix Tezanos is associate professor of sociology at the University of Madrid. His works include *Estructura de classes y conflictos de poder en la España postfranquista* (Madrid, 1978) and *Alienacion, dialectica y libertad* (1977).

Joop Th. J. van den Berg has been director of the Dr. Wiardi Beckman-stichting, the Research Office of the Dutch Labour party, since 1981. He was appointed in 1971 to a teaching and research post in the field of parliamentary history at Leiden University. He is the joint author of a critical study of Dutch politics, *Crisis in de Nederlandse Politiek* (1974) and of a study of the working of the Dutch Parliament. He has recently completed a doctoral dissertation at Leiden University on the social background of members of the Dutch Lower House from 1848 to 1967.

Klaus von Beyme studied political science, sociology, and history at the universities of Heidelberg, Munich, Paris, and Moscow. He has been professor of political science at the University of Heidelberg since 1974. From 1973–1975 he served as president of the German Political Science Association. His major publications include *Challenge to Power: Trade Unions and Industrial Relations in Capitalist Countries* (Sage, 1977) and *Political Parties in Western Democracies* (St. Martin's Press, forthcoming). He is also editor of *German Political Studies* (published by Sage). He has published numerous articles in such journals as *German Studies Review, Government and Opposition, International Political Science Review,* and the *Journal of Politics.* Von Beyme is currently the president of the International Political Science Association.

DOES
WHO GOVERNS
MATTER?

Introduction: A Statement of the Issues

Moshe M. Czudnowski

This is the first of two volumes of political elite studies resulting from the International Mosca Centennial Conference held in September 1981 at Northern Illinois University, with the participation of thirty-five scholars from fourteen countries. This conference also provided the incentive for the establishment of the *International Yearbook for Studies of Leaders and Leadership*, a series intended to serve as a forum for research reports on the study of social and political leaders across nations and as a vehicle for the promotion of individual and collaborative research. The two volumes of the Mosca Centennial papers constitute the beginning of this *Yearbook* series.

The theme common to the studies published in this first volume, under the title *Does Who Governs Matter?*, is, in the phrase coined by Vilfredo Pareto, the "circulation of elites." An additional focus is provided by the fact that the data-based papers in this volume examine political elites in European countries, with an emphasis on a longitudinal perspective. Two theoretically and historically oriented papers precede the case studies: Shils's critical assessment of political elite roles in contemporary societies and Schmidhauser's discussion of two competing interpretations of the circulation of judicial elites. Shils's main argument will be more appropriately put into perspective after a survey of the major dimensions underlying the case studies in this volume. Schmidhauser juxtaposes Weber's model of the formal, rational, and politically independent legal system conceived as a neutral mechanism for conflict resolution to a model based on political and economic world-systems reflecting center-periphery relations and processes of penetration and domination; in the latter model, the legal system protects the interests and institutions essential to the functioning of the "core" nations and their economies. These competing models are the frameworks for a longitudinal examination of the circulation of judicial elites in two sets of nations. Schmidhauser's study sets the stage for a series of more detailed and extensive investigations.

Does Who Governs Matter? is not meant to be a rhetorical question. It is intended to indicate a perceived need to articulate the theoretical and empirical parameters within which "does who governs matter?" is a legitimate question and the answer thereto a relevant finding. As so frequently happens in the academic enterprise, this is not how or why this collective effort began; these studies offer at best some partial and tentative answers. In fact, the purpose of the Mosca Centennial Conference was to monitor the current state of the art and to allow for an evaluation of desirable theoretical goals and directions of research; this is also the purpose of presenting these studies to the reader. In doing so, it might be useful to examine some of the issues suggested by the title question of this volume.

Critics of the predominant patterns in recruitment and elite studies have pointed out that the preoccupation with social background characteristics and career ladders of politicians is theoretically barren unless it posits—and attempts to demonstrate—relationships between such characteristics on the one hand and policy positions and outcomes on the other. In response to this criticism it has to be said that no promising hypotheses about such relationships can be suggested without the information and analyses provided by these patterns of studies, and, many observed regularities notwithstanding, this information reveals a complex and changing scene. Obviously, the question "does who governs matter?" is central to the preoccupations of this field of the discipline, and it has been asked. This, by itself, indicates a stage of maturation in a field which believes that its efforts are not trivial and is therefore shifting its focus to issues of relevance in the next stage of its development. Theoretical relevance is, of course, the goal of any scholarly enterprise; but to reach the theory-building stage one needs building-blocks and road signs, and these are provided by case studies. The need for such road signs is particularly great in the study of political elites, given the dynamic characteristics of societies and social organizations—changes in social stratification systems, modernization, the increasing complexity of government, etc. The relevance of "who governs?" is very sensitive to change in social and cultural infrastructures, and to the rate of such change; so is the second half of the question, i.e., "does it matter?" What the association is between rates of change in social input and rates of change in political output is, of course, an empirical matter and one of the major objectives of elite studies.

Subdividing the question into "who governs?" and "with what consequences?" is not only a useful device for identifying the relevant variables and parameters; it also illustrates two approaches to the study of the impact of governing elites. Traditional political science, following the "founding fathers" of modern political sociology—Mosca, Pareto, Weber, Michels—represents what may be termed the sociological approach to elite studies; the second approach is that of the "new political economy," which examines the macroeconomic consequences of regime change and differences in output between administrations, cabinets, and coalitions within regimes. In a recent volume, Bunce[1] has taken this line of analysis one step further by making comparisons between "political business cycles" in capitalist and socialist nations. Practitioners of these two different approaches have not yet established a joint research program, and while traditional elite studies have all too often failed to answer the question "with what consequences?", political economists have not shown much noticeable concern for the programmatic input of political leaders and their social and ideological support-bases. It is noteworthy, however, that these two perspectives quite adequately reflect, respectively, the relatively open-ended potential for change at the sociological end of the flow chart relating, "who governs?" to "does it matter?" and the political and economic constraints, both domestic and international, which seem to contain policy outputs within relatively incremental and often cyclical change, at least when no sudden or violent collapse of a regime is involved.

The question "who governs?" may seem somewhat ambiguous, but once one specifies the social and political structures to which it is addressed, the referents of the question are easily identifiable. In the emerging constitutional democracy it may have been a ruling class, or, more likely, certain factions within that class. When political parties started to represent social classes or otherwise identifiable socioeconomic groups, there was, as von Beyme points out, a relevant association between the social background of ruling elites and their policy outputs, or at least policy stands. The appearance of mass parties, and "catch-all" mass parties, as well as the broadening of the middle classes as a result of public education, greatly diminished the importance of social background. Ideology and political programs became much better predictors of partisan attitudes and government policies, although severe economic crises could polarize social cleavages. After World War II, the so-called "end of ideology" was proclaimed; it proved to be a brief period of doubt about the continuing relevance of the cleavages of a previous generation. Cultural liberalism and "post-bourgeois" values superseded the economic attitudes of a generation that had experienced the Great Depression, but under the impact of inflation and economic slowdown in most Western societies, they were soon displaced by a "neoconservative" ideology. Environmental protection, nuclear energy and arms, and the security of health, income, and old-age protection added new dimensions of ideological discord.

Thus, at the "who governs?" end of the flow chart, one can identify three major tendencies:

(1) Where social stratification is relatively rigid and social change

relatively slow, the social background of ruling elite is still a valid predictor of policies and political outcomes.

(2) In increasingly pluralistic societies, where mobility and change are relatively high, the social background of decision-makers becomes a diminishing indicator of political affiliation and attitudes. Political parties tend to recruit a more heterogeneous membership which eventually translates into a more heterogeneous leadership.

(3) Under the impact of social and economic crises, however, ideologies and party platforms reclaim their predominance and reflect social differences or cleavages, even if only temporarily.

All three tendencies are documented in the case studies presented in this volume. The first is apparent in the analysis of regime transition in Spain by del Campo, Tezanos, and Santin and in Legg's chapter on political elites in Greece. Cotta's study of Italian elites shows the effects of differential leadership continuity between parties in a country with uneven rates of modernization and political mobilization across regions and social groups. Daalder and van den Berg describe tendencies (1) and (2) as they apply to a long-term perspective on parliamentary elites in the Netherlands (1848–1967). As the analysis reaches the post-World War II period, it reveals that despite the fragmentation of Dutch society into "social pillars," "the make up of the different party groups had become increasingly similar to one another." Analyzing a relatively shorter time span (1956–1975), Eldersveld's examination of party members and activists in Western Germany shows the close association between social change and political involvement—confirming tendency (2)—as well as the persisting socioculturally determined differences between the Social Democratic party (SDP) and the Christian Democratic Union (CDU)—confirming tendency (3). Although Cayrol and Perrineau provide comparisons with the Third (1871–1940) and Fourth (1945–1958) French Republics, they focus primarily on the Fifth Republic and are able to document in detail both tendencies (2) and (3) at the parliamentary, cabinet, and civil service levels, including changes associated with the return to power of the Socialist party in 1981. Substituting cross-level for longitudinal analysis, Rochon is able to demonstrate that at the level of local party activists in the Netherlands, the attitudes of consociational accommodation politics of the Dutch parties and "social pillars" have not survived the modernizing impact of tendency (2), which had become predominant at the national level; yet subcultural integration in the social pillars persists.

There is one dimension that remains insufficiently analyzed in the sociological perspective: the conscious efforts of governing elites to build political institutions, such as electoral systems, designed to maintain or strengthen their positions. At this point, perhaps, one ought to mention the difference in the relationship between long-term and short-term observations, on the one hand, and rates of social change on the other. Methodologically speaking, the slower the rate of change, the safer it is to take a long-term view without missing even relatively subtle changes in elite recruitment; and the more rapid the pace of change, the more likely it is that short-term observations are required to detect elite transformation and circulation. The same distinction applies to electoral and recruitment mechanisms. In the long run, the ups and downs of institutional manipulations have been unable to contain the broadening of the politically involved strata, and political mobilization has been linked to modernization, urbanization, and industrialization. In the short run, however, a change in the electoral system can block access to governmental power or legislative influence for considerable segments of an established or emerging elite. Intraparty manipulations of ladders of mobility have similar effects. Harasymiw's study of elite recruitment in the Communist party of the Soviet Union sheds some light on the possible tensions between societal change and political influence in the closing stages of the Brezhnev regime.

The tendency to ensure continuity is not necessarily the consequence of deliberate actions by a "political class" attempting to react to a changing social environment. Even in the context of twentieth-century modernization, there are islands of traditionalism in the political systems of Western Europe, and traditionalism is, of course, a concept denoting culturally embedded attitudes furthering continuity and stability. From the viewpoint of recruitment to the "political class," or even only segments thereof, the major component of traditionalism that helps maintain continuity is the persistence of social networks of communication, exchange, and support, such as patron-client relationships. These, in turn, are reinforced by the location of members of the political class at, or near, the centers of charismatic authority and effective decision-making power. In the chapter on the political elites in Greece, Legg describes the role of these networks in the continuing survival of the core of a political class across regime changes. Only with extensive use of mass media communication was it possible for Papandreou and his party to win the 1981 election without reliance on traditional networks.

The French Fourth and Fifth Republics, in which efforts directed at economic and administrative modernization (including the restructuring of the political institutions in the Fifth Republic), were relatively successful, display the fact that modernization, too, has its built-in mechanisms for continuity by creating a new and fairly homogeneous elite. Cayrol and Perrineau document the role of the "Grandes Ecoles" (Great Schools), and especially the Ecole Nationale d'Administration, in establishing a class of high-level civil servants who have penetrated the political arena as members of the "cabinets" of Ministers (the teams of aides to members of the Government), where they hold 60 percent of the available positions, and, increasingly, by running for elective positions in the legislature as an additional power base on the pathway to the highest level of political leadership. Their economic and technological training, combined with administrative and managerial experience, has also increased cross-elite circulation which includes the military establishment and business corporations. The role of certain prestigious universities in creating and maintaining a fairly homogeneous elite is known from the British experience; however, occurring at a more recent point in time, the French case seems to be leading to the institutionalization of a modernizing elite. Whether, and how, modernizing policies can be institutionalized is a different matter. Moreover, will the substantial revival of the "Republique des Professeurs" after the Socialist victory in 1981 be a modernizing or stabilizing factor in this development? There also is a large contingent of members of the teaching profession in the post-Franco Spanish political class; del Campo *et al.* report that university professors alone accounted for 30 percent of the legislature elected in 1977. It remains to be seen how this elite will allocate resources between social reform and industrialization.

Finally, there seems to be another "traditionalist" factor of continuity in the Spanish political system: the regional and cultural diversifications, with their localist attachments. Such historical and cultural differences are reinforced by unequal stages of economic development. The politicization of these cleavages will continue to provide obstacles in the integration of the new elites and, consequently, in the formation of a national consensus on priorities and policies, as still evidenced by the Italian political elites, despite Italy's longer democratic experience, more institutionalized political parties, and longer continuity in the national leadership of the Christian Democratic and Communist parties, which Cotta analyzes in his study.

Thus, from the sociological perspective, both short-term and long-term observations reveal elite transformation and circulation in European democracies, albeit with marked differences in continuity and in rates of social change. We don't have systematic evidence of how these transformations are reflected in governmental outputs. In this volume there are two contributions that deal explicitly with this issue, though from different vantage points; both challenge the assumption that in a modern, pluralistic, and technological society, not only the social bases of political parties but also the social characteristics of members of the political elite, are safe predictors of policy stands and governmental outputs, even when social bases and party ideologies differ to a significant extent between parties.

Analyzing types of legislative output with reference to the ruling party or party coalition in Germany between 1871 and 1971, von Beyme documents the divergences between elite input, in terms of social classes or group interests, and governmental output. The most striking example of political determinants of such divergences is the unprecedented social welfare and workers' protection legislation in the 1880's enacted under Bismarck's conservative-aristocratic and bourgeois coalition, as a measure intended to take the wind out of the sails of a strong and growing Social Democratic party. Less dramatic but equally relevant are the far-reaching redistributive measures of the CDU-led government for the integration of about twelve million refugees from East Germany in the 1950's to counter a potential Communist threat to the liberal capitalist system of West Germany. Other measures intended to benefit various middle-class groups were strongly supported by the Social Democratic opposition party.

Frequently, there have been coalitions between otherwise competing and mutually hostile interests in order to protect themselves from economic stagnation or crisis, e.g., agriculture and industry at the turn of the century. Such ad hoc coalitions can be more easily explained in the period of increasing similarity in the social bases of the major parties, when the labor wings of each party tend to cooperate with each other on economic policies, and only middle-class intellectuals are not as "center oriented" as the top leadership of their respective parties; many of the "SPD innovations" after 1969 had been planned or initiated by the "grand coalition" of CDU and SPD in 1967–1969. The German experience discussed by von Beyme also includes coalitions in foreign policy, but deviations from foreign policy programs are less germane to this argument. Deviations from domestic programs presented as necessary consequences of changes in international relations, however, are another example of the relative independence of national policy and of divergence from outcomes predicated on party platforms and on the interests of the social groups supporting them.

To summarize the argument: not only do individual background characteristics of members of a political elite become unreliable predictors of policy stands and government output, especially when parties tend to recruit a heterogeneous membership, but even the social interests to which parties appeal and the ideologies and programs by which they articulate them are insufficient indicators of policies in which parties will engage. Does that mean that even when there are genuine policy alternatives (which is by no means universally the case) party programs are primarily devices for generating electoral support, whereas actual governmental decisions, being subject to the constraints of specific situations or taking advantage of new opportunities, should not be expected to be consistent with proclaimed party platforms and programs? Perhaps accepting even this loosely formulated conclusion is stretching the argument too far.

Political elites, party leaders, and legislators articulate policies, but political decisions are enacted within parameters of growing demand, conflicting claims, and limited resources. The professional politician, and sometimes a political party in power, survive on compromises more or less favorable to some of their specific programmatic demands or commitments. The question "does who governs matter?" can be asked meaningfully only with reference to major shifts in policy or major shifts in emphases. Even emphases can sometimes be achieved only incrementally. What "matters" is the reordering of priority rankings and who is affected, and to what extent, by such reorderings. Occasionally, a leader whose party cannot afford to rebuke him, or who is not accountable to a narrowly defined partisan constituency, can deviate from, or even reverse, a policy he was expected to pursue by followers and opponents alike. In certain cases, such actions are subsequently considered instances of "great statesmanship," which indicates that these were exceptions to the regular political process. But how many Bismarcks have there been in modern history? Or the de Gaulle of 1958, who turned the tables on the colonels and the French Algerian nationalists who made his return to power possible? How many Sadats? The latter, and most of the other examples that come to mind, are related to foreign policy that is less sensitive to domestic partisan differences. Moreover, such exceptions refer to problems that had remained unresolved for a relatively long period of time under the regular political process. The normalization of relationships between the U.S. and the People's Republic of China is no doubt a case in point.

It is precisely the problem-solving ability of political elites under the regular political process that Shils questions in his seminal critique of elite roles in the age of "mass society, collectivist liberalism, and social democracy." Shils argues that the conditions under which the roles of the political elite can be performed with efficacy "no longer obtain in any country, advanced and rich or backward and poor. Everywhere there are clamorous demands for a great variety of governmental actions reaching deeply into society and extending over its entire breadth, and everywhere governments have undertaken to attempt to satisfy these demands. It is a hopeless undertaking . . . it is difficult for any group to stay in power for long except through yielding to demands. . . . These are among the reasons why the rate of inflation is so high in so many countries and why the rate of growth of investment in the maintenance of physical capital lags behind the rate of growth of consumption." The wisdom and good judgment in the art of politics required of the political classes to which Mosca and Pareto were addressing themselves are insufficient for dealing with decisions involving technological innovations under conditions of uncertainty. The tasks which contemporary political elites have undertaken "are in many respects beyond human power . . . [they] require foresights into a future which cannot be

predicted." Moreover, they are "aggravated by the unceasingly critical and demanding scrutiny which the . . . apparatus of knowledge
and . . . the aggrieved assertiveness of the . . . population direct
toward the political elite."

One may add that recent studies of the short-term, four-year policy
cycle do indeed demonstrate that in many cases even relatively un-
dramatic policy changes do not survive much longer than the "hon-
eymoon period" of new leaders. These findings suggest two possible
interpretations. Is it likely that in this complex technological age it
takes much longer for new policies to be well thought-through, then
debated, enacted, organized, and implemented, and that little time
is left to monitor their effect and unintended consequences before
the political cycle has been completed? Or has the rate of change
gone beyond the capability of the political process to deal with its
ramifications and consequences?

Reverting to Shils's argument and restating it in terms of the title
question of this volume leads to the following conclusion: *it is not
who governs that matters, but what we mean by "governing," what
we expect from government.* Are modern pluralistic and technological societies ungovernable? Are they ungovernable only when the
political elite is subjected to processes of intensive and extensive
scrutiny and political accountability? I don't think Shils argues against
accountability. He also points at the fact that the Communist party
of the Soviet Union, which has maintained a closed political elite
capable of sustaining itself in power and even imposing its regime
on other countries, has been unable to solve its domestic economic
problems; authoritarian measures, or even the use of force, are of no
avail in this policy area. Shils argues for "limited government" in
Western democracies but leaves us with the question of whether and
how, under mass democracy and mass communication, a rational,
charismatic elite of "wisdom and good judgment" can emerge and
survive.

The critical component in Shils's concluding question is perhaps
not the quest for political leaders with "wisdom and good judgment
in the art of politics," but the expectation of rationality. Not the
rationality of individual political leaders, but the conditions under
which leadership can be rational in the governance of a pluralistic,
individualistic mass society. The concept of rationality is predicated
on priority rankings. It is well known that aggregating more than two
different priority rankings, let alone multiple and conflicting rankings, can lead to unstable equilibria and cyclical majorities. It is also
known that, given the interdependence of economic factors, the rational but separate pursuit, by different groups, of even the same
priorities can lead to unintended consequences that jointly defeat
their separate endeavors. *What, then, is rational leadership in the
democratic governance of a mass society?*

If technological development and increasing complexity are irreversible trends, have we no other choice than either "limited government," which could amount to hiding one's head in the sand, or advancing irreversibly along the path leading to the "Tragedy of the Commons"? On second thought, even these are not completely mutually exclusive alternatives.

Notes

1. Bunce, Valerie. *Do New Leaders Make a Difference?* (Princeton: Princeton University Press, 1981).

The Political Class in the Age of Mass Society: Collectivistic Liberalism and Social Democracy

Edward Shils

I

The idea of an elite is as old as discourse about human societies, about their rulers, and about the relations of their rulers to their gods and to their subjects. The word did not become established in the English language and in the social sciences until the writings of Pareto and Mosca became known in English-speaking countries. The first social scientist in the United States and Great Britain to use the term freely and centrally in his writings was Harold Lasswell,[1] who was much influenced by Pareto and Mosca.

The word as we know it is a French word, but it did not appear in the titles of works in the social sciences until the publications of Max LeClerc, who wrote on *élites* in Germany and Great Britain and who used the word to designate the coincidence of higher education, wealth, high political position, and high prestige. LeClerc was a "Le Playist" who was perturbed by the dangers of a decay of French institutions and character, and he attributed much importance to the role of *élites*, not just in making decisions, which has become a major interest of American political scientists, but in their influencing, guiding, and dominating the mass of the population. This idea of the productive and guiding function of *élites* was prominent in the late 19th and early 20th century discussions in the Latin countries but fell out of the discussions in the English language. The self-interestedness of *élites* came to be taken for granted—indeed humanitarian and protective attitudes were regarded as marks of moral decay. Sorel and Bourget, from somewhat different standpoints, thought that only elites who fought for their interests and who were not reluctant to use force to maintain their ascendancy were estimable.

There was a similar tough-mindedness in Harold Lasswell's early employment of the term. Elites were simply those who got the most income, deference, and safety. Their functions, aside from accumulating these valued objects and conditions and their techniques of aggrandizement and defense in the pursuit of these ends, were not much considered. The studies of "elite-recruitment," "decision-makers," and of "power-structures," which came to the forefront of academic political science in the United States and also in other countries, did not change this focus markedly. These were still primarily studies of "who gets what, when, and how," as Harold Lasswell defined politics.

The Paretian and to a lesser extent the Moscan way of conceiving elites has provided an illustrious intellectual tradition for this tendency in modern political science. It is difficult to say whether Harold Lasswell's work was the link that bound the early European tradition to the later American tradition. Lasswell's interest in "who gets what, when, and how," was strengthened by his knowledge of German studies of "elite-recruitment," particularly the studies of Giese and Kurella.

There was something slightly mischievous about Lasswell's study of elites, especially in the 1930's. He seemed to be very pleased to be saying things that might be disconcerting to ordinary, more or less egalitarian democratic rationalists—his psychoanalytic interest played a similar part in his relationship to conventional progressivistic liberalism. When Lasswell's ideas came to fruition in the work of younger scholars in the second half of the 1940's and in the 1950's that tension seemed to have been dissolved. The studies of elite-recruitment were conducted without any overtones of censure or pleasure. They were simply matter-of-fact, statistical summaries about the higher probability of the offspring of incumbents of certain groups or occupations to attain positions of high authority, eminence, and remuneration than the offspring of incumbents of lower positions. Studies of "community power" seemed to have a sharper edge of censure. They had an overtone of disapproval of the inequalities of opportunity which gave certain sections of the population better chances of making decisions affecting the community than other sections.

The study of elites, regardless of whether they were called studies of "decision-makers" or of "power elites" continued the traditions of the studies of social selection of which Frances Galton might be regarded as the founder. They derived from Darwinian ideas about the struggle for existence. The eugenical implications which they had in Galton's work on hereditary genius and in the work of Havelock Ellis on the genesis of great men dropped out. Social scientists either accepted the inevitability of inequality of capacity, inequality of opportunity, and inequality of attainments; or they regarded them as evidence of the injustice of present-day societies.

II

One cannot discuss the study of elites without being aware that in the past thirty years a neologism has entered the English language:

it is the word "elitism." It has spread throughout our society and is not confined to the United States. It is a very muddled notion. It seems to assert that a properly conducted society would not have "elites"—except those in the worlds of football, baseball, basketball, and track. In other more serious spheres of human activity, those who use the term "elitism" in a pejorative sense deny both the desirability and the inevitability of elites. They seem to think that inequalities in the exercise of authority are evil; indeed, they seem to think that authority itself is evil since it is by its nature an unequal relationship. Those who use the term think that it is "elitist" to grade students for their work in primary and secondary school, implying or asserting that no significant distinction should be made between competent and incompetent students. They are against examinations that discriminate between those who perform better and those who perform worse. Those who oppose "elitism" oppose inequality of reward; they oppose inequality of power. They wish to abolish inequalities of reward and power. They think that the decisions which affect the entire society should be made by the entire society, whatever that might mean. Their thoughts are not well worked out, but sometimes they suggest that participatory democracy is the answer to the problem posed by the unavoidability of making decisions that affect the wider reaches of society. They espouse the cause of "the people"; they are in favor of "science for the people," critical science, critical philosophy, extra-parliamentary opposition, nonviolent civil disobedience. In their more extreme variants, they praise the effort of the "cultural revolution" in Communist China to obliterate the distinctions between peasants and scientists by sending peasants to scientific laboratories and by sending scientists to do the work done by peasants.

The anti-elitists regard any reference to inequalities of human capacities as elitist, i.e., as morally repugnant. They regard any judgment that some persons are more talented or more moral or superior in courage to others as elitist. They think that any effort to classify and assemble in one or in a single set of institutions, individuals who have more talent or more skill or more courage is elitist, i.e., evil because it refers to inequalities and implies that some individuals are superior in some respects to other individuals. The critical attitude implicit in the use of the term elitism as it is now used treats as repugnant any reference to existing facts of inequality of endowment or performance, if not accompanied by a denunciation of those facts (again with the exemption of inequalities of performance in games and athletic activities). It treats as repugnant any arrangements to further outstanding achievements or any approval of such arrangements. It treats as repugnant any argument that inequalities may in various respects be beneficial to persons other than those who are themselves superior.

These various attitudes toward inequality represent a general out-look that is almost diametrically opposite to the attitudes which lay behind the studies of elites by academic social scientists, publicists, and private scholars in the latter part of the 19th century and much of the 20th century.

The very subject of the study of elites is anathema to the anti-elitists. Mosca and Pareto have always been suspect among progres-sivistic, collectivistic liberals and radicals, partly because they were suspected of having been Fascists, partly because some Fascists in-voked them as witnesses to their oligarchical ideals and their admi-ration—and practice—of brutality. But, in fact, the study of elites is an evaluatively neutral subject. Insofar as it confines itself to the description of what happens between two or more generations, it is silent at the question as to whether inequality in the distribution of opportunities and rewards is inherent in the nature of societies. Indeed, the descriptive accounts contained in elite studies are quite compatible with the beliefs that inequalities are inevitable and with beliefs that they are necessary and useful or at least have advantages which more than compensate for their disadvantages. They are quite compatible with beliefs that the distributions which they disclose are good or evil.

III

Mosca certainly regarded the kinds of inequalities that he discov-ered in his studies as inevitable. He thought there could be no soci-ety without elites and that elites perform functions which are absolutely fundamental for the working of society. He thought more-over that they could not be dispensed with and that some of their vices were an inevitable concomitant of that existence. These did not seem to be controvertible issues to Mosca, nor indeed did they take a central position in his thought. He was more concerned with the conditions under which political elites were effective. This seems to me to set the proper problem in the study of elites. The demo-graphic or "elite-recruitment" studies find their justification when the information that they bring is put to the task of explaining the success or failure of elites in maintaining their domination over their societies and avoiding violent disruptions in their tenure. Mosca did not conceive of the tenure of a particular set of individuals; he thought of tenure as running beyond the lifetime or the political careers of single individuals, conceived simply as individuals. He thought of the success of elites as political lineages or political classes. The ruling or political class was not the aggregate of all individuals par-ticipating in political life; it was not the aggregate of all those sec-tions of the population whose members participated in politics. The ruling or political class was narrower than the latter; it was more a collective than the former. The political class was, according to Mosca, marked by a sense of political vocation, which was shared by its individual members who, at the same time, perceived that sense of vocation in the other members of the class. There was, on this basis, a sense of solidarity of individuals with each other, even though the political class as a whole was divided by rivalries.

The concept of a political class referred to a cluster of families or, to a lesser extent, professions and institutions from which the individuals who held important elective and appointive positions in the government came. Membership in these lineages or membership in these professions or the fact of having been a student at certain schools or colleges or universities offered to their members a sense of identity as parts of a loose collectivity whose "business" was ruling the society. The concept of a political class refers not only to the families, professions, and schools from which politicians and political organizers come; it refers to more than these and to the sense of identity focused on the shared right and obligation to rule. It is also a reference to an accumulating tradition of outlook and skill. The tradition provides each new generational group in the lineages, the professions, or the schools and the protégés of these groups, with the knowledge and skill that it needs to remain in power, to contend for power if it is not in power, and to do its job of exercising power with sufficient effectiveness to enable its collectivity to survive, to leave the peripheries of the ruled, in their significant parts, sufficiently satisfied and, if not satisfied, then sufficiently impotent so as to leave the political class at the center of society.

Mosca—and Schumpeter—seemed to think that these traditions of ruling provided the dispositions and attitudes needed to rule effectively, the self-confidence in confronting the decisions inherent in ruling, the ability to weigh and calculate the chances of success, and the knowledge of human beings with whom one must collaborate and against whom one must act. They thought that political experience is the best teacher of the art of politics and that the accumulated experiences of generations, concentrated into streams of traditions which flow into and through institutions, such as lineages, professions and schools, colleges and universities, are the sources of the knowledge which enables political classes to be successful. The idea of a political class is relevant to the understanding of politics because it implies that certain kinds of attitudes and knowledge are necessary for effective rule and that the sources of recruitment are connected with the qualities that make for effectiveness or ineffectiveness of rule.

Mosca wrote his great book a century ago, and he looked back over all of human history in the way in which an educated man in the Italy of his time, well read in the classics and in history, could do. He wrote in a period that was on the verge of political and social developments which made the existence of the kind of political class which he had in mind more difficult. Political classes in Mosca's sense are greatly attenuated in the West, to the extent that they exist at all. And the tasks which they would have faced, and which their successors do face in the second half of the 20th century, render the efficacy of rulers more difficult.

IV

Let us imagine that political classes of the old type still existed. What kind of world would they face in the last part of the 20th century? Even if we grant the correctness of Mosca's views about the abilities of political classes, could they have been effective in governing the "new kind" of societies?

Let me first indicate some of the features of this "new kind" of society. The new kind of society is no longer a society with the mass of the population living in the countryside or in small villages as peasant cultivators, small farmers, and many agricultural laborers, craftsmen, petty merchants, and a small number of great landowners; and in the city, a large number of industrial workers and handicraftsmen, some lawyers and doctors, small merchants and civil servants; in both countryside and towns, many clergymen and fewer school teachers, numerous civil servants and a tiny number of university teachers. Most of these strata still exist, but they have changed markedly in their proportions within the total. The main changes are the great diminution in the proportion of peasants and landless laborers and a great increase in the proportion of town dwellers.

The occupations, the incumbents of which have increased in their proportion in the total population, are generally occupations which were accorded greater deference, and they were generally the less laborious occupations as well. (Perhaps these two properties are related, "mental" occupations being more esteemed than "physical" occupations.) These prospering occupations tended also to be located in towns and not in the countryside. Many of these occupations required literacy for their performance and hence a higher level of education. These occupations are very heterogenous. Manual occupations are also to be found among them, mainly in transportation. Many of them involve the exercise of intermediate authority. Others are in communication in which more knowledge is involved, and hence more education. Some of these occupations are primarily cognitive, concerned with acquiring knowledge, storing knowledge, transmitting knowledge, and using knowledge.

Literacy, a higher level of education, more deference, and living in cities—all of these are connected with a greater sense of being closer to the center of society. "Being closer" to the center of society is partly a state of mind; it is a condition of self-consciousness about one's own value in relation to that which is most highly valued, and it is an assessment of that value as being relatively high. It is also a conception of the self as being part—even not a very central part—of the center, as sharing in the right to rule or at least to be heard and heeded by those who rule. In its most tangible form, it has been expressed in the demand for the universal adult franchise and in the growth of populistic, socialistic, and collectivistic political parties, pressure groups, and trade unions.

This would never have been possible without the increase in agricultural and, later, industrial productivity. The increased productivity in agriculture and industry in Western countries made it possible to maintain a larger proportion of the population in these "tertiary" occupations. It made it possible to maintain a larger set of institutions not directly participating in agricultural and industrial production, namely schools, which conferred the qualifications needed for these new occupations.

All of these coincident consequences and preconditions of a more productive economy—urbanization, the growth of the literate and cognitive occupations, the increase in the amount of education received by the population, the increased production and acquisition of things, images, and information from a distance, and the increased amount of human travel and of the transportation of goods—have been accompanied by the further realization of national societies and the retraction of local societies. The economies are more oriented toward national than toward local and regional markets. Aspirations for careers are oriented more toward national opportunities—both in higher education and in employment. The focus of attention is directed more to national events and personages, i.e., events occurring and persons acting in wide dispersion over the territory within the national boundaries, and events and personages at the center of society.

The further realization of or the increased preponderance of the national society is partly a function of the visibility of its center. This was barely feasible before the age of greatly increased literacy, relatively inexpensive printing, and incomes sufficiently high to permit the acquisition of literacy and the purchase of the products of the printing press, especially newspapers and periodicals. In more recent decades, radio and television broadcasting have furthered this process.

The visibility of the center, made possible by technological innovation and increased wealth, is accompanied by the increased demands on the part of the individuals whose image of themselves emphasizes their dignities, their own potentialities, and the forthcomingness of the world.

The combination of the visibility of the center, belief in the primary reality of the national society, increased self-esteen and the increased demand for acknowledgment, the provision of all sorts of "things" and the demand for more "things" lies at the basis of the collectivistic liberal state and of modern "popular democracy." (By "popular democracy," I mean "national" and "populistic" democracy.)

This is a very different situation from the one faced by political classes of the kind that Mosca analyzed and appreciated. The kinds of societies over which political classes ruled, although always smaller in size, were characterized by a much larger radius between center and peripheries. The populace was less demanding and less considered.

For many reasons, the threshold of acceptibility has risen. Indignity, psychic misery, physical pain, boredom, restrictions on desire are no longer as bearable as they once were. Grievances are more easily aroused and more readily expressed; it is thought that grievances should be remedied. Remedies for ills and grievances seem to be within human powers, if only the right arrangements are made. Providence and its inscrutability no longer counsel patience or resignation.

The peripheries of the societies ruled by political classes were less audible and less visible and they were less frequently and less distinctly called on to attend to the center. They were under the dominion of more local centers which were dimly seen to be linked with the national center insofar as there was a national center at all. The absence of stimulus and of opportunity held in check the desire to become part of the center in any way, except for a tiny number of individuals whose ascent was then gradual. Each part of the center— within which the political class and its divisions existed—was far more attentive to other parts of the center than it was to the peripheries. The peripheries were present; without them the society could not function at all. But theirs was not such an active presence, and the center, although never totally indifferent, did not have to be very attentive to them.

V

Whatever the complex of conditions that brought forth the present situation of "popular democracy," collectivistic liberalism, and social democracy and whatever the differences among these, the present situation is one that requires a tremendous concentration of power in the government to assemble and dispose of resources and to cope with a very high level of demands in various parts of the population.

Contemporary Western governments have taken the responsibility for full employment and economic growth, as well as for the provision of goods and services beyond those provided by the market, for the fostering of individual happiness and personal development, for the care of health and the conservation of nature, for the progress of scientific knowledge and the promotion of technological innovation, for the well-being of the arts and the quality of culture and for social justice—not just the rule of law—and for the remedying of past wrongs. This is a tremendous distance from the welfare state as it was conceived in Germany in the 19th century and by humanitarian reformers in the United States and Great Britain at the beginning of the 20th century. There is scarcely any sphere of life into which modern governments have not entered as a result of their own conception of their obligations and their sensitivity to the imperfections of man's life on earth and in response to the demands of various parts of the electorate and the prevailing intellectual opinion as to what governments should do and how they can do it.

No "political class," when political classes were still the reservoirs from which governing political elites came, ever had to cope with such a situation. The situation is a novel one; the tasks placed on and accepted by or actually sought by government are to some extent novel in substance and certainly unprecedented in scope. Moreover, the tasks change rapidly. Tasks are redefined. Failures must be remedied by renewed and more extensive measures. The undertakings of governments are so numerous and so comprehensive are the responsibilities that have been demanded of or proclaimed by governments as their "programs" that tasks of coordination of unexampled complexity arise. Governments have long ceased to regard governing as their first, perhaps even their only task; every government on its accession to office has a program of positive actions intended to carry further its past achievements, to broaden them and to improve on them. (Mistakes of one's own commission are seldom admitted.) On the rare occasions when an ostensibly less expansive government accedes to office, its program of undoing some of the arrangements instituted by its more expansive predecessors is as complicated as the positive program it would cancel. Furthermore, programs of cancellation of the arrangements of previous governments are never as comprehensive as the programs of preceding more positive administrations.

How different this is from the budget of tasks that political classes, when they still existed, accepted and were expected to accept! Even in the "absolute" monarchies of the ancien régime, government aspired to nothing comparable in scale and intensity to what contemporary Western governments accept as their objectives.

The great merit of the political class was its inheritance of a tradition of the arts of politics and ruling. The knowledge borne by that tradition was wisdom; it was not technical knowledge. Governments formed by political classes did not use much technical knowledge, and they used practically nothing of what would now be called scientific knowledge and scientific technology. Details of road building, the maintenance of waterways, the registration of titles to property, the construction of tax rolls, and the keeping of accounts of revenues and expenditures could be left to officials; decisions at the higher levels of government, insofar as they drew on this kind of knowledge, could be made by delegation of authority or by placing oneself in the hands of "expert advisors." Turgot and Colbert knew as much of the "science of economics" as anyone in France at that time. The fact is that there was little "science" which was thought to have bearing on the affairs of state; the challenge to know it and to incorporate it into decisions was not a burden which the "political class" had to bear. That burden is, however, one which contemporary politicians must bear.

The kinds of problems with which government dealt were not beyond the cognitive possessions of the political class. The failures of a political class could not be attributed to its failure to master and use an available stock of scientific knowledge. The problems political classes faced, to the extent that they faced them, did not lie outside the powers gained from the assimilation of the traditional political and governmental wisdom available to members of the political class and their own experience.

To do all the things which are demanded of them and to which they have committed themselves, legislators of the present century have called into being an immense bureaucracy. The bureaucracy, competent or incompetent though it might be in taking these tasks in hand, is certainly able to hold its own with the legislators who are constitutionally the rulers of Western societies, whether they be systems of parliamentary government dominated by a cabinet made up of the leaders of the dominant party or the presidential system which provides for an independent legislature and an independent executive. It was long ago pointed out by Max Weber that the bureaucracy would become the dominant power in government, unless it could be held in check by a system of competitive parties which, through elections and the competition in parliament, brought charismatic leaders to the fore. The American Congress, not knowing how to generate charismatic politicians, has sought a makeweight against the bureaucracy through the expansion of congressional staffs. They have now become dependent on a bureaucracy of their own making which is nearly as dominating over its superiors as the bureaucracy of the civil service. The President, to cope in his turn with the civil service on the one hand and with the legislature, which is increasingly wagged by the bureaucratic tail of its own creation, has created a large bureaucracy of his own in the Executive Office of the President.

There was in the past, much conflict within the political class. The conflicts were those between families, between individuals, and between the proponents of different policies. The conflicts took place within a consensus concerning the value of authority. Opposition from outside the political class took the form of resistance to particular measures and to whole sets of measures, but generally it raised no question regarding the necessity and rightfulness of authority as such. Revolutionary religious sectarians were exceptions to this; but they were infrequent, and their resistance in an intense form was shortlived. "Anti-elitism" was to be found only among religious antinomians.

Present-day antinomianism is not confined to particular Protestant or other religious sects. These are indeed the least of the antinomians of the present day. The distrust of authority that has been a characteristic feature of modern liberalism in its classical form was quite moderate. It was concerned with the establishment of restraints on the excessive actions of persons in authority. It was not derogatory toward all authority; it did not regard authority per se as iniquitious. It was not egalitarian, whereas the present-day reviling of authority is sustained not so much by a concern for the evil actions of authority as by a rejection of the very principle of authority because it infringes on the principle of equality, radically interpreted.

Present-day anti-elitism is not just a catch-phrase of educationists, sociologists, political scientists, and intellectuals of the "new Left." It is a phenomenon that is very widespread. It has a long tradition in the United States. It was manifested in the Articles of Confederation and became well established in the United States with the universalization of the adult male franchise and other features of the Jacksonian revolution. It is, of course, a major feature of populism in all countries and not least in American populism. It has been a recurrent feature of progressivism in all countries. It is indeed an inherent potentiality of political democracy. Populism was not, however, antinomianism, and it was not as unqualifiedly egalitarian as the ill-thought-out anti-elitism now current. In the United States, populism was also not entirely opposed to individualism and the assessment of individuals by the merits of their achievements.

Of course, populism never had its way in any of the countries in which it flourished; its proponents espoused other attitudes as well. It was only in the United States that it had a marked influence on governments in the 19th and early 20th centuries. In Russia, the government responded to it by the suppression of its more active proponents. In the rest of Europe, it scarcely existed. It has to wait until well into the second half of the 20th century to begin to have some influence on governments.

Governments have almost always had an eye open for the movements of public opinion, but they did not think that they had to be guided by them. It is a sign of the shortening of the distance between center and periphery that the "voice of the people" has become the "voice of god" (vox populi, vox dei). Sensitivity to opinion outside the center, not as an object to be managed but as a command to be heeded, is a characteristic of present-day rulers in Western countries: not always, of course, but frequently. This was not the case with the political class. Even in the 19th century, when liberalism and the newspaper and periodical press became powerful forces, they were assimilated into the political class. They felt themselves to be part of the political class even when they criticized their rivals very acrimoniously. The political class did not feel itself to be so much on the defensive *vis-à-vis* public opinion as its successors have since become.

This distance between the ruling powers and their critics has become deepened by the anti-elitism of the media of printed and spoken words and the electronically transmitted image. It has been further aggravated by the entry of a new force in public opinion, the literary intellectual on the one hand and academic social scientists on the other. At the height of the glories of the political class—a rather ill-defined stretch of time—universities and their teachers either did not exist at all or led rather confined existences. In the 19th century, conditions changed at certain universities in a few countries because of the sustaining structure of the political class, for example, Oxford University in the 19th and 20th centuries, the Ecole libre des sciences politiques and the Ecole nomale supérieure in France and perhaps the University of Berlin in Germany. Today, however, the teachers in universities have become more numerous than ever, and the antinomians, egalitarians, and anti-elitists in their ranks have become numerous enough and outspoken and challenging enough to form a very hostile component of the center and of many subcenters within society. Rulers today are, therefore, more subject to stringent and often vituperative criticism. What is more, their own ranks are riddled by exponents of these critical attitudes.

A question is therefore in order: What particularly is the effect of anti-elitism in a society in which government is expected to be omnicompetent and omniprovident to regulate, intervene, and initiate in all spheres of social life?

It would take a political class with much more scientific knowledge—which, in fact, does not yet exist—than any political class has been able to acquire hitherto, and it would take far stronger, more charismatic characters than most members of the political class have been to withstand the pressure of incessant scrutiny and criticism, to cope with the immense, terribly complex and overpoweringly numerous tasks which modern governments have accepted, and in doing so to hold its own in the face of the bureaucracies and the expertise with which it is surrounded. It is easier to add more staff members and to enact new legislation than it is to carry out the policies that are intended. It is much more difficult to summon the force of character needed to drive through these policies, to call forth the assent and cooperation of the ruled, to discredit criticism by achievement, and to rally ones subordinates to support and aid the execution of policies. It requires the self-confidence of a charismatic person and the wisdom of long and successful political experience to know when to refuse to pursue certain policies, even though they are much demanded by the populace, by external critics, and by internal advisers and permanent officials.

The situations Mosca thought of when he considered the efficacy of a political class no longer obtain in any country, advanced and rich or backward and poor. Everywhere there are clamorous demands for a great variety of governmental actions reaching deeply into society and extending over its entire breadth, and everywhere governments have undertaken to attempt to satisfy those demands. It is a hopeless undertaking because practically none of the attempts measures up to the intention of its instigators and none avoids repercussions, which bring disadvantages to various sections of society. Where the measures are unsuccessful, they give rise to severe criticism and dissatisfaction; where they are reasonably successful, then more is demanded. Under these circumstances, it is difficult for any group to stay in power for long except through yielding to demands as they arise—if the demanders seem to be important enough to be influential in future elections—and allowing the devil to take the hindmost. These are among the reasons why the rate of inflation is so high in so many countries and why the rate of growth of investment in maintenance of physical capital lags behind the rate of growth of consumption.

Would these injurious social effects have been avoidable had the regime of political classes survived? That is a question which is unanswerable in empirical terms because there are, at present, no countries in Western civilization which possess political classes, in Mosca's sense. There are many professional politicians in all these countries; many persons who make a livelihood from politics. There are some who, in Weber's terms, "live for politics." But these are not the same as political classes. There are a few who represent fragments of what were once political classes. Hence, we have no way of comparing the achievements of politicians who are formed by their membership in a political class with the achievements of those who have not been so formed, both types of political elites acting in societies of the type common in the second half of the 20th century. Political classes in the sense in which Mosca conceived them no longer exist.

Yet it is not pointless to speculate on the question whether, had they continued to exist, they would have been able to avoid the crises into which all societies have fallen, the crises of pervasive and restless dissatisfaction, of the numerous failures of bravely undertaken schemes, and of the ineffectiveness of political elites in governing their societies.

I am skeptical about whether political elites such as political classes nurture would have been much more successful than the political elites who have governed Western societies in the past half-century. The qualities that political classes nurture are the capacity to conciliate potential rivals or to isolate them and render them powerless, the self-confident bearing by which the politician possessing it may impose himself on his followers, the deference which is called forth by birth in distinguished families, and the solidarity of persons who have been together and worked together for long periods and whose families did the same before them. All of these are valuable qualities and would be valuable under present circumstances as under any other.

But these qualities are not the same as systematic knowledge of extremely complicated matters; they are different from scientific knowledge about a great number of such matters. Wisdom and good judgment are irreplaceable, but they are not the same as technical, scientific knowledge. Wisdom in the art of politics, about how to get on with colleagues, subordinates, rivals, and enemies and about how to placate subjects and to help them to be loyal and submissive is different from deciding on a policy of capital investment that entails dealing with technological innovations under conditions of uncertainty. It is no moral superiority on the part of modern political elites that they deal with such matters—they frequently deal with them poorly—but the fact remains that political classes did not deal with such subjects at all. Had they had to deal with them there is no reason to think that they would have done them any better than contemporary political elite in any Western country.

The tasks which contemporary political elites have undertaken are in many respects beyond human powers. They are tasks which require foresight into a future that cannot be predicted. (Who, for example, can predict correctly the demand for electrical energy in the year 2000, the amount that will be available from hydroelectrical installations and at what cost, the amount that will be available from the use of coal and at what cost, and the amount that should be provided for from nuclear energy installations and at what cost.) Predictions are made and decisions are taken, but they usually turn out to be clearly wrong long before the date of fulfillment has been attained. Political classes when they flourished did not try to make such decisions.

It should finally be emphasized that political classes, or rather politicians nurtured in the culture of political classes, were not all that successful. Turbulences were common in the *ancien régime*, disastrous wars were also common, failure and frustration were the common lot of political classes. Yet it is also true that they produced many wise statesmen who were shrewd, relatively far-seeing and reflective, who were brave in the making of decisions and who could surround themselves with loyal and intelligent coadjustors and subordinates. But there were very few Richelieus or Bismarcks. In fact, there was only one of each.

VI

In any case, we no longer live in the age of political classes. The Soviet Union is the only country that can be said to have a political class—a very limited circle of long duration from which the highest political elite is chosen by co-optation and calculation. It is not a political class in Mosca's sense because it lacks the element of recruitment from lineage, but this is a secondary matter. The present Soviet elite comes from a political class, the higher ranks of the Communist party of the Soviet Union; it comes primarily from Russia. Its members were not born into the Soviet political class, but they must enter it very early in their careers and make those careers within it and through the patronage of its then reigning leaders. It is a closed circle; intrusions from the outside are not compatible with its continued existence. Progress within the political class is dependent almost entirely on decisions within the political class which, having the formal organization of the Communist party of the Soviet Union as its frame, maintains—at least thus far—a strict control over succession.

Has the Communist political class been successful? In certain important respects, it has been successful. It has remained in power for about two thirds of a century; it has avoided subversion or replacement from outside itself. It has succeeded in achieving this success by ruthlessness, in brutal suppression of even mild-mannered internal criticism. In this sense, it goes beyond one of the features of political classes. Whereas political classes could assimilate some of their potential rivals or antagonists and could bring them into the system—this is how constitutional liberalism came to live together with monarchically centered conservatism in the 19th century in Western and Central Europe—the Soviet political elite suppresses potential rivals.

Since remaining in power is one of the tests of success of a political elite or of a political class (which is the variant of concern to us here), the Soviet elite has been successful. But one of the features of modern political elites is that they possess programs which they claim to be able to realize. The Soviet elite has certainly been quite successful in its external policies, in its intrusions into other countries. It has possessed the readiness to use force, corruption, manipulation, and conspiracy in the pursuit of its ends abroad, and it has done so with self-confidence. In this respect it has had all the qualities of relatively successful political classes of early modern times up to almost the end of the 19th century; these were the features of political classes which Mosca, and especially Pareto, admired.

Communism is, however, an ideal arrangement of the internal affairs of a society, and it is through the establishment everywhere of such a system that the Soviet elite justifies its extrusions beyond its own boundaries. There it has not been successful, neither within its own boundaries nor in the regimes which it has established and maintained in power outside those boundaries. There, all the qualities which are sustained by the culture of a political class have not helped it—with the exception of its readiness to suppress by the harshest methods those who appear to endanger it. In those fields of activity, like the economic sphere, in which force is not sufficient, the Soviet political class and those lesser political classes which it supports have not been at all successful. Being a political class is thus not anything like a guarantee of success, although it does have certain advantages.

VII

When we turn away from Communist regimes and consider the political elites of modern Western countries, we contemplate a scene which is fairly devoid of the qualities of organization and culture characteristic of political classes. Modern liberalism, with its emphasis on individual achievement, modern taxation, and the changes in the technology and organization of agriculture have doomed one of the pillars of the system of political classes, namely the great landowning families which in many large societies supplied cultural centers of interaction and much of the personnel of the political classes.

The church, the religious orders, and lay, para-ecclesiastical organizations once constituted a set of adjuncts of the political class, particularly in Roman Catholic countries in the *ancien régimes* and to a smaller, but still some, extent in Protestant countries. This has changed greatly in Roman Catholic countries as a consequence of anti-clericalism and more recently as a consequence of radicalism in the priesthood; priests in some Latin countries have become the enemies of what remains of the political class. In Protestant countries too there has been a clerical withdrawal from the political elite.

The political elites have become less self-enclosed, and their different and rival sectors have become less conciliatory toward each other than when they formed a political class. The fate of the system of *versuiling* which prevailed for more than a century in the Netherlands illustrates this process. As long as the political elites of the various "vertical" sectors of Dutch society maintained their ascendancy in consequence of the compliance of their following, they could collaborate more easily with their rivals or competitors of the other "vertical" sectors. When the rank and file of the various parties became more demanding, more consciously "self-esteeming," and more insistent on their being heeded by their leaders, the political class of the Netherlands lost some of its self-enclosedness, its control over recruitment, and its self-assurance. Similar developments, *mutatis mutandis*, have occurred in other Western countries. The churches have become uneasy about their links with the center of their respective societies. They have sought to disavow their participation in the earthly center in order to espouse the causes and to seek the approval of the peripheries of society, while claiming thereby to affirm their link with the transcendent center of all existence.

Lineages ceased to be as significant in the self-consciousness of individuals and in their influence on the conduct and loyalties of their members. Churches became somewhat dissociated from the centers of society—either by the constitutional separation of church and state or through voluntary withdrawal and disavowal by the churches.

Great Britain and France were the only countries in which educational institutions served to form and rally the political class. In the former, the great public schools—above all Eton, Harrow, Rugby, and a few others—and Oxford University (also Cambridge to a lesser degree) provided places for inculcation of the outlook of the political class, a sense of solidarity—the "old school tie"—and places of recruitment into the political class. In France, in different ways, a few of the great *lycées* in Paris, e.g., the Lycée Louis le Grand and the Ecole libre des sciences politiques and, around the time of the First World War, the Ecole normale supérieure, played a similar role.[2] More recently, the Ecole d'administration has been added to the set of formative institutions of the French political elite. (The Ecole polytechnique, important though it has been in the administration of the country, does not seem to have been quite as important in the formation and maintenance of the political elite in contemporary France, although it is conceivable that the technological, scientific training which it offers might lead to its displacement of the more humanistic Ecole normale supérieure. The same applies to the forward movement of the Ecole nationale d'administration.)

Neither the United States nor Germany have had any higher educational institutions which have performed approximately similar functions. No German university, despite the intellectual achievements and the nationalistic devotion (sometimes excessive) of German professors, ever played a role like that of Oxford in Great Britain. The role of the universities in the United States is somewhat similar. In some of the states, the state university played a part of some importance in the formation of a state-wide political elite. (I think particularly of the University of Wisconsin and, with less certainty, of the University of Minnesota.) Harvard University has never been in a position in national political life in the United States comparable to that of Oxford or the French *grandes écoles*. It has, from time to time, appeared to be on the verge of that situation, for example, during the administrations of Theodore Roosevelt, Franklin Roosevelt, and John Kennedy. Many of its members would have liked it to be such, and, recently, the Kennedy School of Public Affairs tries to perform a partial function of an institution which contributes to the formation of a political class through its courses for newly elected members of Congress. Nevertheless, despite aspirations and occasional flickerings, Harvard has not attained that position, and no other American educational institution has come even that near.

The United States is too large and, despite the recent aggrandizement of the national center, it is still too decentralized in its interests, functions, and loyalties for a political class to emerge. Populism would have resisted it. But even without populism and the diversity of American society, local and regional interests and the local and federal structure of the American governmental system would have prevented it. The local and state political machines did create some of the constitutive elements of a political class, but the weakness, between presidential elections, of the national institutions of the two major parties has also stood in the way of the fusion of these constituents into a national political class.

Insofar as the United States has a political class—and it has one only in a most rudimentary and partial form—it does so through its national legislative bodies. Of these, the Senate is by far the most important in many respects. The United States Senate and the British House of Commons have each claimed or, had claimed for them, the standing of "the best club in the world." A club has its atmosphere and its rules; it has its own distinctive culture which new members must acquire and through which they acquire "the art of politics." It is, however, another matter as to whether the "best club in the world" can generate and sustain the skill, knowledge, solidarity, and self-confidence necessary for keeping on top of the problems which the demands of the electorate and of the particular interests within it, and their own ideas about the rightful sphere of government, have presented to modern politicians for solution.

The strain on the political culture of the main centers of Western societies is aggravated by the unceasingly critical and demanding scrutiny which the contemporary apparatus of knowledge, on the one side, and demanding and increasingly aggrieved assertiveness of the mass of population on the other, directs toward the political elite.

When Mosca discussed a closed or a partially closed political class he had in mind primarily the reservoir of recruitment and the extent to which that reservoir was open to persons who came from outside the main political families, institutions, and circles. Modern political life under conditions of popular democracy is too open for the generation and maintenance of a political class. Mosca's emphasis on the partial closedness of recruitment as a condition of the existence and continuity of a political class might also have been extended, and it should now be extended to include closedness from external scrutiny.

Bentham conceived of the "eye of the public" as "the virtue of the statesman," but he never conceived of that eye as having such a depth of penetration, such brightness, and such constancy as the present eye of the public represented in the professional staffs of the mass media of communication. Like many of the critics of the closure of the political classes of the 18th and 19th centuries who wanted a pattern of government more open to the public gaze, he did not imagine how imaginative, how powerful, how detailed, and omnipresent that eye would become.

It would be very difficult for a political elite, nurtured by a combination of open and closed recruitment, to withstand that insistent eye, especially under conditions in which the minds and voices behind that eye demand so much and demand it so insistently and censoriously. The invention of sample surveys of the political attitudes of Western societies, the frequency of those surveys, and the specificity of the objects on which they seek to discover the distribution of attitudes mean that political elites have to think unceasingly about whether their measures are popular. Popularity of measures becomes a criterion of the success of a measure, long before it has had a chance to become effective. Effectiveness and popularity are not the same thing, and their divergence renders the formation of a political class in Mosca's sense impossible. A political class in Mosca's sense did not have to be continuously on the alert to its popularity, and since it did not try to do as much as contemporary political elites in societies dominated by collectivistic liberal and social democratic beliefs and demands, it was easier for it to be effective. Neither of these conditions is present today.

VIII

These reflections seem to lead to the conclusion that Mosca's conception of a political class is no longer applicable in our contemporary societies. Certainly, the structure of a political class as Mosca understood it is a phenomenon which can scarcely be realized at present. It is more appropriate to the analysis of oligarchical and constitutional regimes with restricted franchise.

Nevertheless, some still vital elements survive from Mosca's conception of the political class. He saw the partially closed structure of the political class as the condition of certain attitudes which are needed by rulers who seek to be effective. Self-confidence and a measure of internal solidarity, determination of will, and a capacity to know when to compromise and when not to compromise are qualities that were nurtured by the system of political classes. These are still of the utmost importance in political life.

Max Weber thought that only the charismatic political leaders who emerge in the competition of parties could save society from the ruinous effects of rule by bureaucracy. In a roundabout way, Mosca was saying the same thing. Neither Weber nor Mosca, nor any of the writers who are linked to them in various ways, like Sorel and Michels, anticipated the "demandingness" of the electorate nor the unremitting pressure of the media of mass communications. Weber was clear about the power of the bureaucracy. Mosca, too, was saying that strength of character was the virtue of the statesman, except that he thought it could be cultivated and supported by the presence of a political class which has its own traditions and which was flexible enough to meet new problems. Mosca emphasized the necessity, if a political class were to persist in responding to new demands and in facing new situations, for it to be open to new talents, regardless of whether they originated within the traditional sources from which the political class was recruited. Max Weber in his emphasis on the charismatic qualities which a politician must have to assure the coherence of his following and to hold the ascendancy over the bureaucracy, did not refer to the diversity of recruitment to the political class in a time of stress. Yet, as he stated elsewhere, charismatic qualities overcome the confines of traditional institutions. It remains a question whether, under present-day conditions of mass democracy and mass communications, rational, charismatic politicians who are loyal to the system of representative institutions can emerge and survive. They certainly cannot be produced by any deliberately contrived scheme.

Notes

1. Harold D. Lasswell, *World Politics and Personal Insecurity* (New York: McGraw-Hill, 1935), and *Politics: Who Gets What, When, and How* (New York: McGraw-Hill, 1936).

2. Albert Thibaudet puts this thesis forward explicitly in *La Republique des professeurs* (Paris: Grasset, 1927).

The Circulation of Judicial Elites: A Comparative and Longitudinal Perspective

John R. Schmidhauser

For many years, the literature of comparative judicial systems has been characterized by most of the shortcomings which Roy Macridis and other modern critics attributed to studies of comparative government in general: that they are descriptive, structural and functional in conceptual emphasis, and generally limited to one non-American system.[1] The investigation of comparative cross-national and intranational judicial elites, lawyers, and legal professions has often shared such limited goals. The emphasis has begun to shift in the past couple of decades, but the number of investigations of judicial and legal elites are few and the conceptual bases of some are rather limited. Consequently, it is the purpose of this paper to (1) summarize some of the current approaches and empirical findings and (2) map some of the prerequisites of two conceptual frameworks which may provide a more comprehensive foundation for such cross-national and intranational investigation of the transformation of judicial and legal elites.

The essential components of any meaningful investigation of such elites may, in their simplest description, consist of a number of nominal distinctions organized in accordance with a variety of conceptual frameworks. Comparisons may be made cross-nationally, intranationally, and within a single nation or one of its political subdivisions over time. The nominal distinctions commonly employed in judicial and legal elite studies in the 1950's, 1960's, and 1970's are summarized in Figure 1, a version of the Chinese Box Puzzle adapted by Kenneth Prewitt.[2] This paper will evaluate the conceptual assumptions and empirical data from investigations of the highest appellate judges of Australia, Great Britain, India, Norway, the Philippines, Switzerland, the United States, and West Germany to determine the extent to which the nominal distinctions in Figure 1 are pertinent. In addition, and more importantly, the paper

FIGURE 1.
Judicial Selection as a Variation on Prewitt's Chinese Box Puzzle

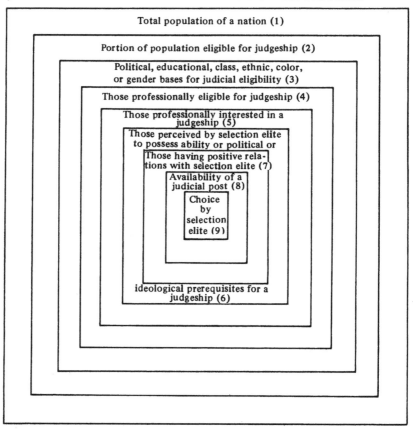

will assess the significance of these findings for comparative analysis of such elites.

The question of whether background and career ladder characteristics are determinants of judicial decision making is beyond the scope of this study, but such variables have been investigated since they are indicators of the characteristics of elite recruitment, of ethnocentrism, and the degree of religious, economic, ethnic, and educational diversity. The description by nation of the variations in such characteristics is a necessary, albeit elementary, portion of the investigations summarized. But more importantly, the distribution of such attributes was assessed in order to determine whether basic theories about law, legal institutions, and legal professionals are confirmed or contradicted. Thus, according to Montesquieu or Savigny, distinctive legal cultures developed as a result of national conditions and the habits and beliefs of the populations of individual nations. Their conceptions emphasized the uniqueness of each nation's legal culture. Conversely, Bentham argued that the universality of basic problems called for universally adopted legal reforms.[3]

More recently, Wilbert E. Moore argued that "the world . . . is a singular system" because professionals in all nations share common educational, economic, and ideological characteristics, including the "rather remarkable concurrence in the ideology of economic development."[4] The validity or invalidity of such sharply contrasting conceptions must ultimately be established on the basis of empirical evidence. Presumably, a universally similar configuration of background characteristics, attitudes, and role orientations across all higher judiciaries in all nations would validate Bentham and Moore, while the reverse would support Montesquieu and Savigny. Developing conceptually equivalent indicators and gathering and evaluating systematically classified data from a large number of nations within the framework of a single research project would, to understate the difficulty and expense, be a formidable undertaking. Therefore, it is not surprising that the data summarized in this paper are derived from separate studies by scholars who were aware of each other's work.

The selection of variables which will provide an empirical basis for the general nominal distinctions summarized in Figure 1 depends upon the conceptual perspectives of the particular investigator. For this analysis of national judicial elites, conceptual frameworks which integrate all major aspects of a nation's judicial and legal system are desirable.

Most conceptual frameworks developed to map the purposes and characteristics of judicial systems and judicial and legal elites are based on the fundamental assumption that these institutions and their personnel evolved or were created in order to institutionalize conflict resolution based upon fair procedure. Indeed, this assumption is an integral part of the "received tradition" in most law school training in the United States. Conversely, most revolutionaries characterize existing judicial systems, judges, and lawyers as instrumentalities of regimes which must be overthrown and replaced. They are viewed as unfair, corrupt, or despotic, as causes of social, economic, and political conflict. This study will explore two conceptual frameworks which embody these contradictory assumptions.

They consist of (1) a modification of Max Weber's model of an ideal legal system and (2) a corollary of Immanuel Wallerstein's World Economic System model. These frameworks are summarized in as parsimonious a form as possible. While these frameworks are derivative of Weber, Wallerstein, and others, strict conformity to their models was not an objective in this investigation.

In broad perspective, Weber's conception of the legal basis for social control and stability embodies several basic attributes: (1) that legal norms may be distinguished from other social integrative norms because they are enforced and (2) that while it is sometimes difficult to distinguish legal mechanisms of social control from nonlegal mechanisms, the presence of a specialized institutional apparatus distinguished such legal from nonlegal mechanisms. These attributes were related to Weber's identification of: legality, formally correct rules, and accepted procedure as bases of political legitimacy.[5] Weber did not posit that capitalism determined the characteristics of Western European legal systems (from which he constructed his ideal model), but he did indicate that an ideal legal system provides the necessary conditions of stability and predictability for the development and maintenance of capitalism. The key criteria employed by Weber for designating such legal systems were "formal" and "rational." The "formal" criterion was met if a legal system's institutional organization and its modes of procedure and decision making were developed and maintained independent of external institutional influences such as political branches of government, political parties, or religious organizations. The "rational" criterion was met when a legal system was characterized by objectivity and impersonality in its modes of decision making.[6] Weber classified governmental authority (in his terminology "domination") in three broad groups: traditional, charismatic, and legal.[7] Many decades before linkage politics became academically fashionable, Weber attempted to demonstrate the integration of political structures and legal systems.[8]

The components of the contradictory conceptual framework were formulated as a corollary of the World System perspective of Immanuel Wallerstein and of other contributors to World System or Center-Periphery conceptions of the impact of a world system of political and economic power and influence which determines the judicial and legal options available to developing nations internally as well as externally.[9] Thus, the development and institutional fulfillment of a World System includes not only its major political and economic characteristics, such as imperialism-capitalism (exemplified by the era characterized as Pax Britannica),[10] but also other forms of penetration by center nations into the polity, economy, and society of underdeveloped or periphery nations. A salient vehicle of such penetration relates to judicial institutions and the legal professions of such nations. Where fundamental political and military power relationships result in outright conquest and colonial development of a previously independent nation or some of its subdivisions, complete replacement of its indigenous judicial system and legal profession frequently occurs concomitantly with military subjugation and economic domination. Or if colonial domination is only partial or is replaced by a client nation relationship, the judicial and legal sectors are in a situation analogous to Gourevitch's realistic description of dual economies. As he put it, "Countries in the periphery develop dual economies: an expanding modern sector tied to the needs of the core, and a stagnant, miserable sector.[11] Similarly, new judicial and legal institutions may be imposed while vestiges of the previous legal system are permitted to exist and atrophy.

The key components of the World System conceptual framework for judicial and legal systems reflect emphasis upon imposed change, center-periphery relations, and economic as well as political power conflicts rather than the conventional basic assumption about conflict resolution. The conceptual model treats significant elements of the judicial and legal systems of selected nations and their relationship to the fundamentals of Wallerstein's World System perspective. In Wallerstein's summation, "A World System is a social system, one that has boundaries, structures, member groups, rules of legitimation, and coherence. Its life is made up of the conflicting forces which hold it together by tension, and tear it apart as each group seeks eternally to remold it to its advantage." Wallerstein distinguishes three varieties of world systems: (1) world empires, in which a single political system controls all or most of the components; (2) the world economy which has existed for five hundred years because the world capitalistic economy "has had within its bounds not one but a multiplicity of political systems"; and (3) socialist world government, which has not succeeded in replacing the second, but which would change the system of economic distribution and political decision making. Within the current world system (the capitalist world economy) the conflicts and tensions which may change or even eliminate a national judicial and legal system are distinguishable in two broad categories. The first involves the conflicts and tensions which Wallerstein deems characteristic of this world system—those growing out of the relationship between the dominant nations (called core states by Wallerstein, center nations by Galtung and others), the peripheral areas, and third, the semi-peripheral areas between these two. The second involves the conflicts and tensions between competing world systems—the capitalist world economy and the socialist world government. At another level of analysis, systemic division-of-labor considerations are also important components of this conceptual framework. Since the division of a world economy involves a hierarchy of occupational tasks, ". . . [the] tasks requiring higher levels of skill and capitalization are reserved for higher-ranking areas."[12] This dimension of the World Economy conceptual framework provides the basis for examining empirically and testing scientifically the validity of Eulau and Sprague's assumption about the convergence of legal and political careers. They had contended that there were "three convergent characteristics" in law and politics "that help to define the structural isomorphism of the two professions—professional independence; a code of ethics; and a norm of public service." They suggest that convergence "seems to be made possible by their integration in the structure of political authority."[13]

In terms of the logic of the World Economy conceptual framework, judicial and legal institutions and personnel are considerably affected or even determined by the conflicts and tensions characteristic of the capitalist world economy and its political manifestations. Independence from external influences (e.g., foreign political and/or economic control) would be the monopoly of the core (center) nations. Modification of the judicial and legal structure, purposes, and characteristics of the personnel of periphery and semi-pheriphery nations or colonial territories would be in accordance with the political and economic needs or demands of the core or center nations.

A detailed examination of the major areas of difference between the two competing conceptual frameworks provides the more comprehensive elements of the World System Model, as well as an item-by-item comparison. These attributes are summarized in Table 1. Because Wallerstein stresses the multiple layers which characterize the World System, references to the requirements of this system pertain to the more complex competitive needs found at various levels of those multiple layers, among them ruling class needs or power bloc demands.

TABLE 1.
What Are the Key Attributes Which Distinguish
These Conceptual Frameworks?

Modified Weberian	Corollary Adapted from Wallerstein
1. Accepts assumption that judicial systems and legal professions evolved or were created to institutionalize conflict resolution based upon fair and objective principles and procedures.	1. Conflict resolution may be a secondary objective, but primary purpose of judicial systems and legal professions is to fulfill needs of world capitalistic economy or its socialist antithesis.
2. The characteristics of judicial systems and legal professions are not the products of deterministic economic and social forces.	2. The characteristics of judicial systems and legal professions are determined by economic and social forces, notably the needs of the world capitalistic economy or its socialist counterpart.
3. Judicial systems and legal professions and their modes of procedure and decision making are developed and maintained	3. Judicial systems and legal professions and their modes of procedure and decision making are developed and maintained

TABLE 1. (cont.)

Modified Weberian	Corollary Adapted from Wallerstein
independently of external institutional influences such as governments, political parties, and religious organizations.	under external institutional influences which seek to maintain the world capitalistic economy or its socialist counterpart.
4. Decision making characterized by objectivity and impersonality in its modes.	4. Objectivity and impersonality in decision making modes may be transcended by compelling need to fulfill goals of world capitalistic economy or its socialist antithesis.
5. Law serves as a neutral arbiter of individual relations between equals.	5. Law protects interests and institutions essential to the optimum functioning of the world capitalistic economy or its socialist equivalent.
6. Legal safeguards for contract and property rights and for noneconomic personal liberties (human rights) are essential.	6. Legal safeguards for property and contract are essential, but noneconomic safeguards are expendable when the bourgeois has achieved effective control of a nation in order to participate in the world capitalist economy.*
7. Predictability and "rationality" were deemed essential to a "legal" system by Weber as components of an ideal system.	7. The "predictability" and "rationality" deemed essential to a "legal" system by Weber were deemed essential by monarchs or other nonrepresentative rulers to encourage commerce and the allegiance of the bourgeois to the monarch.†
8. Judges and elite legal professionals are trained and socialized to develop goals of predictability and rationality.	8. Judges and elite legal professionals are trained and socialized to maintain and develop the world capitalist economy or the world socialist economy.

*Michael E. Tigar and Madeline R. Levy, *Law and the Rise of Capitalism* (New York: Monthly Review Press, 1977).
†Ibid.

In a number of instances, the attributes of these two conceptual frameworks are directly contradictory, notably items related to (1) conflict resolution; (2) the determinants of the characteristics of judicial systems and legal professions; (3) judicial independence or the lack thereof; (4 and 5) legal neutrality and objectivity; and (6) the essentiality or expendability of nonproperty human rights. But in others, the differences are more subtle. For example, it has been argued that the world capitalist economy stimulates convergence "by subjecting all societies to the same forces" and stimulates "divergence by creating different roles for different societies in the world stratification system."[14] The homogenizing thrust is generally interpreted as resulting from the needs of the world capitalist market economy, the thrust toward diversity from world division-of-labor imperatives. Judicial systems and legal professions are uniquely related to the world needs of the capitalist economic system. Therefore, while it might ordinarily be assumed that a branch of a national government (and the professional group most intimately related to the judicial branch) would fulfill a divergent, nationalistic institutional role, it is hypothesized here that this is the one sector of national governments most likely to fulfill the particular legal needs of the world capitalist economy. The framework and pattern of such legal and judicial fulfillment are set by legal professionals, law schools, or their equivalents, and judicial institutions of the core nations; they are generally adopted in the periphery and semi-periphery nations. Consequently, the highest ranking judges and most successful attorneys in these nations are likely to be cosmopolitans, well-trained in the most prestigious of the leading schools of core nations (or in domestic schools modeled after the elite schools of the core nations), and intellectually part of an international community of similar elite jurists and legal professionals. Although many periphery and semi-periphery nations are strongly nationalistic in international policy-making and governmental elite recruitment, judicial recruitment often reflects greater emphasis upon the legal needs of the world economic system. The legal framework based upon the World Economic System perspective, in contrast to that of the modified Weberian model, incorporates the fundamental assumption that judicial systems and legal professions play a very direct role in either a world capitalistic or a world socialist economic system.

In accordance with this preliminary theory, the judicial systems and legal professions of core nations enjoy and maintain relative equality of power and influence, while those of semi-periphery and periphery nations do not share such power and influence. The primary task of the judicial systems and legal systems of core, semi-periphery, and periphery nations is the maintenance of either the world capitalist economic system (which currently is most pervasive) or the countervailing world socialist economic system. The two

systems oppose each other in terms of power, influence, and fundamental assumptions; both the capitalist and socialist nations are
characterized by their own principles and procedures, which accommodate the fundamental prerequisites of their respective economic
systems and which serve to restrict intrusion of principles or practices considered detrimental or contradictory to a capitalist or a socialist legal system. Inga Markovitz's comparative analysis of doctrines
developed by courts in East and West Germany in regard to owner-
ship and sharing of public offices, housing, and worker compensa-
tion provides several pertinent examples.[15] The hierarchy of judges
in the highest appellate courts and the leaders of the bar associations
in the core nations establish and maintain institutional influence
and appropriate doctrinal ascendancy. Similarly, legal education
within either the world capitalist or the world socialist core nations
is oriented to engender the professional behavior, attitudes, and doctrinal commitments which will maintain the integrity of the two
systems.

The characteristics of judicial personnel in a legal system which
provides the stability and predictability requisite to a capitalistic
system were identified by Max Weber as primarily those of a modern
professional elite. These key attributes consist of specialized educational training with emphasis upon abstract, universal principles
and recruitment and professional advancement based upon demon-
strated ability rather than kinship or other ascriptive factors. Weber's
emphasis was upon career ladder attributes as well as background.
In accordance with this model, judicial selection is based upon merit
determined within the context of an institutional framework which
maintains formal independence from the political branches of government. This conception was derived in part from the training and
career patterns of judges in the continental European judicial systems (such as in late nineteenth century Germany and France) that
had provided the contextual basis for Weber's ideal conception. In
fact, the realities of judicial selection were often ascriptive and, as
Weber fully recognized, they were also manifestations of capitalistic
class dominance rather than the fulfillment of the goals of an independent meritocracy.[16] In assessing the realities of recruitment for
the federal appellate judiciary in the United States and for the highest appellate courts of Australia, India, Norway, the Philippines,
Switzerland, and West Germany, the extent to which such judicial
recruitment approximates the Weberian model or the partially contradictory model has to be explored.[17]

The relationship between the social structure and the holding of
higher appellate judicial office in these nations may thus be considered first as part of the broader relationship between socioeconomic
and political stratification. Consequently, models of elite composition deemed appropriate for such analysis are utilized. If ascension

to higher appellate judicial office is independent of such attributes as parental occupation, elite education, elite family background, sex, religion, ethnicity, kinship, or region, then presumably each of these categories is proportionally represented within these courts. Conversely, if ascension to the federal appellate judiciary is contingent upon high status rankings in all these attributes, a perfect example of the ruling elite model is created, and each of the categories is disproportionally represented. For most societies, these models represent diametrically opposed extremes compared to the middle ground of reality found between them. The most open or permeable avenues of recruitment are associated with the first model, which is essentially democratic, while the more restrictive is the second, ruling elite model.[18]

These higher appellate courts were never conceived by their constitutional or statutory progenitors as representative institutions, at least in the sense that legislatures may be deemed representative. But Murphy and Tanenhaus have appropriately suggested that "national constitutional courts typically display a large element of representation" because political leaders who control the appointing authority may "consciously try to staff constitutional courts with personnel of diverse background characteristics that are more or less shared by the various politically relevant groupings within the polity."[19] In a somewhat different sense, sociologists may investigate the extent to which the characteristics of the personnel of particular political institutions proportionally represent the variety of identifiable groups in a particular society to determine whether these groups are politically relevant. Indeed, the inclusion of individuals from their ranks as appointees on higher appellate courts is a key indicator of political relevance for some ethnic groups. One objective of this study is to determine the extent to which regional, ethnic, religious, occupational, and educational groups are represented on the courts investigated.

The empirical bases for this exploratory application of these conceptual frameworks is derived from the following studies of judicial elites: (1) Neumann's collective portrait of the High Court of Australia (2) Gadbois's analysis of the Supreme Court of India, (3) Torgersen's investigation of the Supreme Court of Norway, (4) Samonte's study of the Supreme Court of the Philippines, (5) Morrison's work on the Swiss Federal Court, (6) Kommer's analysis of the West German Federal Constitutional Court, and (7) Schmidhauser's investigation of the federal appellate judiciary of the United States.[20]

Regarding social origins, paternal occupation, family economic circumstances, and status, it is highly unusual in any of the nations for which data are available to find a justice who did not come from an economically comfortable upper-middle-class background. Some national selection processes, notably those of Switzerland and India, stress ethnic, language, or religious diversity in order to insure or attempt to insure political stability. The Swiss Federal Court consistently includes German, French, and Italian representation. The Indian Supreme Court, while overwhelmingly Hindu, has maintained Moslem and Christian representation, though omitting Sikh. Conversely, the Philippine Supreme Court has consistently omitted justices from the sizable Moslem minority. Table 2 provides a summary of these data. From the perspective of class and family origins, higher appellate judicial elites conform to the ruling elite model, with India, the United States, West Germany, and Australia the least permeable systems and Norway and the Philippines somewhat less closed.

Elite transformation resulting from direct political action may be more frequent than is commonly assumed even in nations which appear to be stable. The relative frequency of such change is sometimes overlooked because a great deal of scholarly emphasis in law is placed upon the system-stabilizing and conflict-resolution functions of law, legal institutions, and personnel. It is acknowledged that the modified Weberian model provides important perspectives on the significance of legal elites in political systems experiencing political, social, or economic changes. None of the nations assessed for this study experienced judicial and legal elite transformations as abrupt and as extensive as the French Revolution or the 1979 Iranian overthrow of the Shah. The first Chief Justice of the United States, John Jay, resigned in 1795 in order to run for governor of the state of New York as the Federalist party candidate. The first Chief Justice of the Islamic Republic, the Ayatollah Mohammed Behesti, was blown to bits by a terrorist bomb at a 1981 meeting of the Islamic Republic party in Teheran. Such terminations of judicial careers may represent polar extremes, but both underscore in different ways the need to examine more closely the impact of political change upon judicial and legal elites.

The consequences of significant transformations of judicial and legal elites have been emphasized by Alexis de Tocqueville, Otto Kirchheimer, and Theodore Becker.[21] De Tocqueville raised a number of questions which provide some intellectual challenges to the conception of the convergence of law and politics. The latter often assumes that (1) the involvement of lawyers in politics was generated largely out of the self-interest of lawyers and that (2) there was ready acceptance by the public of legal professionals as judges and legislators because of the skills and/or reputations of these professionals. De Tocqueville discussed other important dimensions as well. On whose behalf did lawyers and judges use their professional talents? Did they become revolutionaries only when their own interests were thwarted or their requests repelled, or did they undertake an independent, relatively altruistic role in behalf of fair legal procedure?[22] Fundamentally, de Tocqueville's questions involve issues both external and internal to each national legal profession. The questions call for comprehensive conventional historical research

TABLE 2.
Summary of Ethnic and Socioeconomic Characteristics of the Justices*

Characteristic	NATIONS						
	Australia 1903–1970	India 1950–1959	Norway 1814–1959	Philippines 1901–1966	Switzerland 1874–1964	United States 1789–1976	West Germany 1951–1972
Upper-middle-class background	77	Approximately 90, at least 40 of that portion high caste Brahmin	60	Upper class / 11 Upper middle class / 48 Lower middle class / 37 Lower class / 4	Large proportion but no precise percentage was provided	82	87
Significant political family background	47	Information not provided	57 (Primarily civil servants)	33	35	45	Information not provided
Primary family occupational background of largest proportion of justices	Professional	Professional	Higher civil service or business	Professional	Professional	Professional in modern times; gentry class before mid-nineteenth century	Professional, with civil servants the largest group (24)
Ethnic, and/or religious origins	British Isles	Hindu – 78 Moslem – 18 Christian – 4 Sikh – 0	Little ethnic diversity during period of investigation	Talalogs, Ilongos, Pampangos, and Pangasinenses	Consistently includes German, French, and Italian judges	Generally some Catholic and Jewish justices after early twentieth century	Some deliberately maintained balance between Protestants and Catholics

Groups excluded	Aborigines and women	Women and Sikhs	Women	Women and a sizable minority of Moslems	Women

First woman seated on U.S. Supreme Court in 1981. No Indian or Hispanic selections to the Court. Limited number of such judges (and a few women) have been chosen for the courts of appeal in the last half

Has generally maintained tradition of having at least one woman on the Federal Constitution Court since 1952

*Numerical data are given where possible in percent.

beyond the scope of this exploratory investigation, but for illustrative purposes two pairs of examples are compared.

An exploratory application of these conceptual frameworks has
been made on the basis of virtually complete data for American
national appellate judges, historical data on major changes in
the American legal profession, and selected cross-national data on
judges and lawyers in core and periphery nations. As Prewitt
and McAllister suggested in discussing "Mosca-Lasswellian notions," the relationship between "theoretically fertile" conceptions
and "empirically testable" hypotheses is often difficult to achieve.[23]
However, in order to take into account the significance of the type of
core-periphery changes associated with the approaches of Wallerstein and others, an appraisal of two pairs of judicial elites in two
pairs of nations with rather different experiences in core-periphery
development will be made here, using data from four investigations
which provide some of the relevant information in chronological
sequence. The data for India and the Philippines provide a limited
but useful basis for the comparison of two supreme courts which
have developed in periphery nations that achieved independence
after World War II. A comparison of the American and Norwegian
Supreme Courts provides a longer institutional transition in nations
that achieved independence before the twentieth century and, after
significant periods as periphery nations, also reached the status of
core nations.

Unfortunately, the periods summarized for India are not extensive,
but some limited observations can be made. Both India and the Philippines maintained strong ties with their respective core nations'
legal education centers in the immediate post-independence era.
During periods of colonial administration by the United States, a
majority of the Filipino Supreme Court consisted of Americans.
Shortly after the early years of the Commonwealth this practice was
discontinued. In a manner consistent with Spanish colonial policy,
the exclusion of members of the sizable Moslem minority was maintained during the American colonial and post-independence era in
the Philippines. In contrast, post-independence India has maintained the British colonial policy of informally but consistently
maintaining Moslem and Christian (but not Sikh) representation on
its Supreme Court. In neither of these periphery nations did the
status of the legal professions or judicial elites undergo serious
changes. In contrast, such changes did occur in the United States
and Norway. From the perspective of a core-periphery analysis consistent with Wallerstein's model, both the American and the Norwegian judicial-legal elites had similar changes. The major
developments in this comparison of American and Norwegian elite
transformation are, first, the unsurprising national changes from a
British or British-oriented to an American judicial and legislative

elite and from a Danish or Danish-oriented to a Norwegian judicial and legislative elite. Second, the general substantive characteristics of the continental mode of legal education were retained, in Norway, providing a professional judicial education differentiated from the education of lawyers. Norway did, of course, develop its own national center for both forms of legal education, first at the Royal University of Frederik and later at the University of Oslo. In the United States, the transition was both national and substantive. Where leading colonial lawyers and judges were often trained in the Inns of Court of London and indeed were often British by origin, after independence the leading attorneys and judges were not only American, but generally trained in the office of a practitioner via the apprenticeship mode of legal education. Later the legal education of the leaders of the profession and the judiciary became dominated by the law schools of which Harvard University was the prototype. Law training for corporate work became the hallmark.[24]

The American and Norwegian experiences were quite different with respect to lawyer representation in legislatures. In colonial America, lawyers were sometimes prohibited from all public offices; when later permitted entry, they were selected in rather small numbers. In colonial Massachusetts, for example, lawyers were not permitted to sit in the legislature before 1691. It was not until 1738 that the first lawyer was elected, and only in 1758 was the second lawyer-legislator chosen. From 1620 to 1760 the legal profession had to struggle for acceptance (and sometimes existence) in Virginia, Pennsylvania, and Massachusetts. It was not until the end of the seventeenth century that lawyers began to replace lay judges in many of the colonies. The reasons for such negative attitudes toward lawyers included political and religious responses to the perceived role of English attorneys allied with the Crown during the periods of political and religious persecution in Great Britain[25] and lay resentment toward those who were viewed as keepers of a professional mystery.[26] The American Revolution of 1775 and especially the establishment of the new federal system under the Constitution of 1789 brought sweeping changes in the status of lawyers. Judicial posts at all but the lowest levels became a permanent monopoly of lawyers although no distinction was made in the education of lawyers for practice or for judicial service. After 1789 lawyers have generally predominated in higher legislative and executive posts. In contrast to the gradual decline of the proportions of judges and lawyers in the Norwegian Parliament, lawyer-legislators have to the present day remained the largest occupational group in both chambers of the American Congress.

The Norwegian Supreme Court has been considerably more insulated from direct political and economic pressures than the federal appellate judiciary of the United States. Consequently, its members were not subjected to the direct political actions which occasionally affected the members of the American federal appellate judiciary.

Elite transformation mirrors fundamental changes in political, social, and economic power in nations. Two major crises directly affected the American federal appellate judicial elite: (1) the transition from the one-party control of the national government of the Federalist party to the establishment of two-party competition, especially as a result of the critical election of 1800, and (2) the emergence of the Republican party to national control in 1860 and the abortive rebellion of the Southern Confederacy. Although American inferior federal judges and Supreme Court justices have Constitutional guarantees of tenure on good behavior, congressional power to abolish courts has been invoked on two occasions, both to abolish courts and remove judges belonging to the political opposition to the party controlling Congress and the Presidency. Thus it was possible for more than twenty federal circuit court of appeals judges selected by President John Adams during the close of his administration to be effectively removed by the elimination of the courts on which they served. Only the Circuit Court for the District of Columbia remained (it had been created under a separate statute). However, in 1862 during the American Civil War, Congress, with the support of President Lincoln, abolished this court and replaced it with a court having the same jurisdiction but called the Supreme Court for the District of Columbia. The three judges of the original court were deemed Southern sympathizers. Prior to their removal via institutional abolition they had been held under house arrest at a Washington, D.C., hotel.[27]

One additional example derived from the American and Norwegian data is illustrative of some of the broad relationships of elite transformation and capitalism which are integral parts of the corollary derived from Wallerstein. For the American analysis, historical periods generally consistent with accepted categorizations by historians were selected. These six distinctive historic eras are: (1) 1789–1828, an era in which government was purportedly dominated by members of the gentry class; (2) 1829–1861, the era in which the Jacksonian social and political revolution was, according to some conventional historical sources, fulfilled; (3) 1862–1888, the era in which accumulated wealth, organized in corporate form, merged with political power; (4) 1889–1919, an era in which corporate influence in government continued to grow, but along with countervailing demands for social justice and regulatory control; (5) 1920–1932, an era of conservative retrenchment and corporate ascendancy in government; and (6) 1933–1976, the period of the purported Rooseveltian social revolution and its aftermath.[28]

The Norwegian historical periods similarly began after national independence was achieved and before the full effects of industrialization were felt. The Norwegian periods are (1) 1814–1884, an era largely dominated by legally trained civil servants directly supportive of the Crown, (2) 1885–1920, an era of conflicting interest group politics with emergent business and corporate influence and countervailing tendencies toward democratization, with the end of Crown control and the establishment of parliamentary government, (3) 1921–1959, an era of greater urbanization and industrialization, further democratization of politics with business leaders developing direct parliamentary influence and a corresponding decline of the influence of higher civil servants. Capitalism was basic in Norway but considerably less strong than in the United States. Table 3 summarizes the relationship of each national development by chronological period to the transformation of each national judicial elite.

These examples from the Philippines, India, Norway, and the United States serve to illustrate possible relationships which approximate some of the characteristics of the corollary derived from Wallerstein. These examples were obviously drawn from investigations which were not designed to explore either of these conceptual frameworks. This preliminary mapping and exploratory endeavor does, however, provide some initial bases for more thorough and extensive investigation. Of particular importance is the desirability for a much closer examination of (1) the circumstances under which lawyers and judges are rejected for public office, (2) the relationship between the recruitment of lawyers as part of each nation's professional elite and the recruitment of lawyers (or, by deliberate choice, the selection of non-lawyers) as judges or legislators, (3) the comparative analysis of the characteristics of lawyers chosen as legislators and lawyers chosen as judges, and (4) the nature of the relationship between successful lawyers in the private sector and higher appellate judges. The necessity to examine more closely the conditions under which lawyers and judges exchange public service for the private sector within capitalistic nations is also an important research goal. The world may indeed be a singular system for the highest appellate judges and top corporate attorneys of the nations assessed, but the scope of investigation must be broadened to include a greater variety of nations, especially representatives of the Soviet bloc, the Middle East, and a variety of Third World nations in Africa, East Asia, and South America. In sum, longitudinal comparative analysis of such diverse legal systems is necessary in the investigation of both the neo-Weberian model and the corollary derived from the Wallerstein framework. Specifically, a sequence of time-series investigations of selected core and periphery legal systems should be designed to determine whether they change from traditional to charismatic to rational-legal (or back) in the framework of a Weberian model or, in the context of the framework adapted from Wallerstein, from pre-capitalist to capitalist, to socialist modes of production and division of labor, experiencing

TABLE 3.
Basic Changes in the Characteristics of American and Norwegian Judicial Elites
by Era of Fundamental Change in Each Nation

Norway		The United States	
Era	Judicial Recruitment	Era	Judicial Recruitment
1. 1814–1884. Era dominated by higher civil servants supportive of the Crown.	Judges chosen from Higher Civil Servant class and supportive of the Crown, nearly half of judges selected to Parliament.	1. 1789–1828. Era of gentry class domination of government.	Justices and judges chosen from the politically active segment of the gentry class.
2. 1885–1920. Era of interest group conflict, end of Crown domination, and establishment of parliamentary government.	Gradual change in judicial recruitment from families of higher civil servants to more from professional families; gradual decline in proportion of judges in Parliament (as well as lawyer-legislators).	2. 1829–1861. Era in which the Jacksonian social and political revolution was purportedly fulfilled.	Justices and judges still, with a few exceptions, chosen from the gentry class.
3. 1921–1959. Era of greater urbanization, direct business influence upon Parliament, and further decline in higher civil servant class.	Continued decline in civil service background and increase in professional background, virtual disappearance of judges as members of Parliament (also considerable decline in the proportion of lawyers).	3. 1862–1888. Era of emergent union of corporate influence and political power.	Decline of gentry class judicial selection and initial increase of selection from professional families.

4. 1889–1919. Era of continuing corporate influence with some countervailing demands for regulation.	Predominantly chosen from professional families, substantial corporate law influence, and the development of a minority of career jurists.
5. 1920–1932. Era of conservative retrenchment and corporate ascendancy.	Virtually all appointees chosen from professional families, most committed to corporate influence (including the minority of career jurists).
6. 1933–1976. Era of the purported Rooseveltian social revolution and its aftermath.	Only minor change in selection pattern from professional families. Roosevelt and in one instance Truman selected some legal professionals who were primarily law professors in order to avoid corporate law influence. After the 1940s the pattern generally represented a reinstatement of corporate-oriented selections.

role changes from periphery to core (or back). Each of these conceptual frameworks appears to contradict the others in certain respects. But each deals with fundamentally different kinds of changes, the first intrasystemic, the latter intersystemic. The possible interrelationships of these frameworks and the potential consequences for judicial elite circulation are thus worthy of subsequent investigation and analysis.

Notes

1. See, for example, Roy C. Macridis, *The Study of Comparative Government* (Garden City, N.Y.: Doubleday and Co., 1966); and Joseph La-Palombara, "Present Trends and Issues: Contemporary Issues in the Theory of Comparative Politics," in *Comparative Political Systems*, ed. Louis J. Cantori (Boston: Holbrook Press, 1974), pp. 26–27.

2. Kenneth Prewitt, *The Recruitment of Political Leaders: A Study of Citizen Politicians* (Indianapolis, Ind.: Bobbs-Merrill, 1970), p. 8.

3. Henry W. Ehrmann, *Comparative Legal Cultures* (Englewood Cliffs, N.J.: Prentice-Hall, 1976), p. 5.

4. Wilbert E. Moore, "Global Sociology: The World as a Singular System," *American Journal of Sociology* 72 (1966), pp. 475–82.

5. Max Rheinstein, ed., *Max Weber on Law in Economy and Society* (Cambridge, Mass.: Harvard University Press, 1954), p. 13; and Max Weber, *The Theory of Social and Economic Organization*, tr. Talcott Parsons (New York: Free Press, 1964), p. 128.

6. Weber, *The Theory of Social and Economic Organization*, p. 77.

7. The initial adaptation of this framework was made in John R. Schmidhauser, "Corruption on the Federal Bench: Mapping the Conceptual Framework in the Context of Weber's Ideal Legal System" (Paper presented at the 1978 meeting of the Midwest Political Science Association, Chicago, April 1978).

8. Guenter Roth and Claus Wittich, eds., *Max Weber, Economy and Society: An Outline of Interpretative Sociology* (New York: Bedminster Press, 1968), p. 883.

9. Michael E. Tigar and Madeline R. Levy, *Law and the Rise of Capitalism* (New York: Monthly Review Press, 1977); Andre Gunder Frank, *Capitalism and Underdevelopment in Latin America* (New York: Monthly Review Press, 1967); Johann Galtung, "A Structural Theory of Imperialism," *Journal of Peace Research* 8 (1971), pp. 81–117. For an approach placing greater emphasis on legal institutions and professions, see also Perry Anderson, *From Antiquity to Feudalism* (London: New Left Books, 1974) and Perry Anderson, *Lineages of the Absolutist State* (London: New Left Books, 1974). A new journal, *Review: A Journal of the Fernand Braudel Center for the Study of Economies, Historical Systems, and Civilizations* (Beverly Hills: Sage Publications, 1980), has been established to develop and criticize the World System perspective.

10. Neville William, *Chronology of the Modern World, 1763–1965*, ltd. ed. (Harmondsworth, England: Penguin Books, 1975); and Albert H. Imlah, *Economic Elements in the Pax Britannica* (Cambridge, Mass.: Harvard University Press, 1958).

11. Peter Gourevitch, "The Second Image Reversed: The International Sources of Domestic Politics," *International Organization* 32, no. 4, (Autumn 1978).

12. Immanuel Wallerstein, *The Modern World System* (New York: Academic Press, 1974), pp. 347–50.

13. Heinz Eulau and John D. Sprague, *Lawyers in Politics: A Study in Convergence* (Indianapolis, Ind.: Bobbs-Merrill, 1964), pp. 143–44.

14. John W. Meyer, John Boli-Bennett, and Christopher Chase-Dunn, "Convergence and Divergence in Development," in *Annual Review of Sociology* 1, ed. Alex Inkeles, James Coleman, and Neil Smelser (1975), (Palo Alto: Annual Review, 1975), p. 223.

15. Inga Markovitz, "Owing and Sharing—The Rightholder's Relation to Society in Bourgeois and Socialist Law" (Paper presented at the 1980 Annual Meeting of the American Political Science Association, Washington, D.C., August 1980). For evidence of short-term accommodation, see Josef Wilczynski, *The Multi-nationals and East-West Relations* (Boulder, Colo.: Westview Press, 1976).

16. Weber's scientific interest in creating an "ideal" model of the administration of justice in a "legal" system did not blind him to the realities of the operation of judicial systems on several capitalistic systems. Indeed, he once noted that:

Formal justice guarantees the maximum freedom for the interested parties to represent their formal legal interests. But because of the unequal distribution of economic power, *which the system of formal justice legalizes,* this very freedom must time and again produce consequences which are contrary to . . . religious ethics or . . . political expediency (Quoted by Roth and Wittich, Max Weber, *Economy and Society,* p. 821; emphasis mine).

17. Since the analysis of most of the American data (through 1976) from the perspective of the modified Weberian model was published in 1979, only a brief summary of some of those findings is incorporated into this analysis. Greater emphasis is given to several exploratory applications of the contradictory model.

18. The democratic model is identical to Putnam's *independence* model, and the ruling elite model coincides with his (and Lasswell's) agglutination model. See Robert P. Putnam, *The Comparative Study of Political Elites* (Englewood Cliffs, N.J.: Prentice-Hall, 1976), pp. 21–22.

19. Walter F. Murphy and Joseph Tanenhaus, "Constitutional Courts and Political Representation," in *Modern Democracy,* ed. Michael N. Danielson and Walter F. Murphy (New York: Holt, Rinehart, and Winston, 1969), p. 542.

20. Eddy Neumann, *The Higher Court of Austria: A Collective Portrait* (Sydney, Australia: University of Sydney Press, 1971); George H. Gadbois, "Selection, Background Characteristics and Voting Behavior of Indian Supreme Court Judges, 1950–1959," in *Comparative Judicial Behavior,* ed. Glendon Schuhert and David J. Danelski (New York: Oxford University Press, 1969); Ulf Torgersen, "The Role of the Supreme Court in the Norwegian Political System," in *Judicial Decision-Making,* ed. Glendon Schubert (New York: Free Press, 1963); Abelardo G. Samonte, "The Philippine Supreme Court: A Study of Judicial Background Characteristics, Attitudes, and Decision-Making," in *Comparative Judicial Behavior,* ed.

Glendon Schubert and David J. Danelski (New York, Oxford University Press, 1969); Fred L. Morrison, "The Swiss Federal Court: Judicial Decision-Making and Recruitment," in Frontiers of Political Research, ed. Joel B. Grossman and Joseph Tanenhaus (New York: John Wiley and Sons, 1969); Donald P. Kommer's Judicial Politics in West Germany: A Study of the Federal Constitutional Court (Beverly Hills, Calif.: Sage Publications, 1976); and John R. Schmidhauser, "The Justices of the Supreme Court of the United States: A Collective Portrait," Midwest Journal of Political Science 3 (1959); and Schmidhauser, Judges and Justices: The Federal Appellate Judiciary (Boston, Mass.: Little, Brown and Company, 1979).

21. Alexis de Tocqueville, The Old Regime and the French Revolution (Garden City, N.Y.: Doubleday, 1955); de Tocqueville, Democracy in America (New York: Schocken Books, 1967); Otto Kirchheimer, Political Justice: The Use of Legal Procedure for Political Ends (Princeton, N.J.: Princeton University Press, 1961); and Theodore Becker, ed., Political Trials (Indianapolis, Ind.: Bobbs-Merrill, 1971).

22. De Tocqueville, The Old Regime and the French Revolution, pp. 116–17; and de Tocqueville, Democracy in America, pp. 321–22.

23. Kenneth Prewitt and William McAllister, "Changes in the American Executive Elite, 1930–1970," in Elite Recruitment in Democratic Politics: Comparative Studies across Nations, ed. Heinz Eulau and Moshe M. Czudnowski (New York: John Wiley and Sons, 1976), p. 118.

24. Erwin O. Smigel, The Wall Street Lawyer: Professional Organization Man? (New York: Free Press, 1964), pp. 112–15; and Otto E. Koegel, Walter S. Carter: Collector of Young Masters or the Progenitor of Many Law Firms (New York: Round Tree Press, 1953).

25. For a full analysis of these significant developments, see Gerard W. Gawalt, The Promise of Power: The Emergence of the Legal Profession in Massachusetts, 1760–1840 (Westport, Conn.: Greenwood Press, 1979); Gawalt, "Massachusetts Lawyers: A Historical Analysis of the Process of Professionalization, 1760–1840" (Ph.D. diss., Clark University, 1969); and Milton M. Klein, "From Community to Status: The Development of the Legal Profession in Colonial New York," New York History (April 1979).

26. Daniel H. Calhoun, Professional Times in America: Structure and Aspiration, 1750–1850 (Cambridge, Mass.: Harvard University Press, 1965).

27. Schmidhauser, Judges and Justices, pp. 46–49.

28. Among the historians who used such time-series categories were Arthur Schlesinger and D. Ryan Fox, eds., A History of American Life, 12 vols. (New York: Macmillan, 1943).

Elite Input and Policy Output: The Case of Germany

Klaus von Beyme

Gaetano Mosca did not believe in mechanisms by which the social origin of decision makers would automatically translate (or convert, if you prefer) into specific political outputs. He criticized Marxism for its social determinism and its tendency to underrate the power of ideas; he believed in the power of factors shaping the policy-makers in a more individual way than the whole ruling class. In Machiavellian terms: *"necessità"* is always limited by *"virtù"* and *"fortuna."* He was also skeptical about the principles of elite recruitment developed by modern parliamentary systems. He considered most parliamentary decisions rather as the impact of plutocratic and corrupt influences than as the result of the social background of the actors or as the reasonable result of political wisdom.[1]

The Italian parliamentary system under the "Statuto Albertino" was corrupted by blurring the traditional party lines under Depretis's "Trasformismo" tactics, mobilizing parliamentary majorities wherever he could get them, even by means of corruption, if necessary. This regime formed the basis of Mosca's analysis. Some of Mosca's followers were even less moderate in criticizing parliamentary systems and claimed that *"i piccoli eroi del suffragio universale"* (the little heroes of the universal suffrage) have even less scruples than autocrats.[2] Mosca, however, remained liberal enough not to recommend a return to autocracy as a promising alternative for Italy.

Modern elite research has again and again asked similar questions, though in a less rhetorical and more "professional" language: "Once again does it pay to study social background in elite analysis?"[3] The analysis of social background data still performs important functions for socialization and recruitment studies. But we have reason to be as skeptical as Mosca about the possibility of predicting governmental output by our knowledge of the social background of the most important political actors.

In light of German data on social background of elites and policy outcomes of the system, my counter-hypothesis is, rather, that there was a much greater *correlation between the social background of elites and policy outcomes in the pre-democratic and pre-parliamentary regimes,* such as the German Empire from 1871 to 1918, than in later periods. Social background "matters" in a democratic system as long as most *parties tend to represent social classes* and strata, or even smaller status groups. However, the most useful focus of analysis is less the social origin of the individual deputies than the social base of the parties. In postwar parliamentary systems, the parties have become catch-all parties, to the extent that they are no longer representatives of social pillars. This does not necessarily mean that the diffusion of social background over all the strata generates a concomitant de-ideologization. The "end of ideology" hypothesis turned into a self-destroying prophecy at the moment it was launched, even in many European systems. But temporary waves of re-ideologization *have weakened the links between social background and policy action of party elites.* Ideology, particularly in socialist and social democratic parties, became more important than social background. Mosca was not able to foresee that "nonrevisionist" Marxist parties such as PSIUP in Italy or PSU in France would have a minimal proportion of worker representation.[4]

Policy output is frequently measured by a typology qualifying the nature of governmental acts and/or parliamentary laws. Most of the typologies have no logical element in common.[5] Therefore, I propose a slightly different typology of governmental output according to the criterion "who benefits" from a measure, "in which area," or "to whom are the measures detrimental."

My typology proposes five categories:

Distributive measures: In contradistinction to Lowi (see n. 5), no attempt is made here to differentiate distributive and redistributive measures. There are few decisions meant to have truly redistributive impact on society in most market systems. There have been quite a few decisions in the initial stage of the Federal Republic which had to impose burden-sharing on citizens who were neither refugees from eastern parts of the country nor affected by air raids and destruction during the war. But the category of "redistribution" after the founding phase of the Federal Republic would count too few cases in order to be meaningful. The category "distribution" contains all the key decisions that entailed the distribution of goods and services for the satisfaction of material needs of parts of the population.

Protective measures: Those governmental decisions that protect the whole population or certain groups and involve major financial rewards to groups. Financial costs tend to be predominantly administrative costs of implementation.

Participatory measures: Those governmental actions that increase the participation of the population at all levels, from industrial enterprises (e.g., "Mitbestimmung") to the national level (e.g., law on parties).

Regulative measures: These include (a) the bulk of the shaping of new institutions and the development of the legal system and (b) the integration of the system within the international community.

Repressive measures: Sometimes every governmental action that limits the freedom of the population or certain groups has been called "repressive." Neo-Marxists included in their typologies of "state activities" even the regulation of the military service as "repressive." A more restrictive sense of the word has been used here: only true limitations of civil rights granted in the Basic Law (the constitution) have been classified as repressive measures.

Counting the key decisions of the first 100 years of a unified German state from 1871 to 1971, and differentiating between regulative measures and institutional innovations, we get the figures present in Table 1 for the measures taken in the average per year.[6]

TABLE 1.
Key Decisions of Governmental Output:
Type of Measure—Average per Year

Regimes	Distrib- utive	Partici- patory	Protec- tive	Regu- lative	Institu- tional	Repres- sive
1871–1918	0.02	0.3	0.5	0.9	0.5	0.6
1919–1932	0.3	0.5	1.9	2.0	1.3	1.5
1933–1945	0.2	0.2	1.7	1.9	1.6	5.6
1949–1971	0.7	0.7	2.6	3.9	1.9	0.4
1871–1971	0.2	0.4	1.3	1.9	1.1	1.3

These figures show that the first three regimes are rather close together in many respects. The most striking deviations from the average figures are to be found in the small number of distributive measures in the Imperial regime and the high number of repressive measures during the Nazi regime. Except for institutional and repressive governmental output, the Nazi regime shows a regressive tendency on all levels, compared to the Weimar Republic. The Federal Republic is on all kinds of decisions above the former regimes— except in the area of repressive measures. Protective and repressive measures in the long run seem to be in balance, but if we compare the regimes, protective decisions show an increasing tendency and are now second in importance to the regulative measures.

If we compare, in quantitative terms, the sum of social, economic, and fiscal legislation with social background data of the decision-makers, we find a high correlation between the two variables. From the protective laws during the Empire to the increasing number of bills which give certain privileges to the middle classes, there is an obvious connection between the social background of the majority of decision-makers and the kind of governmental or parliamentary decision in Germany. Paradoxically, this process did not continue under the Nazi regime, which was most decidedly in favor of the lower middle class in its propaganda. Though the system intentionally tried to promote the interests of the lower middle classes, especially craftsmen, retailers, and farmers, the ambitious plans for autarky and foreign and military policies had functionally the opposite results: the absolute and relative importance and security of these groups declined under the Nazi rule.[7] Especially after World War II, these groups had a political influence far above their proportional importance for the German economy under the dominance of the CDU (Christian-Democrats). The CDU-governmental output was characterized by an unusually high proportion of "private bills" and special regulations for the professions, with farmers and other groups of the middle classes predominating.[8] But this alone cannot explain the correlation between the middle-class background of the CDU decision-makers and the benefits granted to the intended middle-class beneficiaries of the CDU legislation. This high correlation can be explained only if we also consider the adaptation of the SPD's (Social Democrats) opposition to the predominating middle-class values, which was not accompanied by an adequate change to middle-class composition in the party as a whole or in the party's elite. The change in ideology that tended to make the formulations of the party program more and more a collection of Sunday speeches, where occasionally lip service was paid to the party's working class character, was in fact characterized by the acceptance of middle-class values that predominated in the parties of the government coalition.

But quantitative correlations between the variables cannot explain the most interesting phenomenon in governmental output: the sudden shifts and innovations in certain policies. It would be tempting to try to associate the six major types of decisions with the predominance of ideological and political groups as follows:

> redistributive decisions with socialist groups
> participatory decisions with radical groups
> protective decisions with social liberal and social conservative groups
> regulatory decisions with liberal groups
> institutional decisions with conservative groups
> repressive decisions with reactionary groups.

Even this, however, would not be very enlightening. If we compare the groups that supported the government in the four regimes, we find an overwhelming predominance of rightist and middle-rightist groups in power, with the exception of 1919, 1928–1929, and 1969–1980. The increases in the frequencies of certain measures do not always correspond to the access of new groups to governmental power, with the exception of the redistributive and participatory categories, which twice (1919 and 1966) increased with the entry of Social Democrats into governmental responsibility. No clear correlation between the predominance of certain political groups and type of governmental output can be found, for the following reasons:

(1) Whereas France was characterized by the "eternel marais" (M. Duverger) of a radical-liberal predominance since 1870, the German governments were predominantly conservative and showed a remarkable tendency and ability to integrate liberal groups into conservative coalitions.

(2) A political system with little constitutional continuity is forced, much more than others (such as Britain, the Scandinavian or Benelux-States), to have a considerable output in institutional and regulatory decisions, in order to stabilize the constitutional systems and to replace the legislations of former regimes.

As far as legislative output is concerned, Germany had one of the busiest Parliaments in Europe during all its regimes. In the first three systems, however, the creativity at the level of institutional outputs showed an inverse proportion to its efficiency. A great deal of institutions—at that time still fairly unique in the Western World—worked rather badly, as for instance the Economic Council (*Reichswirtschaftsrat*), the referendum, the beginnings of constitutional judical review, and the other governmental outputs (especially regulation of business and economics). These failures have largely contributed to the instability of political regimes in Germany, though so far only one system, the Weimar Republic, collapsed without pressure from outside.

Certain decisions cannot be strictly associated with the predominance of one political ideology, since they are closely interrelated. This is true, most specifically, of protective measures, which usually entail regulatory and institutional arrangements as well. Still more striking in Germany is the correlation between protective and repressive measures. Some periods characterized by many repressive measures, such as the 1880's, the periods of the World Wars, the beginning of the twenties in the Weimar Republic, and the end of the sixties in the Federal Republic, show that a system that reacts flexibly to pressures from protest movements and social unrest tries to combine repressive and protective measures with a certain subtlety in order to survive. This can be noticed even in periods of aggressive foreign policy, so frequent in recent German history.

Some historians[9] have interpreted the German Empire as a Bonapartist regime—as Marx was the first to do—characterized by aggressive penetration of foreign systems, the muting of social unrest through a foreign policy of national glory, protective measures in favor of the petty bourgeoisie combined with verbal hostility against capitalism but secret indulgence toward the expansion of its power, and by a combination of attacks on the rights to participation and plebiscitarian demagogy with protective measures for certain groups of the poor.

The Bonapartism of the German Empire has been overrated by leftist historians: social and plebiscitarian demagogy did not play the same role as under the Second French Empire. The predominance of the old elites was more striking in Prussia-Germany than the attempts of Louis Napoleon to create a new elite loyal to his system from very different parts of society. Germany, more than the Second French Empire, was characterized by an alliance of two powerful interests, agriculture and industry, which seemed to be hostile toward each other in the first years of the regime, as long as the economic boom lasted (until 1873).

In the years of crisis and economic stagnation, agrarian and industrial interests discovered certain common interests and formed an alliance under the flag of protectionism; in 1898, we find the first clear alliance between industry and landowners. At the turn of the 20th century, there even existed an agrarian faction within the industrialists' organization, which represented agrarian industries such as sugar, liquor, and fertilizers. Several times, the movement for a coalition of all conservative interests led to a "rapprochement" of these interests, having fought bitter controversies over the question of tariffs and antitrust-legislation until 1905 and 1907.[10] In 1913, the industrial organization "CVDI," the farmers organization "BdL," and the middle-class organization "Mittelstandsverband" tried to form a "coalition of creative classes" (*Kartell der schaffenden Städe*) under an ideology of common interests of the three groups.

In spite of the different social bases of expansionist policies in the German and French Empires, the model of "social imperialism" for the German Empire under William II is still valid. Comparing the whole period of Imperial Germany, however, the aggressive components of German politics differed from period to period. Five phases can be singled out:

(1) Bismarck's policy was aggressive until the foundation of the Empire. After 1871, he was keen to avoid further confrontations with the other big powers and was therefore reluctant to acquire colonies for Germany. One of the key nondecisions was the decline of an offer of protection by the Sultan of Zanzibar in 1874.

(2) After 1884, Bismarck was pushed by social and colonial interests in the country to participate in colonial expansion.

(3) By the end of the century the coalition of agrarian and industrial interests realized that the direct acquisition of colonies and strongholds created too many financial and political burdens for the Empire; the way of peaceful penetration via trade was therefore preferred.

(4) At the beginning of the 20th century, a new period of increasingly autocratic rule by William II led to new demonstrations of aggressiveness and gun boat diplomacy, as in Venezuela, Morocco, and China.

(5) The period of militant intentions to change the rules of the game in the international sphere at the brink of the First World War.

Even in periods of nonaggressive politics in Germany there is still some association between repressive and protective or even distributive measures. This is true even for the Federal Republic especially at the beginning of the 1950's and the end of the 1960's. Much weaker than the association between the type of decisional output and dominating party is the correlation between elite recruitment and governmental output. Paradoxically, in Germany some of the greatest innovations have been made possible with a rather conservative elite, without major changes in composition. The same seems to be true of certain times in British history under conservative governments (such as Disraeli, Churchill, and Heath).

Only the first key decisions of the four regimes in Germany after 1871 can be explained by a change in the composition of elites. This applies, for instance, to the programmatic statements in the constitutions, party programs, and the first legislative steps undertaken by the three constitutional regimes. The most important among the key decisions in the respective German regimes, however, can hardly be explained in terms of changes in elites composition. Among these key decisions are some of the most innovative redistribution measures.

In the 1880's when Imperial Germany introduced the first laws for the protection of the working classes (1883: health insurance, 1884: accident insurance, 1889: old age pension), which were far ahead of all constitutional regimes in the world that were, in other respects, much more developed than Germany in that period.[11] These measures cannot be explained by a change in elite composition. They represented a clear deviation from the ideologies of the predominantly liberal bourgeois and conservative-aristocratic elites in government and in the Reichstag, and can only be explained as a countermeasure against the different ideologies against which Bismarck's regime was fighting. The first purge was directed against those who were suspected of being liberals. After 1862, Bismarck got rid of about 1,000 officials in order to ensure complete conformity.[12] The second purge was initiated in the period of protectionism against the liberal free-traders of the Dellbrück-era. The third purge was a countermeasure against the Social Democrats under the pressure of

the most rapidly increasing and the most well-organized and re-
spected socialist party of that period.[13] Only the measures against
the Social Democrats were directed against different strata of society,
whereas the suspected liberals belonged more or less to the same
elite groups as the government that brought about the different policy changes. The Social Democrats never fully accepted Bismarck's
social legislation program, and the workers' party was severely criticized by the bourgeois parties for having opposed social measures
on several occasions.

In the 1950's the Federal Republic introduced legislation to idem-
nify the expellees from the Eastern territories, which was unique in
its successful reintegration of over 12 million underprivileged ex-
patriates into West German society. It was one of the best organized
measures of social redistribution without violence in history. These
measures were not due to changes in elite composition, neither were
they due to the pressures of the organization of the expellees, however efficient its propaganda may have been.[14] The representation of
the expellees in the political elite was not disproportionately high,
and their representatives could be found primarily in lower positions in the hierarchy, rather than among the top decision-makers.
The success of the huge innovative legislation was predominantly
due to the Communist threat and the necessity to preserve social
peace in order to stabilize the capitalist system in West Germany.[15]
In both cases, pressure from outside or inside the system, and its
impact on mass behavior, was more decisive for innovation than the
recruitment patterns of the elite, which changed at a much slower
rate than the increase in the urgency of the problem.

The next examples apply to the most important innovative measures in Germany as far as political participation is concerned, which
was second in importance only to obtaining a share in the increasing
wealth for the so-far underprivileged. There were several periods in
which German states made concessions to the participating demand:

> After 1914, when the First World War forced the government to
> recognize the trade unions as equal partners (*Hilfsdienstgesetz*);
> After the revolution of 1918, when the workers' council system was
> legalized;
> After 1967/1968, when social unrest among students and workers
> forced the government to concede participation rights in the facto-
> ries and universities.

All three processes were unrelated to changes in the composition of
elites.

The only innovative period—apart from the 1918 Revolution—
that was clearly accompanied by changes in the elite composition
was the change of government in 1969. But most of the innovations

initiated after this governmental change (reform of the penal code, new insurance laws, adaption of pensions, law for urban planning, federal and Länder-university laws, protection of tenants and others) had been prepared by the great coalition of the CDU and the SPD and were not exclusively associated with the changes in elite recruitment.

When we consider not only key decisions but the whole governmental output for the period of the Federal Republic (1949–1976), comparing the performance of CDU- and SPD-led governments, we arrive at the following conclusions (Table 2).

(1) The changes in the social composition of parliaments do not explain the variance in output. The number of workers did not increase in the Bundestag; the predominance of civil servants and employees continued to grow under SPD governments.[16]

(2) The CDU governments of the four first legislatures showed a higher legislative output in distributive measures. From this, it cannot be concluded that the SPD was less distribution-oriented than the CDU for the following two reasons:

(a) The bulk of distributive measures was during the first legislature (1949–1953)—radical distributive laws in order to settle emergency problems for 12 million refugees, millions of citizens whose houses had been destroyed by air raids, and millions of families without a male wage-earner.

(b) Most of the distributive measures that were not just favors for certain groups of the middle classes were supported by the opposition. If we do not only count the measures but also compare the majorities for certain laws, we see that of an average of six redistributive laws per year, almost three (2.8) were carried by the whole house, and one (1.1) had such a large majority that even beyond rare cases of roll calls it can be concluded that most of the SPD members of the house approved the bill. The SPD governments since 1969, on the other hand, had less support from the opposition of Christian Democrats. Among 3.5 distributive laws passed on the average per year by the Bundestag, only about one-half (1.7 per year) were carried also by the CDU-CSU members of the house (for absolute figures, see Table 2, rows 1–7). Support for redistribution became stronger under the CDU leadership of Barzel and Kohl than it had been in many respects under SPD-opposition leaders such as Schumacher and Ollenhauer.

(3) The amount of regulative measures—which is the category most neutral toward party ideology—shows hardly any differences between SPD and CDU. Participatory measures also show little variance between the two major parties.

(4) Declining growth rates have contributed to a shrinking number of distributive measures under SPD-led governments and to an

TABLE 2.
Types of Political Decisions, 1949–1976

Number of legislature and years of session	Distributive			Participatory			Protective			Regulative			Repressive		
	total	u.*	g.M.†	total	u.	g.M.	total	u.	g.M.	total	u.	g.M.	total	u.	g.M.
I 1949–1953	69	31	12	3		3	31	17	7	73	29	26	1		1
II 1953–1957	13	5	1	5		1	27	13	3	37	14	2	4		1
III 1957–1961	4	2	1				9	6	2	11	6	2	1		
IV 1961–1965	9	5	3	3	2	1	16	12	3	19	12	2	2		
V 1965–1969	7	1	6	3		3	14		14	23		23	2	1	1
VI 1969–1972	8	4		2	1	1	16	7	1	16	6	1	1		2
VII 1972–1976	13	6		5	1	1	33	26		38	20		1	1	1
	123	54	23	21	4	10	146	81	30	217	87	56	12	2	6
CDU government I–IV year by average	6.0	2.8	1.1				5.1	3.2	1.0	9.0	4.0	2.1			
SPD government VI–VII year by average	3.5	1.7	0				8.2	5.5	0	9.0	4.3	0.2			

*u. = carried unanimously (votes where only one or two deputies voted against have been subsumed in this category).

†g.M. = a great majority carried a bill, which means that large parts of the opposition may have approved the measure.

For the calculation of the CDU and SPD performance, the Vth legislature (1966–1969) has been excluded. During the years of the "grand coalition," one cannot attribute any measures to one of the governmental partners. All the laws in this period belong to the group carried with large majorities.

increase in protective measures in many fields. Again, the governmental parties cannot boast of having carried these innovations against the opposition. Five and one-half protective laws out of more than eight (8.2) per year in the period of SPD-led governments were also approved by the CDU-CSU, whereas the SPD in opposition had approved about three (3.2) of five (5.1) protective laws carried by the CDU governments per year during the first fifteen years of the Federal Republic.

(5) Repressive measures were started under the great coalition and cannot be attributed to any of the two major parties. They reached a peak during the students' movement and in the period of terrorism in the early 1970's. There was rarely unanimity among the party elites as to the countermeasures, but normally no simple majority—which did not include the bulk of the opposition—was sufficient to carry a law.

(6) On the whole, parties and their ideologies matter much more than the social composition of party elites or parliamentary groups which predominantly carry certain types of governmental measures. The social composition of the two "catch-all" parties is becoming more similar than in other systems, where a conservative party (instead of a Christian-Democratic party, which always has less characteristic features of a class-party than conservative parties) is facing a workers' party. The remaining social differences are less important. The workers in both parties tend to strengthen the conservative wings, and the middle-class intellectuals are frequently more leftist than party elites coming from a more humble social background. Unlike Britain, the gap in terms of specialists in different fields between the two major German parliamentary groups is small. The tradition of German parties is also apparent below the level of national politics, at the level of the Laender governments: the SPD tends to initiate and support measures in the field of the social and educational distribution of opportunities; but, at the same time, it has a law-and-order tradition of its own, which leads it to spend more money on internal security than the Christian Democrats.[17]

Mosca was rather pessimistic about the future of parliamentary democracy. Democratization of the system for him was tantamount to lowering the intellectual and moral level of the elites. Mosca thought that the representatives would become more similar to those whom they represent. The necessity of doing favors for a democratic clientele was for him the beginning of the decline of politics.[18] Mosca did not see that the representative character of the regime might be replaced by the "responsiveness" of elites. This is one more reason for the fact that social background matters less than ideology—but Mosca tried to protect himself by an immunization of his prognoses: "Nessuna cosa in politica e più difficile delle profezie"[19] ("Nothing in politics is more difficult than prediction").

Notes

1. Gaetano Mosca, *Elementi di scienza politica* (Bari: Laterza, 1947), chap. XVI, sect. 3; chap. X, sect. 8.

2. Ettore D'Orazio, *Fisiologia del parlamentarismo in Italia* (Turin: Einaudi, 1911), p. 444. Cf., for an analysis of the whole pre-Fascist antiparliamentary sentiments, Klaus von Beyme, *Die parlamentarischen Regierungssysteme in Europa* 2d ed. (Munich: Piper, 1973), pp. 190 ff.

3. Uwe Schleth, *Once Again: Does It Pay to Study Social Background in Elite Analysis?*, Sozialwiss. Jahrbuch fur Politik. (Munich: Isar, 1971), pp. 99–118.

4. Cf. Charles Hauss, *The New Left in France: The Unified Socialist Party* (Westport, Conn.: Greenwood, 1978), pp. 82, 78; L. Radi, *Partiti e classi in Italia* (Turin: Societa editrice internazionale, 1975), p. 97 ff.

5. Th. J. Lowi, "American Business: Case Studies and Political Theory," *World Politics* (1963–1964), pp. 677–715.

6. Compiled after *"Reichsgesetzblatt"* and *"Bundesgesetzblatt,"* and some collections of German laws. A systematic overview of the older German laws can be found in U. Dehlinger, *Systematische Ubersicht Uber das Reichsgesetzblatt, 1867–1932 und die Notverordnungen des Reichspraesidenten.* (Stuttgart, 1933) and *Die wichtigsten Gesetze seit 1918: Kurschners Jahrbuch.* (Berlin-Leipzig, 1928), pp. 162–74; J. V. Munch, *Gesetze des NS-Staates.* (Bad Homburg: Gehlen, 1968).

7. Cf. D. Schoenbaum, *Die braune Revolution. Eine Sozialgeschichte des Dritten Reiches* (Cologne: Kiepenheuer & Witsch, 1968), pp. 223 ff.; C. W. Guiliebeaud, *The Social Policy of Nazi Germany.* (Cambridge: Cambridge University Press, 1942), p. 117; W. Fischer, *Deutsche Wirtschaftspolitik.* 1918–1945 (Opladen: Westdeutscher Verlag, 1968), pp. 77 ff.

8. H.-H. Hartwich, *Sozialstaatspostulat und gesellschaftlicher Status quo* (Cologne: Westdeutscher Verlag, 1977)[3], p. 121.

9. H.-U. Wehler, *Bismarck und der Imperialismus* (Cologne: Kiepenheuer & Witsch, 1969), p. 463.

10. H. Kaelble, *Industrielle Interessenpolitik in der Wilhelminischen Gesellschaft. Centralverband Deutscher Industrieller. 1895–1914* (Berlin: Duncker & Humboldt, 1967), p. 128; F. Fischer, *Bundis der Eliten. Zur Kontinuitat der Machtstrukturen in Deutschland. 1871–1945* (Dusseldorf: Droste, 1979).

11. P. Flora and A. J. Heidenheimer, eds., *The Development of Welfare States in Europe and America.* (New Brunswick, N.J.: Transaction Books, 1981).

12. B. Chapman, *The Profession of Government* (London: Allen Unwin, University Books, 1966), p. 31.

13. F. Lutge, *Deutsche Sozial- und Wirtschaftsgeschichte* (Berlin: Springer-Verlag, 1952), p. 391.

14. R. Fritz, "Der Einflu der Parteien und Geschadigtenverbande auf die Schadensfeststellung im Lastenausgleich." Ph.D. dissertation, University of Berlin, 1964.

15. V. Grafin v. Bethusy-Huc, *Das Sozialleistungssystem der BRD* (Tubingen: Mohr, 1965); Hartwich, *Sozialstaatspostulat,* p. 197.

16. Figures on Parliaments under CDU government: K. von Beyme, *Die politische Elite in der BRD.* 2nd. ed. (Munich: Piper, 1974), p. 53. For the

social composition under the SPD government: K. von Beyme, *Das politische System der BRD* 3rd. ed. (Munich: Piper, 1981), p. 135.

17. M. G. Schmidt, *CDU und SPD an der Regierung. Ein Vergleich ihrer Politik in den Landern* (Frankfort: Campus, 1980), pp. 129 ff.

18. G. Mosca, *Partiti e Sindacati nella crisi del regime parlamentare* (Bari: Laterza, 1949), p. 306 ff.

19. Ibid., p. 309.

Changes in Elite Composition and the Survival of Party Systems: The German Case

Samuel J. Eldersveld

The social profiles and political orientations of elites are the focus for much theory about the transformation and survival of systems. Mosca's theory laid great emphasis on this. The theory specifies that the ruling class is responsive to system change, differently reflected in the credentials and characteristics of elites in systems at different points in time. The ruling class incorporates and represents a "balance of social forces." Elites are "on probation," their ascent or descent linked to their representation of social norms, needs, and interests. There are always those out of power who aspire to elite status. Elites may resist social renewal for a time, but eventually—unless they adapt to, and express, the new social forces in their composition—their structures, in the absence of coercion, will deteriorate. The new social forces, particularly the "lower classes," are waiting to be absorbed. This is the way the minority ruling class maintains its power and its system.

This theory of elite transformation linked to system survival can be applied as well to party structures in the party system. Party elites at the middle and lower levels of systems may, indeed, be considered that secondary stratum of leadership referred to by Mosca—a layer of subelites in partnership with the top elites and, because of the subelites' greater proximity to the public, a sector on which top elites are much dependent and through whom they maintain contact with the changing "balance of social forces." This paper will focus on these party elites, using the theory of elite transformation and adaptation as a basic perspective.

Implicit in this theory are two major concepts. The first is that the composition of elites must change *over time* as the society changes and, hence, demands new, or modified, credentials for elites. Thus a continuous renewal takes place, and must take place. If aristocracies continue to select "their own," they will die and be replaced. If they co-opt more representatives from the "dark crucible of the lower classes"[1] into their elite cadres, they may survive; but in the process the character of the ruling class will change, and new social groups will find an expression in elite decision making. A second concept implicit in this theoretical perspective is a hierarchical one—that as individuals move up to elite status (or from the pool of eligible elites to subelite status and eventually to the ruling class), they will represent the new and emerging interests, needs, and norms of the society. But at the same time, as aspirants to power, they will be cognizant of the "elite cultures," with its norms and orientations toward politics into which they wish to move. Thus those who are upwardly mobile will reflect a dual set of characteristics: they are different because of their proximity to the new "social forces," but they are also conformist to their perceptions of what it takes to achieve elite status. Both are necessary for the survival of systems, although one could assume that conflict will inevitably occur in systems undergoing such a process of elite transformation. It is an interest in both aspects of elite change—longitudinal responsiveness and hierarchical differentiation—which constitutes the viewpoint of the analysis presented here.

The survival of party systems in the West has constituted a puzzle for many scholars, because of the continuity, even the freezing of such systems despite significant social change. Lipset and Rokkan's 1967 statement about the frozen nature of party systems despite new social cleavages posed what was for them the key question:

How was this possible? How were these parties able to survive so many changes in the political, social, and economic conditions of their operation? How could they keep such large bodies of citizens identifying with them over such long periods of time, and how could they renew their core clienteles from generation to generation.[2]

They then suggest that we need to know much more about "the internal management and the organizational functioning of political parties" if we are to answer this question.

While it is true that in Western Europe (and the United States) the continuity of party systems in overall systemic terms does seem striking, much change actually took place in these parties in the 1960's and 1970's. One need only note the decline in pillarization in Dutch party politics, the appearance of *poujadism* in Denmark in 1973, the current schism in the British Labour party, or the gradual emergence of a two-and-a-half party system in West Germany as instances of dramatic or moderate change. In election statistics one notes the decline in the Socialist party vote from the 1950's to the 1970's in all Western European countries except Austria, Germany, and perhaps the Netherlands (and in the cases of the latter two, the exceptions may now be questioned). During this same time span, the phenomenon of the rise of small parties has occurred in all these countries except Austria and Germany; the Netherlands shows a recent decline also.[3]

In the specific case of the German party system the transformation which has occurred in the past thirty years is considerable. The data in Table 1 indicate this change.

From the table one sees clearly the disappearance of the smaller parties and the rise in the strength of both major parties to a dominant position, but one also sees the resilience of the FDP as the party of the middle. The system has been modified considerably while the two major parties have increased their control of the electorate.

Despite these indications of unfreezing and some volatility, the basic character of party system alignments has not been so modified that system replacement has occurred. And above all, the major parties in these systems, while sometimes threatened, have been able to survive, and *in the face of significant social change.* Many theories have been advanced to explain these developments. What will be explored empirically here is the possibility that the changes in the composition of party organizational elites, particularly at the lower levels of these party structures, have been functional to party structure survival. And, alternatively, it follows that the decline in parties and in their status in systems may be attributed to the incapacity of the party organization to reflect in their leadership the new social forces making demands upon them. After all, parties are presumably, at least in democratic societies, mobilization structures. Theoretically, they consist of base unit personnel and working cadres who know what changes are taking place, where the votes are (and are not), and how to appeal to them. While reinforcing party loyalties among old supporters, the local cadres are presumably in touch with new interest groups and potential supporters, representing them in the organization, and mobilizing their support, particularly if their older clientele groups are declining, either numerically or in loyalty. A viable organization is thus in a state of dynamic renovation in the composition and orientations of its organizational elites; a declining organization is not socially adaptive in its elite composition. Figure 1 shows the trends in the numerical relationship between party members and party supporters (voters) for the CDU/CSU and the SPD between 1949 and 1978.

Data by which to attempt an exploration of these theoretical concerns are available from German research on local party elites. The German material comes from a rich data archive made available by the Institute of Applied Social Sciences (INFAS) in Bad Godesberg (under the direction of Klaus Liepelt). Since 1962 the Institute has conducted monthly national surveys in which party members and activists were identified for the SPD, CDU/CSU, and FDP. In addi-

TABLE 1.
Changes in Party Votes, 1949–1980*

	1949	1957	1961	1965	1969	1972	1976	1980
A. Major Parties' Vote								
CDU/CSU	31.0	50.2	45.3	47.6	46.1	44.9	48.6	44.5
SPD	29.2	31.8	36.2	39.3	42.7	45.8	42.6	42.9
Total	60.2	82.0					91.2	87.4
B. FDP	11.9	7.7	12.8	9.5	5.8	8.4	7.9	10.6
C. The Smaller Parties								
Percent	27.8	10.3		5.7	3.6	5.5	0.9	2.0
Votes	6,608,419	4,533,185					333,595	749,378

*Throughout this paper, party acronyms have been used, as here. The parties referred to, by acronym, are the Free Democrats (Liberals) (FDP); the Christian-Democratic Union, Christian-Social Union (CDU/CSU), and the Social Democrats (SDP).

FIGURE 1.
Political Cycles in Postwar Germany

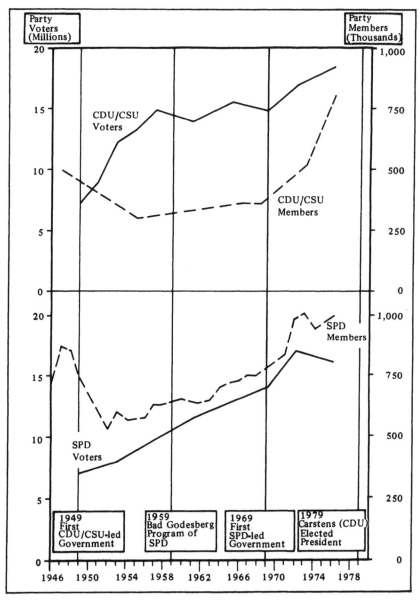

*The sources of these data from party headquarters and official statistics are com-
pilations in Ursula Feist, Manfred Gullner, and Klaus Liepelt, "Implementation of
Ideology: Party Elites in Post-industrial Society," *Transfer* 2 (Wiesbaden, 1976);
and in Max Kaase and Klaus von Beyme, eds., *Elections and Parties* (Sage Publications, 1978).

tion, in 1968 and again in 1977, the Institute conducted a full-scale survey of SPD and CDU party functionaries and members. In 1968, in a project directed by Professor Diderichs, who became a member of the Bundestag, 1,046 leaders were interviewed (492 CDU/CSU, 554 SPD). In 1977 INFAS conducted a study of 2,534 SPD and 483 CDU/CSU members, among whom were a large enough number of functionaries to permit a separate analysis. These data, then, though not perfect and containing many gaps, permit a longitudinal analysis. To a limited extent they also permit some hierarchical analysis. They will be used selectively for both purposes here.

The Gradual Diversification of German Party Cadres

Membership development in the two major German parties sets the stage for this analysis. In 1946 the CDU had enrolled about 500,000 members and the SPD just short of 750,000. This differential has remained with the exception of brief periods when the gap narrowed.

Both parties dropped in membership in the fifties: by 1959 the SPD was down to 580,000, the CDU to 300,000. Both have increased in size since then. Since its 1969 loss of power, the CDU has been undergoing a rebuilding of the organization. By 1976 it was approaching 800,000, while the SPD had increased to more than 950,000. What have been the characteristics of these membership cadres as they have changed from the early 1960's to the mid-1970's?[4]

Table 2 presents changes in selected characteristics of the membership cadres at three points in time. In the 1960's there were more union activists and regular churchgoers in both parties. By the mid-seventies the parties declined in both respects although the CDU/CSU continued to have a bare majority of active Catholics. Both membership groups were younger. But it is the increase in the middle-class character of the SPD which is particularly noticeable, while the CDU has become more middle-class than ever. The SPD became rather evenly split between middle-class members and those identifying with the working class.

 When one looks at these developments in relationship to the changes taking place in German society, the linkage becomes more precise. For example, the occupational distributions of the German population and of these membership cadres seen in Table 3 are useful to make this point. From this, one can see that between 1956 and 1976 the blue-collar proportion of the German population declined from 52 percent to 45 percent, while there was a great surge in white-collar employment, which increased from 22 percent to 41 percent. The response of the parties, as far as the recruitment of their membership and cadres is concerned, was basically in the same direction. But the shift was much greater in the SPD. What is particularly interesting is that both parties mirrored the occupational structure

TABLE 2.
Changes in Social Characteristics of German Party Members

	SPD Members			CDU/CSU Members		
	1962–1963	1969–1970	1974–1975	1962–1963	1969–1970	1974–1975
A. Religion						
All regular churchgoers	32	23	20	95	77	62
Active Catholics	10	8	7	75	59	52
B. Age						
Over 50 years of age	50	44	38	46	43	44
C. Union membership (Activists)	55	41	39	30	18	12
D. Identification with middle or upper class	35	45	50	65	58	79
N =	138	283	481	75	168	313

TABLE 3.

Changes in the Occupational Characteristics of German Party
Members, Compared to Population Changes, 1956–1976

Occupational Categories	1956 (in percent)	1976 (in percent)	Change 1956–1976 (in percent)	Distance from Total Population 1956 (in percent)	1976 (in percent)
Total Population					
Blue collar	52	45	− 7		
White collar	22	41	+ 19		
Self-employed	26	14	− 12		
SPD Members					
Blue collar	66	42	− 24	14	3
White collar	23	50	+ 27	1	9
Self-employed	11	8	− 3	15	6
			Mean	10	6
CDU Members					
Blue collar	11	15	+ 4	41	30
White collar	44	53	+ 9	22	12
Self-employed	45	32	− 13	19	18
			Mean	27	20

of the German society better in 1976 than in 1956. The SPD was particularly adjustive in this sense; occupationally, it became the most representative party.

Another way to demonstrate this differential adaptiveness is to look at elite composition in relation to loyal support groups. That is, to what extent is the membership cadre congruent with, or distant from, those voters who are the stalwart partisans? These developments can be illustrated as in Table 4 by using both subjective social class data and union activism data for the SPD and class data plus active Catholicism for the CDU. From such data one can see that while in terms of class analysis both parties were responsive, there was a lag in the membership cadre's response on both the union

TABLE 4.
Changes in Social Characteristics of German Party Members in
Relation to Loyal Support Groups

Social Characteristics	1962*	1969*	1974*	Change 1962–1974*	Distance from Loyal Voters 1962*	1969*	1974*
A. SPD loyal voters							
Middle class	32	47	41	+ 9			
Active union members	18	17	13	− 5			
SPD members							
Middle class	35	45	50	+ 15	3	2	9
Active union members	55	41	38	− 17	37	34	25
B. CDU loyal voters							
Active Catholics	53	45	45	− 8			
Middle class	64	49	64	0			
CDU members							
Active Catholics	75	59	52	− 23	22	14	7
Middle class	65	58	79	+ 14	1	9	15

*The data are presented in percent.

activity and active religion variables. Thus, for the SPD we found as
follows:

Percent of Active Union Members	1962	1974	Distances 1962	1974
Party Cadre	55	38	37	25
Loyal Supporters	18	13		

The distance is narrowed, but the difference continues. The same
was true for the CDU's composition in religious terms. These data
suggest, then, that considerable change was taking place in German
party activist groups, as a sort of lagged response to changes in the
German population and to the party activists' own voting support
groups. The movement toward the middle majority seems clearly
evident in both parties: the SPD is less a Genossenpartei of union
activists and blue-collar workers, whereas the CDU is less a Catholic
and upper-middle (and upper class) party.

Another type of analysis by which to examine changes in the social backgrounds of party cadres is the use of eras of entry. The data used here are from the major study in 1977, in which respondents were asked to indicate when they entered the party. Several generations are, of course, represented in any party cadre, ranging in the 1977 German study as follows:

Time of Entry	SPD Members (in Percent)	CDU Members (in Percent)
Before 1949	14	6
1950–1959	10	13
1960–1966	15	13
1967–1971	22	18
1972–	30	34

Since these entrance times span four decades, they provide an opportunity to see the gradual change (shown in Table 5) in the characteristics of these members. Cumulatively, the shifts are indeed striking, as in the case of educational level:

Percent Having Middle or Higher Education	Percent Entered in the 1940's	Percent Entered in 1976–1977
SPD	20	45
CDU	52	72

Equally notable was the movement of Protestants into the CDU—8 percent among those joining between 1945 and 1948, but as high as 42 percent of those joining between 1972 and 1975. This, of course, occurred simultaneously with a striking decline in the number of active Catholics in the CDU—83 percent of those joining between 1945 and 1948, compared with 33 percent between 1976 and 1977.

The social profile of the SPD cadre which entered in the 1970's was more female (as high as 26 percent), was better educated, had fewer labor union memberships, and was more middle class. Yet there still were active SPD members who had joined previously and who were union actives (as many as 40 percent), active churchgoers (25 percent being the highest number), as many as 50 percent with Volksschule education, and those identifying with the working class. Similarly, the CDU cadre was also heterogeneous in generational terms: about 30 percent older activists with Volksschule education only and as many as 20 percent higher status types still identifying with the upper class. While the parties were sociologically more adaptive, they were perhaps more sociologically conflicted.

The same type of generational analysis can be used to examine changes in elite attitudes over time. One does find some evidence of

TABLE 5.

Social Characteristics of German Party Members by Era of Entry
into the Party (Time of Entrance from 1977 Data)

	1976– 1977 (in Percent)	1972– 1975 (in Percent)	1967– 1971 (in Percent)	1960– 1966 (in Percent)	1949– 1959 (in Percent)	1945– 1948 (in Percent)	Before 1945 (in Percent)*
Women							
SPD	26	23	18	13	13	27	13
CDU	21	30	18	9	12	13	—
Education— two highest levels							
SPD	45	42	50	33	27	23	17
CDU	72	70	71	65	69	52	—
Subjective social class SPD— working and lower class	35	42	35	49	47	47	57
CDU— upper class	11	19	16	16	25	23	—
Religion Protestants							
SPD	54	51	52	54	59	58	50
CDU	36	42	32	28	25	8	—
Religion— church attendance Active Catholics CDU	33	22	33	45	54	83	—
Union membership							
SPD	40	46	59	61	70	65	74
CDU	18	18	24	26	40	29	—
SPD N	211	555	553	372	264	175	173
CDU N	31	125	122	79	67	23	—

*In the CDU study the earliest category used stopped with 1945.

what might be considered increasing liberalism in the CDU for example, by comparing the views of the earlier entrants with those who came to the party later. On seven selected issues, ranging from more taxation of large incomes to worker "codetermination," we find this comparison:

Average Liberalism Score (1977 Data)		
	1976–1977 Entrants (in Percent)	Percent Entered before 1960
CDU Members	33	26
SPD Members	58	55

Although there is a slight change, it is the homogenity of positions by party, *irrespective of time of entry*, which stands out. This suggests a socialization and/or self-selection process rather than a differentiation by generations.

Age Contrasts as an Approach to Party Elite Change

Differences in elites and potential elites if partitioned by age cohorts can be useful to detect and predict party structural change. This is particularly so if the youngest age cohort can be visualized as upwardly mobile and aspiring to elite positions which it does not hold at the particular time. In a sense the data permit two types of interpretation:
1. It tells us whether, and in what respects, the "next elite" will differ from those presently running the organization and, hence the conflict potential as elites circulate.
2. It tells us what credentials those moving up in the system perceive to be necessary for achieving a position of influence.
The 1977 study permits us to make such an analysis. The youngest age cohort in the SPD (under 25) hold very few party positions (only 2 percent in 1977), while the middle-aged cadre (aged 35 to 44) hold over 30 percent of the positions. Further, we can contrast these with the oldest cohort (age 65 and above) who hold few positions (6 percent in 1977). The CDU data permitting such comparisons are similar, as tables 6 and 7 show.

A careful inspection of these data for the SPD (Table 6) reveals that the youngest age cohort was much better educated than those in the age cohort holding party positions. Fewer were in the working class, one-fifth were still students, and one-third were union members (compared to about one-half of the middle-aged cohort). But they tended to be Protestants, as did those in the middle-aged group, and not regular churchgoers. Their activity level was high, suggesting

TABLE 6.
Age Cohort Comparisons for SPD Members (1977 Data)

	% Youngest Cohort (Up to Age 25)	% Middle-Aged Cohort (Ages 35 to 44)	% Oldest Cohort (Age 65 and Over)
A. Percentage of Top Positions Held in Local Party Organization	2	32	6
B. Social background of cohorts			
1. Education: Beyond Volksschule	60	37	19
(Abitur +)	(26)	(15)	(5)
2. Subjective class: Working and lower	30	42	55
3. Occupations			
Blue collar	17	31	38
Students	22	0	0
4. Union members	36	48	55
5. Religion: Protestants	58	53	52
attending church weekly	2	3	3
6. Sex: women	20	15	21
C. Political activity levels Participated in election meetings	47	48	35
House-to-house canvassing	12	12	10
Recruited friends for party	55	54	42
Average for 13 activities	21.3	23.0	14.3
D. Political orientations			
1. Values: more social justice	45	46	43
less inequality	39	29	19
more democracy	22	16	12
more freedom	19	6	5
more economic growth	5	11	11
2. Reasons for entering party			
"It was always so in my family."	19	22	41
"People of my social class belong in my party."	20	32	41
"I can work for important causes."	44	34	35
3. Ideological direction: "liberal"	73	52	43
4. Satisfied with role in the party organization	47	66	66
N	219	584	545

TABLE 7.
Age Cohort Comparison for CDU/CSU Members (1977 Data)

	% Youngest Cohort (Up to Age 25)	% Middle-Aged Cohort (Ages 35 to 44)	% Oldest Cohort (Age 65 and Over)
A. Percentage of Top Positions Held in Local Party Organization	3	33	10
B. Social background of cohorts			
1. Education: beyond Volksschule	82	65	61
(Abitur +)	(52)	(17)	(25)
2. Subjective social class:			
Upper and upper-middle	19	13	22
Middle	72	77	68
3. Occupations			
Professional, business	8	23	29
Blue collar	10	7	8
Students	32	0	0
4. Union members	15	29	23
5. Religion: Catholics	71	61	58
attending church weekly	38	42	58
6. Sex: women	25	12	18
C. Political activity levels			
Participated in election meetings	75	83	61
House-to-house canvassing	45	28	31
Recruited friends for party	72	75	64
Average for 13 activities	43.4	46.9	29.9
D. Political orientations			
1. Values: more social justice	45	23	37
less inequality	20	14	11
more democracy	3	10	7
more freedom	11	5	8
more economic growth	20	23	14
2. Reasons for entering party			
"It was always so in my family."	8	6	20
"People of my social class belong in my party."	19	24	34
"I can work for important causes."	71	59	51
3. Ideological direction: "liberal"	52	50	38
4. Satisfied with role in the party organization	88	68	65
N	47	132	66

that they were well aware of the expectations of organizational and campaign involvement if they were to be recognized in the party.

They seemed committed to working in the party for particular causes and were there much less because of family tradition and social class expectations. They were more liberal in their issue positions (73 percent, compared to 52 percent of the middle-aged cadre), *and* they were less satisfied with their role in the party! Hence, if these young activists get party positions (and are not otherwise socialized in the process), they may indeed lead the party in a new direction. There appears here to be a possible new dynamism in the SPD membership cadre with significant implications for change if this young cohort achieves elite status.

For the CDU/CSU (Table 7) there are certain similarities but also sharp contrasts to this picture for the SPD. The CDU young cadre was also very well educated, but the members did not identify at all with the new working class or hold union membership, diverging somewhat from those now in power in these respects. It was also an extremely activist cadre, in values and ideology quite bourgeois. In fact, it seems to be split down the middle as to the proportions who were liberal and conservative in ideological direction. Only in its emphasis on the value of social justice did it diverge significantly from the middle-aged cohort now holding many of these party jobs. The young cadre was clearly committed to activity at this time because of an interest in political objectives and causes, and, as with the SPD young membership, less because of family tradition. If this cadre achieves party elite status, it appears that it will be more asymmetric in relation to the SPD young cadre in terms of ideological direction but more congruent with the SPD in education and social class. Another striking difference is also, of course, the high proportion of Catholics and regular churchgoers, although this proportion has been declining in both instances.

In short, these data present evidence of potentially important differences in the future for both parties, as well as evidence of conformism in terms of certain credentials. (Union membership and religious confession are examples.) Further, the oldest cohort in each party exhibits the characteristics of a declining elite, strikingly at odds with the characteristics of the rising young elites.

A special analysis of the young Socialists (Jusos) in the SPD highlights these observations. In the 1977 study there was a large enough sample (127) of Jusos in the SPD membership cadre to permit separate examination. Some of them had already achieved a position in the party at the local level (22 percent), and 5 percent were chairing the local Ortsverein. These are the members who presumably have been causing much of the controversy in the party, provoking Helmut Schmidt and other leaders. It is interesting, therefore, to look at their characteristics and orientations. They were the best educated group, 77 percent having gone beyond Volksschule (49 percent Abitur or higher). Only one-fourth saw themselves in the working or lower class, but 45 percent reported that they were union members. They were more active than the youngest age group (an average score of 35.0 for 13 activities, compared to 21.3). They really attended party meetings (68 percent), recruited friends (64 percent), and engaged in many other types of campaign work. And they were liberal—80 percent, even higher than the 73 percent of the youngest age group. The Jusos, incidentally, are not all in that youngest cadre below age 25. They divide as follows: 40 percent from the under 25 age group and 56 percent in the 25 to 34 age cohort. Many (45 percent) entered the party in the 1972–1975 period and 27 percent in the 1967–1971 period. Only 15 percent entered after 1975. A final key observation is that the Jusos were not very happy with their status. Few (15 percent) felt they had a great deal of influence in the party organization (though 32 percent said "some" influence), and one-half were dissatisfied. They did not feel that the "dominant political direction" in their Ortsverein is "Left" (only 15 percent said it was), but a much larger percentage felt it should be "Left" (43 percent, compared to only 23 percent of the youngest cohort and 9 percent of all members). Clearly they felt "the Left" should have more influence and were working hard to that end. As a potential elite they displayed (and continue to show) characteristics that would modify the party's orientation even more than if the youngest cadre took power.

Hierarchical Variations in Elite Composition

We can even more explicitly contrast established party elites and the emerging or potential elites by presenting the data in hierarchical format. In both the 1968 and 1977 studies it was possible to isolate those who held different types of party positions, or mandates from those who held none. Among the latter, it was further possible to distinguish active, upwardly mobile, and aspiring party members from those who were inactive and had no power aspirations. We know that functionaries differ from members in certain important aspects. The key question here is whether those aspiring to elite position come from similar background and hold similar views about politics, and if not, in what respects the would-be elite is distinctive.

The 1968 study provided an opportunity to explore this matter in some detail. In Table 8 we present the proportions of each element or level in the hierarchy possessing a particular credential—education, religious activity, class identification, union membership. The contrasts between the functionaries who now hold a relatively high

TABLE 8.
Differential Credentials of German Party Activists: Functionaries, Aspirers, and Inactives (1968 Data)

The Hierarchy	CDU/CSU			SPD		
	Percent Having Higher Education (Beyond Volksschule)	Percent Religiously Active*	Percent Who Identify Working or Lower Class	Percent Having Low Education (Volksschule)	Percent Holding Union Membership	Percent Who Identify Working or Lower Class
Functionaries	70	46	15	72	78	61
Chairmen of Ortsverein	63	59	16	61	78	55
Most active members	63	69	13	64	81	55
Aspire to higher position	68	59	9	65	66	49
Never held a position	44	65	19	72	58	60
Inactive members	48	68	22	73	57	58
Nonaspirers	41	68	21	73	59	59
Summary measures						
A. Homogeneity for top levels†	4.0	11.0	2.7	5.0	7.3	4.7
B. Distance between functionaries and nonaspirers	29	22	6	1	19	2
C. Distance between functionaries and aspirers	2	13	6	7	12	12

*"Religiously active" means that those listed attend church weekly.
†The "homogeneity" measure is simply the average difference between the top four levels, from level to level.

position in the local or regional party organization and those who do not can be seen from these data. The contrasts are particularly striking as regards educational level and regular church attendance in the CDU and as regards union membership in the SPD. Further, one notes that the actives and aspirers are congruent with the functionaries on certain attributes but divergent in certain respects also. Class identifications are very similar for the CDU, but in the SPD those who are upwardly aspiring are more middle class already in identification (this was in 1968). There appears to be considerable homogeneity in class and educational credentials but much less so for religious activity in the CDU hierarchy and union membership in the SPD. Finally, one notes also that the distance between functionaries and aspirers seems greater in the SPD than in the CDU. That is, if change did not take place in the characteristics of these subgroups in the hierarchy, one might expect a certain amount of class conflict within the SPD and more religious disagreement in the CDU *if those who were aspiring in 1968 did achieve elite position!*

This expectation makes the direct comparison of 1977 with 1968 much more relevant. Table 9 presents, again hierarchically but in more abbreviated form, the comparisons over time for the echelons in the hierarchy. From the table one can see immediately that *there has been* a striking change in the class composition of the SPD functionaries (from 61 percent to 37 percent working or lower class), a movement toward the middle class which occurred at all levels of the party. The greatest adjustment (+ 24 percent), however, occurred at the functionary level. The same was true in the decline of union membership, noted particularly among functionaries (− 26 percent) and active members (− 30 percent). At the same time the educational level was dramatically increased. Indeed, in terms of what was happening "below" in the party, one might almost say the top SPD elite overcompensated and became less working class and more educated than its most active cadres.

What was happening to the CDU in this ten-year period from 1968 to 1977? Basically, the least change was taking place at the top. But in a sense this meant that the active cadres had to catch up, because the top functionaries were already less religious in 1968 and strongly middle and upper-middle class. Table 10 shows that if we look at educational data for the CDU, we see the same phenomenon. As a result, the CDU hierarchy became more congruent *without great change* by the top organizational elites, while the SPD became somewhat more congruent *because of great change* by the top organizational elites. The contrast in the developments in the two parties appears also in Table 11, which exhibits age cohort data. The younger cohort had by 1968 already infiltrated the apex of the local party hierarchy of the CDU, but this was not true for the SPD until later.

TABLE 9.
Contrast in Social Characteristics of German Party Activists*

	CDU/CSU								
	Middle or Upper Class		Union Members		Weekly Church Attendance		Percent of Difference (1968–1977) in		
							Class Status	Union Member-ship	Religious Activists
	1968	1977	1968	1977	1968	1977			
Functionaries	85	87	30	17	46	41	+2	−13	−5
Orts chairs (or Mandatsträger)	81	85	31	20	59	46	+5	−11	−13
Active members	78	83	32	18	69	40	+10	−14	−29
Inactive members	86	92	15	17	63	43	+6	+2	−25
Difference									
Functionaries and inactives	1	5	15	0	22	2			
Functionaries and actives	7	1	2	1	23	1			

	SPD								
	Percent in Working or Lower Class		Percent of Union Members		Percent with Education beyond Volksschule		Percent of Difference (1968–1977) in		
							Class Status	Union Member-ship	Educational Level
	1968	1977	1968	1977	1953	1977			
Functionaries	61	37	78	52	23	51	+24	−26	−28
Orts chairs (or Mandatsträger)	55	33	76	62	26	57	+22	−14	−31
Active members	57	41	81	51	22	41	+16	−30	−19
Inactive members	58	44	57	48	22	35	+16	−9	+13
Difference									
Functionaries and inactives	3	7	21	4	1	16			
Functionaries and actives	4	4	3	1	1	10			

*The contrast here is achieved from the point of view of hierarchical status.

TABLE 10.
Education beyond Volksschule in the CDU

	1968 (in Percent)	1977 (in Percent)
Functionaries	70	74
Mandatsträger	63	73
Active members	63	71
Inactive members	48	59

TABLE 11.
Age Cohort Analysis, SPD and CDU, 1968 and 1977

	Percent under 35 Years of Age			
	SPD		CDU	
	1968	1977	1968	1977
Functionaries	17	32	35	31
Ortschairmen	21	33	19	16
Active members	12	30	19	32
Inactive members	14	27	30	16

Concluding Comments

One must interpret these data in the light of the developments in German society and politics since World War II. One must remember that the Nazis proscribed all parties of the Weimar and earlier periods (except the National Socialists). The task of rebuilding the German party system after the war was therefore considerable. The SPD returned at once as the party of the working class, with only a minority of those with white-collar occupations in the fifties becoming members of the SPD. Under the leadership of Willy Brandt the party gradually changed its exclusively working-class image, and our data document this reorientation. The CDU/CSU also established itself quickly after the war as a dominant conservative party, under the leadership of Konrad Adenauer. In the fifties it was always seen as a middle class party, and only one out of ten of its members were blue-collar workers. Over 80 percent were Catholics. But that, too, began to change in the period beginning in the late sixties.

The SPD finally achieved governmental legitimacy in the late sixties. The first SPD-led government was formed in 1969, after the CDU and SPD were together in the Grand Coalition from 1967 to 1969. The system status of both parties was thus undergoing major change, both in fact and in the public's mind. As that was happening, and as the German society was changing, both parties began to appeal to, and attract, supporters from "opposite" clienteles—the

SPD from the middle class, and the CDU/CSU from Protestants and blue-collar workers. While this had been going on, tensions developed within both parties, tensions which have become particularly apparent in recent years. There have been problems between the SPD and its coalition partner, the FDP, which are considered by some to be linked to the ideological protests on the Left in the SPD. The conflicts within the CDU/CSU have also been apparent, manifest recently in the lukewarm attitudes of some supporters to the 1980 campaign of their candidate for the Chancellorship, Franz Joseph Strauss of the CSU. Major redirections in the German party system were thus taking place at both the leadership and the ideological levels in the postwar period, changes which our data at the local organizational level document and mirror very well.

While change has occurred in the German society and in the German party system, the major parties have maintained and strengthened their status in that system. In the October 1980 election, change in the party system was again not major, despite the unpopularity of CDU-CSU candidate Strauss. The CDU/CSU dropped 4.1 percentage points; and the SPD gained only 0.3, in an election with a turnout of 87 percent. The new "Greens" party secured only 1.5 percent of the vote.

The viability of the major German parties, on the basis of our analysis, appears in part to be a function of the gradual changes in the types of people they attract into their party cadres and to whom they eventually give party positions. The social backgrounds and profiles of these organizational activists have changed radically over the years, their changes linked to changes in German society. Our longitudinal analysis clearly reveals this, both at the membership and the functionary levels. This suggests that these structures are dynamic, open to social renewal, vote-maximizing, and providers of incentives for activists to join and to work and to move upward in the organization. It suggests also that these parties are indeed combative, rival cadres, in composition as well as in campaign activity, opposing each other effectively by recruiting and deploying base unit personnel where needed on the German political terrain.

There are caveats, however. What this analysis does not demonstrate is the relevance of elite compositional changes to the changing nature of party fortunes from locality to locality. Is it elite composition which counts, or is it campaign activity, or is it the communication of party ideology, or the involvement of citizens in organizational opportunities which are socially gratifying? These are matters yet to be investigated. In a high-turnout culture such as Germany has, is elite composition as it changes to be viewed primarily as a response to changes in the character of loyal support groups, or is it to be viewed as functional to vote mobilization? Perhaps both, but our analysis here does not permit an empirical answer.

A final comment concerning the relevance of changes in elite composition for the intensification of internal organizational conflict is also necessary. Our analysis suggests here that conflicts certainly arose in both parties as the activist cadre changed—for example, the presence of more Protestants in the CDU/CSU and of fewer labor union members in the SPD. The conflict which has developed in the SPD between the Jusos faction and the more moderate and less doctrinaire ideologues is strongly suggested by our data. In this case the transformation process in the absence of integrative and socializing forces may be dysfunctional in terms of party unity. The SPD faces the need for negotiating an organizational consensus between the Jusos, the middle class moderates, and the old comrades from the labor unions who are the stalwarts of the party of the past. Elite transformation, thus, while responsive to social change and contributing to the durability of the party's status in the system, can impose serious strains on organizational consensus.

Notes

1. Gaetano Mosca, *The Ruling Class*, trans. H. D. Kahn (New York: McGraw-Hill, 1939).

2. Seymour M. Lipset and Stein Rokkan, *Party Systems and Voter Alignments* (New York: Free Press, 1967), pp. 50–51.

3. The percentage of the vote received by small parties from the 1950's to the 1970's increased as follows: Britain, + 3.2; France, + 11.6; Sweden, + 2.6; Italy, + 14.6; Belgium, + 10.2; and Switzerland, + 3.8.

4. Figures for the early years of the Federal Republic are based on the analysis by Ursula Feist and Klaus Liepelt, "Implementation of Ideology: Party Elites in Post-industrial Society" (Paper presented at the IPSA conference in Edinburgh, Scotland, August 1976). See also reference sources for Figure 1.

Governing Elites in a Changing Industrial Society: The Case of France

*Roland Cayrol and
Pascal Perrineau*

The present regime in France, the Fifth Republic, dates from 1958. This period in French history breaks with previous periods in two basic aspects. First of all, it has been a time of considerable economic and industrial modernization—the socioeconomic structures of the country have changed more in twenty years than during the whole of the last century. Second, it has been a time of new institutional stability, since the 1958 Constitution established a stable majority system founded especially upon the preeminence of a president of the Republic elected for seven years. This economic and political modernization has been able to depend on a ruling class that has been particularly adapted to this double mission and whose adaptation has continued throughout these years. In May-June 1981, a further change affected French political society, as after twenty-three years with a conservative majority,[1] a Socialist majority took over.[2]

The purpose of this study is to characterize the specificities not of the French ruling class as a whole but of what we shall call the *governing elites* of the Fifth Republic, that is to say, those categories of the elites that have been responsible for directing and controlling the affairs of the State. We shall, therefore, include within this definition the institutional political elites (ministers, members of Parliament, leading local representatives), the administrative elites (high-ranking civil servants, members of ministerial secretariats),[3] and the party elites of the ruling majority parties. We shall endeavor to describe the characteristics and the specificities of these governing elites on four levels: their recruitment, the contacts and connection between them, their reciprocal means of representation, and their systems of values.

Our intention is to draw up a balance sheet for the governing elites of the conservative Fifth Republic at each of these levels, starting from empirical research data, and to measure the change which has taken place in 1981 with the coming to power of the socialists. It will be seen that these draft balance sheets, and an assessment of the recent change, will enable us to deal with some of the classical theoretical problems of political science applied to elites, whether it be recruitment channels, institutionalization mechanisms, the uniqueness of governing elites, or the survival of these elites.

I. The Recruitment of French Governing Elites

Within governing elites in Western democracies, there is always a tendency to over-represent the privileged categories of the population, i.e., the most "well-off" categories in socio-professional terms and the most favored in terms of their cultural level. France, of course, is no exception to this rule of representative regimes; but, notably, since the foundation of the Fifth Republic in 1958, it presents a certain number of original characteristics. The conformity with a general tendency, and the specificity, can be measured on three dimensions: that of the social recruitment of the governing elites, that of their educational and cultural backgrounds, and that of the processes of social mobility through which they have advanced. We shall attempt to draw up the balance sheet for the Fifth Republic (1958–1981) and to evaluate what type of change may result from the fact that in May-June 1981, the Socialist party won both the presidency of the Republic and a majority of seats in the National Assembly.

Governing Elites and Social Reproduction of the Ruling Categories

From the data shown in Table 1, it is obvious that the upper classes are considerably over-represented among the political personnel, and all the more so as one climbs the hierarchy of political elites. From as far down the scale as the mayoral level, and consequently in small communes, the working class is practically excluded from political representation.[4] As for the peasants, they are better represented than their relative "weight" in society, at least at certain levels: those that tend traditionally to favor rural communes, municipalities, of course, and also general councils and the Senate.[5]

Even the middle classes, which accounted for 38.6 percent of the population in 1978, are under-represented as soon as one reaches the categories of those political elites located in the capital (members of Parliament, Senators, members of the National Cabinet). It is indeed the upper classes who have the largest share at this level, and they almost completely dominate the highest offices of the State, both at the central and at the regional levels. The phenomenon is

TABLE 1.
Objective Social Class and French Political Personnel

	Active Population (1978)	Mayors (1977)	General Councillors (1976)	Members of Parliament (1978)	Members of Parliament (1981)	Mayors of Cities of More Than 30,000 Inhabitants	Senators (1977)	Chairmen General Councils (1979)	Chairmen Regional Councils (1981)	Members of the National Cabinet (1979)	Members of the National Cabinet (1981)
Upper classes	8.1%	16.7%	50.5%	66%	82%	57%	55%	69%	95%	89%	86%
Middle classes	38.6	21.5	21.2	17	10	27	15	14	5	—	6.5
Working classes	45.1	4	3	2	3	13	1	1	—	—	4.5
Farmers	7.6	39	12	4	2	1	20	14	—	5	—
Various, unclassifiable, absence of information	0.6	18.8	13.3	11	3	2	9	2	—	6	3
Total	100	100	100	100	100	100	100	100	100	100	100

We have classified industrialists and important businessmen, professional people, managerial staff and teachers (higher and secondary education) as the "upper classes." As the "middle classes," artisans, tradesmen, elementary schoolmasters and employees; and as the "working classes," laborers, farm workers and people working in the service industries. Farmers are classified separately, through lack of data on the size of farms.

Sources: Documents kindly supplied to the authors by V. Aubert (Contemporary French Political Life Study Centre) based, for the most part, on the analysis provided by the Ministry of the Interior and on information taken from the Official Gazette (*Journal Officiel*) and *Who's Who* in France. The authors have added the data concerning the Members of Parliament elected in 1981 and the present Mauroy government (formed after the parliamentary elections held in June 1981).

massive and indisputable; the French democratic system is a representative one in which the elites in power, elected to office through universal franchise, are recruited to a very considerable extent from among the privileged classes of society. Among these privileged classes, we must now identify the strata of society which, in order of priority, supply their members to the various governing elites; we must also measure whether these last decades reflect an evolution with regard to French republican tradition.

The first element, in reply to these questions, is provided by the figures concerning the occupational origin of *National Cabinet* personnel (Table 2). This sociology of French ministers demonstrates a clear development in recruitment, and the Fifth Republic shows indeed significant breaks with the past. Until 1958, the self-employed—employers in industry and commerce, farmers, and professional people—provided the majority of government members (52 percent between 1870 and 1958). Since 1958, the situation has been reversed, and employees have become the majority. The tendency has even increased progressively, in spite of a check in this increase under Georges Pompidou's presidency in 1969–1974. The composition of the government elite, therefore, reflects a process of salarization, that is to say, of industrialization and, therefore, a modernization in French society.

Among the categories whose representation has proportionally declined the most with the establishment of the Fifth Republic, we find members of the legal profession, as if the end of the Third and Fourth Republics marked the disappearance of a certain type of democracy leaning heavily on speeches and on debates that leave a large part to oratory and wild gesticulation (considering the preponderance of Parliament), giving way to a new, more technical and managerial type of democracy, founded on the predominance of the Executive.

This fact is to be compared with a third element: the growing presence of civil servants (first of all of teachers[6] and especially high-ranking civil servants)—in government positions. We shall return later, in more detail, to this increasing interpenetration of the political elite and the civil service. But we must insist here on a dual specificity of the Fifth Republic regime, at the historical and at the geographical levels. Historically, General de Gaulle's appointment as President of the Republic in 1958 enabled one system to lead on to another. It was the catalyst that hastened the inversion of the power structure between professional people and members of the civil service. From de Gaulle onward, one can talk about a real "duopoly of teachers and high-ranking civil servants,"[7] with a predominance of the latter.

The inclusion of civil servants in the political personnel to such a great extent has few equivalents in Western democracies. It is clear that in this respect the preponderance of civil servants in

TABLE 2.
Occupational Origins of Ministers

	Industrialists, Tradesmen, Artisans	Farmers	Medical profession	Legal profession	Other professions, Engineers & Executives in the Private Sector	Journalists	Senior Civil Servants*	Middle or Lower-Ranking Civil Servants	Teachers (all levels)	Employees	Working Men & Women	Others	Total
1870–1940	7%	1.5%	5%	38%	5%	7.5%	19.5%	1%	11.5%	1%	1%	2%	100
1944–1958	17	5	6	23	7	8	14	—	14.5	1	1	1.5	100
1958–1969	18	1	2	12	10	7	29	—	21	—	—	—	100
1969–1974	16	1.5	6	9	16	1.5	39	—	9	—	—	2	100
1974–1976	8	—	5	5	17	8	44	3	5	—	3	2	100
1979	13	5	8	5	10.5	2.5	34	—	16	—	—	6	100
1981	2	—	2	11	9	9	25	—	34.5	—	4.5	3	100

*Army officers: 11.5% in 1870–1940, 2% in 1944–1958, 2% in 1958–1969, 2% in 1969–1974, and 3% in 1974–1976.

Sources: For the period from 1870–1974 and for 1979, documents supplied to the authors by V. Aubert, based mainly on the analysis of data collected by M. Dogan, "Les filières de la carrière Politique en France," Revue Française de Sociologie (October–November 1967); E. G. Lewis, "Social Background of French Ministers, 1944–1967," The Western Political Quarterly (September 1970); and on research based on the analysis of Who's Who in France. For the period from 1974–1976, see P. and J. D. Antoni, Les ministres de la Ve République (Presses Universitaires de France, 1976). For 1981, statistics compiled by the authors.

government service in France is considerably facilitated by the legal privileges enjoyed by members of the civil service, and enjoyed by them alone.[8]

On the other hand, and this is the last characteristic that we would like to emphasize at this stage, there are few people from the management side of private business among members of the French government personnel. As is often the case in France, the pathways of political and economic modernization go mainly through the State.

The available data concerning *parliamentary* personnel (Table 3) lend additional weight to all that has been noted above.[9]

There is a clear trend toward an increase in the number of employees in political recruitment: 69 percent of all members of Parliament for the period from 1871 to 1893 were self-employed; the percentage was still 59.6 percent for the 1919–1936 period; it went down to 42.3 percent in 1945–1958 and to 43.5 percent in 1958–1978. One should note that it was during the Fourth Republic, and not the Fifth, that people who were self-employed exceeded the 50 percent mark in the Assembly. In 1981, the movement accelerated even more: only 23.8 percent of the members of Parliament elected on June 21, 1981, are self-employed. We must also point out a relatively unique aspect of the Fourth Republic: between 1945 and 1958, 11.9 percent of all members of Parliament came from the working class. This may be accounted for by the large number of Communist members and by the system of proportional representation used at the time.

The decrease in the number of professionals in Parliament is also obvious. It concerns, above all, members of the legal profession. Here, too, the Fourth Republic reflects the clearest break with the past, with 1981 constituting a further point of acceleration, since lawyers made up 33 percent of the Assembly in 1871–1893, 25.2 percent in 1919–1936, 12.7 percent in 1945–1958, 10.9 percent in 1958–1973, and only 5.3 percent today.

Last, the increase in the number of senior civil servants is obvious, and, here again, this is a phenomenon specific to the Fifth Republic. It is becoming all the more significant as this Republic continues on its course, insofar as the direction taken by French political careers is changing, and a growing number of high-ranking officials in the civil service (especially members of ministerial secretariats) begin their political careers in the entourage of a member of the National Cabinet, and later run for elective office themselves.[10]

To these elements concerning the social recruitment of individuals exercising a full-time political activity (ministers and members of Parliament), one should add data about one last stratum of political personnel whose role among the ruling political elites is not negligible: *officials of the majority political parties*, delegates at the National Congresses. Leaning on government action, providing it with a relay within the party, constituting a breeding ground for the recruitment of new staff at the local or national level, and contributing,

TABLE 3.
Occupational Origins of Members of Parliament

	Industrialists, Tradesmen, Artisans	Farmers	Professional people	Journalists	Managerial Staff, Private Sector & Engineers	Senior Civil Servants*	Middle or Lower-Ranking Civil Servants	Teachers (all levels)	Employees	Working Men & Women	Others	Total
1871–1893	21.5%	6.7%	40.8%	5.8%	3.4%	13.2%	0.8%	3.9%	0.5%	1.3%	2.1%	100
1919–1936	16.8	9.1	33.7	6	5.1	7	1.5	9.8	3.5	5.8	1.7	100
1945–1958	11.8	12	18.5	5.7	8.6	5.3	2.7	14.8	6.3	11.9	2.4	100
1958–1978	12.3	7.3	23.9	4.1	9.8	12.3	3.3	13.2	3.3	2.7	7.8	100
1981	5.7	2.3	15.8	3.4	10.7	— 18.6† —		33.9	1.8	3.2	4.6	100

*Army officers: 5.8% in 1871–1893, 3.4% in 1919–1936, 1.6% in 1945–1958, 1.2% in 1958–1978, 0.6% in 1981.

†Represents combined total of senior civil servants and middle or lower-ranking civil servants.

Sources: For the periods from 1871 to 1893 and 1919 to 1936, figures established from M. Dogan, "Les filières de la carrière politique en France," Revue Française de Sociologie, no. 8, 1967; for 1945–1958, V. Aubert, "Etude sur le personnel politique francais," sociology thesis, 1973, quoted in P. Birnbaum, Les sommets de l'Etat (Paris: Ed. du Seuil, 1977), p. 71; for 1958–1978, figures calculated by the authors from the Parliamentary election White Papers published by the French Ministry of the Interior; for 1981, see R. Cayrol, "Beaucoup plus d'enseignants, moins d'industriels et de paysans," Le Monde, June 23, 1981.

to a certain extent, to the choices made by the leaders and holders of political office, the militants and officials of the majority parties make up a significant percentage within the governing elites and benefit from a relative autonomy when compared with those encumbered by the institutional apparatus.

Officials of the parties that supported the policies of the conservative Fifth Republic (1958–1981), i.e., those from the Gaullist Rassemblement pour la République (RPR) and the Giscardian Union pour la Démocratie Française (UDF), seem to come from social environments comparable to those of the other political elites (Table 4). Once more we are dealing with members of the privileged classes (the working classes are practically absent from their ranks). Farmers, too, are under-represented. Senior civil servants constitute one of the three largest categories in this elite.

There are, however, two major "deviations." The first is shown in a comparison between the UDF and the RPR. Gaullist officials are self-employed more often than their opposite numbers in the UDF. Moreover, within the "civil servant–teacher duopoly," senior civil servants are better represented in the UDF, while the neo-Gaullists display a greater proportion of elementary schoolmasters and teachers at higher levels.

The second "deviation" distinguishes between Gaullist and Giscardian party elites as a whole and parliamentary and government elites: officials coming from the private sector make up the largest category in the party elites of the RPR and the UDF, in sharp contradistinction to the elites in the institutional structure of government. There is an important difference here which can be explained by the difficulty for a Frenchman in the private sector to adopt a full-time political career, inasmuch as the "return ticket" to his original occupation, or to any other prospective career, is not available to him. The possible ambition to be part of the power elite is not sufficient to counterbalance the drawbacks, first, of a parliamentary salary that is often barely more than a decent salary earned by a member of the managerial staff in the private sector and, second, of a serious risk that one's career prospects may come to an end if one is not re-elected.

With the Socialists now in power, it would be interesting to find out whether these characteristics of the French governing elites in the conservative-led Fifth Republic will be perpetuated or fundamentally altered. One's reply to that question must today be a guarded one: there is indeed a genuine change, but there also is considerable continuity with the past.

An examination of Tables 2 (composition of the Mauroy government in June 1981) and 4 (occupational origin of Socialist officials) shows that the political leaders of the Socialist party are recruited just as much from the privileged strata of the nation as the former majority parties—even if the electoral support and the membership

TABLE 4.
Occupational Origin of Majority Party Delegates at National Congresses

	Industrialists, Company Directors, Tradesmen, Artisans	Farmers	Professional People	Journalists	Managerial Staff (Private sector & Engineers)	Senior Civil Servants	Middle or Lower-Ranking Civil Servants	Teachers (all levels)	Employees	Working Men & Women	Others*	Total
RPR (Neo-Gaullists)	13.5%	3.8%	13.8%	—	26.9%	11.3%	4.4%	12.8%	4.1%	2.2%	7.2%	100 (n = 347)
UDF (Giscar-dians)	10.1	1.8	13.2	1.8	27.6	17.3	4.3	7.6	3.6	1	11.7	100 (n = 442)
PS (Socialists)	1	2	5	1	23	7	8	34	5	5	9	100 (n = 669)

*The "Others" column is essentially made up of non-working members of the population (housewives, students, etc.).

Sources: Surveys carried out by R. Cayrol and C. Ysmal using questionnaires distributed to delegates at the National Congresses of UDF in 1979, RPR in 1980, and PS in 1981, within the framework of a European survey of political party congress members led by K. Reif (Mannheim University) and R. Cayrol.

of the party are to be found further down the social ladder.[11] Moreover, the Socialist members of Parliament elected on June 21, 1981, are rarely of working-class origin (0.7 percent are working class men and women), or even middle-class origin (11.3 percent); 86 percent come from the upper classes, and there are only 0.4 percent farmers. Thus, the transfer of power to the Socialists has not led, so far, to the promotion of working- and middle-class people within the political elites and in the institutional apparatus of the French State.

Nevertheless, changes are occurring in the power structure. On the one hand, the percentage of employees has further increased, whereas the share of industrialists, professional people, and peasants has been reduced. On the other hand, while the Socialists still emphasize the preponderance of the "duopoly of teachers and high-ranking civil servants," they are beginning an internal readjustment to the advantage of the teachers, since the latter make up 34 percent of all middle-grade party officials, 34.5 percent of government officials, and 47 percent of their parliamentary party.

Governing Elites and Cultural Channels

It is a commonplace to note that educational and cultural levels are the highest in socially favored categories. It is, therefore, not at all surprising to find that French political elites, which, as has been said, over-represent the privileged social categories, are largely recruited from among those sections of the population that have had the benefit of higher education.

We have not enough space here to relate the "elitist" characteristics of higher education in France[12] and to specify the impact of the dual system of higher education, where special, or "great" schools (grandes écoles) which run parallel to the universities, favor the reproduction of the ruling elites.[13] Let us limit ourselves to pointing out three characteristic elements of the governing elites in Fifth Republic France. First, scientific training (exact and natural sciences) is utterly in the minority among ministers, members of Parliament, party officials, and senior civil servants alike. As an example, only 5 percent of all ministers have had a predominantly scientific educational background and no more than 1 percent of all members of the ministerial secretariats.

Second, one type of training dominates government elites, and that is a legal and economic one. If one adds the diplomas from the Paris Institute of Political Studies (Institut d'Etudes Politiques de Paris) and the National Administration School (Ecole Nationale d'Administration, E.N.A.) to university courses in these subjects, he will conclude that one fifth of all socialist and Gaullist officials, one third of all Giscardian officials and of all members of Parliament, and more than half the ministers and senior civil servants have gone through these educational channels and patterns.[14] Thus, the language and the terms of reference of the governing elites are very similar and homogeneous, due to a largely identical training which is precisely that which teaches one of the workings of the machinery of the State.

Finally, within this training, the special schools play an eminent role as one climbs the hierarchy of political and governmental offices; no fewer than 28 percent of all ministers for the period from 1959 to 1974 and 36.5 percent in 1979 graduated from a special school.[15] Among these special schools, one can notice the growing importance of the E.N.A., which provided not only 14 percent of the ministers between 1958 and 1974 and 19 percent between 1974 and 1976 but 33 percent of all members of ministerial secretariats as early as 1968. This, of course, confirms what has been said on the importance of senior civil servants in the political elite of the Fifth Republic, a subject to which we shall return when we address the issue of the circulation of politico-administrative elites.

One must not rule out the possibility that this situation may some day change, due to the coming to power of the Socialists, whose civil servants are more often members of the teaching profession. However, the importance of a legal and economic training in their middle-ranking officials, like the weight of graduates of the E.N.A., in the Mauroy government, and within the ministerial secretariats set up in May-June 1981, lead one to assume that there again the change can only be a relative one, altering but little in a situation that is basically being perpetuated.

Governing Elites and Social Mobility

Fifth Republic governing elites are recruited from among the favored categories with regard to their occupational and cultural backgrounds and are mainly from privileged family backgrounds also. Table 5 lists, as an example, the socio-professional background of the fathers of the various members of the political and senior administrative personnel. For the current elite itself, the E.N.A. has, since 1945, provided the essential elements of the body politic[16] and the higher ranks of the civil service. On reading this table, it is easy to see that the family antecedents of the politico-administrative elites belong, in their majority, to the upper classes and that this is all the more obvious as one moves up the political hierarchy. Even if one groups together the descendants of middle- and working-class families, these only make up approximately one third of the fathers of members of Parliament, chairmen of General Councils, mayors of large towns, or graduates of the E.N.A.; they constitute no more than a quarter of all Giscardian and a fifth of all Gaullist middle-ranking officials and only 15 percent of all ministers. It should be

TABLE 5.
Social Mobility: Occupations of the Fathers of Members of the Political and Administrative Elites

	Fathers of Members of Parliament (1978)	Fathers of Chairmen of General Councils (1979)	Fathers of Mayors of Towns of More than 30,000 Inhabitants	Fathers of Middle-Ranking Giscardians Officials UDF (1980)	Fathers of Middle-Ranking Gaullists Officials RPR (1979)	Fathers of Ministers (1979)	Fathers of Graduates of the E.N.A. (Classes of 1947 to 1969)
Industrialists, Important businessmen	19	13	18	18	16	23	7
Professional people	11	10	16	9	8	18	9
Executives	19	7	8	24	22	29	32
Teachers (all levels)	4	5	6	4	2	12	*
Artisans, tradesmen	10	8	9	7	8	3	7
Middle-ranking managerial staff	8	8	11	12	11	6	24
Employees	6	15	11	6	8	—	12
Working men	9	7	9	9	11	—	5
Farmers	11	22	6	9	12	12	4
Politicians	2	5	4	—	—	3	—
Various	1	—	2	2	2	—	—
Total	100	100	100	100	100	100	100

*Higher and secondary education teachers are included in the executives; elementary schoolteachers are included in middle-ranking managerial staff.

Sources: For the fathers of members of Parliament, ministers, mayors, and chairmen of general councils, figures were calculated by V. Aubert from biographies published in Who's Who in France and by the newspaper Le Monde. For the fathers of middle-ranking Giscardian and Gaullists officials, figures were taken from the previously quoted surveys by R. Cayrol and C. Ysmal. For the fathers of graduates of the E.N.A., see J. L. Bodiguel, Les anciens élèves de l'E.N.A. (Presses de la Fondation Nationale des Sciences Politiques, 1978).

noted in passing that contrary to certain generally accepted views the recruitment sources of Giscardian and Gaullist party members are very similar.

Access to the governing elites has, therefore, been available, in the conservative-led Fifth Republic above all, to the sons of the most comfortable families who have been able to benefit from an appropriate type of education enabling them to take up an administrative or elective career or an administrative career leading to an elective one.

On this level, too, one may wonder whether the fact that the Socialists have come to power in France is likely to alter the configuration of French governing elites. In this respect, changes are likely to be more obvious. While it has been pointed out that the Socialist elites do not have a very profoundly different socio-background than Gaullist and Giscardian elites, various data seem to indicate that they reflect somewhat different processes of social mobility. Indeed, a study of the parliamentary parties covering the period from 1968 to 1973[17] has already shown that whereas Gaullist and Giscardian members of Parliament generally come from the wealthier families, their Socialist counterparts are more often recruited from the middle or working classes. Nineteen percent of all Gaullist members of Parliament in this study and 15 percent of all Giscardian members, but 48 percent of all Socialist members, had a father belonging to one of these classes. Were one to construct a "social origin index" with the occupations of the two grandfathers, the father, and the original occupation of the member of Parliament himself as components of the index, the results would show that the index of belonging to the ruling classes was 0.26 for the Socialists compared to 0.52 for the Gaullists and 0.60 for the Giscardians (0.02 for the Communists). The corresponding index for the working classes was 0.22 for the Socialists, against 0.06 for the Gaullists and Giscardians (and 0.54 for the Communists).

Similarly, it was noted that in 1970, 43 percent of the members of the Socialist Party Executive, as well as 28 percent of the federal secretaries (party officials at the department level), were sons of working people or members of the middle class.[18] In addition, 28 percent of the members of the Executive in 1974[19] and 25 percent of the party delegates at the national conference in 1977[20] were from working-class backgrounds.

These data as a whole seem to indicate that the massive election of Socialists into the governing elites has not, so far, resulted in the promotion, within these elites, of individuals belonging to the lower classes of society, but of individuals whose *origins* are often in these classes and whose academic and occupational attributes and skills were already, even before their joining the politico-administrative elite, the result of a process of upward social mobility.

II. Circulation within the Ruling Elites

Beyond the structural links uniting these various fractions of the governing elites, we must now consider whether there are links resulting from the circulation of the actors between the different sectors of political power. An evaluation of the degree to which the State is independent with regard to economic and political elites clearly depends on the answer to such a question. This empirical approach to the question of the degree of the State's autonomy raises two essential problems: (1) that of the independence or interdependence between the political and administrative sectors and (2) that of the independence or interdependence between the administrative and economic sectors.

Circulation between the Political and Administrative Sectors

French republican tradition is very attached to a strict separation between political and administrative fields. This attachment was born in reaction to a regime in which a confusion of powers was the order of the day, under the July Monarchy (1830–1848). At that time, more than half the members of Parliament belonged to the Administration, which then had no autonomy whatsoever since it was impregnated by the world of business and strictly controlled by the holders of political power. The introduction, in 1848, of universal franchise (for men only) allowed the gradual emergence of new political personnel, less attached to the bourgeoisie and to government bodies. With the advent of the Third Republic, this new political personnel was to enter both the legislative and the executive branches. This enabled it to acquire a real autonomy and to dissociate itself from the Administration. This distinction between political and administrative personnel was to continue until the end of the Fourth Republic. As Pierre Birnbaum writes, "Senior civil servants and, in particular, members of the main elements of the Body Politic, became less common in the parliaments of the Third and Fourth Republics, giving way to a professionalized political personnel, born of universal franchise."[21] One may ask what the position is in the Fifth Republic. The answer to this question will be given by examining successfully four essential components of political power: the cabinet, the ministerial secretariats, Parliament, and the majority parties.

Civil Servants and National Cabinet Personnel. Within the framework of the parliamentary regime of the Fourth Republic, the National Cabinet closely depended on Parliament. This dependence went as far as the socio-professional composition of the National

Cabinet, which relatively faithfully reflected that of Parliament. The dominant groups of the Assembly (lawyers, teachers, industrialists, journalists, and doctors) were also well represented in the National Cabinet.

Civil servants were represented in the National Cabinet essentially through teachers. The "Republic of teachers" that Albert Thibaudet referred to in 1927 was still flourishing.[22] It was, on the other hand, profoundly disputed when General de Gaulle came to power. As early as the appointment of the last National Cabinet of the Fourth Republic, General de Gaulle affirmed his intentions by recruiting 69.5 percent of his ministers from the civil service (more than two thirds of which came from the highest ranks of the civil service and less than a third from the teaching body) (Table 6). The era of senior civil servants in the political personnel had begun.

Top members of the administration entered the National Cabinet, and a close interpenetration between political and administrative elites reappeared more than a century after the fall of the July Monarchy. The administrative personnel that "colonized" the offices of political power was over 75 percent composed of senior civil servants.[23] Three main reasons can be found for this "invasion" by the senior civil service into political power.

The first is circumstantial and is due to the defeat of the parties of the Left in 1958. Indeed, the teachers, of whom there are very many in the left-wing parties, were to be the first affected by the failure of the Left in 1958. Their role became a marginal one in Parliament and was to be even more diminished in the government, where they were to be replaced by senior civil servants. Their position tended to weaken even further throughout the Fifth Republic, while that of the senior civil servants was to be strengthened.

The second reason for the increasing role of senior civil servants within the National Cabinets of the Fifth Republic is a political one. General de Gaulle, as early as 1946, considered that the weakness of the State resulted from the excessive power of Parliament. Thus, in his opinion, it was necessary to establish the preeminence of an executive power freed from Parliament's tight control and, therefore, from that of the professional politicians who go to make it up. The founder of the Fifth Republic wrote: "It is necessary, too, that the Executive, which is destined to serve the entire community, should not proceed from Parliament, which brings together the delegations of private interests."[24] This concept of constitutional organization was to lead General de Gaulle to recruit his ministers mainly from outside the parliamentary breeding ground and above all in the highest ranks of the civil service, the guarantor of the continuity of the State. There was to be a particularly large number of senior civil servant and nonparliamentarian ministers during the presidencies of de Gaulle and Valéry Giscard d'Estaing, even if many of them, having been appointed to ministerial office, then wished to receive

TABLE 6.
Analysis of the Civil Servant Section (Fifth Republic)
(in absolute numbers)

National Cabinet	de Gaulle (1958)	Debre (1959)	Pompidou (1966)	Pompidou (1966)	Couve de Murville (1968)	Chaban Delmas (1969)	Messmer (1973)	Chirac (1976)	Barre (1976)	Mauroy (1981)
Number of ministers coming from civil service	16	13	12	14	18	17	25	22	22	26
Senior civil service	11	9	9	10	12	15	19	15	17	10
Other civil servants	—	—	—	—	1	—	1	5	1	1
Teachers as a whole	5	4	3	4	5	2	5	2	4	15
Proportion of civil servants in each government*	69.5%	52%	43%	50%	58%	43.5%	66%	62%	64%	59%

*This total of civil servants includes teachers.

Source: F. DeBaecque, L'interpenetration des personnels politique et administratif, p. 17 and Le Monde, June 25, 1981.

the consecration of being elected by universal franchise in the next parliamentary election.

Last, and parallel to this evolution in the political stature granted to the Executive, a new ideology developed among civil servants. The traditional ideology, whereby the administration is closely subordinated to political power, was gradually superseded by a technocratic ideology putting forward two advantages held by the administration over political power—technical competence and stability.

Civil Servants and Ministerial Secretariats. These politico-administrative bodies, like the governments, have been "invaded" by high-ranking civil servants, who made up 79 percent of their members in 1968. An empirical study of the 307 members of the civil secretariats (i.e., personally and politically appointed "cabinets") of presidents of the Republic and prime ministers from 1959 to 1974[25] shows us that professional men and women, people working in the private sector, and teachers are practically excluded from them. All together, these three categories constituted only 3.1 percent, 4 percent, and 3.5 percent, respectively, of the total number of civil secretaries of the presidents and prime ministers from 1959 to 1974.[26] As Pierre Birnbaum remarks, "This recruitment greatly contributes to the autonomization of the politico-administrative machine which is dissociated from the professionalized traditional world of politics and from private interests."[27] These ministerial secretariats often constitute a stepping stone to a ministerial career: about 40 percent of the Fifth Republic's ministers have held positions in such secretariats. In this way, an extremely homogeneous politico-administrative personnel is formed of senior civil servants, who became politicians themselves or who work with them before doing so. The channel of parliamentary recruitment, which was dominant during the Fourth Republic, has given way to that of the ministerial secretariats, which have become a sort of waiting room for positions of political power.

We must now consider whether or not this contamination of the world of politics by the administration has also reached that stronghold of professionals constituted by Parliament.

Civil Servants and Parliamentary Personnel. Countless books and articles on the decline of the French Parliament have been published since 1958. The Constitution of that year set up a legal structure severely limiting Parliament's powers in favor of the Executive. Largely freed from the control of the legislative branch, the Executive was strengthened by relying on the senior sections of the civil service and reducing the influence of the professionalized political personnel.

In spite of this marginalization, Parliament has not been neglected by these senior civil servants, and that for two main reasons: democratic legitimacy and political apprenticeship. Many ministers who are also senior civil servants have indeed been known to run for

Parliament so as to add a sort of democratic legitimacy to their technical legitimacy. This was the case for Georges Pompidou, Raymond Barre, and Robert Galley, among others. Finally, young senior civil servants already installed in the corridors of power became candidates for election by the people in order to complete their political apprenticeship and, later, to reach higher office. This step was taken by Valéry Giscard d'Estaing, Jacques Chirac, and Alain Peyrefitte. Thus, senior civil servants have not neglected Parliament in the past twenty years; there were five times as many of them as members of Parliament in 1978 as at the end of the Fourth Republic. No social group has progressed so markedly during the Fifth Republic. In 1978, they and the teachers were the best represented social group in the National Assembly (13 percent for the senior civil servants and 15 percent for the teachers).[28]

However, whereas senior civil servants have provided the Fifth Republic with a third of its ministers and four fifths of the members of its ministerial secretariats, they only go to make up one eighth of its members of Parliament.[29] The further one goes from the heart of political power (presidency, government, ministerial secretariats), the scarcer senior civil servants become. In 1978, they only made up 8 percent of all general councillors and 4 percent of all majors.[30]

The distribution of senior civil servants among the political groups is very uneven. Attached to the Fifth Republic regime, which has opened the doors of power to them more widely than before, these senior civil servants are principally to be found in the right-wing groups.[31]

Civil Servants and Party Elites. Senior civil servants are extremely well represented in the right-wing parliamentary parties, and it will be interesting to see whether they are as numerous in the ruling machinery of the two great right-wing parties, the Rassemblement pour la République (RPR) and the Union pour la Démocratie Française (UDF). The UDF, which is a combination of several small center- and right-wing parties is, in fact, closely linked to its parliamentary party. A previously mentioned survey shows that senior civil servants made up more than 15 percent of the delegates at the 1980 UDF Congress. The senior civil service is, therefore, not absent from what used to be called the "President's Party." The same result occurs when one considers the occupations of the candidates at the March 1978 parliamentary election:[32] between 7 percent and 14 percent of the candidates in the different component parts of the UDF were senior civil servants. If one considers the Gaullist party, more than 10 percent of the candidates were senior civil servants. Last, at the highest level of the RPR, the Central Committee, one can note among the 18 percent of the civil servants, 5 percent who were senior civil servants (March 31, 1979) (Table 7).[33]

Thus, senior civil servants are present even in the circles sur-

TABLE 7.
Socio-Professional Composition of the Candidates for National
Assembly in 1978 (in percent)

	RPR (Neo-Gaullists)	PR (Giscardians)	PS (Socialists)	Total (candidates from the seven main parties)
Senior civil servants	10.4	10.6	4.3	5.7
Industrialists, tradesmen, and artisans	15.2	17.1	4.3	9.7
Executives and engineers	21.1	17.2	13.7	13.8
Professional people (total)	21.8	28.8	11.3	15.4
Lawyers	4.7	9.6	3.4	4.7
Doctors	10.6	13.6	5.4	4.8
Middle-ranking managerial staff	15.1	11.1	17.7	16.0
Teachers (all levels)	10.2	8.6	39.8	21.7
Farmers	3.5	3.5	2.3	2.8
Employees	2.2	0.5	4.1	4.8
Working men and women	0	1	1.1	9
Others	0.5	1.6	1.4	1.1
	n = 407	n = 198	n = 444	n = 1,812

Sources: G. Fabre-Rosane, A. Guede. "Sociologie des candidats aux elections leg-islatives de mars 1978," Revue Francaise de Science Politique, 28, no. 5 (October 1978): 854.

rounding the power structure, in the parties that went to make up the old majority. There are more of them at the leadership level than at the grass roots level, and more of them as candidates than as mere militants.

The fact that senior civil servants have penetrated the political structures is, therefore, an important element of the Fifth Republic. This penetration is complete at the heart of the power structure (presidency, government, ministerial secretariats) and somewhat less so in Parliament and in the parties, the structures whose power was reduced by the 1958 Constitution. Nevertheless, it is not negligible even there, and becomes greater as soon as the power stakes are more obvious (conservative parliamentary parties, ruling party circles, election candidacies).

In the spring of 1981, power changed hands. François Mitterrand and the Socialist party won the presidency, the premiership, and a majority in the National Assembly. France's political scene looks completely different. It will be interesting to find out whether this change means the end of this "senior civil servant Republic."

The Socialist Breed. A good many commentators believed that the preeminence of senior civil servants in the Fifth Republic's political class marked the final end of that Republic of teachers which had had its hour of glory during the Third Republic. But now, with the Socialist victory in 1981, these teachers, who had been somewhat forgotten, are reappearing in full force at every level of the political class. They make up a good third of the new National Assembly, and almost 30 percent of the secretariats of the President and Mauroy National Cabinet. After a reign of more than twenty years, could the Republic of senior civil servants have given way to the Republic of teachers?

In this respect, two elements are noteworthy: first, that teachers had never completely disappeared from the corridors of power, and second, that senior civil servants had penetrated the circles of the opposition of yesterday, which is today's party in power.

Indeed, despite a definite reduction in their influence, teachers have always represented between 5 percent and 15 percent of National Cabinet members, 3.5 percent of the Prime Ministers and the President's secretariats, and between 9 percent and 20 percent of the members of Parliament between 1958 and 1980. Each swing to the left at the electoral level was reflected by an increased number of teachers in the National Assembly (in 1967, 1973, and 1978). Thus, the growing interpenetration between senior civil servants and the political class in the Fifth Republic had reduced, but not eliminated, the weight of the teachers in the governing elite. All the preconditions for a massive return of the "Republic of teachers" were present.

The opposition parties, and particularly the Socialist party, had not gone through twenty years of the Fifth Republic without being profoundly affected in their strategy, their workings, or in their composition by the characteristics of the regime (the majority system, the importance of the president, and the growing influence of senior civil servants). Among these effects, the increasing role of the senior civil servants within the Socialist party must be emphasized. Indeed, this is discernable at different levels of political responsibility: senior civil servants constituted 4.3 percent of the Socialist candidates in the 1978 parliamentary election, 7.9 percent of the Socialist mayors in 1977,[34] and 18 percent of all members of the national secretariat established at the 1979 national congress. This presence of senior civil servants in the ruling circles of the Socialist party increased still further with the 1981 election victory, as there are now 23 percent senior civil servants in Pierre Mauroy's National Cabinet and 36 percent in François Mitterrand's secretariat. This presence is certainly more modest than in Barre's last National Cabinet (34%) and in Valéry Giscard d'Estaing's secretariat (68%), but it is important enough to be able to describe the Socialist Fifth Republic as a regime in which two dominant groups—senior civil servants and teachers—now control the centers of political power. Since the 1981 elections, it has been possible to talk about a "Republic of civil servants" in which senior civil servants and teachers live side by side, and where the influence of the private sector has been considerably reduced (there are no industrialists in the Mauroy National Cabinet and only 4% in Parliament). The osmosis between senior civil servants and the political class has been replaced by a broader base of interaction between agents of the State and politicians.

The Connection between the Administration and the Para-Public and Private Sectors

While the Fifth Republic has been and is characterized by a profound interpenetration between the political staff and senior civil service, a second characteristic is an increased movement of certain members of the administration toward the private and para-public sectors. This movement was all the more original because it went against the weight of tradition, which did not take kindly to this "merging" between the public and private sectors. In France, the administration and the private sector have long held each other in mutual distrust.

This growing interaction between the two sectors has gone together with the greater and greater intervention and commitment of the State in the economic life of the country. Through the development of a large public and para-public sector, its growing role as a regulator of the economy, and its policy of training economic as well as administrative elites, the State has initiated "private vocations" among its civil servants.

Exchanges between the State Apparatus and the Public and Para-Public Sectors.[35] The public and para-public economic sectors are the privileged area of interpenetration. While senior civil servants take over preferably the highest positions in public companies, the absence of homogeneity among the staffs of these companies leads to a coexistence between the administrative directors and the private-sector directors who have joined them.

Despite a hardly negligible contribution of executives from the private sector,[36] the main part of the managerial staff in the public and para-public sector comes from the senior civil service. These senior civil servants who work for a State employer are aware of the demands of industrial development and believe in an ideology in which acknowledged management principles in the private sector (competition, efficiency) are entirely recognized and accepted. This ideological symbiosis facilitates the movement of the managerial staff in public companies toward the private sector. In the Birnbaum et al. survey[37] of the French ruling class, 44 percent of those who head an industrial company belonging to the public sector subsequently make their way into the private sector. Thus, it may be said that for some senior civil servants, the time spent in the public and para-public economic sector is only a step on the way to the private sector. The public and para-public economic sector is not only a meeting ground where private and administrative staff merge, it is also a stepping-stone for public administrators heading toward the private sector.

Exchanges between the Administrative Sector and the Private Sector. Unlike the public and para-public economic sector, the administration takes in only a minute number of individuals coming from the private sector. This "exchange of elites" is a one-way road and concerns only senior civil servants who join the private sector. The phenomenon has increased continuously since the 1950's. It included 20 percent of all senior civil servants in 1954 and 28 percent in 1974[38] and is most frequent among senior military men (41 percent of all senior officers left their military affiliations in 1974 to take up positions in the private sector). They are followed by other senior civil servants: members of the great technical corps (Civil Engineers and Mines), top administrative executives in public companies, and senior civil servants in the central administration. This movement also affects senior civil servants in the basic institutions of the body politic: in 1974, 16 percent left their original departments to join the private sector.

The massive movement of the military toward the private sector can largely be explained by their technical training (Polytechnique, Saint-Cyr), which predisposes them to take up careers as engineers or as directors in private industrial corporations. That of other senior civil servants can also be explained by the technical training received by some of them (engineers who have been through the Mining School or the Civil Engineering School) or their occupational predisposition (directors of public companies for whom the public and para-public sector is simply a waiting room on the road to a career in the private sector). As far as the aristocracy of the senior civil service is concerned, i.e., the members of the main elements of the body politic, their less frequent movement in this direction can be explained by their position of power in the State. This position is not easily relinquished, even if they are offered superior material advantages in the private sector. As C. Brindillac writes: "The Director of the Treasury may receive a salary which is considerably inferior to that of the Director General of a private bank, but he has vastly superior power. And this power is exercised in a much broader field, which affects the whole nation. These great servants of the State like to be among the hundred people who debate the business of the country between themselves and consider it much more fun, to paraphrase Cicero, to command the rich than to be rich themselves.[39] However, this hesitation to leave the body politic is not experienced by all its members, since there is a continuous tendency to join the private sector, especially as far as the Treasury is concerned (Table 8).

TABLE 8.
Movement to the Private Sector of Members of the Administrative Sections of the Body Politic

	1954		1964		1974	
Council of State	4%		9%		4%	
Audit office	10		6		10	
Treasury	31	(of which 15% is banking)	26	(of which 14% is banking)	32	(of which 24% is banking)
Prefects	10				74	
Diplomats			5			

Source: P. Birnbaum et al., La classe dirigeante francaise, p. 70.

Thanks to this movement, there is a close connection between the highest levels of the State and the largest private or public companies. A study of the managerial staff of the 100 biggest French companies reveals that 42 percent of them come from the civil service (14 percent from the main elements of the body politic).[40] Thus, over and above similarities in social origin and channels of socialization, a physical closeness is created between the heads of the public and the private sectors. This profound interpenetration of the two sectors leads one to dispute the argument developed by Raymond Aron, according to which the diversity of France's ruling categories makes it impossible to speak of a certain degree of homogeneity and unity within the ruling class.[41] The relative merger of personnel is accompanied by a palpable development of a senior servant's ideology, in that there is a certain "privatization" and an attenuation of the frontiers between the private and public sectors.

"For senior civil servants, public service is thus less an end in itself than a step toward other political or economic responsibilities. To spend one's whole career in the service of the State is somewhat considered as an admission of failure, evidence of one's incapacity to use one's technical competence to his advantage, and this perception does reveal a certain weakening of the Salience of the State."[42] With the 1981 victory of the left-wing parties, in which the State appears again as a central value, one may wonder about the future development of this trend. It is possible that over the next few years, senior civil servants may return en masse to their ideology of public service.

III. Interrelations between Segments of the Governing Elites

Concerning the ways in which the various segments of the governing elites view each other, French sociologists have few empirical data at their disposal. We are trying to find out here how the various segments of the elite perceive one another. Do these perceptions conflict or not? Is the relative social homogeneity of the elites reinforced by a psycho-sociological homogeneousness?

The Private Sector as Perceived by Senior Civil Servants

Henry Ehrmann has noted that under the Fourth Republic, a mutual hostility characterized the relationship between employers and the highest ranks of the administration.[43] "The feelings of the highest ranks of the Administration towards the employers are not entirely devoid of a certain ambivalence. Civil servants have no practice and experience of business, it is said. Civil servants consider that employers are hypocritical when they deplore the political demagoguery which favours the small man." More than twenty years later such statements would distort the truth. Indeed, throughout the Fifth Republic, the distinction between the public and the private sectors has become less and less obvious. More than 90 percent of all senior civil servants believe that communication between the two sectors is easy,[44] and only 13 percent of these senior civil servants feel that a separation between them is desirable. Asked the same questions, directors in the private sector give similar answers, the percentages being 90 percent and 3 percent. One notes here an important change in mental attitudes, especially on the part of senior civil servants, who have long been attached to a tradition of the preeminence of the State, which was considered the only depository of impartiality and of the general interest against the competition of selfish private interests.

This genuine transformation of mental attitudes is shown in practice by easier and more frequent contacts between senior civil servants and directors in the private sector and groups representing various interests. Seventy percent of all senior ministry officials meet members of different lobbies very often or daily.[45] For them, these meetings are, above all, an opportunity to assess different interests. Senior civil servants feel less and less entrusted with a predefined mission of general interest. The latter no longer springs ready-made from the brains of civil servants; instead, it is the result of an arbitration between various industrial demands. Only 18.6 percent of the senior civil servants who were interviewed believe that the purpose of these contacts between the administration and different lobbies is, above all, to explain and justify decisions that the administration has already made by itself. One third among these senior civil servants think that these contacts "lead to a discussion between various interests and facilitate policy formulation and implementation." No one thinks that these contacts "offer no advantage."[46] The conception of an all-powerful administration, which sees no room for agreement and concerted action, is accepted only by a very small minority.

The Political Sector as Perceived by the Senior Civil Service

As representatives of the State, senior civil servants do not always feel much affinity for the politicians who represent the nation. For them, the State unites and gathers people together, while the nation is divided. This old conception seems to have persisted and has not evolved at the same rate as that concerning the relationship between the public and the private sectors. Indeed, there are many senior civil servants who believe that the political and administrative fields ought to be clearly separated. Only 30 percent of all senior ministry officials interviewed think it is desirable for senior civil servants to hold political office. Over 65 percent think that it is not desirable.[47]

This mistrust of all that is political is also reflected in the very negative judgments made by top ministry officials about the politico-administrative entourage that surrounds the ministers—the ministerial secretariats. Seventy-nine percent of these officials believe that the ministerial secretariats encroach upon the offices of the administration. Over 60 percent of them see the secretariats as a screen between themselves and the minister. Only 32.1 percent think of them as a useful intermediary between the minister and his administration.[48] The senior civil servants who run the ministries, therefore, believe that these politico-administrative bodies, called ministerial secretariats, are detrimental to the smooth working of the administrative machine.

The image of members of the French Parliament, in the eyes of these same senior civil servants, is not much better and reflects the decline in the position of parliamentarians during the Fifth Republic. On a scale where members of Parliament were compared with businessmen, professional people, and senior civil servants, members of Parliament, in the almost unanimous opinion of the senior civil servants, find themselves right at the bottom as far as prestige, freedom of action, the importance of the tasks accomplished, and the preparation for these tasks are concerned.[49]

For most senior ministry officials, the parliamentarian is merely the representative of the different categories of interests in his constituency. Only 3.7 percent consider him the representative of the national interest.[50] The member of Parliament is a victim of this mediocre image and of the constitutional system of the Fifth Republic, which establishes the supremacy of the Executive, and sees the officials devote only a small part of their time and duties to dealing with legislative matters, and far more to the field of rules and regulations. Fifty-nine percent of all senior ministry officials say they devote only a quarter of their time to legislative matters, while 58 percent of them spend three quarters of their time on activities related to rules and regulations.[51] The 1958 Constitution, which extended the field of executive and administrative legislation at the expense of that of the law, has had a strong impact on the higher ranks of the administration by separating them further and deeper from Parliament and its legislative powers and processes.

Senior Civil Servants as Perceived by Members of Parliament

Members of Parliament do not, by any means, have the same poor opinion of senior civil servants as the latter have of them. Indeed, the vast majority of members of Parliament express the opinion that senior civil servants play a very important role in political decision making.[52]

Given the low importance that members of Parliament assign to themselves about their weight in political decision making, it is obvious that they have become conscious of their reduced role in the institutional system that was set up in 1958 and that they recognize the preeminence of the upper reaches of the State administration and of the elected chief Executive. This new awareness is particularly keen among opposition members (in 1968, Communists and Socialists) who are "victims" of the new majority system whereby, since 1962, no parliamentary alliance has been dissolved during the term of a legislature.

This brief summary of the images that the different sectors of government elites have of each other seems to highlight three fundamental elements.

First, the growing movement of senior civil servants toward the private sector is accompanied by a relative psycho-sociological homogenization of the two spheres. After decades of mutual suspicion, a time of peaceful coexistence seems to have arrived. One can even think of it as harmony and the beginnings of a series of common values. The interesting question for the coming years will be whether or not the Socialists' conquest of the machinery of the State will deeply challenge this relative "privatization" of the ideology of senior civil servants.

Second, and contrary to what has happened between the highest ranks of the administration and the private sector, the growing amalgamation of senior civil servants and political elites has not drawn the two closer together. The poor image that the administration has of the political class is no better than it ever was. It is difficult to see how this image could improve in the near future, since the senior civil service now occupying the State machinery under the Socialists, was profoundly fashioned by twenty-three years of Gaullist and Giscardian power, which held members of Parliament and the political parties in rather low esteem.

Third, the reduction of the parliamentarians' role during the Fifth Republic has been reflected in the realization of their own powerlessness. It will be interesting to find out whether the reevaluation of Parliament's role, as the Socialists now propose, is likely to alter the members of Parliament's feelings of powerlessness or whether the weight of the institutional tradition established in 1958 will be stronger.

IV. By Way of a Conclusion: Governing Elites, Values, and Society

It is well known that post-1958 France has experienced an extraordinary period of economic and political modernization. The main elements of this are a rapid economic growth, the establishment and implementation of the European Common Market, the progressive disappearance of antiquated structures in industry and agriculture (and a corresponding reduction in the rural population), the development of oligopolies, the renovation of commercial structures, the development of capitalist banking, decolonization, and the setting up of political institutions guaranteeing government stability and the preeminence of the Executive.

What has been called the "French economic miracle" has taken place—as has often been the case in France's history—under the control and tutelage of the State. By turning upside down the reluctance and hesitation of the former economic elites, the elites of traditional capitalism, small- and medium-sized companies and family-run farming enterprises, by controlling most of the credit, and through concerted action with the important industrial sectors, the State has greatly contributed to the success of the "industrial imperative."

In this modernization policy, the State was able to rely on the governing elites, which were made to measure and particularly adapted to the task. This highlights the importance of the study of governing elites; it allows one to assess whether the processes of modernization of a society are effectively relayed by the political personnel, the function of which it is to translate the goals and orientations of the ruling class into governmental decisions. Everything in this report about the sociology, the training, and the systems of representation of these elites clearly illustrates how adequate the political and administrative officials were for that particular period in French history. The interpenetration of political and administrative personnel and the movement of administrative elites toward the economic and industrial sectors were equally functional. The dominant concepts within these governing elites do constitute the driving ideology of this period of modernization. One has only to run through the lists and summaries of the courses and seminars available to students of the Paris Institute of Political Studies and the E.N.A. in the last few years to get a grasp of the notions that have become the stock-in-trade common to all the country's ruling elites: an attachment to the industrial policy, the need for economic efficiency and competitiveness, fair prices in public companies, an opening up to the world market (with foreign trade a priority), and the decline in the traditional notion of public service as the guarantor of the general interest, in favor of an image of the public sector as an orchestrator of a policy of modernizing the economy and organizing industrial relations.

It is not difficult to understand why the French governing elites see themselves as the image of their own success and that of the system they maintain. Indeed, Ezra Suleiman's survey, carried out among the directors of large companies, senior civil servants, officials of the body politic, and members of the teaching staff of the special schools, gives the impression of a ruling class that is sure of itself and of the system it runs.[53] It does not dispute the system of special schools. In answer to the question, "France is one of the few countries where two parallel systems of higher education coexist (i.e., the universities and the special schools). All things considered, do you think this is a good thing or a bad?", 87.7 percent of those from the public sector in E. Suleiman's sample said it was a good thing (46.6 percent very good, 41.1 percent quite good); and 82.2 percent of those from the private sector gave a positive answer, too (42.0 percent very good, 39.3 percent quite good).

This ruling class does not question the role of the different elements of the body politic: 83.6 percent of the administrative elites and even 68.3 percent of the private sector elites feel that these different elements "certainly" or "probably" make up the main innovating force in a system which, in other respects, is very bureaucratic. Quite simply, 79 percent in the public sector and 67.8 percent in the private sector consider that these elements are indispensable to the smooth working of society as a whole.

This elite is sure of the system and the principles of authority and hierarchy on which its power is founded. Over 76 percent of the managerial staff in the public sector interviewed, as well as 87.9 percent in the private sector, think that "for an organization to function efficiently, a strongly hierarchical structure is needed, with just one person at its head if necessary." Over 93 percent in the public sector (and 91.6 percent in the private sector) agree with the idea that "in all organized life, there are those who command and those who obey, and this is how things should be."

Fully subscribing to the values that underlie and are the foundation of the French social system, the governing elites thus seem both a closed world, withdrawn into itself and into its certainties, and also a remarkable collective agent for the transformation of the country in the industrial age. Does that mean that the governing elites are in the process of making the picture that we have presented in these pages stand still forever, or else, will elements of question, mobility, and change reappear?

It is absolutely true, as E. Suleiman said, that "no major structural reform has been envisaged, be it by the Left or by the Right, as both recognize that the elitist system is not without advantages. It provides the State with relatively competent, devoted and loyal servants who consequently constitute an element of stability."[54] In this respect, the large-scale recruitment of new Socialist elites from the very same areas as the governing elites of the conservative Fifth Republic and the Socialist officials' first declarations about the institutionalization of the elite[55] do not suggest any fundamental change.

Still deeper factors likely to challenge present recruitment mechanisms, institutionalization, and the system of values of the elite seem to be at work, and these might eventually lead to diversification or even renewal. We would like to mention five such factors.

First, the weight of the working class in the organization of society. The choices of economic and industrial modernization have been made in the last few decades, we are told, by the governing elites of the State in conjunction with those of the most important industrial sectors. Concerted action between them has largely reached deadlock over the factors toward whom this policy had been detrimental: the owners of antiquated means of production in industry, agriculture, and commerce, on the one hand, and the working class on the other. While the former hardly seem able, at the present time, to play a leading role in the choices of society, the situation of the working class is more ambiguous. The parties it votes for are now in power. That alone is not a guarantee for change, and many European examples of social-democratic management are there to remind us of that fact. Much will no doubt depend on the capability of the French trade-union organizations to redefine their role now that the parties of the Left are in power. A very small number of union leaders have accepted positions of responsibility in the apparatus of government. Above all, the nature of the industrial relationship between the State, the employers, and the workers' organizations is in the process of being redefined. There is, in this, an interesting element, a new one for France, and that is the possible opening up of the governing elites and, at any rate, the possible modification of their practices and their system of values.

The second factor is the slackening of the stranglehold of the centralized Jacobin State. It is a well-known fact that the tradition of a centralized state has, for centuries, constituted a fundamental explanation of the specificities of French political society and a powerful stimulus for the unification movements of its governing elites. Certainly, such a tradition has inspired mechanisms, processes, and reflexes that cannot be expected to disappear overnight, even after the implementation of the Socialist party's plans for decentralization and regionalization. Nevertheless, the direct election of regional assemblies by universal suffrage, the transfer of economic competence from the State to the regions, and the autonomy of decision that is to be given to the local authorities are bound to create a new situation. A new stratum of elites may emerge which—if the specifically French phenomenon of accumulating political offices at different levels of government can be kept within reasonable limits—could bring about a new relationship between the central State authorities located in Paris and the citizens across the country.

The weight of "post-materialistic" values in a crisis situation is the third factor. The system of values of the governing elites is, as we have said, largely founded on the principles of economic growth, industrial modernization, authority, and hierarchy. But growth is slowed down or stopped in a Western world stricken by a long and deeply rooted crisis, although French means of production are largely modernized. Under these circumstances—without being able to speak about rapid evolution or agonizing revisions—one can now witness an opening up of the young French governing elites to values already present in the French mind.[56] This is shown by the relative progress made by the conservationist, ecologist electorate, the development of the political platforms of parties calling themselves socialistic and far left, and the actions of feminist and regionalist movements. In a society in which quantitative economic progress appears more difficult to make, anti-hierarchical values and concepts of freedom and right may, on the contrary, make great strides and affect a larger number of ruling groups, because these values are sheltered from immediate quantitative tests.

The fourth factor concerns the influence of putting one's thoughts and ideas on a worldwide level. France has always liked to play the role of the Messiah on a world scale. French governing elites have always wanted to consider themselves as the center of the universe. More than any other in Europe, the French governing elite is closed to external influences. However, the decline in the use of the French language (and the corresponding need for French elites to learn and speak other languages), the development of exchanges within the European Common Market, and the increase in foreign trade with every region (developed or not) in the world place French governing elites in the position of taking the whole world into consideration in their reflections and in their references. This is not to say that the increased number of journeys undertaken by a sizable proportion of the French ruling class to Brussels, Strasburg, and Luxemburg (the main seats of the European institutions), as well as to New York, Moscow, Algiers, or Peking, have already profoundly altered attitudes, which were essentially parochial. But, the preconditions for development do exist.

The fifth and final factor is the accession to power of the Socialists (and the Communists). It is in this context that, while taking all the previous factors into consideration, the change brought about by the victory of the Left in 1981 must be taken into account. First of all, this change is associated with an accentuation of the inter-generational processes of social mobility and with restoring the balance within the privileged groups to the detriment of the self-employed (industrialists, tradespeople, or farmers) and to the advantage of the teachers. This sociological shift may, in fact, have some effect on the system of values, insofar as teachers are often more doctrinaire than the elites, even the Socialist elites, in the private sector.

But the effects of the Socialist party's (and its minority Communist allies') accession to power on the systems of values, the practices of the elite, and its degree of openness toward society as a whole may be much greater, if this accession to power can act as a catalyst on the other four factors—the weight of the working class, the slackening of the centralized State's stranglehold, the set of post-materialistic values, and the new worldwide criteria.

In this respect, it is important to know who exactly will govern within the Socialist strata. With the Socialists, and the massive return of the teachers, is France coming back to a less "modern," less pragmatic, and more ideology-oriented policy? As a matter of fact, the intellectual tradition of French teachers is deeply marked by reluctant feelings toward industrialization and the managerial mind. But in this recent period, the PS has also been reshaped by its technocracy: the internal discussions of the Socialist cabinet during its first six months have shown that a large number of its cadres are today believers in economic competitiveness and in a compromise with the economic powers. Therefore, it seems important to analyze both the outline and the contradictions of the different elite categories within the new Socialist ruling class.

Through the integration of new individuals into elites, through their plans for changing structures and mental attitudes (decentralization, freedom, women's rights, worker participation, democratic planning, etc.), through the extension of the public sector (nationalizations), and through the need to preserve a competitive economy while satisfying the working classes who elected them, the French left-wing parties may be getting ready to create the objective conditions for a diversification of the governing elites of their country and of their ways of perceiving reality; on one condition, of course, that the Socialist governing elites, who have until now benefited from the privileges of an elitist French society, agree to see some of their privileges challenged by the implementation of their own programs.

Does who governs matter? In modern France, the answer to this question is, without any doubt, an affirmative one. It appears to be one of the main questions allowing us to test the efficiency of the political system. The adequacy of the composition and values of the governing elite to the socioeconomic program supported by a majority of the people shapes the ability of the political system to implement this program.

Notes

1. Presidents Charles de Gaulle (1958–1969), Georges Pompidou (1969–1974), and Valé Giscard d'Estaing (1974–1981) were supported by right-wing majorities, including, in various combinations, parties calling themselves Gaullist, center parties, and classical right-wing parties.

2. Mr. François Mitterrand (Socialist) was elected President of the Republic on May 10, 1981. The Socialists, on their own, won more than 50 percent of all the seats in the National Assembly on June 21, 1981. After that parliamentary election, the President appointed a government of 44 members, led by Mr. Pierre Mauroy, composed of forty Socialists (or left-wing radicals) and four Communists.

3. To each French minister is attached a team of aides (appointed at his discretion) known as the ministerial secretariat. See notably J. Siwek-Pouydesseau, "Les Cabinets ministériels," in Siwek-Pouydesseau et al., Les Superstructures des administrations centrales (Edition Cujas, 1973).

4. The "lower classes" are better represented at this level in large towns (where there are over 30,000 inhabitants) than elsewhere, because of the influence of the Communist party in certain large working-class cities.

5. We must remember that France is divided administratively into 36,334 communes (elected mayoral level), 3,526 cantons (elected General Councillor level), 96 departments (Chairman of General Council level), and 22 regions (Chairman of Regional Council level). The Senate, which is composed of 284 senators, is elected by a two-tier system of universal franchise, by an electoral college which clearly over-represents the rural communities. The National Assembly, the main House of Parliament, is directly elected by universal franchise. Since 1958, voting procedure has been a two-round majority ballot. At the present time, there are 491 seats in the National Assembly (of which 474 represent mainland France and 17 the overseas departments and territories).

6. In France, the vast majority of teachers are employed by the State.

7. V. Aubert, J. D. Parodi, "Le Personnel politique francais," in Projet, no. 147 (July-August 1980).

8. Above all must be mentioned the possibility open to every civil servant (including teachers) to be "temporarily released" so that he may take up the office of minister, member of Parliament, senator, or member of a ministerial secretariat, and be fully entitled to return to his previous job at the end of his term of office.

9. Since the various data used in this article have not always been

122 122 DOES WHO GOVERNS MATTER?

gathered with the same classification criteria in mind, it is unfortunately not possible to achieve a strictly homogeneous presentation of these data.

10. See especially R. Cayrol, J. L. Parodi, C. Ysmal, *Le déuté francais* (A. Colin, 1973).

11. See R. Cayrol, J. Jaffré, "Party Linkages in France: Socialist Leaders, Followers and Voters," in K. Lawson, ed., *Political Parties and Linkage* (Yale University Press, 1980), pp. 27–46.

12. Let us note that in 1974–1975, 11.6 percent of all French students were of working-class origin, while working men and women then made up 37.8 percent of the active population. See H. Ehrmann, *Politics in France* (Little, Brown & Co., 1976), p. 86.

13. See, for example, P. Bourdieu, "L'Ecole conservatrice: les inégalités devant l'école et devant la culture," *Revue Francaise de Sociologie,* 7 (1966); P. Bourdieu and J. C. Passeron, *Les Héritiers* (Ed. de Minuit, 1974); P. Bourdieu, and J. C. Passeron, *La Reproduction* (Ed. de Minuit, 1970).

14. For the ministers, statistics established by V. Aubert; for the members of Parliament, R. Cayrol, J. L. Parodi, and C. Ysmal, *Le député francais;* for the UDF and RPR, survey by R. Cayrol and C. Ysmal; for the PS, survey by R. Cayrol, previously quoted; for the ministerial secretariats and directors, J. Siwek-Pouydesseau, *Le personnel de direction des ministères* (A. Colin, 1969).

15. P. and J. D. Antoni, *Les ministres de la Ve Republique* (Presses Universitaires de France, 1976), p. 26 for 1959–1974; 1979 statistics supplied by V. Aubert.

16. The Treasury, the Council of State, the Audit Office, and, to a slightly less illustrious degree, the diplomatic corps and the prefectorial body.

17. R. Cayrol, J. L. Parodi, and C. Ysmal, *Le député francais.*

18. P. Bacot, *Les Dirigeants du Parti Socialiste* (Presses Universitaires de Lyon, 1979), p. 181.

19. M. Benassayag, *"Deux ou trois choses qu'on sait de lui,"* *Nouvelle Revue Socialiste,* n. 1 (April 1974).

20. J. M. Lech, "Cadres: de vrais 'sabras,'" *L'Unité,* no. 257 (1–6 July 1977).

21. P. Birnbaum, *Les Sommets de l'Etat,* Essai sur l'Elite du pouvoir en France (Paris: Ed. du Seuil, 1977), p. 33.

22. A. Thibaudet, *La République des professeurs* (Paris: Grasset, 1927).

23. By senior civil servants, we mean those belonging to the important administrative or technical elements of the body politic: the Council of State, the Audit Office, the Treasury, the Prefectorate, the Foreign Service, the Department of Civil Engineering, and the Department of Mines.

24. C. de Gaulle, *Mémoires de guerre,* Vol. 3 (Paris: Plon, 1959), p. 240.

25. A. Coutrot, *Les Membres des cabinets des Présidents de la République et des Premiers ministres.* Table ronde des 30 novembre et ler décembre 1979 sur "L'Administration et la Politique en France sous la Ve République," Paris AFSP, IFSA. In his book *Les Conseillers du Président* (Paris: PUF, 1980), p. 45, Samy Cohen notes that 80 percent of Valéry Giscard d'Estaing's advisers were senior civil servants.

26. Ibid., p. 13.

27. P. Birnbaum, *Les Sommets de l'Etat,* p. 93.

28. During the Fourth Republic, the senior civil servants constituted only 3.7 percent of the National Assembly.

29. In the Senate, or Upper House, representing, above all, rural France, senior civil servants only represent 2.5 percent of the senators.

30. F. De Baecque, L'interpenetration des personnels politique et administratif, Table Ronde des 30 novembre et ler decembre 1979, "L'administration et la politique en France sous la Veme Republique," Paris, AFSP, IFSA, pp. 44–46.

31. Ibid., p. 35.

32. G. Fabre-Rosane, and A. Guede, "Sociologie des candidats aux élections législatives de mars 1978," Revue Francaise de Science Politique, 28, no. 5 (October 1978): 854.

33. F. De Baecque, L'interpenetration des personnels politique et administratif, p. 41.

34. P. Garraud, Le Renouvellement des élites politiques locales socialistes: les maires des villes de plus de 15,000 habitants, AFSP, Groupe d'études sur le socialisme, 6 June 1980, p. 30.

35. All together, in one legal form or another, French public companies today occupy nearly 15 percent of the working population.

36. The authors of La Classe dirigeante francaise consider that there are 15 percent of these people who have changed over from the private sector in the population to the category "other senior civil servants," which includes "directors of public companies."

37. P. Birnbaum, M. Bellaiche, C. Barucq, and A. Marie, La Classe dirigeante francaise (Paris: PUF, 1978), p. 78. This survey considers that the ruling class includes "ruling fractions of the dominant class, that is, senior civil servants, the highest ranks in the military and the owners and managers of the means of production and of banks. . . ." Bearing this definition in mind, the authors, in a historical perspective, have constituted three samples of 1,000, 1,700, and 2,300 individuals from the 1954, 1964, and 1974 editions of Who's Who.

38. P. Birnbaum et al., La Classe dirigeante francaise, p. 64.

39. C. Brindillac, "Les Hauts Fonctionnaires et le capitalisme," Esprit (June 1953).

40. D. Danic-Careil, Les Dirigeants des cent premières entreprises francaises, D.E.S. de Science Politique, Université de Paris II, 1975.

41. R. Aron, "Classe sociale, classe politique, classe dirigeante," in Archives européennes de Sociologie, Vol. 1 (Paris, 1960), pp. 260–81.

42. J. Chevalier, L'Idéologie des fonctionnaires: permanence et/ou changement, Table Ronde des 30 novembre et ler décembre 1979 sur l'Administration et la Politique en France sous la Ve République, Paris, AFSP-IFSA, p. 46.

43. H. W. Ehrmann, La Politique du patronat francais (1936–1955) (Paris: A. Colin, 1959), p. 227.

44. E. N. Suleiman, Les Hauts Fonctionnaires et la politique (Paris: Ed. du Seuil, 1976) (adaptation of Politics, Power and Bureaucracy in France, Princeton University Press, 1974); Les Elites en France: Grands Corps et grandes écoles (Paris: Ed. du Seuil, 1979) (adaptation of Elites in French Society: The Politics of survival, Princeton University Press, 1979).

45. E. Suleiman, Les Hauts fonctionnaires et la politique, p. 188.

46. Ibid., p. 189.

47. Ibid., p. 101.

48. Ibid., p. 92.

49. Ibid., p. 155.
50. Ibid., p. 158.
51. Ibid., p. 173.
52. See R. Cayrol, J. L. Parodi, and C. Ysmal, *Les députés francais et le systéme politique,* Paper presented at the 1973 Montreal International Political Science Association World Congress, pp. 5 and 32.
53. E. Suleiman, *Les Elites en France* (Paris: Ed. du Seuil, 1979) and his very similar American version *Elites in French Society: The Politics of Survival,* (Princeton: Princeton University Press, 1978).
54. Suleiman, *Les Elites en France,* p. 281.
55. See particularly an interview with Catherine Lalumière, the Socialist Minister of the Civil Service in the first Mauroy government, about the E.N.A., published in *Le Monde* (6 June 1981 issue).
56. See, for example, R. Inglehart, *The Silent Revolution,* (Princeton: Princeton University Press, 1977).

The Spanish Political Elite: Permanency and Change

Salustiano del Campo, José Félix Tezanos,
and Walter Santin

I. From the Restoration to the Second Republic

In the period 1874–1936, the Spanish political system went through three different regimes—the constitutional monarchy, the military-civil dictatorship of General Primo de Rivera, and the Second Republic, which, in turn, had different stages. In the context of the discontinuity of political regimes and their stages, the theme of the continuity of the political elite becomes particularly relevant. In effect, if the discontinuity of the political process is evident, the question turns to knowing to what extent that phenomenon is reflected in the continuity—or discontinuity—of the political elite.[1]

At the end of 1874, General Martínez Campos proclaimed Prince Alfonso de Borbón as King of Spain, making General Serrano and his government abandon an ephemeral Republican presidentialist attempt and turn the power over to the party supporting Alfonso and the presidency of the government to Cánovas del Castillo. The bloodless nature of the Canovist victory, the disintegration of the 1868 revolutionary coalition, the profound crisis experienced by the First Republic, the short number of years that had passed between 1868 and 1874, and the liberalism of Canovas all contributed to a marked continuity in the political elite. In fact, the constitutional monarchy presents a continuity of its political elite with the immediate past, to an extent unsurpassed by either the dictatorship or the Second Republic; the latter regimes made far greater breaks with the past and removed the preceding political elites from their positions.

In this context, it is not surprising that a good part of the political elite of the Restoration had antecedents in Parliaments previous to that of 1876; it will even include some leaders of the Republic, such as Castelar, a former Republican President. Of the 388 members of the first Parliament elected by universal male suffrage in 1869, 72, i.e., 19 percent, were members of the first Parliament of the Restoration—from 1876 to 1879. In the second Parliament of the regime—from 1879 to 1881—23 percent had been members in pre-Restoration Parliaments. In addition, of the 13 presidents of the Council of Ministers who succeeded one another until 1910, 10 had been members of Parliament before 1874 and half of them had been ministers before the return of Alfonso XII. These continuities could be observed in practically all political parties.

Under the constitutional reign of Alfonso XIII—from 1902 to 1923—there is a period of relative homogeneity that goes from the electoral law of 1907[2] to the dissolution of Parliament by General Primo de Rivera in 1923 and includes seven legislatures. During this period, the total number of seats to fill through elections was 2,765, and the number of persons elected reached 1,338. Of these 1,338 members of Parliament, 49 were elected seven times, 42 six times, 52 five times, 77 four times, 115 three times, and 234 twice. A little more than half of the 1,338 members of Parliament, exactly 770, were elected only once, a fact that seems to indicate a degree of renovation of the political elite in that period.[3]

By 1923, the system of the Restoration was already mortally wounded. The military-civil dictatorship of General Primo de Rivera did not carry out structural reforms, either economic or social, but it disrupted the evolution of the political system by removing the political elite of the Restoration to such an extent that only a very small part would return in the Second Republic. This was a deliberate policy of the dictator. When he created his party—the Patriotic Union—in 1924, he sent out a circular to the civil governors giving instructions for recruiting members to the new party and defining the potential social bases of the same in these terms: ". . . persons who have not taken part in politics; those who deceived, abandoned it [the previous regime], and those who were honest politicians."[4] Similarly, when the regime made an attempt at institutionalization through the election of a National Assembly in 1927, it did not accept the former political elite but only men who were apparently not political but rather representatives of the different sectors, including some leaders of the UGT (General Workers' Union).[5] Thus, we will find in the Assembly only 71 ex-members of Parliament of the last period of the liberal monarchy (from 1916 to 1923) out of a total of 429 assembly members, i.e., 17 percent. This proportion differs very little from that represented by the 116 ex-members of Parliament of the monarchy (12 percent) among the 992 representatives in the three legislatures of the Second Republic, even though the dictatorship was much closer in time to the monarchy. These results seem to indicate clearly that the discontinuity in the political elite was created by the dictatorship and not by the Second Republic.

Another symptom of the radical break with the former elite is apparent in the fact that of the 159 persons who were ministers under the constitutional reign of Alfonso XIII, only 14 were subsequently appointed as members of the assembly. It seems, therefore, that the *coup d'etat* of 1923 was made against the old parties and the old elite and also that the regime felt close to the politicians of the Conservative sector.

The dictatorship did not have enough time to create a single party and a solid political elite, even though it is also true that it did not dedicate much energy to these tasks. The very few assembly members who appear in the three legislatures of the Second Republic do so for the greater part in the Spanish Renovation party: 8 of 19 persons and 12 of 29 seats. The CEDA, the center-Right of the Second Republic, regains only five assembly members. This trend will be reversed during the Franco regime: even though a decade has passed, 5.6 percent of the assembly members will reappear in the Parliament of 1943, and one of them will be its President.[6]

The Second Republic was proclaimed on April 14, 1931. The military uprising that would bring about the Civil War and the triumph of Franquism in 1939 occurred on July 18, 1936. During these five years of Republican rule, three parliamentary elections were held—in 1931, 1933, and 1936. The discontinuity of the political elite between the last period of the constitutional monarchy (the five legislatures from 1916 to 1923) and that of the Second Republic is great: in 1931, of the 470 representatives, only 64 (13.8 percent) had been members of Parliament; in the second Republican legislature, in 1933, there were 70 ex-members of Parliament (15.5 percent), and in the Parliament of 1936, 59 (12.5 percent).[7] Among the 88 ministers of the Second Republic, only three had had this post under the monarchy; of those 88 ministers, *none* was appointed again under Franco.

Before the proclamation of the Republic, the Republican parties had not had a considerable representation in Parliament. This is an important factor in explaining the low proportion of ex-legislators—31 of the 305 (10.1 percent) who formed the majority that voted for the Constitution of 1931. In 1933, the representation of the Right in Parliament does not show continuity either, except for a small sector of the extreme Right (Traditionalists and Spanish Renovation) and a small party of the center-Right (the Agrarians). In 1936, only two parties had a share of more than 10 percent of ex-legislators of the monarchy: CEDA and Republican Union.

If the continuity between the political elite of the Second Republic and that of the monarchy was low, the stability of the Republican parliamentary elite itself was also low: in the three legislatures from 1931 to 1936, there was a total of 1,384[8] seats occupied by 992 people; of this group, 671 representatives (67.6 percent) were elected only once; 250 (25.2 percent), twice, and 71 (7.1 percent), three times.[9] These facts are full of political significance; they reflect, at the elite level, the convulsions of the Second Republic and its inability to achieve a minimally stable political life.[10]

II. The Political Elite during the Franco Regime

The political elite of the Franco regime has been the object of a fair amount of attention on the part of social scientists, many of whom published their research during the last years of Franco's life. This can be explained, in part, by the longevity of the Franco regime and by the historical context (regarding its relationship with European Fascist regimes in the period between the World Wars) in which it will be considered in the future by sociologists and political scientists. On the other hand, the considerable development of sociology in Spain during the 1960's and 1970's did allow a large part of the social scientists' uneasiness about the Franco phenomenon to find appropriate expression in sociological and political analyses.[11]

Some Characteristics of the Political Elite under Franco

In a historical context of noticeable political discontinuities, with some logical parallel discontinuities in the political elite, one cannot be surprised at the fact that the Franco regime displayed a clear break with regard to the political personnel of previous periods, especially as a consequence of the Civil War of 1936–1939 and of the following repression politics in the early forties. In this sense, one must bear in mind that the Civil War brought about the violent deaths of 70 representatives of the Republican Parliament—along with many other citizens with diverse political responsibilities—and prison or exile for practically all of the representatives of the Republican parties. Of the remaining representatives of the parties of the Right, only 26 would be members of Franco's first Parliament in 1943, and a total of 31, that is to say, 3.1 percent of all representatives elected under the Second Republic,[12] would be reelected to one of the legislatures after 1943. Although seven of these representatives became ministers of Franco's,[13] the government of Franco displays considerable discontinuity, even regarding the previously most conservative and right-wing political elites.

On the other hand, during the forty years of Franco's rule, the dynamics of the political elite has allowed those who study it to speak of a moderate line of continuity, along with important renovations, especially in specific historical periods. In order to understand the significance of these renovations of the political elite under Franco, one must take into consideration both the long duration of Franco's domination and the important changes brought about in the international context and in the economic and social situation of Spain, which were to bring about a series of changes in political orientation and in the organization of the Franco system, and which were also to be reflected in the ten legislatures of Parliament and in the ten governments appointed by General Franco.[14]

The average tenure of office of legislators (*procuradores*) under Franco was greater than two legislatures (six years), and the average survival rate for each legislature was around 60 percent.[15] The impression of a renovation which these figures give should be contrasted with a twofold fact: on the one hand, the moments of greatest renovation were times of high political import—in 1946 (after the defeat of the Axis), again in 1958 (politics of economic liberalization and the beginning of the rise of the *Opus Dei* technocrats), and in 1967 (new constitutional laws); on the other hand, the continuity of the *procuradores* was much higher among a rather defined group which can be considered the true nucleus of the political elite under Franco and which remained in its positions throughout various legislatures. This is the group that has been called by some "*procuradores*-leaders" (members of the board of the Parliament and of the National Council, members of the permanent Commission and the boards of other commissions, etc.) and also the *procuradores* appointed directly by the Chief of State and the National Advisers. Most members of this group remained in Parliament until their death.

Table 1 describes the specific occupations of the members of legislatures under Franco in comparison with those of previous pe-

TABLE 1.
Occupations of the Spanish Parliament Members in Various
Legislatures

Occupation	1879*	1907*	1914*	1927*	1931*	1971†	1977†	1979†
Entrepreneurs and businessmen	15%	9%	7%	10%	5%	18.4%	16.4%	10.6%‡
Farmers	15	11	13	2	2	5.2	1.7	—
Military personnel	8	5	4	10	3	6.6	0.5	—
Public servants	10	13	13	30	16	34.7	33.9	30.5
Engineers and architects	5	4	3	10	5	2.5	2.7	5.2
Physicians	—	2	1	5	10	4.4	6.9	4.8
Lawyers	33	34	39	16	35	13.7	17.4	23.3
Manual laborers	—	—	—	—	9	1.3	7.3	4.6
Others and unknown	14	22	20	17	15	13.2	13.2	21.0

*Source: Juan J. Linz, *Spanish Cabinet and Parliamentary Elites: From the Restoration (1874) to Franco (1970)* (Bellagro, 1970), quoted in Informe FOESSA, 1975 (Madrid: Euramerica, 1976), p. 1298.
†Source: Personal research based on the sources of information quoted above. Only the main occupation of the Parliament members has been coded in order to compare them to the previous distributions.
‡Includes farmers.

riods. During the Restoration, lawyers were predominant in the legislative political elite, with a noticeable presence of farmers and business managers. In the Assembly of the dictatorship of Primo de Rivera (1927), the proportion of lawyers is much lower. This is also true of the farmers (who, we assume, represented in a good measure part of the network of influential people in the small towns during the Restoration), while the number of public servants, and military personnel is very high. In the first legislature of the Second Republic, the proportion of military personnel, public servants, and even business managers decreases noticeably, while the number of lawyers increases, reaching proportions very similar to those of the Restoration period. An important innovation in these Parliaments of the Second Republic is a large proportion of doctors and professionals, and the presence, for the first time in a Spanish Parliament, of a notable number of manual laborers, a fact which reflects the process of industrialization and the emergence and rise of a strong Socialist party (PSOE). During the Franco regime there is a return to a type of legislative elite which is very similar to that of the dictatorship of Primo de Rivera—predominance of military personnel and public servants and also a larger number of business managers.

Concerning the top of the political elite (those who have formed part of the governments), an evolution can be detected which Amando de Miguel has subdivided into three periods: first, the *blue stage* (1938–1957), characterized by a strong military presence (35.4 percent of the ministers of the period), complemented by public servants and engineers and other professionals. A second stage, which he calls the *technocratic* (1957–1973), in which the presence of military personnel, although still large, diminishes noticeably (28.6 percent), accompanied by an increase in the number of ministers with ties in the business world and the technical professions (engineers, architects, etc.) and by the largest proportion of university professors in the ministerial cabinets of Franco (16.7 percent). Finally, during the third and final stage, that of the *public servants* (1973–1975), the military presence is reduced to three ministers who occupy the military ministries while the proportion of public servants, already rather large in previous periods, reaches its highest quota: 79.2 percent of the total number of ministers, i.e., almost the total of the civilian ministers.[16]

The Dynamics of the Elites under Franco—Politicians and Technocrats

As has often been pointed out, the political dynamics of the entire period of the Franco dictatorship have been strongly marked by the very "particular" concept of politics that Franco had. This conception, which originated from a rejection of politics itself and a negative and even irritating image of politicians, developed during his years of military life in the Spanish Morocco. One must also take into account that Franco belonged to the group of military men in Africa who had had a special colonial experience in a country that had been subjected to a civil-military domination and in which the idea of the administration of public services and of military domination were one and the same.

When Franco gained control of all the resources of power, he acted in conformance with what his experience had taught him, and during the three years of the Civil War, this turned out to be extremely "functional." Such political inertia fitted in rather well with many of the ideological assumptions of fascism, which, as is well known, strongly influenced the first phase of the dictatorship (the phase of maximum ideological exaltation).

Thus, the recruiting of political elites during the Franco regime was to be based on the prior establishment of a distinction between "politicians" ("those who turn politics into a means of personal benefit" and will be the object of much harsher remarks)[17] and "public servants" (of whom impartiality "above party quarrels" is expected and whose technical competence and capacity help them to identify with the general interests of the State). These concepts will lead Franco to substitute an "elite of public servants" for the classic "political elite," in such a way that even the former leaders of the parties of the Right will see themselves isolated from and left out of the decisive political offices.

The range and ultimate political sense of this practice in the recruitment of the elites has been brought out in a rather illustrative manner by Pi-Sunyer: "The predominance of the public servants—civil and military—is already a first indication which reveals the 'remedial character' of political personnel under Franco, in the measure in which it supposes the displacement of the 'former politicians' and of the professional categories from which the political personnel were traditionally recruited to the benefit of 'experts' and technicians, characterized as being apolitical. No one will be refrained from seeing the influence that these apolitical principles have in the recruitment of public servants, technicism, predetermined organic functionalism, elitism, political activity as 'public service' (not as representation), discipline, subordination, and hierarchy."[18]

The dynamics produced by the sociological character of the elites during the Franco regime, which, as we have already noted, will add certain differentiating traits to each one of its historical phases, do not allow, however, any of these phases to be characterized specifically as "a period of public servants." In fact, this "public servant nature" is precisely the true uniting thread in the logic of the recruiting of elites during this historical period, although, surely, with different stages of predominance of one or another group of public servants. An irrefutable proof of this is given in the information provided by Pi-Sunyer, referring to the period of maximum ideological exaltation and fervor (1936–1945), according to which, of a total of 1,614 political officeholders analyzed, 70 percent were civil or military servants (and, of these, 41 percent military and 59 percent civil servants).[19]

The internal dynamics of the political elites of this period were strongly impregnated by the hierarchical organization of the public administration groups, which made the political careers of the elite under Franco rather long: one "ascended" from one post to another, step by step, in such a way that one reached the highest political positions after having achieved a certain brilliant record of "services rendered." Furthermore, careers depended on the measure in which one was involved in some of the diverse coteries which formed throughout the period of the dictatorship and which, at some moments, reached the point of even colliding violently among themselves.

This configuration of "apolitical-political careers" explains two of the features of the highest level of the political elite under Franco— on the one hand, the tendency to remain in positions of political responsibility for long periods of time and, on the other, and as a consequence of the same fact, the higher posts of responsibility were reached at rather high ages (especially after 1957). However, the average ages of Franco's ministers did remain at a rather constant level—around 51 years of age at the time of appointment for civil ministers and over 60 years of age for the military.

For many foreign observers of Franco's regime it is often difficult to understand why a regime that apparently cultivated the technical qualities and competencies of its elites did not obtain more brilliant results in practice in its administration, and, above all, why these results were below expectations, especially in the last period of the regime—the so-called "technocratic stage"—in which there was an attempt to magnify the image of technical competency. To answer this question, one must begin by pointing out that the impression that Franco surrounded himself with a well-trained elite is, in fact, true. It must be remembered, as Amando de Miguel has underlined in his study of Franco's ministers,[20] that of the total civil ministers, 28 were recipients of "honors" in their studies or won first place in "competitions" (state examinations). However, the expected potential of "technical competence" did not produce the desired results. Franco preferred collaborators who placed loyalty to his person above all else over those who were either "apolitical," or not very critical, although they had a great capacity to develop initiatives and innovations. That is to say, "efficiency" primarily meant efficiency to obey orders or follow instructions, which were more or less general, and not the ability to solve problems. In the same way, the "ideological-personal" loyalty was more important than any other political quality.

During the last period under Franco, these ideas of loyalty, discipline, and submission to the centers of power were perpetuated to a large degree by the group of "technocrats of Opus Dei," who added to personal loyalty to a commander, a certain spirit of sect or coterie. The way in which the political elites acted during this time has been the object of diverse economic, political, and sociological studies[21] and constitutes, in great measure, the central point of what analysts consider to be the final chapter in the crisis of the Franco government. This crisis will open the way to the first governments of the monarchy.

III. The Political Elites of the Transition to Democracy

On November 20, 1975, Franco died. Juan Carlos de Borbón became King of Spain on November 22, 1975, in a solemn act that has never been confirmed to have been a proclamation, a restoration, an installation, a swearing-in, or a mechanical application of the Law of Succession upon the person designated by Franco, but it raised neither doubts nor controversies. In fact, the constitutional monarchy of Juan Carlos I is one of the few points which is today a source of rare unanimous acceptance in Spain.

On November 18, 1976, the Parliament of the X legislature of the organic democracy approved the Law for Political Reform, which received the approval of the citizens on December 15 of the same year. According to this reform, Parliament would be composed of two houses, the Congress and the Senate. Election to the Congress would be by universal, direct and secret suffrage. In the Senate, a number not greater than one fifth of the senators would be appointed by the King. Congress will be elected by a proportional representation system and the Senate by majority ballot. The duration of a term would be four years.

On June 15, 1977, the first democratic Parliament of the monarchy was elected; it became a Constituent Assembly. This date can be taken as the beginning of the democratic transition in Spain. The Parliament of 1977 drafted the Constitution, which was approved by referendum on December 6, 1978, and sanctioned by the King on December 27 in a joint session of the two Houses. On March 1, 1979, new parliamentary elections were held, now under the Constitution. These were the elections to the present Parliament, the term of which extends to 1983.

The whole process took place with Adolfo Suarez acting as President of the Government from July 4, 1976, the day on which he was appointed by the King, to January 29, 1981, the date on which he resigned. Throughout this period, five governments followed one another. *Fifty-eight* ministers took part in these various governments. The duration of tenure in office varied considerably from one minister to another.

The Parliamentary Elites of the "Consensus"

The Parliament of 1977 was composed of 349 representatives and 247 senators.[22] The political options and ideologies of the members of Parliament are reflected in their alignment with different parliamentary groups:

Congress
Union de Centro Democrático (Central Democratic Union)	166
Socialistas del Congreso (Socialists of the Congress)	102
Minoría Catalana y Vasca (Catalunyan and Basque minority)	22
Comunistas (Communists)	22
Alianza Popular (Popular Alliance)	16
Socialistas de Cataluña (Socialists of Catalunya)	15
Others	8

Senate
UCD (Central Democratic Union)	116
Socialists of the Senate	47
Independent Progressists and Socialists	21
"Entesa dels Catalans"	16
Independent groupings and Independents	23
Basque Senators	10
Others	14

In the case of the Upper House, it must be remembered that this included the group of 41 senators chosen by the King.

The following is the composition of Parliament, by age and sex:

Age
Between 21 and 30 years old	2.4%
Between 31 and 40 years old	22.9
Between 41 and 50 years old	35.0
Between 51 and 60 years old	23.5
Between 61 and 70 years old	13.0
Over 70 years old	3.2
	100.0

Sex
Male	96%
N = 596	

The large majority of the members of Parliament are between 40 and 60 years old, and there are far fewer members under 30 years of age than there are parliamentarians of 60 years or older. In turn, the total number of women is only slightly larger than the number of men under 30. The average age in Congress is 44.2 and in the Senate

(considering only elected senators), 49.6 years; the senators designated by the King were somewhat older, with a mean age of 56.9
years. The overall average age of the Parliament is 47 years, which
is below that known in the last legislatures of the organic Parliament.

Regarding age, it is to be noted that there is a greater similarity
between the Parliaments of 1977 and 1910, than there is with that of
1968 (Table 2).

TABLE 2.
Comparison of the Ages of the Members of Parliament

Age	1910 (Congress)	1968	1977 (Congress)
Under 40 years	42%	9%	39%
From 40 to 49	32	32	34
From 50 to 59	20	39	17
60 or over	6	20	10
	100	100	100
	N = 352	535	349

Another fact of general interest is the residence of the members of
the 1977 Parliament in their electoral districts; 80.9 percent of the
555 members* resided in their electoral districts, whereas 19.1 percent did not. About one fifth of those elected declared that they lived
outside of their district, and almost all of these live in Madrid; add-
ing these members of Parliament to the senators designated by the
King who live in Madrid and to the representatives of the capital,
we find a relatively large percentage of Parliament members who are
residents of Madrid.

Let us now explore how the parliamentary elite of the first democratic legislature compares with the elite under Franco in their relationships with the bureaucracy.[23] Slightly over one fourth of the
members of the 1977 Parliament (27.9 percent) are members of the
high organisms of the State; the percentages are somewhat higher in
the Senate than in the Congress (Table 3).

This constitutes a considerable decrease in the bureaucracy present in Parliament compared to the Franco regime, but the proportion
of high-level public servants still is quite significant. For those who
believe that the process of removing the public servants of the cen-
tralist and dictatorial state in Spain has been completed, this seems
to be a counter example: more than one quarter of the members of
the first democratic Parliament belong to this group. Almost two
thirds of the positions of bureaucrats occupied by members of Parliament are in nine high-status professional groups, as shown in
Table 4.

*The 41 royal senators, not bound to an electoral district, are not included.

TABLE 3.
Number of Bureaucrats and Nonbureaucrats in the 1977 Parliament

	Total	Bureaucrats	Non-Bureaucrats
Congress	N = 349	85	264
	100%	24.4%	75.6%
Senate	N = 247	81	166
	100%	32.8%	67.2%
Parliament	N = 596	166	430
(Congress and Senate)	100%	27.9%	72.1%

Sixty-three percent of the bureaucratic positions occupied by members of Parliament were in these high-status professions. Among these nine groups, that of full professors of universities should be especially noted, since it represents more than one fourth of the bureaucrats in Parliament. This seems to reaffirm the elevated prestige of the state organisms. The basic fact is the outstanding political

TABLE 4.
Members of 1977 Parliament Who Belong to Nine High-Status
Bureaucratic Groups

Bureaucratic Profession	Congress	Senators	Royal Senators	Total Number	Percent
Diplomatic corps	5	2	1	8	3.7
Full professor of a secondary education institution	3	6	—	9	4.1
Agricultural engineer	5	2	1	8	3.7
State lawyer	10	3	1	14	6.5
Full professor at a university	17	30	11	58	26.9
Associate professor at a university	3	3	—	6	2.7
Technician of civil administration	10	8	2	20	9.3
Lawyer of the state council	4	1	1	6	2.7
Labor inspector	5	1	1	6	3.7
Military	4	5	4	13	6.1
Others	27	32	7	66	30.6

power of these groups, which, in a large measure, maintain the positions they had under Franco's regime, especially full professors of universities, technicians of civil administration, and state counselors.

Seventy-seven members of the Parliament of 1977 served in the organic Parliament of the Franco regime, some of them on several occasions, as shown in Table 5. In the elections, a larger concentration of candidates with experience in the Franco Parliaments was noted in the provinces, which are predominantly agricultural and, in general, less developed, especially in the Castilles, Leon, Galicia, and Extremadura. The four *procuradores* aspiring to become members of Parliament obtained 39 seats in the Congress and 22 in the Senate. To these who were elected, 16 appointed senators who already had experience in the organic Parliament have to be added.

TABLE 5.
Previous Legislative Experience of Members of the 1977 Parliament

Experience in Legislatures	UCD	AP	PSOE	Otros	Royal Senators	Total
1	21	3	—	3	2	29
2	17	4	—	—	4	25
3	5	—	—	1	4	10
4	1	3	—	—	2	6
5 or more	—	3	—	—	4	7
Total	44	13	—	4	16	77
Percent of parliamentary group	16.30	72.22	0	4.03	39.02	
Percent of total Parliament						12.99

One should note the high proportion of ex-*procuradores* in the AP (Popular Alliance), a rightist group, and the absolute absence of the same in the PSOE (Spanish Socialist Workers' party). Also, only 44 of the members of Parliament in UCD (Central Democratic Union), 16.3 percent of the total, have been in Franco's Parliament. This fact should not be interpreted to mean that a majority of the members of Parliament in UCD have not had anything to do with the elite under Franco. While it is true that some sectors of UCD had no relationship with the Franco government, and even formed the ranks of the moderate democratic opposition, it is also true that a biographical study of the members of Parliament in UCD reveals that a large part of them had some ties with the previous regime. It can be confirmed that at least 119 of those members of Parliament, that is to say, 44 percent of the total, occupied diverse political posts during the Franco government,[24] especially in the intermediate levels of central executive power, as well as in the areas of local government and the syndical apparatus. Among these members of Parliament, there is a good number of ex-general directors, mayors, lieutenant mayors, committee presidents, delegates of the syndicates, etc. If we add the high proportion of public servants among the members of Parliament in UCD, we can conclude that middle level elites under Franco can be found in this party, while the highest level elites are in the AP.

In the Parliament of 1977, as shown above in Table 1, social and occupational sectors that had become marginal under Franco regained considerable importance: manual laborers, technicians, public servants, and other professions. The participation of executives and businessmen is also important. On the other hand, the percentage of military personnel is practically nil.

The high degree of interdependence and intercommunication among the political and economic elites in Spain is a well known fact, although difficult to prove rigorously down to the last detail. In this context, it is not strange that among the members of the first democratic Parliament, there are people who also appear as members of a large number of boards of administration[25] (Table 6). In this information, as in that referring to the long life of the *procuradores* under Franco, two extremes should be pointed out: on the one hand, the high proportion, 37.5 percent, of members of the rightist AP, and, on the other, the practical nonexistence of economic ties of the members of Parliament in the PSOE (Spanish Socialist Workers' party).

TABLE 6.
Members of Parliament with Economic Ties*

Group	Total Seats	Number with Economic Ties	Percent of Total
AP	16	6	37.5
UCD (CDU)	282	31	11.0
PSOE (SSWP)	164	2	1.2
PCE (SCP)	20	—	—
Others	114	21	18.4
	596	60	10.1

*Calculated on the basis of DICODI, 1977.

The Present Parliamentary Elites

On March 1, 1979, the first Parliament of the constitutional monarchy was elected,[26] and its term extends to 1983. The ideological description and the political options of the members of the present

Parliament are expressed in the following distribution of seats among the different parliamentary groups:

Congress	Seats
UCD	165
PSOE	96
PCE	23
Catalunyan Socialists	16
Conversencia Democrática	9
Mixed	14
Catalan Minority	9
Basque	7
Basque Socialists	6
Andalusian	5
Senate	
UCD	118
PSOE	68
PNV (Nationalist Basque party)	8
Others	14

The distribution of the members of Parliament according to their ages is shown in Table 7.

TABLE 7.
Distribution by Age of the Members of the 1979 Parliament

Ages	UCD	PSOE	Others	Total
Under 30 years	1.1%	5.3%	1.2%	2.5%
From 30 to 34	6.6	23.3	7.2	12.4
From 35 to 39	22.4	22.2	16.9	21.5
From 40 to 44	19.6	18.0	8.4	17.4
From 45 to 49	23.4	7.9	20.5	17.8
From 50 to 54	11.9	6.4	8.4	9.5
From 55 to 59	8.4	5.8	13.2	8.2
From 60 to 64	3.1	3.7	12.1	4.6
65 or over	3.5	7.4	12.1	6.1
	100.0	100.0	100.0	100.0
	N = 286	189	83	558

Examination of the data in Table 7 reveals that the average age for members of Congress in UCD was 43.6 years, and in the Senate, 48.0. For PSOE members, the average age in Congress was slightly younger, 39.5, and in the Senate, approximately the same as UCD, 48.3. For all other parties combined, the average ages are 49.6 in the Congress and 51.4 in the Senate. Considering all members of Parliament, the average age results become 43.2 years in the Congress and 48.5 years in the Senate. Average age for UCD members in both Houses was 45.4, for PSOE, 42.7, and for all other parties combined, 50.2. It is evident that the Socialist representatives in Congress are younger, their average age being under 40. In the Senate, there are practically no differences between UCD and PSOE. The comparison of ages of members in the 1979 legislature with the previous legislature yields the information shown in Table 8.

TABLE 8.
Comparison of Ages of Members of the 1977 and 1979 Parliaments

Ages	1977–1979	1979–1983
Under 40	28%	36%
From 40 to 49	35	35
From 50 to 59	22	18
60 or over	15	11
	100	100

Between 1977 and 1979, Parliament has become "younger," even with the high percentage of Parliament members (60 percent) who were reelected. The rejuvenation factor lies in the 40 percent of the members who were not returned for various reasons, and in the low average age of the new representatives elected in 1979. Thus, the average age of 44.2 years in the Congress in December of 1977, has changed to 43.2 in December of 1979; in the Senate, the average of 49.6 in December of 1977 has become 48.5 in December of 1979.

The presence of women in Parliament is still minimal. Only 25 of the 558 seats of Parliament are occupied by women. In the Congress, the 19 female representatives represent 5.4 percent; the six women in the Senate represent only 2.9 percent.

Madrid continues to be a source of residential attraction for members of Parliament. In order to indicate the magnitude of this phenomenon, it suffices to remember that around 25 percent of the members of Parliament have their stable residence in Madrid, the city where they carry out their professional activity.

The relationships between place of birth, habitual residence, and the province for which the members of Parliament have been elected, which are detailed in Table 9, indicate the degree to which the representatives have ties with the area of their representation, as well as the level of parliamentary "colonialism" in some regions. The highest proportion of ties between the members of Parliament and their region of representation is for the areas of greater local autonomy and in the islands, where the geographic conditions make this relationship easier.

As has been stated previously, a high proportion of the members of the 1977 Parliament were reelected in 1979. In Congress, 230 members of Parliament of the previous legislature continued, 22 of them coming from the Senate. Sixty percent of the members of Par-

TABLE 9.
Relation of Birthplace-Residence-Election of Members of the 1979
Parliament, by Region

Region	Seats	Birthplace	Residence	Birthplace-Residence-Election*
Catalunya	11.2	8.8	11.5	73.0
Andalusia	17.4	16.0	14.5	69.1
Madrid	6.5	9.7	24.8	44.4
Valencian	7.3	6.8	6.8	70.7
Castilla–Leon	15.8	14.7	10.2	46.6
Galicia	7.7	8.2	6.3	72.1
Basque–Navarra	7.5	7.5	6.7	76.2
Castilla–Mancha	7.3	7.4	4.3	46.3
Aragon	4.7	5.2	3.4	65.4
Canary Islands	4.3	4.1	4.1	91.7
Asturias	2.5	3.2	1.8	71.4
Extremadura	3.6	3.1	2.2	50.0
Murcia	2.2	1.3	1.6	50.0
Balearic Islands	2.0	2.0	1.6	81.8
Abroad	—	2.0	0.2	—
	100.0	100.0	100.0	

*This column indicates the proportion of members of Parliament having all three characteristics.

liament elected in 1977 were elected to a seat in Parliament for 1979–1983.

Table 10 displays the legislative experience of the members elected in 1979, who had served under the Franco regime.

TABLE 10.
Experience in Previous Francoist Legislatures of Members of the
1979 Parliament

Experience in Legislatures	UCD	CD	Other Right-Wing Parties	Total
1	17	1	2	20
2	11	1	—	12
3	4	1	—	5
4	2	1	—	3
5 or more	—	3	1	4
Total	34	7	3	44
Percent over the group	11.89	58.33		
Percent over total of Parliament				7.88

The most outstanding feature is the high percentage of members of Parliament in CD who have had experience in the Organic Parliament. Of this total of 44 members of Parliament who had served in the Organic Parliament, 37 also served in 1977–1979. Also, it is of some importance that one representative and five senators of the present Parliament had been members of the Parliament of the Second Republic.

Of the 558 members of Parliament who compose the present Parliament, 154 (27.6 percent) are bureaucrats.[27] This proportion of bureaucrats is practically the same as in the 1977 Parliament, where the percentage of bureaucrats was 27.9. Around 80 percent of the bureaucratic positions held by members of Parliament are associated with only a small number of institutions, as shown in Table 11.

TABLE 11.
Members of 1979 Parliament Who Belong to High-Level
Professional Groups

Professional Group	Posts	Percent of Total
Diplomatic corps	7	4.6
Full professor of secondary education	7	4.6
Other professors of secondary education	6	3.9
State lawyers	11	7.1
Full university professor	33	21.4
Other university professors	42	27.3
Civil administration technician	9	5.8
State council lawyer	5	3.2
Labor inspector	2	1.3
Others	32	20.8
	N = 154	100.0%

In this table, the high percentage of those who are in the teaching profession stands out: 57.2 percent; 48.7 percent of these are university professors. Thus, full professors at the universities, the State Counselors, and the technicians of civil administration continue to maintain their previous power.

Fifty-nine members, i.e., one out of every ten members of Parliament, are industrial or agricultural entrepreneurs. In addition, a majority of the representatives and senators of the "Center"—UCD, PNV, etc.—have ties with firms on their boards of administration. The professions of the members of Parliament are shown in Table 12.

Regarding the level of education of the members of Parliament, it

TABLE 12.
Occupations of Members of Parliament Elected in 1979

Profession	Percent of Total
Industrial and agricultural entrepreneurs	10.6
Merchants and small businessmen*	2.5
Public servants	30.5
Engineers and architects	5.2
Physicians	4.8
Lawyers	23.3
Economists*	3.8
Other professionals with higher degrees*	3.6
Cadres and technicians	6.5
Manual workers	4.6
Others and unknown*	4.6
	100.0%
	N = 558

*Computed from "Funcionarios en las Cortes actuales" ("Public servants in the Present Parliament"), Revista MUFACE (MUFACE magazine), No. 19 (April 1981).

should be pointed out that 79 percent of them have a university education, 14 percent have a high school education, while 7 percent have only a primary education or trade school studies. In this respect, this Parliament is more educated and enlightened than the Parliaments under Franco. By profession, lawyers—23.3 percent of the members of Parliament—stand out, and the number of those with a law degree but not practicing is even higher. They are followed by the teaching professions, included here among the public servants. Finally, the extremely low proportion of "blue-collar" workers—4.6 percent—should be brought out, with the UCD not having any member of Parliament in this category.

Characteristics of the Ministers under Suarez

From July 4, 1976 to January 29, 1981, Adolfo Suarez Gonzalez was President of the Government. During this period, five cabinets and some ministerial adjustments, in which a total of 58 mninisters entered and left the government, followed one another. The fact is that the 30 ministers who were in their positions for more than one year totalled more than 75 percent of the total number of days that the 58 ministers held that post. The fact that practically half (28) of the ministers had such a short term reflects both the recurrently critical nature of that period in the political history of Spain and the use and abuse of the assignment of ministers as an expedient for achieving minimal cohesion at the top of the government party.

These 58 ministers, who have been members of five governments, were younger than the 118 members of all the cabinets under Franco. Table 13 shows the average ages of the members of the five Suarez governments. Even if we take the highest average age of the civil ministers, that of the fourth government, we find a difference of 3.3 years in comparison with the average age of the civil ministers during the last stage of the Franco government.[28] There has obviously been a significant rejuvenation of the personnel of the highest political elite, at least until now.

TABLE 13.
Average Ages* of the Members of the Governments of Suarez

	All the cabinet	Only civil ministers
First government	49.6	45.6
Second government	45.0	43.8
Third government	45.6	44.7
Fourth government	46.5	45.8
Fifth government	45.0	44.1

*Computed by taking into account the age at which they became ministers for the first time.

In terms of education, almost two thirds of the 58 civilian members of Suarez's cabinets held a law degree (50 percent of all 73 cabinet ministers). A law degree has traditionally facilitated access to the "grands corps" of the civil service, through the state examination competition, and this has become an important step in the careers of the highest level political elite. As for occupational background, the largest single category among the civilian cabinet ministers is a full university professorship (about 25 percent). One should also add that 15 of these ministers had studied in prestigious European and North American universities and that many held high academic honors achieved during their studies.

Most of the 58 ministers also have personal and family ties with the business world, and at least 38 have held positions as corporate executives[29] or have had direct relations with the banking community. It is, however, difficult to ascertain in detail the links between economic and political power.[30]

The politically most interesting fact is that 36 of the 58 Suarez cabinet members had held political office during the Franco regime; 12 of these had also been decorated by the Falangist National Movement. Members of the democratic opposition to Franco constitute a small minority in this top executive elite. Despite regime change and ideological change, the highest political elite displays considerable continuity, as a consequence of the civil service and technocratic orientation in the last stages of the Franco administration.

IV. The Spanish Political Elite: Some Concluding Observations

The Sociological Characteristics of the Political Elite of the Transition

The historical dynamics of the Spanish political elite seem to be marked, as we have seen, by two great breaks provoked by the dictatorship of General Primo de Rivera and by the regime of General Franco. The Second Republic was based on the removal of the political elite of the Restoration and, in turn, the Franco regime swept away the Republican political elite.

However, in the present democratic transition, the political personnel of the Center and the Right shows an important continuity with the political elite under Franco, including many very famous family names. This continuity often seems to be concealed, by the rise of politicians, who occupied secondary positions during the Franco government, and by the eclipsing of the majority of the great political figures of the Franco regime. It can be said that the transition has brought about a paradoxical situation: while an official attitude of accentuated lack of confidence and clear contempt regarding the "professional politician" existed during the Franco period, once Franco died, the political elite of the Center and the Right has been constituted, in part, precisely by the generation of the most clearly "professional" politicians who entered politics and developed under Franco. Some of the most typical examples can be found in the ranks of former members of the so-called "blue" sector of UCD.

One of the innovations introduced by the parliamentary elite of the dictatorship of General Primo de Rivera was the large proportion—nearly a third—of public servants. This fact differentiated the elite of the dictatorship clearly from the traditional elite of the Restoration. The Republic returned to a type of elite which, in this respect, came very close to the former elite of the Restoration. The Franco regime reintroduced a technocratic elite, with the result that, from this point of view, the elites of the Restoration and of the Republic are similar to each other, and both are differentiated from the elites of the dictatorship and the Franco regime. One of the consequences of this peculiarity of the democratic transition process in Spain has been the establishment of an important continuity in the bureaucratization of the elite, especially in the ranks of the political elite of UCD.

It is necessary to underline that the bureaucratization of the political elite, in general, and of the parliamentary elite, in particular, have consequences that are not at all negligible. One of them, perhaps the most socially noticeable, is the difficulty that any proposal in Parliament may encounter, which declares the incompatibility between exercising bureaucratic positions and holding an elective legislative seat. Thus, social reality crosses the formal separation between executive and legislative powers, thereby challenging the principle of the political neutrality of public servants.

The elites of the Left also present a certain continuity with the elites acting in opposition to the Franco regime, despite the attempts on the part of the Senate apparatus of Franco to dismantle their organizations. Yet there are some rather clear differences within the ranks of the Left: while the PCE (Spanish Communist Party) presents more continuity, since many of its leaders were already in the forefront during the civil war, the PSOE (Spanish Socialist Workers' Party) has been subject to an intensive renovation of leadership, a renovation that parallels the transformation and amplification of the party's political clientele (middle classes, Catholic, and regionalist sectors, etc.)

In both leftist parties, the present elites have benefited from the political climate in the universities during the last stage of the Franco regime, which led to the incorporation of many former university students into these political parties. In general, it can be said that the student struggle and university struggle, from its beginning in the fifties to the very last days of the regime in the seventies, constituted a source of leadership recruitment that strengthened the parties of the Left and, above all, of the PSOE.

Although it is difficult to make any forecasts as to what the dynamics of the political elites in Spain are going to be once the transition cycle has come to a close, a good number of analysts agree in pointing out the risks resulting from the lack of permeability and renovation of the elites. Thus, the large proportion of public servants in the political elite constitutes a climate that does not favor a spirit of initiative and innovation; the public servant, in general, operates under the criteria of loyalty, hierarchy, and subordination and usually transfers the principles of bureaucratic order to the political sphere. This results in a good part of the political elite orienting their activity according to criteria that make it an elite of "power professionals," always open to an ideologized loyalty toward those who occupy the highest positions of political decision-making. For many politicians, the center of gravity of their loyalties is not in the political parties, or in their leaders, or in the ideals that these embody, but in the realities and structure of power. This leads to certain "easy loyalties," and therefore dangerously transitory ones, and at the same time generates a tendency, in specific political circles to act with an esprit de corps that may create obstacles to any process of elite renovation.

In turn, the present electoral system of closed lists has facilitated influential schemes of co-optation and recruitment of loyal elites that can eventually produce routinification, political paralysis, and an impoverishing of the elites, a period of intense social change and political uncertainties.

Political Elite and Economic Elite

During the Franco government, economic expansion and expansion of the state apparatus were carried out jointly, the one imbricated in the other. Thus, a series of channels of intercommunication and interdependence between political power and economic power was developed. A relatively small elite concentrated noticeable power in each one of these spheres, from which they exercised a great influence over other spheres. As a consequence, the power of the economic oligarchy has manifested itself in its influence on political and social life, while at the same time certain high-level bureaucratic elites have developed great power beyond the strictly political sphere, and particularly in the economy. In this manner, members of the political and bureaucratic elite have become outstanding members of the economic oligarchy, a fact that has reinforced the political power of the oligarchy.

The democratic transition has taken place in a period of economic crisis and has produced only a few changes in the intercommunication between politics, economy, and bureaucracy. Thus, the high political elite of UCD, the 58 ministers of Suarez, constitute a group that has intense ties with the bureaucracy and also appears to be connected, although not as strongly, with business and banking.

If we consider the present map of political forces in Spain, we must recognize that the adjustment of interests and representations is being produced in a manner that it is difficult to determine with precision. This is due to the particular manner in which the democratic transition has come about and the role played by specific political circles, "professionalized" under the Franco government, in the articulation of some political interests, in the impact of the power bureaucracy of the State, and in the recruitment of "loyal" political elites from certain groups of this bureaucracy. The special weight exercised by the State in the development of any party, if not corrected by a greater adjustment among the social and economic interests and their corresponding political demands, could become one more element in the traditional gap between official Spain and real Spain.[31]

An example of this gap is the lack of trust on the part of the population in the development of the so-called "State of Autonomies," a product of the best efforts of the political class. The growing abstention in electoral consultations, including those concerning regional autonomy, is equally impressive. It seems, therefore, that we may be fatally heading in a direction that will reach a point in which the political class will no longer express political Spain, in a way analogous to how our stock market reflects nothing about how our economy is actually functioning.

The Role of Institutions

At present, the monarchy has met with, and continues to exercise, an essential role in the democratic tradition. As an institution, it has both continuity and discontinuity with the Franco regime, so its legitimacy is of a plural nature. On the one side, the monarchy predicates its continuity with the previous regime on the so-called "successorial provisions." On the other, it has been an essential force of political change in the transformation from the Franco regime. In addition, the King has inherited the rights of dynasty from his father, the Count of Barcelona. And, above all, in spite of the fact that the institution has not yet been subject to a formal referendum, the monarchy has received daily popular legitimization from the Spanish people through the leaders of all parties within the constitutional span, parties which receive an overwhelming majority of the national vote.

In like manner, the monarchy brought with it a decisive impulse for the renovation of the elite, primarily due to the age of the King. One of the greatest problems of dictatorial regimes is the aging of their elites. For this reason, at the beginning of the transition period, citizens began to perceive the new image of "the generation of the King," and the speculations that at the time of appointing the President of the government, the age of Adolfo Suarez (the youngest of all candidates) was one of the motivations of the monarch, turn out to be quite believable. This consideration takes on real meaning when we remember that this decision was a matter of giving the Right a leader of the same age as Felipe Gonzalez, the majority leader of the Left. The last crisis of government opened the way to an aging of the governmental elite: the currrent President of the Government, Leopoldo Calvo Sotelo, is six years older than Adolfo Suarez, and he projects a notably more aged image (and is perceived to be closer to intermediate generations) than the leader of the opposition.

Finally, in evaluating what the whole process of transition has meant, one must also take into account the fact that the monarch has played his role in a very modern style. The King has known not only how to comply with his constitutional role, with discretion and with decisiveness when it was necessary, but also to keep the institution uncontaminated from great pomp and courtly displays.

The Political Elite and Pressure Groups

The analysis of political elites does not exhaust the topic of *power*, and the sociological study of power must include elites in other sectors of society, who are wielding power and exercising influence on the political system.

The democratic transition process in Spain cannot be explained without understanding the behavior and attitudes of the social powers that have been called in Spanish political life, the poderes facticos (factual powers, or, pressure groups). Among these, the Army occupies an outstanding place, given the role it has played in the transition by supporting the King.[32] Without this support, the transition would not have been possible. It is important here to point out two facts: first, at the beginning of the process of change, the military supporting the monarchy was a small group; second, during the period of transition, important changes took place in the high military command when a good part of the most recalcitrant supporters of Franco were removed from the main command positions for reasons of advanced age.[33] Recent events have made it evident that in this area the danger of further tensions has not yet disappeared.

The Spanish Catholic Church, experienced a long and slow disassociation from political power under the Franco regime. From a total support of the regime, sanctified as a crusade and glorified in the ideology of national Catholicism, to the progressive separation from the official positions which it expressed in some attitudes of open opposition after Vatican Council II, the Church diametrically changed its course in the face of the Franco regime. At the death of General Franco, important legal ties between the Church and the State continued to exist, particularly the right of presentation by the Chief of State in the appointing of Bishops, a right which the King renounced in the first year of his reign. With this, a new secularizing trend in the relations between the Church and the State began which would be expressed in the Constitution of 1978. During the transition, the Church did not initiate or support the establishment of a Democratic Christian party, nor did it resist its creation, although at present it seems to be reconsidering this position and is attempting to exercise a greater influence in certain aspects of political life.

The Church and the Army are not the only points of reference for an analysis of interest and pressure groups, but they are certainly the most important, and they offer an indication of the tensions and adjustments between the various elites. A thorough analysis of these interactions would have to include economic power groups, as well as the impact of—or rather absence thereof—the Spanish intellectuals in the democratic transition.

The lack of a minimally effective participation of the intellectuals stands in contrast not only to the earlier experience in democratization in Spain's recent history but also to the role the intellectuals played in the opposition to Franco. Universities had been the center of continuous criticism of the regime, and one would have expected a more active involvement of the intellectuals in the post-Franco period. Instead, the gestation and the unfolding of the transitional process has remained under the influence and direction of a professionalized political elite. While it is true that many professionals, academics, and distinguished university graduates have themselves become members of this elite, it includes very few intellectuals in the strict sense of the term, and their influence is extremely weak. Some intellectuals, apparently not well integrated into their respective political parties, have recently associated themselves with a platform entitled *Foundation for Progress and Democracy*; this action, however, merely highlights the difficulties they have encountered in their attempts to gain some political influence for their views. There seems to prevail a "disintellectualization" of politics, which may have important consequences for the development of the political process in Spain.

The Dynamics of the Spanish Political System

In modern Spanish political history, the present democratic transition constitutes the first progressive change of regime without the government's being controlled by the Left. At the risk of somewhat simplifying realities, it can be said that it is the first and most genuine historical experience of "continuist reformism," and although its end result cannot be determined yet, it will have a decisive influence on the future of the Spanish political system.

The crisis of government in February 1981 gave birth to a new cabinet of 15 ministers who had already held cabinet positions under Adolfo Suarez, a politician of the former regime who has the virtue of not being the formal leader of his party and of not having reached the highest office through an electoral process. The Spanish people voted for UCD in 1979 under the leadership of Suarez, and the UCD members voted for Rodriguez Sahagun and Calvo Ortega in their Congress of 1981.[34] The tensions that this situation creates in UCD itself, together with those generated by the political dynamics of the country, make it difficult, if not impossible, to predict the direction in which political life in Spain may go in the near future. All seems to indicate, however, that this government may lead to an early election, which could bring about changes in the balance between UCD and PSOE.

Notes

1. For this topic, see the studies of Juan J. Linz, "Continuidad y discontinuidad en el elite política española: de la Restauration al régimen actual," *Estudios de Ciencia Política y Sociologiá-Homenaje al Professor Carlos Ollero* (Madrid: Facultad de Ciencias Políticas y Sociología, 1972), and M. Tuñon de Lara, *Historia y realidad del poder, El poder de las*

"*elites*" en *el primer tercio del siglo XX* (Madrid: Edicusa, 1975). For the historical aspects, see M. Martinez Cuadrado, *La burguesia conservadora (1874–1931)* (Madrid: Alianza, 1976), and R. Tamames, *La Republica, La Era de Franco* (Madrid: Alianza, 1977).

2. Cf. Cuadrado, *La buerguesia conservadora*, pp. 401ff.

3. Cf. Linz, "Continuidad y discontinuidad," p. 370.

4. At another level of the political elite, that of the civil governors, Bernard Richard has made two important studies: "Etude sur les gouverneurs civils en Espagne de la Restauration à la Dictadure (1874–1923)," *Melanges de la Casa de Velázquez*, vol. VIII (Madrid: Casa de Velázquez, 1972), and "Notas sobre el reclutamiento del alto personal de la Restauration (1874–1923): El origin geográfico de los governadores civiles y su evolucion," *in* M. Tuñon de Lara *et al.*, *Sociedad, política y cultura en la España de los siglos XIX y XX* (Madrid: Edicusa, 1973). In the latter, he affirms: "It is important, for the understanding of this period, that the Restoration has thusly recruited a large part of its high personnel in especially agricultural and often poor regions, while, on the contrary, other much more prosperous and dynamic regions, the population of which was more mobilized, have not supplied more than a small part of that personnel."

5. Quoted by M. Tuñon de Lara, *Historia y realidad del poder* (Madrid: Edicusa, 1975), p. 126.

6. The UGT (General Workers' Union) and the PSOE (Spanish Socialist Workers' party) flatly refused participation in the National Assembly. Cf. Cuadrado, *La buerguesia conservadora*, p. 456.

7. For details regarding the displacement which the dictatorship made of the old elite of politics, see J. L. Gomez, M. T. Gonzalez, and E. Portuondo. "Aproximación al estudio de las elites políticas en la Dictadura de Primo de Rivera," *Cuadernos Económicos de Información Comercial Española*, No. 10 (1979). In this study, the authors affirm: "But if we wished to conclude with a hypothesis that the partial information available to us seems to confirm, we would dare to venture that the modification of political elites that comes about in the dictatorship points toward a certain displacement of the political hegemony in favor of the sectors of the financial-industrial bourgeoisie. . . . In summary, if the representation of the great landowners is not modified, a slow advance is produced at their side, slow but firm, in the direct or indirect political representation of the most economically advanced sectors of the Spanish economy."

8. Cf. Linz, "Continuidad y discontinuidad," p. 385.

9. Ibid., p. 394.

10. For other important information on the political elite of the Second Republic, see J. L. Garcia de la Serrana, "Los intelectuales en la II República," *in* M. Ramírez, *Estudios sobre la II República española* (Madrid: Tecnos, 1975); O. Ruiz Manjon, "Autoridades locales y partidos en Andalucia durante la segunda República," *REIS* 5 (1979), pp. 167–81; and M. Ramírez Jimenez, *Los grupos de presion en la segunda República española* (Madrid: Tecnos, 1969), esp. pp. 43–69.

11. A summary of the sociological literature on the topic of the Franco government can be found in José Félix Tezanos, "Notas para una interpretación sociologica del franquismo," *Sistema* 23 (1978).

12. When comparisons are made between the Parliament of the Second

Republic and those under Franco, it should be taken into account that
there is a substantial difference—in the former, the representatives were
elected by universal suffrage, while in the latter, the determining factor
for presence in Parliament was political ambition.

13. Information from Linz, *"Continuidad y discontinuidad."*

14. In the last of these governments, presided over by Arias Navarro,
there were changes in diverse positions of ministers in October 1974 and
in March 1975.

15. Jesús M. de Miguel and Juan Linz, *"Las Cortes Española, 1943–
1970. Un análisis de cohortes, Primera parte. Las cohortes," Sistema*, No.
8 (January 1975).

16. Information from Amando de Miguel, *Sociología del franquismo*
(Euros: Barcelona, 1975).

17. Franco liked to disqualify his opponents with the mere dialectical
recourse of speaking of them as "politicians" and, on more than one oc-
casion, he stated in his speeches—as a decisive argument—that those who
did not agree with his regime really wanted to occupy the highest political posts in the ministries. The official propaganda amplified these opinions, and during this period, expressions like "policastros" (a negative
way of saying "politicians"), "ambitious politicians," "professionals of
politics," etc., were commonly used in the propagandistic dialectic.

18. C. Viver Pi-Sunyer, *El personal político de Franco (1936–1945)*
(Barcelona: Vicens Vives, 1978), pp. 64–68.

19. Ibid., pp. 69 and ff.

20. de Miguel, *Sociología del franquismo.*

21. As an example of what the technocrats' administration involved in
reality (one of their favorite topics), see Salustiano del Campo and Manuel Navarro, *Crítica de la plantificación social española (1964–1975)*,
(Madrid: Castellote, 1976).

22. B. Díaz Nosty, *Radiografí de las Nuevas Cortes*, Equipo de Docu-
mentatión Política (Madrid: Sedmay, 1977); M. Baena del Alcázar and J.
M. Garcia, "Elite franquista y burocracia en las Cortes actuales," *Sistema*
28 (January 1979); and *Quien es quien en las nuevas Cortes* (Madrid:
Dossier de Actualidad Económica, 1978).

23. Bureaucrats here signifies the public servants of the Central State
Administration who pertain to groups in which a higher university degree
is now required for entrance. This includes the military, for it is now felt
that study in military academies is equivalent to a university degree.

24. J. F. Tezanos, *Estructura de clases y conflictos de poder en la España postfranquista* (Madrid: Edicusa, 1978).

25. DICODI 1977. Keep in mind that this publication only gathers information concerning societies with more than 2,000,000 *pesetas* of notarized capital.

26. B. Diaz Nosty, *Cortes Generales 1979–83*, Equipo de Documenta-
ción Política, Jose Maya, ed. (Madrid: 1979); and *Quien es quien en las
Cortes Generales 1979–83*, Documentación Española Contemporanea
(Madrid, 1980).

27. Figures from "Funcionarios en las Cortes Generales," MUFACE,
No. 19 (April 1981).

28. J. Figuero, *UCD: "La Empresa" que creó Adolfo Suarez* (Barcelona:
Grijalbo, 1981)—and de Miguel, *Sociología del franquismo.*

29. Figuero, UCD, pp. 180 ff.; J. Muñoz, S. Roldan, and A. Seranno, *La internacionalización del capital en España* (Madrid: Edicusa, 1978), pp. 417 ff.

30. In the DICODI of 1973 and 1977, 20 ministers appear as holding posts as directors of companies with notarized capital of more than 2,000,000 *pesetas.*

31. This distinction refers back to that made by Ortega y Gasset in 1914 between official Spain and vital Spain. See José Ortega y Gasset, *Vieja y nueva política* (Madrid: Revista de Occidente, 1963), pp. 13–63.

32. It must be taken into account that the true power that the Constitution grants to the King is that of Commander-in-Chief of the Armed Forces. The exercise of this power on the part of the monarch on February 23, 1981, was decisive in preventing the *coup d'etat.*

33. The recently approved Law of Active Reserve will produce a notable rejuvenation of the military commands.

34. President Leopoldo Calio-Sotels has become UCD chairman and has appointed a new cabinet in December 1981. Fifty-six percent of its members are residents of Madrid, and 62 percent hold a law degree; no less than 72 percent are civil servants.

The Italian Political Class in the Twentieth Century: Continuities and Discontinuities

Maurizio Cotta

I. Empirical Studies of Elites and the Classic Theory of the Ruling Class

Since the first formulations of the theory of the ruling class in the writings of Mosca, Pareto, and Michels at the beginning of this century, a burgeoning of studies concerning those "who govern" has indeed taken place. The behavioral revolution of the fifties undoubtedly deserves special credit for the continuously expanding amount of increasingly detailed collections of empirical data on social backgrounds, careers, attitudes of politicians in general and of members of legislative assemblies in particular, produced in the last two decades.

A dispassionate evaluation of these developments cannot, however, dispel the impression that the growth of the field of elite analysis has often been quantitative more than qualitative. In front of the wealth of data collected (in itself a blessing, of course), the elaboration of theoretical frameworks for interpreting them has clearly lagged behind.

A comparison of the present situation of elite studies with the classic theory at the beginning of this century reveals a dramatic reversal in the balance between theoretical formulations and empirical analysis. The boldness and scope of Mosca's and Pareto's generalizations, often based upon a scanty and methodologically rather haphazard empirical documentation, provide a striking contrast with the limited attention given by many contemporary students of political elites to the theoretical meaning of their empirically sophisticated studies.

Given this situation, it is not a surprise that the question of the relevance of elite studies itself has been raised from time to time.[1] But are we really to reach the conclusion that it is not worth studying elites? In fact, more than questioning the legitimacy of elite studies as a whole, these criticisms are directed against a too simplistic theoretical framework accepted more or less implicitly and without discussion by many empirical studies. It is to this framework, therefore, that we must explicitly address our attention. The substance of its argument may be described in the following way: the role of political elites in the political system is interpreted without the mediation of further intervening variables. Relations between society and political elites on one side and between political elites and policy outputs on the other side are interpreted as direct links. As for the first relationship, the consequence is that the main criterion of analysis and evaluation will be that of sociological representativeness. From this, obviously, follows the overwhelming attention paid in empirical studies to social background characteristics of elites. As concerns the second relationship, individual sociological characteristics of elite members are assumed to be the major explanatory variable of policy outputs. This assumption, accepted implicitly by many empirical studies of elites (even if most of them stop short of analyzing outputs), is paradoxically enough often shared by the very critics of these studies. Having found weak correlations between political outputs and sociological profiles of elite members, they question the whole meaning of elite studies instead of this simplistic framework. In recent years, however, the need for a more articulated scheme for interpreting the role of elites in politics both on the input and on the output side has become increasingly felt.

On the input side, the search for a less simplistic interpretation requires that attention be paid to the intermediary role played by other variables between society and political elites. Among these variables, those related to party organizations are particularly important. Instead of a direct relationship between society and political elites, which is perforce deemed to be interpreted in terms of sociological representativeness, we have to look for an indirect relationship within which parties play a "translating" role. Consequently, the attention will be focused more upon the political than upon the social characteristics of politicians—or, in any case, to the latter only insofar as they can be used as indicators of the former. The concepts of political professionalization and political career acquire a crucial role in this perspective.[2]

Regarding the output side of the problem, the step that needs to be taken is to move from an approach using the analysis of political elites for explaining in a direct way the contents of policy outputs and political behavior to a more indirect one, applying this analysis to the understanding of the structure and functioning of the institutional settings within which policy outputs and political behavior are produced. It is the road followed, for instance, by a number of studies of parliamentary elites trying to apply their results to the evaluation of the institutionalization of parliament.[3] This perspective suggests, moreover, that we need to study elites not only as simple aggregates of individuals but as structured entities. The pure sum of individual characteristics is not enough to understand the behavior of elites.

A further development in the field of elite studies should be mentioned since it goes in the same direction of the search for a more meaningful theoretical perspective to guide empirical research. We want to refer to the the shift from static or short-term to diachronic and long-term analyses of elites. The common perspective underlying efforts of this kind[4] is that studying the continuity and discontinuity, then the stability and change, of political elites through a time span of considerable length (more than one generation) provides a favorable vantage point for understanding developments of the whole political system.

In some ways, then, we could conclude that the new trends emerging in the field of elite studies signal a renewed interest for the broader themes typical of the classic theory, but of course without forsaking the heritage of empirical rigor left by the behavioral revolution.

This article is a modest attempt to rethink some of the theoretical intuitions of the classic theory of the ruling class and to use them more or less as a springboard in the quest for a theoretically meaningful interpretation of certain elite-related phenomena of Italian history of this century.

II. The Classic Theory of the Ruling Class and the Problem of Elite Renewal

When reading Mosca's and Pareto's major works in this field,[5] one aspect of their analysis comes immediately to the fore as having a central role: the dynamics of elites. In sharp contrast with much of the empirically oriented research of more recent times that has directed most of its attention to a static analysis of individual properties of elite members, the classics assigned a preeminent role in their theory to the processes of reproduction, change, renewal, and disintegration of elites conceived as structured wholes. They see what they call "circulation of elites"[6] as a crucial variable for explaining continuity and discontinuity, functioning and malfunctioning of political systems. However different Mosca and Pareto may be in cultural background, style, and scientific perspectives, strong resemblances are apparent in the substance of their theoretical formulations on this subject.

Let us see very briefly how this theme is discussed by Mosca. A first and very general empirical observation that he makes is that in the dynamics of the political class, we can detect periods of great stability (and little quantitative and qualitative renewal), followed by other periods of much greater change.[7] The second step made by Mosca is to look for an explanation of these two different situations. Here Mosca finds a principle that, according to him, applies to all political elites. A sort of "inertia law" is at work in every political elite and stimulates in it a tendency to perpetuate itself. Hence, a low turnover and some hereditary arrangement are a common character of established elites.[8]

However, as Mosca is ready to acknowledge, this principle is far from absolute. Otherwise, as he writes, "the history of humanity would be much simpler," and we could not explain why the old ruling classes lose their power and are replaced by new ones.[9] The factors that bring about the fall of an old ruling class can be for Mosca both external and internal. The first are related to the social environment (changes in the nature of soceity and, therefore, of the qualities required from the ruling class).[10] The second have to do with the organization of the political class itself: when a political class has become too close and there is too little renewal, a decay of the political class itself will take place.[11] This means that when the principle of continuity goes beyond a certain point, it can trigger its own reversal.

The third step that Mosca's analysis undertakes is to evaluate the meaning for the political system of the renewal process and of its changing rhythms. As we have already seen, too little change and an excess of continuity of the political class, according to him, have negative effects on the functioning of the political system, since they produce a qualitative decline of the ruling class. The consequence will be the emergence, sooner or later, of an antagonistic ruling class, since the old one was not able to co-opt within itself and appease the leading elements of the ruled classes. The result will probably be a regime crisis and an abrupt displacement of the old political class. On the other hand, too much openness of the political class, while it might bring into the political play elements of innovation, would, on the other side, damage the structure of the existing political system and dissolve it.[12] Clearly for Mosca, who on this point follows the classical tradition of moderate government, some balance of the two principles (democratic principle = renewal; aristocratic principle = continuity) will determine, by combining the advantages of both, the most favorable conditions for the stability and good functioning of a political system.

As for Pareto, his argument starts with a broad division of elites into two general categories defined on the bases of the motivations and principles that guide them and of the skills and qualities they command. It is the well known distinction between "foxes" and "lions," "speculators" and "rentiers."[13]

But the discussion of the qualitative profile of elites is only the first step in Pareto's analysis. The question to which he immediately turns his attention is that of the persistence through time of governing elites. Under what conditions do they maintain their hold upon government, and under what conditions are they displaced? The general explanation offered by Pareto for the circulation of elites is an imbalance between ruling class and ruled class. The nature of this imbalance is rooted in the distribution of motivations and skills between the two classes. Pareto believes that every governing elite is deemed to undergo a process of qualitative homogeneization and decay.[14] Unless it is able to restore its qualitative balance by incorporating new elements from the ruled class, it is therefore bound to face a crisis and submit to revolutionary change. Such abrupt change will take place typically when two conditions are in place. First, the governing elite has become predominantly composed of "foxes," i.e., by politicians governing with bargaining, clientelistic, and often corrupt means. These politicians exert a limited symbolic appeal upon the population at large, refraining from the use of coercion out of what Pareto calls, with some disdain, "humanitarianism." The second condition is that from the ruled class, a new elite has emerged that can command a larger popular allegiance with the help of powerful political ideals and sentiments and which is ready to make use of coercive means in the political play. As a result of this disparity, the new elite is bound to displace the old one and a new elite cycle will begin.[15]

We may stop here and try a summary appraisal of the value that Mosca's and Pareto's analyses may have for our purposes. Their weaknesses are immediately apparent. The first is obviously the extremely high level of abstraction of their sweeping generalizations on the dynamics of elites. This high degree of generality makes these formulations difficult to falsify, but at the same time their explanatory power of empirical events is limited. An overstretching of concepts (and particularly of the concept itself of elite and ruling class) is often apparent. Another criticism that can be addressed to both authors has to do more with the substance than with the methodology of their analyses. Their theory of political elites pays too little attention to the institutional side of politics. For them, political elites are the key variable for understanding the process of politics. But as a consequence of the little attention paid to the institutional environment, within which elites necessarily operate, their key variable runs the risk of a sort of disembodiment; and it becomes difficult to identify in less general and more specific terms their relations, both active and passive, with society and the political system. Our approach would, therefore, be less reductionist: neither elites nor institutions can be reduced entirely to one another. On the contrary, they provide two complementary points of view for understanding politics; these gain from being combined. Having raised these criticisms, we must still say, however, that Mosca's and Pareto's analyses have kept a very rich power of suggestion in spite of the passing of time. They point to the crucial processes of every political system: how power holders manage to keep their position and how they are displaced. What is needed, therefore, more than rejecting their generalizations, is to develop their stimulations and to bring them nearer to an empirical theory.

In order to make a small step in this direction, we shall apply an analytical perspective centered on the dynamic processes of political elites to the history of the Italian political system during this century. As is well known, the Italian political system has gone in this period through three very distinctive stages: (1) the liberal regime on its way to a full democratization (from the beginning of the century until 1922–1924); (2) the authoritarian, Fascist regime, becoming a fully established regime in 1924–1926 and ending in 1943;[16] and (3) the redemocratization and consolidation of the present democratic regime, starting with the years 1943–1946. This analysis will be focused mainly on the proto-democratic and the democratic stages, but some attention will have to be paid also to the intermediate regime because of its impact on the other stages.

The problem to be discussed is the relationship between the process of reproduction and renewal of the political class and the discontinuity of the democratic regime. This means looking into the intersections between the elites and the institutional articulations central to this regime, in order to search for the role they play and the changes they undergo during these transitional phases. The matter is not of little theoretical interest if we think of the number of countries which have gone through sequences of regime transition comparable to that of Italy (Austria, France, Greece, Germany, Japan, Portugal, Spain, Venezuela) or which might in the future follow a similar path (Argentina, Chile, Brazil, Uruguay?).

Within this general question, three points deserve particular attention:

1. Can the process of elite renewal be in some way related to the crisis and fall of the democratic (or proto-democratic) regime that open the way to the authoritarian rule?

2. How extensive is the destruction of the old democratic political class produced by the authoritarian phase? At the end of this, are there survivors left from the previous democratic experience to ensure some degree of continuity with the past in the rebuilding of the new democratic regime and of it political class, or must this process start from scratch? And further, is this to be considered a blessing or a drawback?

3. How successful is the stabilization of the new democratic political class; and what is its role in ensuring the consolidation of the new regime?

III. The Italian Political Class and the Crisis of Pre-Fascist Democracy: The Risks of Renewal

In discussing the role of the political class variable in the fall of pre-Fascist democracy, we might borrow two different and apparently contradictory suggestions from the classic theory. The first is that too close a political class faces the risk of declining quality and may be displaced by a newer and antagonistic political class; the second, that too much openness and renewal may also produce a crisis in the regime. Which, if either, of the two alternatives is relevant for the breakdown of the democratic regime in the Italian case?

Two problems immediately appear. The first concerns the meaning of the concept of *openness* (or of *closeness*) of the political class. The concept may have both quantitative and qualitative aspects. Does it mean that there is a high level of turnover among the members of the political class, that the renewal of the political class brings in new politicians with different characteristics, or both? Second, which are the thresholds for saying *too* close or *too* open? A third problem ought to be added: how do we operationalize the concept of *political class*, which both Mosca and Pareto leave ill-defined?

Starting from the last point and given the historical context under analysis, we shall consider the political class as composed mainly by the members of Parliament. To these should be added a few party leaders and government members insofar as they do not yet belong to the first group. It may well be granted that some elements of the political class will be missed by this delimitation. It cannot be denied, however, that in order to understand the functioning of the democratic regime, these institutionally defined groups are crucial. A further aspect that should not be forgotten and to which I will return later, is that, within this fairly large class of politicians, by no means all have the same weight: there are leaders and followers. We shall leave the first two points mentioned above for the moment without an answer and look first at the empirical evidence.

The quantitative dimension of elite renewal provides a first approach to the problem. At the turn of the century, the rate of turnover among members of the Italian Parliament had a rather low level: the average percentage of new members at each election was under the 25 percent mark (general election of 1895: 19 percent; 1897: 24 percent; 1900: 24 percent). This low level of renewal is matched by a great continuity of incumbency, as shown by the fact that in this period nearly a third of all the members had five or more parliamentary terms.[17]

We have said "low level of renewal"; but can we say also "too low"? Since we do not have a sufficiently established generalization concerning the interpretations of quantitative thresholds of elite turnover, we are not able to give a definite answer to that question. We may, however, offer some elements of evaluation by comparing the Italian data with those available for other countries. The data collected for the French Third Republic by Mattei Dogan show a little higher rate of newcomers at general elections during a similar period: between 1893 and 1919, an average of 29 percent.[18] And a comparable level of turnover is documented by Linz for Spanish elections before the First World War.[19]

If we look at the anglophone area, we have, in fact, a rate of renewal for the U.S. House of Representatives at the turn of the century that is significantly higher than in the Italian case (36 percent between 1891 and 1903). But in the following years, the mean percentage of newcomers declines to levels even lower than the Italian ones.[20] As for the United Kingdom between 1918 and 1951, the average of MPs elected for the first time was 28 percent.[21]

From these comparisons, we may conclude that while the level of renewal of the Italian parliamentary class at the end of the nineteenth century was surely rather low, it was not, however, radically different from other political experiences. But, in any case, if an absolute evaluation of a given level of renewal raises problems that are not easily solved, a step toward a meaningful interpretation of these data may be made by looking at them in a diachronic perspective. We must look, then, for the stability or change in the trends of elite renewal. From this perspective, we can see that the period of low turnover rates that we have mentioned was but the beginning of a trend of increasing renewal of the parliamentary elites (see Figure 1). Starting with the election of 1904, the rate of newcomers would never be under the 30 percent level. However, until World War I, the increase was only moderate. It was the first postwar election of 1919 that brought about an absolutely unprecedented level of renewal. The members elected for the first time were more than 60 percent of the total number. The ratio between old and new members had reversed. While in the past a large majority of politicians survived from one legislature to another, in this case, only a minority managed to do so and a large majority left the scene.[22] As a result of a number of factors that cannot be discussed here in detail (the introduction of a proportional electoral system, the First World War, the establishment of a Catholic party), a break in the continuity of the parliamentary elite took place.

The following election (1921) indeed brought a certain stabilization in the process of renewal; the percentage of newcomers dropped to 38 percent. However, the turnover was still a good deal higher than at the beginning of the period we are discussing. And in the next election, held in 1924, the renewal reached again a very high level (54 percent of the members of Parliament were elected for the first time).[23]

FIGURE 1.
Percentage of New Elected Members of the Italian Lower Chamber

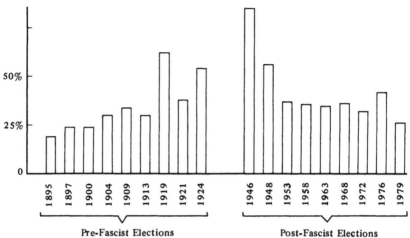

Thus, from the quantitative point of view at least, the years preceding the fall of the democratic regime in Italy display a trend of increasing renewal rather than a declining openness of the political class. Of the two generalizations concerning the relationship between elite renewal and regime stability that we found in the classic theory and more specifically in Mosca, it is then the second, pointing to the destabilizing effects of a too hasty elite circulation, that could apply to the Italian experience. Or perhaps we could suggest a somewhat more complex formulation taking into account both aspects. A period of low (and inadequate) levels of renewal of the political elites, such as the one we have detected in Italy at the turn of the century, has left the political class lagging behind the changing conditions of society and has, therefore, prepared the ground for an abrupt elite circulation, the affect of which is the disruption of the institutional foundations of the regime. A large replacement of the political class takes place not only *after* the transition to a new regime (as might be easily expected), but also in the years immediately preceding it.

It is interesting to point out that in at least two other cases the breakdown of democracy came after a period of high turnover in the political class: this was the case during the last years of the Weimar Republic[24] and also in Spain during the Second Republic.[25]

Of course, this is still not enough for saying that a high level of turnover of the political class is *the* cause of the fall of a democratic regime. There are, in fact, other instances where a large renewal takes place without endangering democracy. For instance, in the United Kingdom the first elections after World War I and after World

War II show abnormally high levels of turnover—48 percent and 53 percent—but do not bring about the fall of the democratic regime.[26] And also during the French Third Republic, the first election after World War I stimulates a higher turnover in the parliamentary elite (52 percent of newcomers)[27] without producing a major crisis.[28] Given such contradictory evidence, a more cautious formulation would be to say that while this variable in itself is not sufficient to explain the democratic breakdown, it might be relevant as one of the elements of the complex syndrome which is responsible for the crisis of democracy.[29] When the other conditions of such a syndrome are not in place, a rapid circulation of political elites may be absorbed without excessive danger for the regime (and may also play a positive role of innovation); but if added to other elements, it might become an unbearable burden.

In order to ground this hypothesis, we must understand the institutional impact of the rate of renewal of the political class and, more specifically, of a change in this rate. In this perspective, it is important to remark that the renewal rate structures the seniority stratification of the parliamentary class; therefore, a significant change of the former means also a change of the latter, with all the implications this may have for the structure of the parliamentary class itself and for its relationship with the parliamentary institution within which it operates. As has been suggested by some authors, the institutionalization of parliament is at stake here.[30]

To discuss this question, we need, then, some operationalization of the concept of parliamentary seniority. For this purpose, the threshold of two terms will be used as a discriminating criterion. Like any other threshold, it has some degree of arbitrariness; but it is not too unreasonable to say that it takes, at the very least, two terms of office for a legislator to become fully master of such a complex institutional machinery as a parliament. Accordingly, a distinction is made here between *junior legislators* (those at their first or second mandate) and *senior legislators* (those with three or more terms).

Even without being too deterministic, it seems reasonable to hypothesize that the institutional socialization of newcomers into the traditional norms, usages, and conventions of the parliamentary system will be easier and smoother when an equilibrium exists between the two components; on the contrary, the more the junior component tends to overwhelm the senior one, the greater will be the chances of a break of the institutional continuity (which may mean extensive procedural changes or a larger restructuring of parliament or even a major disruption of its functioning).

If we look at the Italian parliamentary class during those years from this perspective, a remarkable change is easily detected. At the beginning of the century, the junior component does not reach even

FIGURE 2.
Seniority Structure of Italian Lower Chamber

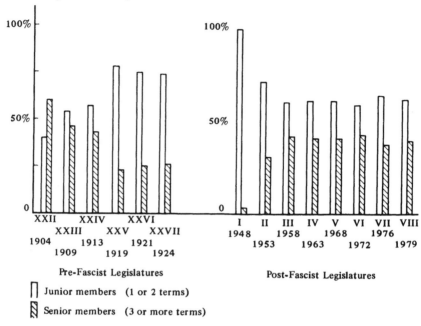

Pre-Fascist Legislatures   Post-Fascist Legislatures

⊓ Junior members (1 or 2 terms)

⊠ Senior members (3 or more terms)

a half of the whole parliamentary membership (40 percent in the Parliament elected in 1904); with the two following elections a moderate rise of the percentage of junior legislators can be noticed. But after the 1919 election, the picture becomes entirely different. The junior component attained an overwhelming majority (78 percent in 1919; 75 percent in 1921; 74 percent in 1924), while the senior legislators share shrank to more or less a quarter of all the members (see Figure 2). Those who could best ensure the institutional continuity have thus become a small minority.

The renewal and rejuvenation do not affect only the parliamentary class at large but also a more selected and institutionally prominent group of legislators: speakers and deputy-speakers of the Chamber of Deputies. If we compare prewar and postwar years, the decline in the parliamentary seniority of this group of institutional leaders is striking. In the twenty-second legislature (1904–1909), their average seniority was 10 terms (the ongoing one included). In the twenty-third legislature (1909–1913) and in the twenty-fourth (1913–1919), seniority was 8.2; but after the war, it dropped to 4.9 in the twenty-fifth legislature (1919–1921), to 4 in the twenty-sixth (1921–1924), and finally to only 2.9 in the twenty-seventh (1924–1929). A further point to be noticed is that none of the legislators who had held such positions before 1919 made a comeback, and most of them were not even reelected to Parliament.

As these data suggest, the quantitative dimension of elite circulation processes during this period of Italian history points in itself to the existence of a situation characterized by a weakening of the factors of institutional continuity. But, as Pareto would suggest, for a full evaluation of the meaning of a process of change in the political class, its qualitative dimension must be taken in consideration along with the quantitative aspect. The question to address is the following: does the high level of renewal of the parliamentary elite combine also with a significant change in its qualitative profile? It is obviously different if a high turnover means only a more rapid circulation of politicians of the same type or, on the contrary, an accelerated substitution of the old political class by a different breed of politicians. In the latter case, a number of questions can be raised. What are the attitudes of the new politicians toward the existing regime and its institutional configuration? How is their coexistence with the remnants of the old political elite going to work in the transitional phase? Is some kind of integration between old and new politicians possible?

In the years after World War I, there are indeed changes also at the qualitative level. The sociological profile of legislators shows some change: a decline of the upper classes and a growth of professional politicians can be noticed.[31] But nothing really dramatic. The most important qualitative features of the political class that changed during these years are connected to the party affiliation of the members of Parliament. The great renewal of the parliamentary class that took place with the 1919 elections went hand in hand with a major earthquake in the party system. The two mass parties, the Socialist party (PSI) and the Popular Party (PPI), made unprecedented headway, and correspondingly, the old established bourgeois sector in Parliament faced an abrupt decline. Such a change in the party system has a direct impact on the political class for a number of reasons. First, the two growing parties are both outside the traditional political establishment; therefore, the political class emerging with them obviously has a very different approach to the existing institutions than do the old liberal politicians: it is not "their" political regime, and they do not feel bound by it in the same way.[32] Second, the new parties are entirely different organizations from those of the liberal and democratic sector,[33] which could not even be considered real parties but rather Parliament-based personalistic groupings. Inevitably, this affected the organizational patterns of the political class. The old personalized system, based on leader-followers relations, gave way to a more formal and impersonal one. This transformation became institutionally visible when, after the 1919 election, the working organization of the lower chamber, instead of being based on individual members as in the past, became centered on juridically recognized parliamentary groups. With this, a new element of discipline, but also of rigidity, was introduced in the functioning of Parliament. Another important consequence of the new type of parties was that, along with the parliamentary groups and their leadership, there was a potentially different leadership, selected by external organizations of the same parties. In fact, during all this period, the recognized political leader of the PPI was not a Member of Parliament. And a clearly dualistic leadership, with parliamentary leaders and party leaders divided more often than not by conflicting political outlooks and strategies, was also apparent in the Socialist party.[34] The meaning and the impact of the renewal of the political class becomes, therefore, much more evident if we look at the two dimensions (quantitative and qualitative) together. The new political class was also a different political class.

The two new parties accounted for a large part of the renewal of the political class. Of the 156 Socialist deputies elected in 1919, 128 (82 percent) were newcomers, and almost the same percentage held for the PPI (81 out of 98, or 83 percent). PSI and PPI were thus new parties, both in terms of their political position (outside the establishment) and their political class. At the same time, their role in the new parliament and in the political process was also new. They had been minority forces in the past;[35] now added together, they constituted 50 percent of the legislators. Against them, no government was possible.

As for the old parties, they had lost almost half their seats; also, within their ranks the renewal had been strong (106 newcomers out of 252, or 42 percent). This means that among them, the number of nonreturning members of Parliament had been particularly high. Consequently, within the parties that represent more prominently the continuity of the political system, the political class faces in these years all the problems of a large-scale re-equilibration.

At the next election (in 1921), a decrease in the renewal rate of the two mass parties became apparent (only 37 percent of newcomers in the PPI and 33 percent in the PSI). But this had no immediate impact upon the seniority structure of their parliamentary groups, where more than 80 percent were still junior legislators. In the parties of the center and the right, taken together, the turnover remained higher (41 percent) but was not equally spread. The old liberal and conservative component had now reached a certain stabilization, together, it must be said, with a serious weakening of its parliamentary weight. But new political groups had emerged—Fascist, Nationalist—with a young leadership lacking parliamentary experience.[36] And, to fully appreciate the role these new politicians ("lions," if we want to put it in Pareto's terms) were to perform, it must not be forgotten that, given the state of the coalitional game in these years and the reciprocal vetoes between some of the major political forces, their weight considerably exceeded their comparatively limited numbers.

Some sense of the fact that the postwar political class was a "new" political class in its political orientations as well can be gained from the following indicator: the requests presented to Parliament for suspending the parliamentary immunity of members indicted for some kind of legal offense. After World War I, the number of cases when the offense had political and institutional undertones (for instance: slander against the state or some of its institutions, incitement to political violence or rebellion, participation in political riots, etc.) becomes significant.[37] We can read in these data not only a sign of the general deterioration of the political climate but also of the part played in this process by members of the parliamentary elite. This fact cannot be dismissed lightly. This conflictional atmosphere did not leave the parliamentary institution itself untouched, as can be learned from the fact that during the twenty-sixth legislature (1921–1924) proposals had to be advanced for strengthening the disciplinary powers of the president of the lower chamber and for creating a special jury to deal with quarrels between members.[38]

When the question of the effects of the political class variable is discussed, attention generally focuses upon "policy effects." There are, of course, good reasons for this: policies are what politics is for. But, as we said at the beginning, we must not forget that policies are produced by institutions and, therefore, depend on the functioning of the latter. The institutional dimension can be overlooked only when institutions can be taken for granted, their existence and working not being at issue. This is, obviously, not the case in Italy during the years we are examining. Therefore, attention has to be addressed to the institutional aspect. We have seen how changes in the circulation processes of the political class had a bearing on this dimension. In order to somewhat bridge the distance between institutional and policy levels, we must pay some attention to a process that has a crucial role as a link between the two: the process of cabinet formation. The consequences of the new situation in the political class after the 1919 election made themselves felt very clearly in this process, which, for a parliamentary regime, is extremely important and delicate.

All experienced politicians who were potential prime ministers belong, of course, to the old political class represented by the traditional parties. However, because of the weakening of these parties, they had become "generals without soldiers." The opposite was the case in the new parties: they now had many soldiers but no generals. They may have had, indeed, some senior political leaders, but these, because of the past oppositional role of the parties, had no experience in the process of building government coalitions. It is typical of this kind of situation that the only politician of the new mass parties (Meda of the PPI) who, in these years, was asked by the King to try to form a cabinet, twice refused to accept this task.[39] In some way, he did not feel ready for the job or capable of commanding enough authority in Parliament. The result was that the "old generals" had to build their governments while relying mainly upon the "new soldiers." But the task was much more difficult for them now than in the past: the new sectors of the political class were more rigid than the old, because they acted more strictly along party lines. Therefore, they were less easily co-opted to support the government on an individual basis. It is no wonder that even the leading liberal politician of the prewar years, Giolitti, who in the past had dominated the government building process, now faced a failure. The "miracle," which he had accustomed both his political friends and enemies to expect (always being able to make a comeback from his self-dictated retirements to find a parliamentary majority), did not occur this time; and he preferred to retire and give way to other, less outstanding politicians.

A measure of how much the cabinet-building process had become more troubled in these years is provided by the average duration of cabinets. While between 1900 and 1919, it was approximately 16 months, between 1919 and 1922, it dropped to only 6.7 months. This situation did not leave the policy-making capability of the executive unaffected. A very simple indicator of the rate of success of legislative proposals submitted to Parliament by the cabinet shows, indeed, a dramatic decline in the postwar legislatures compared to the rates in the years before the war.[40] Moreover, the decline in the rate of legislative success also included legislator-initiated proposals; the crisis affected both government and Parliament.

We have noticed before that the new groups of the political class were organized more rigidly, along formally defined party lines. This, however, does not mean that they were always very cohesive and united. On the contrary, during this period both the Popular and the Socialist parliamentary groups faced deep cleavages within their ranks, precisely on the question of their participation in the government. The dissension produced at first a lack of political flexibility in both groups, which greatly reduced their possible roles in the solution of the governmental crisis, and, at a second stage, formal splits of groups of dissenters. The splits in the PSI were so serious as to generate three different parties (Unitarian Socialists, Maximalist Socialists, and Communists) with conflicting strategies concerning participation in governmental coalitions. As for the Popolari, they lost a fairly large group of deputies who, at a crucial moment (the vote for the electoral reform of 1923), decided to support the Fascist proposal against their party line.[41] It is reasonable to suggest that the enormous growth of the two parties and of their political class had provided the breeding ground for internal dissension on the divisive problems of the postwar period.

Less difficult social problems than those faced by the Italian democracy in those years would, perhaps, have granted the new political class more time to consolidate its structure and to overcome its heterogeneities. It might have delayed the crisis, as in the German case where the Weimar political class lasted ten more years, or perhaps it could have even been possible to avoid the breakdown of democracy. But for a number of reasons which cannot be discussed here in detail, there was not enough time and a new anti-democratic political class was able to shrewdly exploit these opportunities to take power and inaugurate authoritarian rule.[42]

Reverting to the classic theory formulations, we may, then, conclude from the Italian experience that if the political class variable played a role in the democratic breakdown, this was mainly the consequence of too abrupt a process of renewal. The coupling of the quantitative and qualitative dimensions of this phenomenon (particularly the much increased heterogeneity within the political class) contributed significantly to weakening the ability of the fragile democratic regime to face the difficult challenges of those years.

While this interpretation of the Italian case seems rather plausible, a more systematic comparison with other cases would be required in order to formulate a general law. In particular, one would need a discussion of those cases where a large renewal of the political class was only a factor of innovation without destabilizing effects.[43] We have to know more about the conditions within which the processes of elite circulation develop and the factors which may counterbalance the tensions arising from a political class undergoing a rapid change.

IV. The New Political Class of Post-Fascist Democracy: The Problem of Consolidation

If we now look at the second democratic experiment in the Italian history of this century—the one starting after the fall of fascism, brought about by its military defeat in World War II—the problems we face are not entirely different, but the perspective and the outcomes are clearly not the same.

The element in common with the experience examined above is that once more the political class is, to a great extent, new (precisely how new is a point we will have to discuss). It is, therefore, a political class that has to undergo a process of consolidation and of institutional learning. However, the relationship between regime change and political class renewal is now reversed. After World War I, a large renewal of the political class had taken place within the framework of the existing political regime; and the regime change which occurred thereafter could, to some extent, be seen as related to that

process. Now the renewal of the political class is a direct consequence of the regime change—or better, of *two* regime transitions:
from democracy to fascism and from fascism back to democracy. The
difference is significant and obviously facilitates the task of the post-
Fascist political class.

In their fight against the old political class, the new politicians of
1919 and 1921 were easily induced also to fight the existing parliamentary regime, thus risking (and in fact leading to) their own self-
destruction. They had been able to emerge under the protection of
the old regime, and with its disruption they were crushed by the
new authoritarianism. On the contrary, the post-Fascist political class
can establish itself fighting against both the old (Fascist) political
class, and the old (Fascist) regime, thus gaining a double democratic
legitimacy.

What can we learn from the classic theorists on the problems of
this phase? We can recall, without going into a detailed discussion
since the question is only peripheral to this analysis, a point in
Mosca's theory which provides a key to understanding the reasons
for the sudden crisis of the Fascist political class. What he says about
the inevitable decline of a political class which has outlived the
political values of which it was the bearer[44] clearly applies to the
Fascist political class. Having come to power on the wake of a nationalistic ideology, it could not survive the worst possible failure of
this ideology: military defeat and foreign occupation.

As for the problem on which we want to focus here, i.e., the establishment and consolidation of a new political class (in our case, the
post-Fascist one), one can find in Mosca and Pareto only general
observations, such as the common tendency of political classes, once
they have reached power, to become increasingly more closed and
to perpetuate themselves through different types of exclusionary
practices, particularly taking advantage of hereditary devices.[45] Up
to a certain point such a tendency, according to Mosca, has a positive
function, since it ensures the transmission of values and qualities
that are required for the functioning of the political system.[46] This
point of view, although couched in different terms, is shared by the
theory of institutionalization.[47] Of course, in contemporary political
contexts, the role assigned by the classic theory to the hereditary
principle seems somewhat outdated. While this principle may have
had, in the past, a large role in ensuring the continuity of a political
class, today other political factors—most prominent among them
party organizations—have taken its place. The hereditary principle
is confined nowadays to a marginal role, which is not to say, however, that family ties are unimportant, as shown, for instance, by the
fact that between 1946 and 1976 nearly 40 percent of Italian deputies
had relatives with political experience of some kind, and 15 percent
had a family member belonging to the parliamentary elite.[48]

Before looking at the problem of the stabilization of a new political class, we have to look at how this class was formed. In particular, we have to answer the following question: how much discontinuity was produced by the nondemocratic regime, or to put it in another way, how *new* is the new political class? This question has, in fact, two dimensions: (1) the degree of discontinuity with the authoritarian political class, and (2) the degree of discontinuity with the former democratic political class. The first aspect may be relevant for evaluating the degree to which the nondemocratic past still weighs in the newborn democracy but also to what extent the transition was an evolutionary one or a *ruptura*. The second may help to answer questions as to how experienced the founders of the new regime in the democratic game are and to what degree memories of the past democracy, with its cleavages and political alignments, will guide their behavior in the new situation.

With regard to the first point, if we confine the analysis to the parliamentary level, the political class of the new democratic regime shows very little continuity with the nondemocratic political class. Of all the members of the Constituent Assembly and of the lower chamber elected between 1946 and 1976, only fifteen had been members of the legislatures "elected" under the Fascist regime. This does not mean that only so few of the new politicians had had some connection with the Fascist regime; it is pretty clear that many more had been politically ivolved in the past regime, but at a lower or local level, not as members of the national ruling class. On this point, the difference between the Italian and the recent Spanish case is considerable.[49] The data concerning the continuity of political elites are consistent with the different types of transition to democracy taking place in the two countries: evolutionary in Spain, discontinuous in Italy.[50] The fact that in Italy the new political class has little or no personal links with the authoritarian regime (except for some members of the small extreme-Right party) means that opposition to the Fascist regime (*Antifascismo*) is shared by all the political forces as a powerful instrument of symbolic action and as a legitimizing device. Its role in bridging certain political cleavages should not be underestimated.

The next point concerns the continuity with the old democratic regime. How large a role have the survivors of the pre-Fascist democracy played in the shaping of the new democratic political class?

We may start with a global measure. In the first parliamentary body elected freely after the fall of fascism, i.e., the Constituent Assembly of 1946, there are 88 (15 percent) legislators with an experience of the old democratic Parliament. This rather small minority became even smaller (only 3 percent) in the lower chamber (*Camera dei Deputati*) of the first regular Parliament, elected in 1948.[51] It is not too difficult to explain the limited number of survivors of the old democratic political class. The passing of time is obviously a first factor. The physiological toll of more than twenty years is perforce extensive. Another factor which may have played a role is the fact that, as we have seen, a large part of the old political class was a "new" political class, which had not yet had the time to take root before the Fascist takeover. It was, therefore, more easily eliminated by that regime.

In comparative terms, however, the group of pre-authoritarian legislators who manage to make a comeback at the first election of the reestablished democracy was not so small. In Western Germany, in spite of the shorter interruption of democratic rule, there were only twenty-eight survivors of the old *Reichstag* elected to the first Bundestag in 1949 (7 percent of all the members).[52] And in France, after only five years of Vichy government, the percentage of legislators of the Third Republic elected in 1945 to the first parliamentary assembly of the Fourth Republic was exactly the same as the Italian: 15 percent.[53] The extremely radical nature of the nondemocratic period in Germany[54] and the extensive reshuffling of the party system in France after World War II are probably the factors responsible for the greater discontinuity in the political class of those countries, considering the time elapsed.[55] Other countries, such as Spain and Greece, show a more linear relationship between the time factor and survival of the old democratic elites.[56]

Returning to the Italian case, it is of some interest to note that in the Constituent Assembly the numerical weight of old legislators was not the same in all political sectors. In fact, it ranged from a minimum of 6 percent among Communist legislators to 14 percent of the Christian Democrats, 24 percent of the Socialists, and to a maximum of 32 percent among legislators of the Right. The parties which already had fascism before an older political tradition now showed a greater continuity with the past. We have, thus, some evidence supporting the hypothesis of an association between survival of the old democratic elite and the degree to which it had established itself before the authoritarian takeover. We can also interpret these data—and there is no contradiction between the two readings—as a sign of the more limited ability of the older political forces to recruit younger politicians.

In order to fully appreciate the role played by the pre-Fascist political class in the transition to democracy, these measures are insufficient. In fact, they lead to underestimation of its influence. For a more balanced assessment, we have to go back several years and look at the "noninstitutional" politics of the years 1943–1946, between the fall of fascism and the first elections. These transition years were indeed crucial for the first shaping of the new political class and for the laying of the foundations for the democratic regime. In these years, the first merger of old and new politicians took place, and political alignments began to take shape. At this time, no true parliamentary body existed and the areas available to the political class were the newborn parties, the government, and the *Resistenza* movement.[57] Each arena was structurally different; and although they were mutually connected, each would generate a somewhat different political class. In the *Resistenza* movement, the old politicians played a very limited part; the preeminent role was that of a young leadership with little experience of the old parliamentary democracy and with a strong motivation for innovation. It is not surprising that members of this group often shared radical ideas about a nonparliamentary democracy based upon popular councils. But in the other two arenas, the role played by old politicians was more important[58] for a number of reasons, among them the military occupation. It was there that the fundamental decisions were made on what would eventually be the new regime.[59]

In the first "political" government since the fall of Mussolini, the second Badoglio cabinet, nine out of seventeen ministers had been deputies or senators in the pre-Fascist period (and three had also been ministers).[60] This high proportion remained more or less the same in the following cabinets of the 1940's. The degree of continuity is significant. Its impact should not be underestimated if one thinks of the central and rather unrestrained role of the government in the rebuilding of democracy during these years, when no Parliament existed to control it.

In contradistinction to this high degree of continuity at the government level, the founding groups of the parties[61] displayed significant differences in the balance between old and new politicians. Of the three mass parties, the Christian Democracy (the successor of the old Popular Party) shows the greatest leadership continuity with the pre-Fascist period. Almost all the founders of the party in the early months of 1943 could claim a political experience in the old Popular Party, either as members of its parliamentary group or of one of the leading bodies of the party organization. Even the last chairman of the old party, before its dissolution, was in place to lead the newborn party. This continuity persisted in the following years but, starting with the first national party congress in 1946, the proportion of new politicians became significant. On the whole, the process of generational circulation in the Christian Democratic Party took place rather smoothly, within a sound framework established by the old politicians.

The case of the Communist party was rather different. None of the members of the small parliamentary group of the pre-Fascist period plays a leading role in the reconstruction of the party. The continuity here was mainly with a younger political class, grown in the clandestinity of the opposition to the Fascist regime. Only the top leader of the party (Togliatti) represented a longer continuity, going back to the original founding group of the party in the early 1920's. This factor, together with his role in the international Communist movement and the Soviet investiture that Togliatti could claim from having been for a long period the representative of his party at the Komintern in Moscow, gave him an undiscussed authority as the leader of the party. This well-defined structure of the political class in the Communist party made the assimilation of a large number of young politicians possible through a process of co-optation that caused very little intergenerational conflict.

Of the three large parties, the Socialist party was the one with the least homogeneous and coherent founding group. It was the party with the largest generational spectrum among its early leaders (an age range of thirty-five years, compared to the dozen years in the PCI). In addition to a number of rather old survivors of the pre-Fascist parliamentary group and party leadership, there were politicians who became active during the transition years between democracy and fascism, and finally a nucleus of young politicians who emerged during the crisis of the Fascist regime, having no direct knowledge of the old party but playing an important role in rebuilding the new Socialist party. To this generational heterogeneity, one should add the fact that none of the most influential top leaders of the pre-Fascist party had survived. The lack of a top echelon of leadership with an undisputed authority made the assimilation of the younger generation and the mediation between old and new politicians much more troublesome than in the other two parties. The multiple splits this party would undergo in the first years of the post-Fascist democracy are probably due, to some extent, to the uncertainty about the authority structure within its political class.

Within the parties of the traditional Right, the survival of old politicians was considerable, and the role they played in the transition years in checking the more Jacobinic models of democracy proposed by the Left is not to be underestimated. But it soon becomes clear that they were rather out of tune with the new politics of the post-Fascist period, which was characterized by a much higher level of popular mobilization than that of the years when these politicians had become politically active. A good indicator of this change is the average turnout at elections: before fascism, it was around 60 percent; after fascism, it reached 90 percent.[62] The consequences were felt very clearly with the first elections of 1946 and even more so in 1948. The parties of the liberal and conservative right were not able to compete effectively with the other parties and gained only a very small share of the electorate, and one which shrank (15 percent in 1946 and 8 percent in 1948, while in the elections of 1921 they still had more than 30 percent). What the classics say about the inevitable disappearance of a political elite that has outlived the social conditions that fostered its ascendancy appears to be particularly appropriate in this case.

To sum up, all the parties showed in this period some mix of old and new politicians. But if we look at the two who were most successful in this phase, the DC and the PCI, both of which gained ground—the first at the expense of the old Right and the second of the Socialist Left—we find that an important element they had in common is the greater initial homogeneity and the certainty, within the political class, of the top leadership structure. It becomes clear from this analysis that in a transitional phase the process of renewal and reconstitution of the political class is highly dependent on the structure of the embryonic groups from which it develops.

From the point of view of the consequences for the newborn regime, it is very important that, in these transition years, the Christian Democracy (DC) attained a central position in the political system between Left and Right and, as a consequence, a dominant role in governmental coalitions (a role which the elections of 1946 and 1948 further sanctioned by giving the DC the status of largest party). This means that the new democratic regime inaugurated its life with a greater equilibrium of continuity and innovation (compared to the old parliamentary experience), at least in the higher strata of the political class, than if success had gone to the Communist Left or to the traditional Right. In the first case, discontinuity would have prevailed; in the second, the weight of the past would have been dominant. A very clear symbol of this coexistence between old and new is the fact that, until his death in 1954, de Gasperi, the leader of the Christian Democratic Party and at the same time of the government (having been prime minister between 1945 and 1953), was the same person who was the leader of the old Catholic party in the last years of the pre-Fascist period; yet he acknowledged the role of the politicians of the younger generation and based the support for his own leadership position on an intergenerational coalition.

Soon, with the beginning of the normal institutional life of the new regime (which also meant a great increase in the number of institutional positions to be filled, compared to the rather elitistic dimension of the transition years), the new political class, with no experience of the past democracy, emerged forcefully. First, it became quantitatively dominant in the lower and broader echelons of the political class. We have seen that at the parliamentary level, but the same happened within the national assemblies of the party organizations. The next step was access to top leadership positions. Among the three large parties, the Christian Democracy was the slowest in replacing the old politicians with new ones in top positions. Even there, however, this substitution was accomplished at the end of the 1950's in the government, in the leadership of the parliamentary groups and in the party executive.

By way of a conclusion, one may point out that during the transition period, the elements of continuity with the pre-authoritarian democratic experience appeared qualitatively, if not quantitatively, significant. An evaluation of what this meant for the new democratic regime may be a matter of debate. It is, however, reasonable to suggest that the presence of a group of politicians who had a personal

experience of the acrimonious dissension between democratic parties in the pre-Fascist years and their calamitous consequences for
the survival of democracy has contributed to the building of a constitutional consensus in the post-Fascist years.

The next point of interest is the stabilization of the new political
class that came into place with the new regime. There are at least
three questions to be answered:

1. Has a process of stabilization of the political class indeed followed the deep renewal produced by the regime transition?

2. How long did it take for this process to be accomplished, and
how long did it last?

3. Did it affect homogeneously all sections of the political class?

The first dimension to be examined will be the quantitative measure of renewal employed for the pre-Fascist period. Looking at the
percentage of newcomers among the members of the lower chamber
of Parliament, one can see that the stabilization of the political class
in its parliamentary component was almost accomplished with the
1953 election (the second election for the "normal" Parliament, the
third if one also includes the election to the Constituent Assembly).
Starting with 1953, and including the next four elections, turnover
oscillates between 37 percent and 32 percent, showing a slightly
declining trend (see Figure 1). As might be expected, these figures
are higher than those of old and well established democratic political systems such as the United States or the United Kingdom.[63] For
a more meaningful comparison, however, one should look at countries that have gone through a similar regime discontinuity. Among
these cases the French Fourth Republic, during its shorter life span,
offers an example of lower levels of stabilization of the parliamentary elite.[64] Western Germany and Japan, however, show a degree of
continuity among Parliament members after the first election, which
is consistently higher than in the Italian case.[65] In these three cases,
the degree of stabilization of the political class seems to fit pretty
well with the degree of stabilization of the regime itself, and Italy
would fall in between on this dimension as well.

With regard to the seniority structure of the political class produced by these circulation rates, the proportion of junior and senior
members, as defined above, was extremely stable between the third
and the eighth legislature of the post-Fascist period (see Figure 2).
This seniority structure (with senior members reaching an average
level of 40 percent) showed indeed, a much greater balance than that
of the years immediately preceding the Fascist takeover; but compared to the German experience after the fall of the Nazi regime, it
still assigned a weaker role to the senior parliamentary component
(see Figure 3).

In spite of the fact that the degree of stabilization reached by the
Italian political class during this period was not higher, but rather

FIGURE 3.
Seniority Structure of the Major Italian Parties (II–VIII Legislatures:
1953–1979)

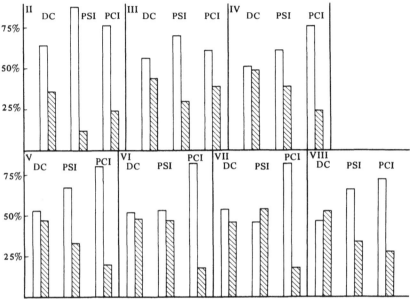

☐ Junior legislators (1 or 2 terms)

▨ Senior legislators (3 or more terms)

lower than in many other democracies, this process has recently undergone a reversal. With the general election of 1976, the turnover rate reached a new high of 42 percent, but the seniority structure has not changed much: between junior and senior members the ratio is now 63:37. Is this to be interpreted as a turning point in the stabilization of the political class, or is it only a temporary phenomenon? It is still too early to say: the election of 1979 seems to give more weight to the second interpretation: the turnover rate dropped to a new minimum (27 percent), and the percentage of junior members also declined somewhat.

For an accurate evaluation of the dynamics of the political class and of its institutional stabilization, the global measures are not entirely adequate, since they may conceal significant differences between party groups. Indeed, leaving aside the smaller groups and concentrating on the three larger parties (DC, PCI, and PSI), it is easily noticeable that the circulation of their parliamentary elite followed rather different patterns, as shown in Table 1. At least from a quantitative point of view, there was stabilization only among the Christian Democratic Party and (with a temporal lag) the Socialist sections of the political class. In both cases, the rates of renewal of

TABLE 1.
Percentages of First-Term Members in the Three Major
Italian Parties (DC, PSI, PCI)*

Election Year	DC	PSI	PCI
1948	46	60	67
1953	30	47	28
1958	35	38	37
1963	22	31	49
1968	31	36	46
1972	22	28	47
1976	42	25	56
1979	19	45	23

*The parties are referred to by acronym. DC is Christian Democrats; PCI, the Italian
Communist Party; PSI, the Italian Socialist Party.
Source: Cotta, Classe politica e parlamento in Italia, p. 324.

the parliamentary class showed a clearly declining trend and reached
levels that are under the average for the whole Parliament. They also
remained rather stable. Only the 1976 election for the DC and the
1979 election for the PSI caused an unusually high level of circulation, as a consequence of internal struggles for the leadership of the
two parties.

On the contrary, starting from the 1958 election, the Communist
parliamentary group was characterized by increasing levels of renewal which were significantly higher than the average. Only the
1979 election showed a dramatic change in this pattern; but it is too
early to say whether this change is of an idiosyncratic nature, explained by the unanticipated call for an election (two years before
the natural expiration of the legislature) or whether it inaugurates a
new phase in the recruitment policy of the PCI. The consequences
of such different patterns of elite circulation are more clearly ap-
praised by examining the seniority structure of the three parliamentary groups (see Figure 3).

While in the first two parties the lower turnover rates produced a
parliamentary class in which the senior legislators increasingly balanced the junior members (reaching in 1972 almost a 50:50 ratio), in
the PCI the institutionally younger component was by far dominant
in quantitative terms and even increased its share with the passing
of time (reaching a maximum of 82 percent in 1972). The heterogeneity is striking, even more so if one compares it with the German
case, which, as Figure 4 indicates, is historically similar.

Can we then conclude against Mosca's suggested general law that
in the Italian experience a large (and in this case increasing) section
of the political class was exempt from the tendency to stabilize and
perpetuate itself? If the quantitative data seem to support this hy-

FIGURE 4.
Seniority Structure of the German Bundestag and of the Two Larger
Parties (CDU-CSU and SPD)

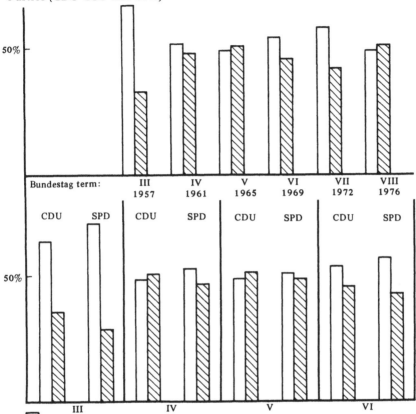

□ Junior legislators (1 or 2 terms)

▨ Senior legislators (3 or more terms)

pothesis, a more qualitative analysis immediately raises some doubts. Both looking at the sociological profile (i.e., the social background) and at the political profile (i.e., recruitment and political career) of the political class, one can see a greater qualitative continuity in the Communist political class, in spite of the extensive quantitative circulation, than among Christian Democratic politicians.[66] One must then assume that the reproduction of the political class was ensured in this specific case through a mechanism different from that of a slow renewal rate among members of the parliamentary group. Further evidence supporting this interpretation can be gained from an analysis of the political behavior of the Communist political class. None of the signs of disruption of its collective cohesion that one might expect from such a high level of turnover was apparent during this period. No major internal dissensions became manifest in the Communist parliamentary group (except for a minor split in the late 1960s); nor has this group shown the tactical rigidity which is often the external sign of a political class that has not reached an internal homogeneity or consensus.

The most promising answer to the question of the stabilization of the Communist political class is that one has to look not at the parliamentary but at the party component, i.e., at the politicians holding the leading offices of the national organization of the PCI. In fact, the stability there has been greater. What is more, it increases as one examines successively higher levels of the political class. Thus, at the level of the membership of the national party assembly, the Central Committee, the average percentage of newcomers at each congress is around 30 percent.[67] But moving upward to the smaller and more powerful *Direzione*, the average percentage of newcomers drops to 21 percent. At the highest level, that of the chairman of the Party, the stability becomes extreme. From the fall of Fascism (but one might as well go back to the 1930's) until now, the PCI has had only three chairmen (Togliatti, Longo, Berlinguer), while the DC in the same period has had eleven and the Socialist Party, seven.

Indeed, the political class which emerged in Italy with the new democratic regime has undergone a process of stabilization, which, while allowing for a certain degree of circulation and renewal, has on the whole put a premium on continuity. The latter aspect is far from exceptional if one looks at established democratic politics. It can also be considered as evidence that in Italy the effects of the democratic breakdown and the authoritarian interval have been overcome. A more peculiar aspect of Italian politics in the period discussed is the fact that the stabilization of the political class has followed two divergent models. Following the first model, which is typical of the DC and of the PSI, this process has been, to a high degree, *parliament-oriented*. It has meant a strict and long-term relationship between parliamentary institutions and political elites; without excluding the role of external party organizations, it has, to some extent, balanced their weight and determined a "dualistic" orientation of the political class. The other model, typical of the PCI, has relied much more heavily on the external party organization for ensuring the continuity of the political class. Except for a minority of Communist politicians, the parliamentary experience has been, in general, a short-term political engagement for this section of the Italian political class.

Explaining the reasons for these differences would require an *ad hoc* discussion focusing on the peculiarities of the Communist party-type and on the permanent opposition role which the PCI has played in the post-Fascist period. As for the consequences of this situation, it is not totally unwarranted to suggest that these differences, which go to the heart of the structure of the political class, have been partly responsible (together with other variables, such as the fragmentation of the party system, the ideological polarization, etc.) for the low levels of decisional effectiveness of the Italian political system, well documented by a number of recent studies.[68] This would hardly be surprising. A political class structured according to contrasting models which reflect different attitudes toward the institutional framework of the existing regime will necessarily encounter great difficulties in cooperating within this institutional framework and in making it work.

After this inevitably cursory discussion of two important periods of recent Italian political history, it is time to draw some tentative conclusions. We started with a number of cues offered by the classic theory of political elites, particularly by Mosca and Pareto. Even if their theoretical formulations may leave us doubtful as to their value as rigorous empirical generalizations, we have seen that they may still be powerfully suggestive, particularly by calling attention to a broader analytical perspective relating the study of elites to the momentous questions of regime change and regime survival. The analysis developed here has touched upon two periods of Italian history— one ending with the crisis and fall of the old democracy, the other starting with the inauguration of a new democratic regime—when regime-related questions have been particularly serious and have played a much larger role in political life than they have done in more stable countries. The evidence presented suggests that studying the dynamic processes of elite circulation may offer a useful point of view for casting further light upon such critical junctures in the life of a political system. In particular, attention has been focused on the rates of renewal of the political elites, the changes they undergo during these transitional phases, and the consequences these factors have on the internal structure of a political class and its balance of continuity and discontinuity, old and new. These features of a political class appear critically related to the ability of the institutions of a democratic regime (especially Parliament and government) to establish themselves and to work according to their constitutional role.

An analysis based on the Italian case alone cannot pretend to establish sufficiently well-grounded generalizations. What we have gained from it is more in the nature of hypotheses and stimulation for further research. Three themes, in particular, would deserve further discussion and a comparative verification. The first concerns the relationship between elite circulation and the stability of a democratic regime. The Italian experience suggests that a very large and abrupt renewal of the parliamentary elites may be a factor contributing to the crisis of democracy in that it brings about an institutional disruption of the central and very delicate structures of the regime itself: primarily Parliament, but also the executive in a parliamentary system. What would require further empirical testing are the thresholds beyond which the negative effects of a large renewal of political elites manifest themselves and the contextual conditions that may enhance or counterbalance such effects. But attention should also be given to the relationship between quantitative and qualitative change in the political elites, since one is likely to find there crucial elements for determining the greater or lesser destabilizing impact of elite circulation.

The second theme concerns the relationship between restoration of the democratic regime after years of authoritarian rule and reconstruction of a democratic political class. For the extremely delicate transition phase between the two regimes, the process by which the new political class becomes structured is obviously crucial. It is, in fact, this political class which will guide and sustain the transition itself. In this phase, characterized by a situation of institutional uncertainty, an early consolidation of a sufficiently clear authority structure within the political class seems a particularly important condition for a successful inauguration of the new regime. The Italian example offers some evidence for the strategic role the survivors of the old democratic elite can play in guiding the first steps of the restoration of democracy, without preventing the co-optation of a large number of new politicians in the following years. On this point, a comparison should be attempted with political experiences where the restoration of democracy could not count upon this element of continuity with the past. Does this make the "learning" of democratic procedures and behavior more difficult?

The third theme to which the Italian case draws attention concerns the long-term process of consolidation of the political class which emerges with the restored democracy. The Italian experience of the first thirty years of the new regime suggests that both in the timing and in the nature of this process the political class of a country may display remarkable differences. In particular, we have seen that the central role in the process of consolidation may be played by different political structures (Parliament, party organizations). What needs to be explored more thoroughly, through comparative research, are the factors explaining this structural heterogeneity in the political class and the effects it has on the working of the central institutions of democracy.

Summing up, the directions of further research to which these themes call attention, if we want to better understand the relationship between political elites and democratic regimes, are the factors governing the "reproduction" process of the political class and the impact that changes in the political class have upon structure and working conditions of the central institutions of democracy.

Notes

1. See Lewis J. Edinger and D. D. Searing, "Social Background in Elite Analysis: A Methodological Inquiry," *American Political Science Review* 57 (1968); Uwe Schleth, "Once Again: Does It Pay to Study Social Background in Elite Analysis?" *Sozialwissenschaftliches Jahrbuch für Politik* 1 (1971); and Klaus von Beyme, "Elite Input and Policy Output: The Case of Germany," in *Does Who Governs Matter? Studies in Elite Circulation,* ed. Moshe Czudnowski (DeKalb, Ill.: Northern Illinois University Press, 1982).

2. See Giovanni Sartori, "Dove va il Parlamento," in *Il Parlamento Italiano* (Naples, ESI, 1963); Mattei Dogan, "Les filières de la carrière politique en France," *Revue française de Sociologie* 8 (1967); Kjell A. Eliassen and M. N. Pedersen, "Professionalization of Legislatures: Long-term Change in Political Recruitment in Denmark and Norway," *Comparative Studies in Society and History* 20 (1978); and Mogens Pedersen, *Political Development and Elite Transformation in Denmark* (Berkeley: Sage, 1976).

3. See Nelson Polsby, "The Institutionalization of the U.S. House of Representatives," *American Political Science Review* 58 (1968); Mogens Pedersen, "The Personal Circulation of a Legislature: The Danish Folketing, 1849–1968," unpublished manuscript, Institute of Political Science, University of Aarhus, 1972; and Gerhard Loewenberg, "The Institutionalization of Parliament and Public Orientation to the Political System," in *Legislatures in Comparative Perspective,* ed. A. Kornberg (New York: McKay, 1973).

4. Among these efforts, at least the following should be mentioned: Mattei Dogan, "La Stabilité du Personnel Parlementaire sous la Troisième République," *Revue Française de Science Politique* 3 (1953); Dogan, "Les filières de la carrière politique en France"; Juan J. Linz, "Continuidad y discontinuidad en la elite politica española de la Restauracion al regimen actual," in *Libro Homenaje al Professor Carlos Ollero: Estudios de ciencia politica y sociología* (Guadalajara: Gráficas Carlavilla, 1972); Wolfgang Zapf, *Wandlunger de deutschen Elite* (Munich: Piper, 1966); and Paolo Farneti, *Sistema politica e società civile* (Turin: Giappichelli, 1971).

5. The first formulation Gaetano Mosca gave of the theory of the ruling class was in his *Teorica dei governi e governo parlamentare,* first published in 1884. The full development of the theory is in his later work, *Elementi di scienza politica,* published in 1896. For this discussion, the fifth edition (Bari, Italy: Laterza, 1953) is used. Pareto's main work on his theory of elites is found in the second volume of the *Trattato di sociologia generale,* first published in 1916. (This discussion uses the third edition [Milan: Comunitá, 1964] as the reference text.) Some anticipations also appear, however, in his *Systèmes socialistes,* published in 1902.

6. Pareto, *Trattato di sociologia generale,* vol. 2, p. 534.

7. Mosca, *Elementi di scienza politica,* vol. 1, pp. 102 ff., and 2, p. 97.

8. Mosca, *Elementi di scienza politica,* vol. 1, pp. 95 ff.

9. Ibid., p. 100.

10. Ibid., pp. 101 ff.

11. Ibid., p. 155.

12. Mosca, *Elementi di scienza politica,* vol. 2, p. 125.

13. Pareto, *Trattato di sociologia generale*, vol. 2, pp. 623 and 667.

14. Ibid., pp. 539 ff., 623, 894 ff.

15. Ibid., pp. 623–26.

16. The chronological delimitation of the first two periods may be a matter of some dispute, since the transition between the two regimes requires a number of steps. The years between 1922 (first Mussolini cabinet) and 1926 (expulsion of opposition members from Parliament and disbandment of all parties except the Fascist) can be seen as a "gray area" during which the transition to nondemocratic rule becomes more and more irreversible.

17. Farneti, *Sistema politico e società civile*, p. 195.

18. Dogan, "La Stabilité du Personnel Parlementaire sous la Troisième République," p. 322.

19. Linz gives the following percentages of newcomers: 31 percent in the 1907 Cortes, 34 percent in 1910, 30 percent in 1914 ("Continuidad y discontinuidad en la elite politica española de la Restauracion al regimen actual," pp. 369–70).

20. Polsby, "The Institutionalization of the U.S. House of Representatives," p. 146.

21. Loewenberg, *Parliament in the German Political System*, p. 146.

22. Domenico Novacco points out that, of the 508 members of the previous legislature, 203 did not even run again for reelection, and 126 were defeated (*Storia del Parlamento Italiano*, vol. 12 [Palermo, Flaccovio, 1967]).

23. The election of 1924 should be evaluated with some caution, since it took place under conditions of diffuse violence and the competition was far from fair. However, since it was not entirely faked and some degree of pluralism was still allowed, it most not be completely disregarded. Its result may help to understand the further steps of the authoritarian takeover.

24. Loewenberg, "The Institutionalization of Parliament and Public Orientation to the Political System," p. 146.

25. Linz, "Continuidad y discontinuidad en la elite politica española de la Restauracion al regimen actual," pp. 394–99.

26. Loewenberg, "The Institutionalization of Parliament and Public Orientation to the Political System," p. 146.

27. Dogan, "La Stabilité du Personnel Parlementaire sous la Troisième République," p. 322.

28. It is interesting to note that among the important political changes produced by the great wars of this century, a larger circulation of political elites is in many countries a common feature.

29. Juan J. Linz, *The Breakdown of Democratic Regimes: Crisis, Breakdown and Reequilibration* (Baltimore: Johns Hopkins University Press, 1978).

30. See Polsby, "The Institutionalization of the U.S. House of Representatives," p. 146; and Loewenberg, "The Institutionalization of Parliament and Public Orientation to the Political System," pp. 145–46.

31. On this point, see Luigi Lotti, "Il Parlamento Italiano, 1909–1963: Raffronto storico," in *Il Parlamento Italiano*, ed. G. Sartori (Naples, ESI, 1963); and Paolo Farneti, "The Italian Parliamentary Elite from Liberal-

ism to Democracy" (Paper presented at the Joint Sessions of the European Consortium for Political Research, Grenoble, 1978).

32. Neither of the parties felt a special allegiance (in this case, rather, a straightforward hostility) toward the monarchical institution. A clear manifestation of this attitude took place when, at the opening of the Parliament, the Socialist legislators left the Chamber at the moment of the King's speech. While such a behavior might have gone almost unnoticed in the past, when the Socialist party was only a minor group, its delegitimizing effect was at this time much greater.

33. It is, in fact, more appropriate to speak of political areas (conservative, liberal, democratic), since the map of the single groups during these years underwent a continuous process of reshuffling along a trend of increasing fragmentation. (See Paolo Farneti, "Social Conflict, Parliamentary Fragmentation, Institutional Shift, and the Rise of Fascism: Italy," in The Breakdown of Democratic Regimes: Europe, ed. Juan J. Linz and Alfred Stepan [Baltimore: Johns Hopkins University Press, 1978], pp. 23 ff.)

34. The effects of this situation were particularly serious for the process of coalition making (which is indispensable for building cabinets). The relations between the old liberal parliamentary leaders and the dualistic leadership of the mass parties were for structural reasons extremely difficult, since the two political elites "lived" under different institutional constraints.

35. The PSI had only 52 deputies in 1913 (10 percent of the lower chamber); a Catholic party did not even exist before 1919; and only a few "Catholic" legislators had been elected through agreements with the Liberal and Conservative parties (the so-called "Patto Gentiloni").

36. Farneti, "The Italian Parliamentary Elite from Liberalism to Democracy," p. 16.

37. In the 1919–1921 legislature, out of 60 requests considered by the Chamber of Deputies, 29 had such a political-institutional character. In the following legislature, 57 out of 106 were of the same nature. In the 1909–1913 legislature, by comparison, the number was only 3 out of 116. (See the reports of the secretaries general of the 1913, 1921, and 1924 Chambers of Deputies.)

38. Camera dei Deputati, La XXVI Legislatura (Rome: Segretariato Generale della Camera dei Deputati, 1924), p. 106.

39. Giuseppe Spataro, I democratici cristiani dalla dittatura alla repubblica (Milan: Mondadori, 1968), pp. 41 ff.

40. Starting with the twenty-first legislature (1900–1904), the success rates for government bills introduced in the lower chamber were as follows: twenty-first legislature: 70 percent (out of 882 bills); twenty-second legislature: 88 percent (out of 933); twenty-third legislature: 89 percent (out of 1,111); twenty-fourth legislature: 33 percent (out of 1,157); twenty-fifth legislature: 13 percent (out of 1,078); twenty-sixth legislature: 33 percent (out of 1,551) (Camera dei Deputati, Manuale dei Deputati per la XXVII Legislatura [Rome: Camera dei Deputati, 1924], pp. 1086–87).

41. Spataro, I democratici cristiani dalla dittatura alla repubblica, pp. 81 ff.

42. Farneti, "Social Conflict, Parliamentary Fragmentation, Institutional Shift, and the Rise of Fascism," p. 26 ff.

43. Michael R. King and Lester G. Seligman, "Critical Elections, Congressional Recruitment and Public Policy," in *Elite Recruitment in Democratic Politics*, ed. Heinz Eulau and Moshe Czudnowski (Sage Publications, 1976).

44. Mosca, *Elementi di scienza politica*, vol. 1, p. 101.

45. Ibid., pp. 94 ff; and Pareto, *Trattato di sociologia generale*, vol. 2, pp. 899 ff.

46. Mosca, *Elementi di scienza politica*, vol. 1, p. 95.

47. See, for instance, Polsby, "The Institutionalization of the U.S. House of Representatives"; Loewenberg, "The Institutionalization of Parliament and Public Orientation to the Political System"; and Richard Sisson, "Comparative Legislative Institutionalization: A Theoretical Explanation," in *Legislatures in Comparative Perspective*, ed. A. Kornberg (New York: McKay, 1973).

48. Maurizio Cotta, *Classe politica e parlamento in Italia* (Bologna: Il Mulino, 1979), p. 152. Where highly organized mass parties have not developed, the role of family ties may be even larger, as the Greek case shows (see Keith Legg, "Restoration Elites: Regime Change in Greece," in *Does Who Governs Matter?*, ed. M. Czudnowski, pp. 188–213.

49. The survivors of the Francoist regime are a rather large group in the Spanish constituent assembly elected in 1977; moreover, their weight is concentrated in two parties: *Alianza Popular* and UCD (Salustiano del Campo, J. F. Tezanos, and W. Santin, "The Spanish Elite: Permanancy and Change," in *Does Who Governs Matter?*, ed. M. Czudnowski, p. 125–153.

50. Leonardo Morlino, *Come cambiano i regime politici* (Milan: Angeli, 1980), pp. 86 ff.

51. Many of the old legislators are appointed *de jure* to the upper chamber (*Senato*) for its first term. In the Senate, the continuity is, therefore, larger.

52. Deutscher Bundestag, *Die Mitglieder des deutschen Bundestages: I.–VI. Wahlperiode* (Bonn: Deutscher Bundestag Wissenschaftliche Dienste, 1971), pp. 154 ff.

53. Patrice Manigand, "Les Députés de la IV République" (Paper presented at the Joint Sessions of the European Consortium for Political Research, Grenoble, 1978), p. 8.

54. Linz, "Continuidad y discontinuidad en la elite politica española de la Restauracion al regimen actual," p. 387.

55. In the French case, another factor that made for a large discontinuity was the fact that the members of the 1936 Parliament who had supported the Pétain government were legally precluded from reelection.

56. Legg, "Restoration Elites," in *Does Who Governs Matter?*, ed. M. Czudnowski, p. 188–213.

57. In September 1945, a consultative assembly (*Consulta Nazionale*) was created, but it was not an elective body. Its members had been designated by parties, economic organizations, or *de jure*. The proportion of pre-Fascist politicians was rather high—27 percent (Lotti, "Il Parlamento Italiano, 1909–1963," p. 147).

58. Cotta, *Classe politica e parlamento in Italia*, pp. 66 ff.

59. It should not be forgotten that the guerrilla movement took place only in northern and central Italy under German occupation, while the government was in southern Italy under Allied occupation.

60. The first Badoglio cabinet (July 1943–April 1944) was a "nonpolitical" cabinet, in the sense that the parties did not take part in it, and its members were mainly high bureaucrats.

61. Under this label, we consider the members of the national directive bodies of the parties which were formed in these years and which were not elected by regular party congresses. The first regular party congresses took place at the beginning of 1946.

62. Giovanni Schepis, *Le consultazioni popolari in Italia dal 1948 al 1957* (Empoli: Caparrini, 1958), p. 98.

63. For the U.S. House of Representatives, Polsby gives an average of first-term members of 17 percent in the elections between 1945 and 1965 ("The Institutionalization of the U.S. House of Representatives," p. 146). For the British House of Commons, the average level of renewal after the election of 1945 (which, coming after ten years, produces a very high level of renewal) is not very different (Gerhard Loewenberg, *Parliament in the German Political System* [Ithaca, N.Y.: Cornell University Press, 1967], p. 88).

64. Manigand, "Les Députés de la IV République," p. 10.

65. In the German *Bundestag*, the percentages of newcomers are as follows: 46 (1953); 34 (1957); 25 (1961); 25 (1965); 30 (1969); 29 (1972); 23 (1976) (Deutscher Bundestag, *Mitglieder Struktur des deutschen Bundestages: I.–VII. Wahlperiode* [Bonn: Deutscher Bundestag Wissenschaftliche Dienste], p. 3; Kürschners *Volkshandbuch, Deutscher Bundestag, VII Wahlperiode* [Darmstadt: Neue Darmstadter Verlanganstalt, 1977]). In Japan, in the lower chamber after the high turnovers of the first elections (47 percent in 1947 and 41 percent in 1949), the stability of the parliamentary elite is very high (23 percent newcomers in 1952, 10 percent in 1953; 12 percent in 1955; 14 percent in 1957; 13 percent in 1960; 14.5 percent in 1963; 21 percent in 1967) (Henry Baerwald, *Japan's Parliament* [London: Cambridge University Press, 1974], pp. 276–77).

66. Cotta, *Classe politica e parlamento in Italia*, pp. 143 ff. and 154 ff.

67. Fulco Lanchester, "PCI: dirigenti e modelli di partito," *Città e Regione* 7 (1981), p. 86.

It should be noted that comparing party congresses with parliamentary elections is not illegitimate, since both have the function of electing a "parliamentary" body: the party national assembly (*Comitato Centrale*) in the first case, the "true" Parliament in the second. In the case of the PCI, the number of congresses held between 1946 and 1979 is not far from the number of political elections (ten against nine). This makes the comparison of turnover rates sufficiently meaningful.

68. See, for example, Franco Cazzola, *Governo e opposizione nel Parlamento italiano* (Milan: Giuffrè, 1974); Franca Cantelli, V. Mortara, and G. Movia, *Come lavora il Parlamento* (Milan: Giuffrè, 1974); and Giuseppe Di Palma, *Surviving without Governing* (Berkeley: University of California Press, 1977).

Restoration Elites:
Regime Change in Greece

Keith Legg

Since the beginning of this century, Greece and other Mediterranean countries have undergone significant regime changes: monarchies have given way to republics, and republics to monarchies; democracies have been replaced by authoritarian rule, and authoritarian rule by democracy. Major scholarly efforts have been directed to explaining conditions facilitating the emergence of authoritarian regimes or to describing their modes of governance.[1] Little consideration has been given to the opposite condition—the problem of democratic restoration. This essay examines continuity and change accompanying alternation of regimes in one Mediterranean country—modern Greece. The more specific concern is the effect of periods of authoritarian rule on political career patterns in the "restored" democratic systems.

Restorations are a special type of regime change. The concept of "restoration" implies a particular sequence of changes.[2] The "original" regime is replaced, usually in some irregular fashion, by a new and different one. Eventually this second regime is replaced, although occasionally in a more tranquil manner, as the "first" regime is "restored." Confusion may arise because the "second" regime may claim to be restoring values and institutions prevailing at some earlier time. In this sequence, the change encountered in the "restored" regime is likely to be inversely related to change produced by the intervening regime. If the "second" regime pursued far-reaching goals of social transformation, few of the values, institutions, or elite personnel of the "original" regime would be likely to survive unaltered. A "restoration" regime would most likely be marked by a similar sharp break with its predecessor. Actually, most regime changes produce modest alterations. The sequence of original regime, second regime, and restoration regime, although marked by political upheaval or discontinuity, may obscure an underlying continuity. This continuity is especially notable in economic, social, and cultural spheres, but some continuity is likely to exist even in the political world.

I. Regime Change: The Greek Case

Since the beginning of the century, there have been a number of political upheavals in Greece, but only two involved relatively long lapses from democracy, and thus qualify as regime changes. The first, the Metaxas dictatorship, lasted from 1936 until 1941; the second was the period of military rule from 1967 to 1974.

Greek politics, or indeed those of most other Mediterranean countries, operate on two levels.[3] One is the level of routine exchange relationships. Here patterns of political exchange, whether in parliament or outside, simply replicate those of the marketplace and other social sectors. These exchanges need not be perceived as mutually beneficial because one side might gain more than the other. The way to temper this war of all against all is to find refuge in the solidarity of the family and in patron-client relationships. Consequently, the routine level of politics is basically selfish and expedient. The other level is the heroic one, where individuals perform selfless acts on behalf of worthy causes. This pattern of activity surfaces in somewhat predictable social contexts, but it is also possible in national politics. In modern Greek history, the worthy cause has been the survival of a rather narrowly defined set of values encompassing certain cultural traditions and the orthodox faith. This second level is activated when these values are perceived to be threatened, either internally by Greeks not sharing them or when foreign elements are poised to attack. The guardian of national values is, of course, the military establishment.

The Metaxas Regime: 1936 to 1941

The Parliament elected in early 1936 was divided between the partisans and successors of Eleftherios Venizelos, the largely republican Liberals, and the largely royalist Populists. The balance of power was held by the small Communist party. The division between republicans and royalists was a bitter and enduring one, stemming from conflicts between Venizelos and King Constantine I over foreign alignment in World War I. The Liberal politicians tended to be drawn from the newly successful commercial and professional elements, and from the more recently acquired parts of the kingdom. The Populists were more likely to be men from old political families and to come from the original parts of the kingdom. By the 1930's, the major protagonists had passed from the scene, the two parties differed little on domestic policy, and both were constellations of individual politicians held together by personal ties and patronage.

The inability of either major party to form a government in the face of considerable social turmoil prompted King George II to appoint a nonpolitical prime minister.[4] General Metaxas, the leader of his own small right-wing party, was appointed Vice-Premier and given the Ministry of War. With the untimely death of the nonpolitical prime minister, the King called upon General Metaxas to assume the office in April 1936. The Parliament confirmed the appointment and agreed to a five-month adjournment to give the new government time to deal with pressing problems of social unrest.

Metaxas saw Communists as both causes and beneficiaries of these disturbances, and this perception was shared by the leaders of the major parties. "Heroic" measures were necessary, but they took longer than planned. Strikes and social unrest continued, and consequently, the king, upon request of Metaxas, dissolved the Parliament before it reassembled. Political parties were abolished, and martial law was imposed. The Regime of the 4th of August was in place. The Italian invasion, the German occupation, and the civil war further delayed the restoration of democracy until 1946.

The Metaxas regime, although often characterized as royalist, was really antipolitical. Metaxas initially justified his dictatorship as necessary to preserve Greece and Greek values from communism. Later, dictatorship was necessary because of international events that portended war. The heroic level of politics required collective opposition—both against internal enemies such as Communists and also to meet threats of foreign invasion. It meant an emphasis on cultural values that stressed internal harmony and differentiated Greeks from outsiders. There was a stress on patriotism, on past history, and on the Greek Orthodox faith. At the same time, other traditional values, those that lead to conflict (particularly those associated with bargaining and exchange), were depreciated.

The regime acted on these goals by closing the single political institution most associated with internal conflict, the Parliament, and abolishing political parties. Communists and others on the Left disappeared to jails, island exile, or underground, to await more propitious times. The traditional politicians, whose excesses and vanities had led Greece to the brink of Communist revolution, were sent into exile or retired to private life. The rest of the state apparatus remained intact. To be sure, ministries were divided, amalgamated, and new ones created, but this followed past practice. An attempt was made to create a national youth movement, but there was no attempt to create a single party on the Fascist model. The military was the preeminent unifying institution. King George II continued to reign.

Specific policies were also directed at emphasizing national unity. Press censorship, monitoring of theatrical performances, and close attention to the content of educational curricula were all aimed at suppressing "non-Greek" values and ideologies and strengthening "national" ones. The traditional bargaining relations of the market-place were attacked, since these were assumed to be a cause of social unrest and labor turmoil. Although not necessarily authoritarian in inspiration, laws were enacted fixing minimum wages, social insurance, and prices for essential commodities. Later, as the international financial position of Greece deteriorated, a full set of currency controls were also introduced. "Heroic" politics are hard to sustain, and the effect of greater regulation, with the discretion it implies, was ultimately to increase opportunities for exchange relationships—particularly for those involved with the state apparatus. Eventually, the Italian attack did induce national unity and legitimized the effort of Metaxas to impose heroic behavior on the population.

Since the regime didn't anticipate transforming national values or substantial institutional change, it is not surprising that the composition and character of the elite was relatively little changed. Throughout the period of republican and royalist controversy, two separate sets of officers, virtually indistinguishable in social background, had alternated in military position. With the restoration of the monarchy in 1935, the process of replacing republicans with royalists had begun, and this was completed under Metaxas. Individuals holding "political" positions and those closely identified with individual politicians or excessive republicanism were dismissed. Professors and students at the university unwilling to accept the government view of appropriate national values were also harassed, dismissed, and occasionally imprisoned. The economic elite, although chafing under higher taxes and government regulation, was certainly not disturbed. The leaders of Athenian society, although unimpressed with Metaxas and his wife because of their relatively humble social origins, were not penalized. The hierarchy of the Orthodox Church, always under government supervision, was left intact.

Quite clearly, the disappearance of parliamentary politics did not mean that the routines of political exchange outside the Parliament were eliminated. Moreover, the antipolitical stance of the regime did not mean the absence of politicians in positions of authority. A total of forty-five individuals held the posts of minister or deputy minister. Twenty-one of these individuals had sought parliamentary office in the past, and nine had actually served. Although apparently disruptive for the traditional political elites, the Metaxas period did not seriously alter patterns of life for other parts of the elite establishment or for the average citizen.

The Democratic Restoration of 1946

The major goal of the Metaxas regime—the strengthening and maintenance of national values—could not be rejected by a restored democracy.[5] In fact, occupation and the civil war rehabilitated the

Metaxas regime and its officials. The perception of Metaxas that the Communists were a threat to the nation had been given reality by the civil war. Other than the restoration of representative institutions, the goals of the democratic regime were imposed by conditions and events: the defeat of the Communist insurgents and economic recovery.

Consequently, institutional alteration was slight. The royalist-republican controversy simmered, but a plebiscite, although disputed, retained the monarchy. The 1935 revision of the 1911 constitution remained in force until a revision was completed in 1952. The highly centralized state apparatus, staffed with the same career officials, remained in place.

The restoration Parliament was the visible center of politics. The office of prime minister and ministerial position were once again the major prizes in the game of politics. Ministries increased in number, in part because of greater demands on government, but in part because new places were needed for patronage purposes. The competition for personal power and position—the routines of political exchange—again marked political life. Although the civil war still required a commitment to heroic politics, the politics of exchange predominated. The civil war was successfully concluded by the military, aided by fortuitous external events, in spite of parliamentary politics. The military and the monarchy, institutional symbols of a narrowly defined nationalism, were always ready to manipulate parliamentary factions to insure against redefinitions of that nationalism. They remained important political actors even in a restored democracy.

The antipolitical mentality of the Metaxas regime was gone, but the democratic leadership retained a definition of "national" that excluded the Left. Rules of electoral eligibility and systems of election were subject to revision. Not only did this permit rules that diminished the possibilities for electoral successes of the Left, it was also useful against traditional political opponents. The 1952 revision of the 1911 constitution was less liberal in the realm of civil rights than the 1927 republican constitution. The decrees and police regulations enacted on top of those from the Metaxas era during the 1947–1949 civil war remained available for use until at least 1963.

Although the usual civil rights—freedom of the press, right of assembly, and free speech—existed on paper, the extensive repertoire of legal restrictions and exemptions, together with possibilities for discretionary enforcement, were used to suppress undesired opinion. Certificates of social belief, secured from the local police and clergy, insured that supporters of the Left were excluded from state employment. Penalties for insults against authority, control of newsprint allocations and newspaper distribution, variable enforcement of health, safety, and labor legislation, and even violence "unnoticed" by the state authorities were all instruments of restored democratic politics. Just as the exigencies of elite political bargaining encouraged a luxuriant bureaucratic growth to increase otherwise scant political resources, so too did the possibilities of discretionary enforcement of regulations.[6]

The bias of the restored regime was toward maintaining politics as usual, but within a particular definition of the Greek nation. There was no interest in transforming or altering the state apparatus or the contours of civil society. Social and economic changes did take place, some very rapidly, but not as a result of rationally designed public policy. The wealthy remained wealthy and the poor remained poor, although there were occasionally dramatic changes of fortune. Refugee Greeks from Turkey still inhabited the ramshackle Athenian suburbs, but they were now joined by other refugees produced by the civil war and later by poor villagers drawn by the attractions of the city. Intellectual and social circles were hardly altered, unless an individual was tainted by left-wing views and sympathies.

The relationship of the restored political elite to the state apparatus and civil society continued as before. Labor and associational life continued to be manipulated and controlled through forms of political exchange. The economic elite was factionalized; the pattern of economic competition simply replicated political competition. One part of the political elite utilized the state apparatus and public policy in the form of tariff protection, state subsidies, import licenses, taxation, and credit to gain support from some sector of the economic elite. As a result, when electoral shifts occurred, the new governors were allied with a different set of industrialists, businessmen, bankers, and shipowners.

The political elite after 1946 looked remarkably similar to that of the pre-authoritarian period, and there was even some continuity from the Metaxas period. Of the forty-five ministers or deputy ministers from that period, over one third ran for parliamentary office in 1946 or afterward (and it should be remembered that a portion of the original forty-five were either dead or very old by 1946). Seven were elected, among them the former Minister of Public Security.

Cabinet ministers in the restored democracy were hard to distinguish from those of the pre-Metaxas period in terms of occupational backgrounds and family political connections.[7] The restored Parliament also looked very much like its predecessor of 1936. Although reliable data on family backgrounds are lacking, the occupational distributions within the 1936 and 1946 Parliaments are quite similar.[8] Social and political mobility did occur, but the social background of the political elite in general remained relatively constant. The one feature that did change, the increased advantage for those with political backgrounds, suggests a restriction of recruitment opportunity and a less open political elite.

The Military Regime of 1967 to 1974

The conditions preceding the military coup of April 1967 were reminiscent of those leading to the earlier installation of the Metaxas dictatorship: a period of parliamentary instability, a perception that left and "non-national" elements were becoming influential, mass agitation and labor unrest, the involvement of the king in parliamentary politics. The coup was undertaken by a group of army colonels with troop commands in the Athens area and ties to the Greek central intelligence agency. The reason for the move, according to the justifications first produced, was the imminent Communist threat. Later explanations and elaborations emphasized the incapacities of parliamentary politicians to deal with pressing social and economic problems, as well as the inefficient, corrupt, and unjust operation of state institutions.[9]

In fact, the election scheduled for late April and the likelihood of a victory for George Papandreou and his Center Union party were the catalysts. Papandreou was very much a traditional politician, at home with familiar patterns of political exchange. His son and heir apparent, Andreas Papandreou, was the problem. Andreas Papandreou had promoted the lifting of political restrictions against the extreme Left, and, more seriously, he had questioned the role of the military and the monarchy as guardians of national values and their role in the political process. Further discomfort had been produced by his criticism of the United States and benefits of continued involvement in NATO. The electoral success of the Center Union would result in modifications in the relationship between the heroic and routine levels of Greek politics.

The colonels had no coherent ideology, but several themes—largely echoes from the Metaxas period—were constant. The heroic and self-sacrificing role of the military was compared to the self-seeking and corrupt character of parliamentary politics. Once again the uniqueness of the Greek nation, both in terms of religion and past history, was emphasized, particularly as a yardstick against which to separate the loyal from the disloyal, the vigorous from the decadent. In addition, there was a populist edge to the rhetoric that conveyed a dislike of the wealthy and well-born and a contempt for intellectuals straying from "true" cultural values. Quite clearly, the values and preferences expressed by the military leaders reflected their village backgrounds and limited intellectual horizons.

The Parliament remained closed and parties banned—politicians imprisoned, exiled, or sent home. A new constitution promulgated and approved in 1968 remained largely inoperative until 1973. This constitution gave the military the right to supervise and intervene in parliamentary politics, but elections and civilian rule were still required. A bloody confrontation between students at the Athens

Polytechnic and the military in November 1973 aborted even these tentative steps toward civilian rule. Eventually, real power was concentrated in the hands of troop commanders in the Athens area and the head of the military police. Representative institutions aside, state structures remained largely as before.

Indeed, in the first years of the regime, even personnel shifts were minimal. The military presence was apparent in appointments to the position of secretary-general in individual ministries, a crucial position usually filled by political appointees. As time passed, as opposition and bureaucratic recalcitrance increased, more substantial personnel changes were made. This was most evident in the judicial system and in higher state councils. Since the leaders of the Orthodox Church were viewed as at least partly responsible for the progress of moral decay in the country, elderly bishops were forced to retire, a new Primate of Greece and a new ruling synod appointed. The normal personnel turnover because of deaths, retirement, and resignations over the seven years of military rule provided substantial opportunity for change. Despite the necessity of approval by the military leaders, replacement nearly always came from inside the ministry or public agency.[10] After the departure of the king and his entourage, those high-ranking officers viewed as close to the monarchy were dismissed or retired. This produced significant opportunities for advancement throughout the officer corps.

Disruption in the economic and social world was limited and temporary. In the first months of the regime, a campaign against tax evasion—directed mainly at wealthy businessmen and professionals—increased tax revenue by 25 percent. After this, the relationships between the business world and the government fell into familiar patterns of political exchange. The peasantry, perhaps not displeased with the apparent assault on Athenian privilege, was also rewarded: peasant debts to the Agricultural Bank were cancelled. Labor in both public and private employment gained financially from pay increases that out-distanced increases in the cost of living but in return lost the right to strike. Above all, the military gained in pay and perquisites.[11]

The intellectual world, a usual forum for dissent, was more directly affected. A few newspapers ceased operations, and those remaining had to publish with care. However, government supervision varied—foreign publications were readily available, and domestic dissent could be disguised in fiction and in reports of foreign events. Institutions of higher education were suspect since individual faculty members and students were in early opposition to the regime. For that reason, government representatives were added to monitor the activities of deans, faculty, and students. New textbooks reflecting the biases and values of the military rulers were authorized.

There were six fairly substantial cabinet changes in this period.

Although the proportion of military officers in ministerial position varies, this does not mean that military control diminished. It is striking, however, that these cabinets were not collections of unknowns, but men of prominence from the judicial system, the bureaucracy, and the academic world. One hundred individuals held office as ministers or deputy ministers during the period of military rule. Fifteen had run for parliamentary office in the past, and nine of these had actually served as members of Parliament. On the whole, these individuals had been associated with right-wing party politics. Several had become involved in elective politics after retirement from bureaucratic careers. (Two ran again after the restoration, and one was elected in 1977.)

The occupational backgrounds were not dissimilar to those found among the members of cabinets during the Metaxas period. There was a large bloc of career civil servants and another of military officers, a sizable contingent of academics, and a sprinkling of professional and technical people. Many had begun careers during the Metaxas period. Only one individual was clearly identified as part of the economic elite. Approximately one half of the cabinet members were prominent enough by the mid-1960's to be listed in a Who's Who published in 1965. Although occupational data for twenty-eight individuals is unavailable, it is known that they were not previously involved in parliamentary politics. They appear to be middle-level bureaucrats who occupied positions of deputy minister. Incomplete biographical data prevent assessments of family political backgrounds.

Several developments during the period of military rule did have long-term consequences. The involvement of military officers in civilian administration and the easy access of others to power soon eroded the military's sense of self-sacrifice. As corruption became more evident and threatened professional standards, tension and factionalism within the military increased. Although some officers, including the prime minister George Papadopoulos, resigned their commissions, the military could no longer be regarded by most of the population as a more virtuous institution than the Parliament, and its activities were certainly no longer heroic. The other institution with heroic possibilities, the monarchy, had been abolished in 1973 and replaced by a powerful presidency designed by Papadopoulos for himself. The attempt to regain heroic stature through armed intervention in Cyprus eight months later was an utter failure. The result was a voluntary abdication of the military from formal political power.

The Democratic Restoration of 1974

The transfer of power from military to civilian leadership occurred at a moment when heroic politics were required. However, it was a traditional politician, Constantine Karamanlis, who was called from voluntary exile in France to fill the role. The major problem was a nationalist one. However, now, instead of a threat from domestic Communists, the threat was from outside. There was a serious threat of war in the aftermath of the Turkish invasion and partition of Cyprus. Consequently, the transition to civilian rule was accomplished without serious upheaval, and a government of national unity was selected to serve until elections could be held. Given the national crisis, no immediate action was taken against the military leaders of the authoritarian regime. Eventually the major conspirators were imprisoned, but others seriously involved were dismissed discretely, "mingled with normal promotions and retirements in such a way as to avoid head-on challenge of the will and collective morale of the officer corps."[12]

Another reason for the tranquil change was simply that most members of the political, economic, and social elite had made arrangements of one sort or another with the military regime in order to maintain their wealth and power. The routines of traditional political exchange had come to link these elements with the military itself. Only a minority had consistently opposed the regime, and some had taken considerable personal risk to challenge it. The vast majority of average citizens had simply accepted it.

Karamanlis did take the lead in redefining national values so that the Left and extreme Left could be considered parts of the national community. External pressures on the military regime, particularly from Europeans concerned with civil rights, made it difficult for a democratic government to continue restrictions on the Communists. In addition, the split of the Greek Communist party into two wings, one "Eurocommunist" and the other oriented toward the Soviet Union, lessened the likelihood of Communist electoral success.

The constitution produced under the colonels was junked, and the 1952 constitution restored. The restoration of the monarchy remained controversial until a plebiscite in December 1974 settled the issue. Over 60 percent of the voters opted for a republican form of government. The king was replaced by a president with limited and largely ceremonial powers. This institutional alteration was significant because the alliance of the military and monarchy existing prior to 1974 could not be reestablished. Not only had the interlude of authoritarian government undermined the status of the military as a "nonpolitical" guardian of national values and institutions, but the loss of the monarchy removed a major point of leverage on the traditional political world.

The rest of the institutional landscape changed very little. Some individuals clearly identified with the military regime were forced out of the state apparatus, and others removed by the colonels were reinstated. The practice of planting state representatives in the administrative hierarchies of educational institutions was abolished.

The hierarchy of the Orthodox church was shaken up once again. However, intellectual life blossomed anew. Those in command of the economic sectors remained in place. A policy of encouraging private enterprise, both foreign and domestic, had flourished throughout the pre-authoritarian period; the colonels had not interfered, and neither did the new regime. Since the routines of individual exchange were not restored to political institutions, they were unlikely to be curbed in the marketplace. Although some portions of the economic elite might be damaged by Greek entrance to the Common Market, this could not be blamed on the transition to democracy.

There were twenty individuals holding cabinet positions after the elections of 1974. Only seven, including the prime minister, had held regular cabinet office before. Unlike past political cabinets, there were four individuals with largely nonpolitical backgrounds, among them a professional diplomat and university professors. (Several had served in nonpolitical, caretaker governments before.) Four individuals with prior parliamentary experience made their first appearance as cabinet officers, and five others became ministers upon their first election to Parliament. Although the men with prior cabinet service had some claims to appointment on the basis of parliamentary tenure and expertise, the new appointments seem to have depended on personal connections with the prime minister. Certainly they were not based on seniority, parliamentary tenure, political experience, or technical expertise. More interesting, of the twenty cabinet members, nine came from political families. Of the five ministers without prior parliamentary experience, three came from political families. These appointments tend to confirm the continued clientelist orientation of the major political party, the New Democracy Party of the then Prime Minister Constantine Karamanlis.

The institutional impact of the democratic restoration on the life of the average citizen was probably slight. The more basic political dynamics, however, were significantly altered, not only in comparison with the military regime but also in comparison with the previous democratic one. The monarch was gone, the military partially discredited, ānd those on the Left were no longer marked as political pariahs. This meant that the mechanisms permitting the activation of heroic politics were dismantled, and the routines of political exchange were clearly ascendant. Some participants, particularly those on the "rehabilitated" Left and some more moderate, had demands that could not be accommodated through traditional politics.

II. Regime Change and Political Career Continuity

The closing of representative institutions and the abolition of political parties are standard procedures for authoritarian regimes. However, legal abolition of parties does not necessarily mean their disappearance. Politics as a mode of activity does not stop, and politicians do not take up other professions. After all, few authoritarian regimes claim permanence; there is always the presumption that democratic politics will be restored and parties will again play visible and influential roles in the political process. Two factors seem to influence the ability of parties to survive. One is related to party organization. The other is simply time—how long does authoritarian rule last?

Most political parties in Mediterranean countries can be classified as either bureaucratic or traditional "notable" organizations. (Some parties combine aspects of both.) The bureaucratic party has visible and formal organization, an identifiable ideology, and probably significant mass membership. Parliamentary participation is usually only one activity among many. Organizational leadership controls placement on electoral lists and, consequently, membership in the Parliament. Such parties depend primarily on ideological appeals for membership recruitment, although control of ancillary organizations such as trade unions or farmers associations may also be important. Both their ideological appeal—since they are usually identified with Marxism—and their organizational capabilities make them obvious targets for suppression. Their very existence is often used as a justification for the termination of democracy and the imposition of authoritarian rule.

Paradoxically, just as their organization and ideology make them highly visible targets, these same features promote survival. A hard core of dedicated members maintain a skeleton organization "underground," ready for rapid expansion once authoritarian rule is relaxed. The authoritarian regime is not the only threat to their survival, however. Typically, internecine ideological conflicts and controversies over international ties create additional dangers.

Parties composed primarily of traditional notables seem to vanish when Parliament is closed. There is little or no formal organization, ideologies are vague or nonexistent, and there is no mass following for the party as such. These parties pose no threat to authoritarian regimes, for they are usually unable to mobilize the masses for demonstrations or manipulate labor organizations to produce strikes. Traditional politicians rarely become resistance heroes. The absence of meaningful formal organization means that the real organization consists of the personal networks of individual politicians. These networks lead into the state apparatus, other public institutions, and the private sector. The abolition of political parties cannot eradicate these personal links—unless all political men were to be imprisoned or exiled.

The concern of the ordinary parliamentary deputy attached to a traditional political party is not the legislative process but constituent service. He may act as patron, client, and broker in these activities, for all these roles create ties of mutual obligation linking the deputy to constituents and to individuals in both public and private bureaucracies. The disappearance of parliamentary institutions does not mean the services provided by the politician are unneeded. Indeed, the politics of patronage, access, and intervention continue, regardless of the rhetoric of the authoritarian leaders. The political resources generated by the legislative process in the form of inducements or constraints that can accrue to individual members of Parliament are probably exaggerated. Instead, the major resource for politicians is knowledge of bureaucratic discretion and the ability to manipulate it. Even without office, the politician acting as patron, client, or broker is in a position to use personal contacts to link constituents with individuals in the state apparatus and to influence the informal organization imbedded in each part of the state apparatus itself. In some respects the politician without a parliament is playing a role not unlike the politician from a non-governing party when parliament exists.[13]

Since these networks are personal, they depend on the survival of the individual politician. Sometimes networks can be transferred to equally trustworthy individuals, often younger family members. Most likely, however, a lengthy period of authoritarian rule will obliterate networks centered on elective politicians, and, in consequence, the restoration of democracy may find new parties based on quite different clientelist networks.

The association of length of authoritarian rule and continuity in parliamentary careers can be seen in Table 1. The longer the authoritarian interval, the more turnover in members between Parliaments.

TABLE 1.
Authoritarian Rule and Career Continuity

	Year of Restoration Parliament	Years of Authoritarian Rule	Number of Carry-over Members	Carry-over Members as Percent of Membership
Spain	1979	38	5	1.4
Italy	1946	23	93	16.0
Greece	1946	10	107	30.2
Greece	1974	7	114	38.9

Source: For Greece, data published by the Greek Ministry of Interior, and personnel records of the Greek Parliament. For Italy, S. Somogyi et al., *Il Parlamento Italiano 1946–1963* (Napoli: Edizioni Scientifiche Italiane, 1963), p. 27. For Spain, calculated from material in Richard Gunther, "Strategies, Tactics and the New Spanish Party System: The 1979 General Election," paper prepared for the International Symposium, Spain and the United States, Center for Latin American Studies, University of Florida. Since Gunther does not provide information for the minor parties in the Spanish Cortes, these figures may be low.

The time factor is modified by several intervening variables. One is simply the age distribution of membership in the "original" Parliament. Without periodic electoral upheavals, the advantages of incumbency insure an aging parliamentary membership. Regime change at a particular point in the age cycle can insure that few parliamentarians are around for the restoration. Conversely, upheaval at another point may permit many parliamentarians to reassemble.

Another intervening variable is represented by the electoral system. The system in place for the original Parliament and that used for the restoration may not be the same. Even if they are, population shifts and increases may significantly alter the effect. Some electoral systems are designed to represent area rather than mere population: rural districts are generally over-represented, urban districts are under-represented. It is easier for individuals representing small populations to manage personal networks of patrons and clients, maintaining them during periods of authoritarian rule and activating them for electoral support. Individuals representing districts with large populations are more likely to depend, at least in part, on formal party organization, or the assistance of trade unions, religious groups, or some other organization to mobilize support. Yet the density of formal organization tends to change during periods of authoritarian rule, and these organizations, too, may be suppressed or leadership changed. Consequently, they may not be available to give organizational support to the politician when restoration occurs. Individuals representing larger districts, usually urban areas, may also rely on the personal support networks of other middle-level patrons. But during periods of authoritarian rule these individuals may choose to develop more direct links to the bureaucracy themselves, thus bypassing the former member of Parliament. Finally, when comparing the data for the three countries in Table 1, it should be remembered that parliamentary size is remarkably similar, despite great differences in state population. Each deputy in the 300-member Greek Parliament represents far fewer constituents than his counterparts in the Italian or Spanish Parliaments.

III. Restoration and Political Career Patterns

Despite regime change, economic and social elites remain intact; the administrative elites continue to occupy the state bureaucracy. There is even some continuity in the political elite from the old democratic regime to the authoritarian replacement. Similarly, when the authoritarian regime gives way to a restored democracy, some figures in the deposed regime participate in electoral politics.

Most members of the political elite do find their lives and careers disrupted, because the single most significant act of authoritarian regimes is the suppression of parliamentary institutions. One evidence of the disruption of traditional politics is the fact that many more parties participate in the first elections after democratic restorations than they do in "normal" ones. The election of 1946 occurred under civil war conditions, but in the first normal election, there was a surge of new parties and candidates (see Table 2). The second democratic restoration in 1974 was also accompanied by an increase in parties and candidates.

The period of authoritarian rule also disrupts individual political careers.[14] Only a minority of members in the last pre-authoritarian Parliament reappear in the first "restored" Parliament. Only 107 members of the 1936 Parliament were elected to the 1946 Parliament, and 84 members of the 1964 Parliament were elected to the 1974 Parliament. This apparent lack of membership continuity reflects the fact that only about half of the membership in either pre-authoritarian Parliament actually ran for seats in the restored Parliament. In 1946, only 172 of the 300 members of the 1936 Parliament ran, and in 1974 only 161 of the 300 members of the 1964 Parliament ran. A more detailed analysis of the 1964 Parliament reveals that a sizable proportion of those who did not run in 1974 were in advanced age categories. Members from left-wing parties also disappeared because most were elected as token representatives of the working class. Data on turnover also reflect changes in the parties contesting and winning elections. A Parliament dominated by the "center" in 1964 was replaced by a Parliament overwhelmingly dominated by the "right" in 1974. The context of elections are never quite the same, and in Greece the electoral rules and party

TABLE 2.
New Candidates and Parliamentary Elections 1946 to 1977*

Year	Number of Parties	Total Number of Party Candidates	Proportion of New Candidates (in Percent)
1946	5†	1211	57.7
1950	12	2178	55.0
1951	7	1666	28.2
1952	5	779	20.8
1956	3	849	26.6
1958	5	1361	39.4
1961	3	900	25.1
1963	4	1164	34.8
1964	3	813	14.6
1974	8	1335	70.5
1977	15	2063	63.8

*Does not include independents and independent lists.
†Obscures number of parties due to electoral coalitions.
Source: Greek Ministry of Interior.

TABLE 3.
Continuity in Parliamentary Membership

Period	Percent of Later Parliament
1936 Deputies in 1946 Parliament	30.2
1946 Deputies in 1958 Parliament	23.0
1958 Deputies in 1964 Parliament	38.0
1964 Deputies in 1974 Parliament	29.2

labels are seldom quite the same either. These factors make it difficult to evaluate the importance of these data without a "norm" for parliamentary turnover.

To facilitate comparison, data on parliamentary turnover over similar periods under democratic conditions are presented in Table 3. These data show that turnover through authoritarian periods is not especially greater than in non-authoritarian periods. The relatively high turnover among Greek parliamentarians suggest that more-enduring factors are at work.

Data on parliamentary turnover are somewhat misleading because the political elites include not only individuals elected to a particular Parliament but also those politicians whose parliamentary service is interrupted by electoral defeat or personal decision. A better measure of continuity, then, is membership in any prior Parliament, not simply membership in the previous one.

Data in Table 4 suggest a somewhat greater continuity in the political elite. In 1946, about half the members had prior parliamentary experience; in 1974, approximately 40 percent had served in Parliament before. What is surprising is the number of members successful on their first try for parliamentary office. In 1946, 34.7 percent of the parliamentary membership were successful on their first try for office; in 1974 the figure was higher, comprising 54.9 percent of the membership. Only a handful were making a first appearance after previous unsuccessful attempts.

TABLE 4.
Parliamentary Members and Prior Political Experience

	Number	Prior Parliamentary Office (in Percent)	Prior Unsuccessful Parliamentary Candidatures (in Percent)	Parliamentary Office at First Attempt (in Percent)
1946	354	50.8	11.6	34.7
1974	288	39.6	7.3	53.1

Two interesting facts emerge—one, the high turnover, and second, the great incidence of initial success in running for parliamentary office. These are explicable if the dualistic character of Greek parties is remembered. Every politician uses personal networks and family ties to gain electoral victory. At the same time, parliamentary candidates must find a place on the electoral list put together by a leader of a major political party. Consequently, success or defeat is only partly due to the efforts or connections of the individual candidate. Public perceptions of party leadership, the consequences of economic and social change, or a sequence of international events can all influence the electoral outcome. Politicians with extensive personal networks have the most secure electoral base. They gain large majorities when the political environment is favorable, and they manage to retain their parliamentary seats when it is adverse.

Members of the political elite of course vary in terms of the mix of family clientage ties and political environmental factors that are necessary for their individual success. But the parliamentary survivors of parties losing elections are most likely to come from families with substantial clientage networks. The total percentage of Greek deputies coming from political families actually increased between 1946 and 1974, as shown in Table 5. This suggests that many deputies are able to maintain political networks for considerable periods of time, and increasingly to pass these networks on to successors—whether sons, brothers, nephews, or even wives and daughters.

The importance of family ties and personal networks for electoral success is examined in Table 6. Parliamentary membership for both 1946 and 1974 is divided into three categories: those who had successfully run for parliamentary office before (although not necessarily in the last Parliament preceding the authoritarian interlude), those who had run unsuccessfully prior to the authoritarian regime, and finally, those who had not run for office before but were successful in election to the first "restored" Parliament.

In 1946 about one third of the parliamentary membership in each category came from political families. If we combine parliamentary experience regardless of family political connections (assuming these individuals have created and maintained some personal political

TABLE 5.
Parliamentary Membership and Political Families

Year	Percent of Parliament Members
1946	35.0
1958	34.6
1964	40.0
1974	44.8

TABLE 6.
Parliamentary Members and Prior Political Experience

	Prior Parliamentary Office (in Percent)	Prior Unsuccessful Parliamentary Candidatures (in Percent)	Parliamentary Office at First Attempt (in Percent)
1946	N = 180	N = 51	N = 123
Political Families	35.6	27.4	37.4
Nonpolitical Families	64.4	72.5	62.6
1974	N = 114	N = 21	N = 153
Political Families	43.8	23.8	45.1
Nonpolitical Families	56.2	76.2	54.9

networks) and add to this those in other categories coming from political families (where they presumably have inherited some type of political network), there is a great deal of continuity in the parliamentary political elite over the authoritarian period.

The importance of family ties and personal networks varies from one party to another. As noted before, the durable part of the major political constellation is disproportionally composed of members from political families. Minor parties and parties of the Left rarely have high proportions of deputies from political families. These points can be clarified with an examination of the two restoration Parliaments in terms of party affiliation (see Table 7). The 1946 election and that of 1974 have some similarities. First, in each case, the proportion of left-wing deputies elected to the Parliament was small. In 1946, the Left was still involved with the civil war, thus even those on the Left that had detached themselves from the Communist leadership of the war were suspect. In 1974, the Left was severely fragmented; consequently, votes were scattered among several parties. In both 1946 and 1974 the center was fragmented, and the Right was relatively cohesive.

Data for the 1946 Parliament are less complete than those for the 1974 Parliament, simply because the electoral records on which evaluation of family political connections are based do not extend as far back. Several other factors reduce comparability. There were more spaces for new faces in 1946 because the chamber had 354 seats rather than 300. Further, the on-going civil war meant that populations were uprooted, electoral registers inaccurate, and party lists incomplete in some districts. The occupation, but especially the civil war, disrupted traditional political networks. In addition, new regionally based political organizations spawned by the resistance movement also contested parliamentary seats. Party comparisons are clouded, however, because two major coalitions fought the

TABLE 7.
Political Parties, Parliamentary Members, and Prior
Political Experience

Year	Party	Number	Prior Parlia-mentary Experience (in Percent)	Prior Unsuccessful Parlia-mentary Candidature (in Percent)	Election at First Attempt (in Percent)
1946		354	50.8	11.6	34.7
	Populists	160	58.1	15.6	26.3
	Liberals	49	77.6	8.2	14.3
	Venezelist Liberals	30	33.3	20.0	46.7
	National Liberals	34	38.2	17.6	44.1
	Social Democrats	27	51.8	7.4	40.7
	National Party	21	19.0	14.3	66.7
	Minor Parties	33	24.2	15.1	60.6
1974		288	39.6	7.3	53.1
	New Democracy	210	38.6	6.7	54.8
	Center Union	57	45.8	5.3	50.9
	PASOK	13	46.2	15.4	38.5
	A.E. (United Left)	8	25.0	25.0	50.0

elections, and the parties in each coalition could not offer candidates for all 354 seats.

The political parties contesting the 1946 elections were led by men heavily involved in pre-war politics. The only major exception was the "National Party" led by a leader of one of the resistance organizations from the occupation. The two parties with the closest ties to the past, the Populists and the Liberals, hasd the greatest continuity. The other parties, primarily factions of the pre-war Liberals, had more successful first-time candidates than the older parties.

The 1974 election was held six months after the collapse of the military regime. All of the parties, including the Left, were led by men with prior parliamentary experience. The majority party had slightly fewer members with prior political experience and slightly more winning elections on the first attempt. The two factions of the center, the Center Union and PASOK (Panhellenic Socialist Movement), had slightly more members with prior parliamentary experience than did the majority party. The Left had the smallest proportion of experienced parliamentary deputies. Only PASOK had fewer than 50 percent of its parliamentary membership in the "election first attempt" category.

The continuity, in terms of membership coming from political families, is apparent, and the importance of family ties for first-time victory is also conspicuous (Table 8). Over two thirds of the mem-

TABLE 8.
Parliamentary Members from Political Families

Party	Number of Members	Percent of Party Delegation from Political Families	Election at First Attempt	Percent Elected at First Attempt from Political Families
		1946 Election		
Populists	160	30.6	42	38.1
Liberals	49	24.5	7	42.8
Venizelist Liberals	30	50.0	14	64.3
National Liberals	34	29.4	15	26.7
Social Democrats	27	37.0	11	45.4
National Party	21	23.8	14	21.4
Minor Parties	33	39.4	20	30.0
		1974 Election		
New Democracy	210	39.5	127	41.2
Center Union	57	64.9	32	69.0
PASOK	13	23.1	7	0
A.E. (United Left)	8	12.5	6	0

bership of the 1946 Parliament either had previous political experience (disregarding family political ties) or, if elected on the first attempt, came from political families.

The great electoral victory of the New Democracy party in 1974 meant that individuals normally rather far down on the proportional representation lists in the urban areas were elected. In addition, the Center Union and PASOK both competed for the votes going to a unified Center Union party in 1964. This competition split votes and enabled New Democracy candidates to win in unlikely areas. The Center Union party, as the minority party, elected only the durable parts of the party—those individuals with family networks. PASOK had some family components, but filled its lists with candidates from families new to elective politics. As one might expect, the party furthest to the left, the United Left, had the smallest proportion of its parliamentary membership from political families.

In the major parties, the incidence of family connections among first-time winners is high. Although the breakdown does not appear on the table, nearly half the members inherited seats directly from fathers. The size of the majority party victory allowed New Democracy candidates with less durable ties to win. Victorious new candidates from the Center Union clearly relied on family ties for success. The Left generally does not elect members with family networks. It is not surprising that the parties of the Left often campaign against the privileges that family ties and social networks are alleged to produce.

For bureaucratically organized and ideological parties—and in Greece this means the Left—the two periods of authoritarian rule were exceedingly disruptive. Organizations were suppressed and members imprisoned, exiled, or suffered from legal disabilities. For parties composed primarily of notables, individuals involved in traditional types of political exchange, the periods of authoritarian rule had less dramatic effects. The general character of the parliamentary elite changed little. The turnover from one Parliament to another was not dramatically different; prior parliamentary experience continued to be important, and family political connections continued to be advantageous for the first-time candidate.

IV. Conclusions

Authoritarian rule seems to have had relatively little impact on dominant values, institutions, or even the character and composition of elites in Greece. A basic continuity in social, economic, and political sectors transcends authoritarian and democratic regimes. Government expenditures have followed incremental logic. Patterns of growth measured by GNP have seemed similarly unaffected by regime change. Unanticipated increases or decreases in either have reflected international economic conditions or problems more than specific domestic decisions. Although spokesmen for each succeeding regime proclaimed new goals, these initial hopes were usually altered or forgotten as maintaining power became the central concern. To some extent, this continuity simply reflected the conservative character of Greek society and politics. Neither the democratic regimes nor their authoritarian replacements had Marxist orientations. More far-reaching changes would have been expected if the ideological distance between succeeding regimes had been greater. In any case, tracking real change was difficult. Announced goals were usually difficult to implement. Old rules may have remained in place, yet they became largely inoperative. Or, the significant change may have been cloaked in a bureaucratic discretion that left few traces when regimes changed.

Yet the fact that authoritarian interludes and democratic restorations have not produced fundamental changes did not mean that alternation of regimes did not have consequences: some individuals, groups, and institutions lost power and advantage, others gained. Although generally of lesser degree, these redistributions of power and advantage also occurred as a consequence of shifts in electoral fortune during democratic periods. Of course shifts in power and advantages accruing to various individuals and groups are not unknown even in authoritarian settings. Some institutions may readily adapt to a new order and consequently retain importance, others may remain in place but impotent. In authoritarian regimes, the military and the police ascend in significance as competitive parties and parliamentary institutions decline and disappear. In the economic sphere, business and banking interests gain at the expense of organized labor. Institutions that encourage debate or express dissent—the media, intellectual associations, and institutions of higher education—are closely monitored or suppressed. Once democracy reappears, of course, the order of importance is likely to be reversed, and the elite networks favored by the prior regime are cast into the shadows to be replaced by new constellations of the influential.

In Greece, cohesion may have been attributed, improperly, to any social institution. Rivalries within the business world, bureaucracies, the labor movement, and the social and intellectual worlds were easily harnessed to one political faction or another whether in an authoritarian or democratic context. Even authoritarian institutions were rarely as cohesive as they seemed, since the disappearance of democracy does not end conflict. Some parts of these social and occupational sectors, some individuals within them, were favored at the very moment that others were persecuted.

For the average citizen not involved in political activities and without membership in suspect organizations, the change from one regime to another had very little direct consequence. People simply endured without appeal, obeying authority because of habit or narrow self-interest. Rarely were the authority relationships between government and individuals significantly altered, nor were patterns of interpersonal relations severely disrupted. In Greece, the political culture has long portrayed the state and its operatives as enemies, and this perception persisted regardless of regime. At the same time, the state was viewed as a source of individual benefit, if only access could be found. This perception, too, continues, regardless of regime. For most Greeks, politics is the exchange relationships that ameliorate government regulation or grant special privileges. Regime changes may alter strategies, but the goal remains unchanged.

Formal changes of regime in Greece have been occasions for the replacement of one set of political leaders by another. The demise of a democratic regime and the emergence of an authoritarian one has meant that an orientation favoring political exchange has been replaced by an orientation toward "heroic" politics. Professional politicians were replaced by a cast of different professionals who claimed to eschew politics. With the downfall of the authoritarian regime, the professional politicians returned to the helm, the military returned to the barracks. But before the retreat, heroic politics had usually slipped into the mundane.

Certainly the closure of representative institutions and the termination of competitive elections did at least terminate or interrupt the careers of individual politicians. However, the bulk of political opportunity lay in bureaucratic rather than elective office. The normal processes of recruitment into these positions continued despite regime change, and the role of personal contacts and clientage networks did not diminish. Those professions and occupations (in addition to bureaucratic ones) that facilitated the development and maintenance of clientage relationships remained important. Individuals continue to perform political roles, even if the parliamentary level was missing.

Recruitment to elective office was largely carried on through clientage networks. With the onset of authoritarian rule, Greek political parties dissolved quite readily into clientelist components. Since these components were based on interpersonal relationships they remained when parties were abolished and could easily reassemble for normal political party activity when democracy was restored. The very lack of formal organization, however, meant that party leaders relied on personal contacts and recommendations from third parties for selecting individuals to fill out electoral lists. Preference was given to those individuals with personal or family clientage networks at the constituency level. This, in turn, meant that advantages accrued disproportionately to former parliamentarians or individuals from political families.

Periods of authoritarian rule did inhibit the growth and development of parties on the left. However, authoritarian rule alone did not account for their weakness in Greece. Late industrialization and urbanization, together with the special historical circumstances of the civil war provide more cogent explanations.

The preference of Greeks is certainly for democratic rather than authoritarian regimes, even though the latter may occasionally engender popular enthusiasm. The assumption that democratic regimes necessarily reflect popular policy preferences more adequately does need some qualification, however. Even though Parliament and competitive political parties make the policy process visible and seem to maintain governmental accountability, these functions are not crucial for most parliamentary deputies or for other members of the "political class." The routines of personal political exchange have remained primary. In the past, most members of the Greek Parliament have abjured real involvement in the policy process. There has been little demand by parliamentarians for the staff or facilities that would enable them to acquire knowledge about issues. Policy formulation remained largely in the hands of a handful of political leaders. Parliamentary divisions did follow party lines, but discipline was due less to fear of electoral retribution than to disinterest. When dissent surfaced in traditional parties it was nearly always over questions of leadership succession. Most often this meant fragmentation; new parties and new party labels were readied for the next election.

Patterns of political exchange continued from one regime to the other despite the occasional abnormalities of heroic politics. For real change to occur in Greece, clientelist modes of activity must cease to predominate in political life as well as in other sectors. The patterns and sequences of economic, social, and political changes that explain the decline of patronage politics and the development of modern organizations in Western Europe were not replicated in Greece. The routines of traditional political exchange not only accommodated the vast economic and social changes of the early post-war period, but were probably strengthened by them.

But in the last ten years, the population has increased and is younger; and the majority reside in a handful of urban centers. Even those left in rural areas are tied to the national center through mass communications and transportation networks. The processes of economic and social change, as well as increased government involvement, have escalated the number and complexity of requests for intervention and amelioration. In fact, the expectations for change that accompanied the fall of the military regime in 1974, particularly since they could not really be accommodated by the restoration of routine exchange politics, undoubtedly created pressures for more fundamental change. Clientelist politics, with its individualist orientation, has been overwhelmed and unable to meet popular demands. Not only do these new problems require long-term and collective solutions, but clientelist forms themselves have begun to atrophy. Modernization reduced incentives for assuming patronage roles at the local level—the essential building blocks for clientage networks reaching the highest levels of politics. This meant a growing number of potential clients at lower economic and social levels for whom no patrons can be found. Consequently, in electoral politics, the strength of the clientelist component has been reduced. On the other hand, the middle and upper classes, who have been the visible beneficiaries of economic change, often retain direct access to the highest levels of political decision-making and bureaucratic discretion through family ties and personal networks.[15] In fact, for them, direct involvement in elective politics is far less important.

The "ideology" of clientelism assumed that everyone could benefit from traditional patterns of political exchange. For those in the lower economic and social strata there is an increasing gap between this ideology and reality. Consequently, the legitimacy of traditional patterns of political exchanges has eroded.

Andreas Papandreou and his political movement, PASOK, became the main opposition party in 1977 and the majority party in 1981. Papandreou and his party capitalized on the pressures for change within the Greek electorate, and their victory appears to end the dominance of clientelist politics in Greece. Paradoxically, a change in political leadership occasioned by a regular democratic election may inaugurate more far-reaching changes in Greece than any past regime change. The new government is the first to publically embrace domestic goals derived from social democratic ideology. It is also departing from past practice in promoting an independent international position, one quite removed from the normal dependency on a great power patron.

Politics itself has been altered. Most Greek political leaders have been adept at "balcony politics" but now the technologies of mass communication, combined with a more molilized population, have produced a nationwide audience. This development strengthens the position of the party leader, for he can use his mass appeal to undermine the clientelist components of his entourage (and even PASOK has some clientelist elements). Candidates can now be selected on the basis of loyalty to the leader or commitment to a policy because electoral success largely depends on the mass appeal of the leader rather than on constituency networks. Given the size of urban constituencies, name recognition rather than clientelist ties becomes a major political asset. Candidates with old and famous names have adapted successfully to the new politics. They have been joined by others who have transferred to political advantage the name recognition gained in other activities.

With the decline of clientelist politics, the elements that provided continuity within democratic regimes and through authoritarian ones, the politician with a personal clientage network ensuring parliamentary survival through party defeats and political survival through authoritarian interludes, are likely to disappear. Although the "personal" element of the clientelist tie has been transferred to mass politics, the organizational element has not. Greek parties, even PASOK, have yet to develop real organizational sinews.

The electoral victory of Andreas Papandreou and PASOK registered a significant change in the character of political parties and electoral behavior. It remains to be seen whether the transformation goals of the new government can be accomplished. Although the routines of exchange may have less appeal in electoral politics, such routines seem likely to persist in the bureaucracy and in other sectors of life. Certainly the advantaged parts of the population are likely to continue to use family connections and personal networks regardless of government policy. Although the ideology of political clientelism may be undermined at the mass level by the failures of past governments and the older generation of politicians to satisfy individual demands, the ideology of mass participation remains imperfectly developed. Moreover, judging by the experience of other more advanced countries, there is likely to be a gap between that ideology and political reality as well. The success of the present government may inaugurate a pattern of politics more like that of other developed western countries; a failure may provoke an even more significant regime change, either one oriented toward an improbable and anachronistic restoration or one with an ideology anchored in an even more radical future.

Notes

1. See especially the essays in Samuel P. Huntington and Clement H. Moore, eds., *Authoritarian Politics in Modern Society: The Dynamics of Established One-Party Systems* (New York: Basic Books, 1970).

2. This conceptualization relies on Robert A. Kann, *The Problem of Restoration: A Study in Comparative Political History* (Berkeley and Los Angeles: University of California Press, 1968), Part I.

3. This discussion draws on William H. McNeill, *The Metamorphosis of Greece since World War II* (Chicago: University of Chicago Press, 1978), chap. 1.

4. The best discussion in English of this period is Yanis Yanonlopoulos, "Greece: Political and Constitutional Development, 1924–1974," in John T. A. Koumoulides, ed., *Greece in Transition: Essays in the History of Modern Greece, 1821–1974* (London: Zeno Booksellers and Publishers, 1977), chap. 2.

5. McNeill, *Metamorphosis of Greece*, chap. 3

6. These practices are discussed more fully for both Greece and Italy in Keith Legg, "Regime Change and Public Policy in a Clientelist Polity," A Paper Presented to the American Political Science Association Annual Meeting, September 1972, Washington, D.C.

7. Keith Legg, *Politics in Modern Greece* (Stanford: Stanford University Press, 1969), pp. 305–7.

8. Ibid. p. 281

9. The most complete material is found in Richard Clogg and George Yannopoulos, *Greece under Military Rule* (New York: Basic Books, 1972).

10. This analysis, as yet incomplete, focuses on the occupancy of bureaucratic positions in ministries and other public agencies, using a yearly series of directories listing governmental personnel. The directories are published by a private Greek public relations firm, "Orizon."

11. McNeill, *Metamorphosis of Greece*, pp. 123–37.

12. Ibid., p. 134.

13. For an extended discussion of the concepts of patron, client, and broker, see Keith Legg, *Patrons, Clients and Politicians: New Perspectives on Political Clientelism* (Berkeley: Institute of International Studies, University of California, 1975).

14. All data on Greek cabinet ministers, members of Parliament, and parliamentary candidates originate in materials published by the Greek Ministry of Interior or from the personal records of the Greek Parliament. These materials collected since 1964 make up a file of approximately 15,000 individual political histories including years of candidatures, party affiliations, and districts. Some material also provides biographical information, particularly father's name. Consequently, it is possible to connect individuals with the same surname running in the same district over several generations. Since systematic data exist only from 1926, the analysis of prior political experience and family connections for the pre-World War II period is less reliable than for the later years.

15. Survey data supporting this assertion can be found in George A. Kourvetaris and Betty A. Dobratz, "Political Clientelism in Greece: Myth or Reality," unpublished manuscript, Department of Sociology, Northern Illinois University, DeKalb, Illinois, 1980.

Members of the Dutch Lower House: Pluralism and Democratization, 1848–1967

Hans Daalder
and
Joop Th. J. van den Berg

In the literature of comparative politics the Netherlands has come to represent the archetype of a consociational democracy. In that model (as elaborated above all by Arend Lijphart)[1] two features stand out: the simultaneous existence of a number of strongly demarcated ideological subcultures (i.e., a Calvinist, a Catholic, a Socialist, and possibly a Liberal one), coupled with a conscious policy on the part of political elites to contain the potentially conflictual tendencies in the system by deliberate coalescent behavior.

Lijphart's model has not remained uncontested. One line of criticism[2] holds that in actual historical record the politics of accommodation did not *follow* the process of social segmentation (as Lijphart holds in what he calls a "self-denying hypothesis") but in fact *predated* it; in that view the traditional pluralist nature of the Dutch elite, nurtured in the pluralist days of the confederal Dutch Republic, could peacefully accommodate the processes of a slowly evolving mass politicization along religious and ideological lines which never had the explosive potential which Lijphart posited.[3] Another line of criticism has preferred to interpret the process of social segmentation (generally known in Dutch as *Verzuiling*) as a conscious and successful policy on the part of political elites to encapsulate the masses—whether to retain their own political position to preserve the role of religion, to safeguard the capitalist system, or any combination of these—thus preventing a full development of class politics by a clear exercise of deliberate social control.[4] Whatever the merits of these alternative readings of Dutch developments may be, they all put considerable emphasis on the special nature of the Dutch political elite and its role in the development of modern mass politics.

In that light the rather small amount of systematic study of political elite groups in Dutch society is somewhat remarkable. There is only one systematic study of the historical recruitment of Dutch cabinet ministers, the 1957 study by Dogan and Scheffer-van der Veen.[5] There are only scattered historical analyses of the background of Dutch Members of Parliament in particular parliamentary periods, but there are no studies covering the entire period of mass politicization.[6] Other elite groups (e.g., high civil servants, judges, military personnel, party leaders, mayors, and other local elites) are treated even more scantily. This gap in the literature for contemporary elites has been rapidly filling in the last fifteen years. We now have extensive survey data with Members of Parliament in 1968, 1972, and 1979.[7] Local government elites have been repeatedly interviewed in recent years.[8] So have senior civil servants,[9] party delegates,[10] and even (former) cabinet ministers.[11] But such material generally lacks a longitudinal perspective.

The absence of such a perspective is regrettable, not least because in a developmental perspective, the Netherlands represents a special case. In Stein Rokkan's macromodel of Europe it is, with Switzerland, the only case of early statehood in the central trading belt of Europe.[12] Its city network caused early burgher rule but resisted internal consolidation and unification until the period of the French revolution. In a comparative perspective parliamentary government came early (1848) but in a period of strongly elitist politics in a relatively stagnant society. The franchise was only slowly extended over a period of seventy years, and both party and other mass organizations came only late and gradually.

This paper on Dutch Members of Parliament between 1848 and 1967 seeks to add some new pieces to the puzzle which the Dutch case of political development represents in a comparative perspective. As such, it forms only one part of a more general attempt to analyze processes of political modernization. This attempt involves systematic study also of other political elite groups (e.g. ministers, senior civil servants, and local elites, notably mayors), as well as more detailed analyses of the character of local and national mass organizations, as they evolved gradually in the late nineteenth and early twentieth centuries.[13]

I. The Data

Since the late 1960's, data on Members of Parliament (as on a variety of other elite groups) have been systematically collected and stored in an increasingly sophisticated automated file. The file now rests with the Parliamentary Documentation Centre, established and directed by Nico Cramer, Professor of Parliamentary History at the University of Leiden.[14] The data collection has proved to be far from easy. Even for such a public group as Members of Parliament, relatively complete information is often difficult to find, as soon as one goes beyond mere demographic data into professional careers and political activities in local government, parties, or social organizations. While such information is generally available for the more prominent politicians, it is not always easily found for the less prominent ones.

We have selected the period 1848 to 1967 for intensive study. The first year of this period saw the introduction of the first directly elected Lower House, the last year, the end of traditional social segmentation. Beginning in 1967 the major religious parties lost rapidly in strength, initially largely toward a variety of newly established political parties but later also directly to their larger traditional political rivals, the Liberals and Socialists. The changes in the composition of Parliament since 1967 are better covered in the three parliamentary surveys[15] than in the general longitudinal file, however.

We present our data in the form of time-series graphs. In interpreting developments over time, one should bear in mind the effect of institutional changes, notably of the franchise and the electoral system.[16] Between 1848 and 1888 the franchise was originally restricted to about 11 to 12 percent of the male population over 23 years of age, on the basis of a census suffrage which was particularly demanding in the larger cities. The franchise was lowered to about 26 percent of males over 25 at the constitutional revision of 1888, to be doubled again to about 49 percent in 1896. From that year the proportion of eligible voters grew in the wake of increasing economic prosperity, until in 1913 it reached about 63 percent. Universal suffrage for men was introduced in 1917, and for women in 1919. The electoral system was also changed: between 1848 and 1888 one half of Parliament was renewed every two years (except when dissolved in its entirety). Usually, members were chosen in two-member districts, but there were also a number of one- and three-member districts. As population expanded, the number of Members of Parliament increased, from 68 in 1851 to 82 in 1879; in 1888 it was fixed at 100. From 1896 all members were chosen in single-member districts with fixed boundaries, with a run-off ballot between the two highest placed candidates, the entire Lower House being renewed every four years. In 1917 the system was changed into a very extreme form of proportional representation, in which for all practical purposes the country formed one district for seat allocation, with a very low threshold (0.5 percent of the valid national vote in 1918, raised to 0.75 percent from 1922 to 1933 to 1.0 percent from 1937 to 1956, but lowered again to 1/150, or 0.67 percent when the number of members of the House was increased from 100 to 150 in 1956). In the presentation of our graphs, we use percentages, rather than actual figures, so as to make figures comparable over time.

In our presentation we shall always distinguish four periods:

1. 1848–1888, when the franchise was limited to about 12 percent of the adult male population

2. 1888–1917, when the suffrage increased from 26 percent in
1888 to 63 percent of adult males in 1913
3. 1918–1937, the interwar period, after the advent of universal
suffrage in 1917
4. 1946–1967, the postwar period.

II. The Distribution of Political Forces

Figure 1 shows the percentage strength of the major political families between 1848 and 1967. To simplify the visual representation,
members representing different parties (e.g., different parties in the
Orthodox Protestant family, assorted Liberals, and various types of
Socialists including Communists) have been added together. Figures
for the nineteenth century are highly debatable, however: until the
end of the century constituencies sent "persons," rather than "partisans," to Parliament. Parliamentary caucuses developed only slowly,
and party organizations outside Parliament arrived even later. One
should therefore recognize that labels like "Conservatives" and "Liberals" represented highly fluid realities, with many transitions and
intermediate shades. For a time (at least until the 1860's), a number
of Catholics figured as ardent Liberals. Similarly, the borderline between Conservatives and Orthodox Protestants remained vague until

FIGURE 1.
The Distribution of Political Forces (Percentage of Lower House Deputies)*

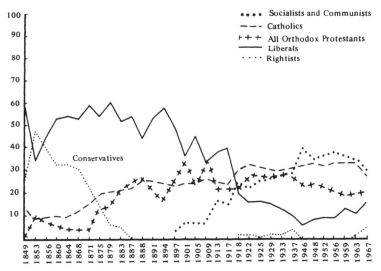

*The Radicals (Vrijz. Democraten, 1901–1940) and D'66 (1967) have been included
with the Liberals. Part of the 1946 jump of the Socialists is explained by the
amalgamation of the pre-1940 Radicals with the Socialists into the Labor party
(PvdA) (1946).

at least 1879, when the Antirevolutionary Party was established as the first clear party organization in Dutch history which associated a distinct group of deputies with organized parties outside Parliament. The Liberals remained split into various groups even after a first alleged national organization was formed in 1885. The Catholics also found it difficult to develop a distinct party organization, even though their religion generally made them a distinct group in the eyes of non-Catholics; their organizational efforts took on more definite form only between 1896, when a caucus was formed, and 1926, when a new national party organization was established to confront the realities of a system of nationwide proportional representation.

With these reservations, one may summarize the picture of Figure 1 in the following terms.[17] Between 1848 and the late 1870's the major division was between Conservatives and Liberals, neither category representing very distinct entities; during that period certain Orthodox-Protestants and Catholics began increasingly to go their own ways. From the late 1870's on, a division between Liberals on the one hand, and members representing distinct religious positions (Calvinists and Catholics) on the other became the major split, with the first group being regarded as occupying the Left of Parliament and the second, the Right. Until 1901 the Liberals were generally dominant, although they were a far from cohesive group. After one earlier Cabinet of the Right (1888), a coalition of by now two Calvinist parties (Antirevolutionaries and Christian Historicals) and the Catholics broke through to a decisive majority in 1901. Jointly, the Right was to retain half or more of the seats of Parliament for the remainder of the period we investigate, except for two Parliaments, chosen in 1905 and 1913, respectively. Already before the advent of universal suffrage and proportional representation (PR) in 1917, the Liberals had begun to experience strong competition from the Socialists, who came to overshadow them numerically from 1918 on, taking about a quarter of the Lower House in the interwar period. After amalgamation with some radical groups in both the Liberal and religious sectors in 1946, the Socialists increased to at most one-third of the Parliament. The graphs clearly reveal the stabilization of the party system, once PR and universal suffrage had been introduced.

III. Regional Origin and Domicile

For all its small size, the Netherlands shows a history of a marked influence on Dutch political life by regional forces. In the time of the Republic, the Estates-General had in fact been a mere assembly of provincial delegates. Even after the definite consolidation of the Netherlands as a unitary state, the principle of representation had remained a geographic one, as between 1814 and 1848 provincial estates served as the electoral college for an indirectly elected Lower

House, eligibility being restricted to persons resident in the same province. The introduction of direct election for the Lower House severed such geographic links. Although a constituency system was introduced, the new constitution did not insist on a residence rule. Yet in the actual election of Members of Parliament regional forces remained a powerful factor, local notables being a particularly conspicuous group in the new Lower House for decades to come.

During the first decades of responsible government the data reveal correspondingly little deviation between place of birth and place of residence at the time of election. That situation changed markedly toward the end of the nineteenth century when more and more Members of Parliament took up residence in the West (which was both the more prosperous part of the country and the one which had the seat of government located in it). Throughout the period under review the figures retain a high proportionality between the place of birth of deputies and the general population, however, suggesting that there was no marked discrimination in representation against certain regions. Also, the internal migration toward the west tended to reverse itself somewhat toward the later period. Theoretically, the introduction of nationwide proportional representation (severing, as it did, any formal geographic link between voters and a particular party or representative) could have led to increased distortion (for instance, in favor of the more central provinces of Holland or Utrecht. In practice, this did not materialize, as parties remained aware of the use of retaining specific links with particular geographic concentrations of voters and fashioned their slates accordingly. The regional origin of representatives of the various political groupings tend to reflect known geographic differences in the electorate.[18]

Another significant finding is that in the nineteenth century, taking place of birth as the criterion, Deputies tended to come in disproportionate numbers from the cities, notably the smaller provincial ones. In later years of rapidly *increasing* urbanization, the proportion of members born in *rural* communities, rose very substantially, a development which might reflect the late emancipation of the countryside in a once heavily city-dominated society.

IV. Social Status and Milieu

The 1848 Constitution abolished all special criteria of eligibility for the Lower House except age (members had to be above thirty), nationality, and the normal enjoyment of legal rights and privileges in civic affairs; it was argued that it followed implicitly from the latter that only males could be chosen (a limitation which was undone in 1917, two years before women received the franchise).

Until 1848 members of the nobility had had a special place in the Dutch constitutional system, as they chose a fixed share of each of the provincial estates which then in turn elected the Lower House. The term "nobility" covers, in fact, two substantially different groups in Dutch society. There were a limited number of ancient noble families, who were generally more numerous and prominent in the more feudal eastern part of the country than in the more prosperous urbanized and burgher-dominated West. After the unification of the Netherlands, the first King William (1813–1840) had deliberately created a new nobility, generally chosen from leading regent families who had already been prominent in the time of the Republic when offices had been reserved to increasingly oligarchical city families. Persons who could show ancestry through the male line of at least three generations in actual governing positions in the established cities of the Republic could also request inclusion in the rank of the nobility at a later date. The old and the new nobility are included in the Nederland's Adelsboek (the Adel), annual red-bound volumes published regularly since 1903. Next to the older nobility and the families newly ennobled in the early nineteenth century, genealogies of other prominent families have been included in the Nederlandsch Patriciaat, annual blue-bound volumes published since 1910. These "patrician" families generally owe their inclusion to their members' occupation of prominent offices in the military, the colonial civil service, or banking, commerce, and industry. The criteria for inclusion are less precise than those of the Adel, however, for at least two reasons. First, not all eligible families are necessarily included (inclusion presupposing a willingness to have ancestry traced, often at not negligible cost). Further, certain families are included as a function not of an early but of a relatively late accession to prominent office. With these reservations, however, the share of nobles and members of the patriciaat is presented jointly in Figure 2.

The picture is quite telling: sons of noble families held generally a quarter or more of the seats in the Lower House throughout the first period, 1848 to 1888; and they retained not much under one-fifth even in the second period, 1888 to 1917, which was a time of a lowering of the franchise and increasing party organization. The share of members from the Patriciaat was larger: often reaching above 40 percent in the first period of responsible government and sinking only under one-third of the Lower House after 1905. Nobles and patricians together amounted to close to two-thirds of the Lower House before 1887, dropping to a figure below 50 percent only in 1913.

These figures are highly illustrative of the relatively narrow social circles from which the Dutch parliamentary elite was drawn for as long as sixty years or more after the arrival of responsible government. Most exclusivist were the representatives of the Conservatives and of the Calvinists until 1888, each group having generally more than three-fourths of their memberships from leading families (the

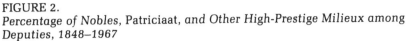

FIGURE 2.
*Percentage of Nobles, Patriciaat, and Other High-Prestige Milieux among
Deputies, 1848–1967*

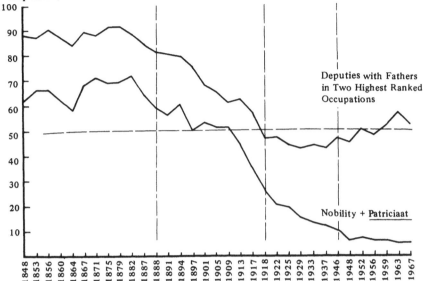

actual nobles forming generally close to one-half of the Conservative
deputies and often two-thirds and more of the still limited number
of distinct Orthodox Protestants). The number of representatives from
less prominent families increased as the share of Calvinist deputies
expanded in the second period, but only after 1909 were more than
50 percent of Calvinist deputies from less distinguished families.
From an early date Liberals included from one-third to one-half of
their membership from less prominent families, and within the Liberal ranks the share of nobles, as against members from the *Patriciaat*, was substantially weaker than that of the Conservatives or
nineteenth century Calvinists. But even in the case of the Liberals,
nobles and "patricians" jointly fell below 50 percent only in 1917.
Catholics (who had been excluded from most offices in the times of
the Dutch Republic) had still a substantial share of noble representatives and other local notables, but the number of sons of prominent
Catholic families in Parliament rarely reached one-half even in the
early period.

Figure 2 also shows the rapid decline of the share of deputies from
prominent families after 1909. This change was due partly to the
entry of Socialists in much greater numbers and to a somewhat increased representation of the Catholics, but also to a process of substantial change *within* the ranks of Liberals and Calvinists, among
whom nobles and scions of "patrician" families dwindled to 20 percent or less in the interwar period and to yet lower figures after 1946.

Adel and *Patriciaat* represent rather specific ascriptive categories. To trace elements of status in parliamentary recruitment further, we have also investigated the social origin of Members of Parliament in a more indirect way, analyzing the occupation of fathers. Basing themselves on an empirical prestige stratification survey of the 1950's, the Leyden sociologists van Heek and Vercruijsse, van Tulder, and others, including Vinke,[19] have divided occupations into six groups ranking from 1 (highest-ranked occupations; e.g., free professions, managing directors of large enterprises, high military officers, teachers in *lycées* and higher education) to 6 (lowest; unskilled labor). The higher graph in Figure 2 shows the percentage of deputies having fathers who had occupations in the two highest-ranked categories (variously estimated at about 7 percent of the total employed population in 1919 and 11 percent in 1954). This graph raises the relatively high social milieux from which Members of Parliament were recruited to even higher figures in the 1848–1888 period. In our second period the graph declines in a similar manner. However, from 1918 this decline halts, to reverse slightly in the postwar period, proving, in general, that close to, or more than, one-half of the members of the Dutch Lower House had fathers with occupations ranked within the two highest categories. If we break down these figures further, it becomes clear that an increase in the membership of Deputies with fathers in lower-ranking occupations started with Catholics and Calvinists, who since 1918 generally held between two-fifths and three-fifths of Members from middle- or lower-ranking milieux. The figure for Socialist Deputies was about three-fifths between the wars (with actual working class milieux rarely forming more than one-fifth, even in the case of the Socialist parties). In the postwar period there is a trend toward recruitment from somewhat higher milieux in Calvinist and Socialist parties; this trend is less marked in the Catholic group. The differences in milieu, as measured by the prestige ranking of fathers' occupations among the three major ideological subcultures—Calvinists, Catholics, and Socialists—practically disappeared in the postwar period, with only the Liberal group showing a continuing (if somewhat diminished) preponderance of higher milieu.

Our findings so far are as follows: in the narrow franchise period of 1848 to 1888, the Dutch Parliament retained a strikingly large figure of Members from milieux traditionally given a special place in Dutch government. The weight of this group diminished somewhat in the following two decades; but a basic shift occurred only toward the latter part of the second period, when political parties became increasingly powerful, and Catholics, Calvinists, and Socialists came to dominate Parliament. Then, the traditional milieux of nobility and *Patriciaat* vanished rapidly. Less ascriptive milieux with a high social prestige ranking retained a substantial share, but all in all the role of lower-ranking milieux (though rarely of actual work-

ing-class origin) became substantial in all three subcultural groupings—Calvinists, Catholics, and Socialists. The Liberal party
maintained a more upper class character for a longer time, but this
tendency became less marked in the postwar than in the interwar
period, at a time when the share of highest milieux in the other three
major groupings again began to increase.

V. Occupation: The Background of Fathers

Given the marked presence after the arrival of responsible government of milieux which for centuries had formed the core of the
governing elites in the Netherlands (i.e., the old and new nobility
and the members of the *Patriciaat*), we have probed further into the
question of the degree to which Members of Parliament were born
into families which had been associated with government in one
way or another. On the basis of the occupation of fathers we have
divided Deputies in three main groups: those with fathers in any
type of government office notably (including, in the earlier period,
the judiciary), those recruited from families active in education and
various social organizations, and those in any type of nongovern-
mental employment (including such varied categories as the professions, commerce, industry, and agriculture). Figure 3 shows the
extraordinarily high share of milieux which were already associated

FIGURE 3.
*Percentage of Fathers of Deputies in Three Different Occupational
Categories, 1848–1967*

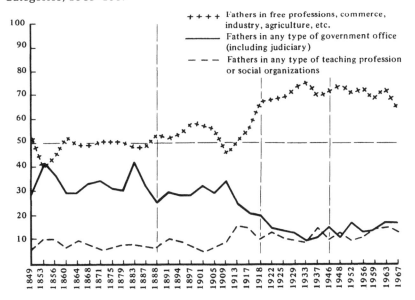

FIGURE 4.
Percentage of Deputies without Father Previously in Executive or
Representative Functions, 1848–1967

with government before the member concerned was elected to Parliament; this was notably the case in the first two periods when government as such took a much *smaller* share of society than it was to do
after World War I, let alone after the Depression and World War II.

To probe this phenomenon further, we have operationalized the
degree of "governmental experience" among fathers in two ways: we
have added together all fathers who had experience in any type of
government office (including work as a high-ranking official and
military officer), and we have similarly investigated to what degree
fathers had served in any representative body (whether in Parliament, provincial, or municipal councils, or the ancient *Polder* boards,
which were public bodies in charge of dykes and the regulation of
water levels). We have called those members who did not have fathers in either category *homines novi*, persons who rose to membership of Parliament without parental prop or prod. Figure 4 shows
that only after 1900 did these *homines novi* begin to be in a clear
majority, the share of members who already had fathers in executive
and/or representative roles in government before that date being very
high indeed. We can underline that statement further if we realize
that among non-government-associated fathers before 1900 between
12 to 20 percent of the persons were in free professions, largely
composed of lawyers who by the nature of their work were also not
far removed from problems of law and government.

VI. Occupations: The Experience of Deputies

Shifting our attention from fathers to the Members themselves, we have portrayed in Figure 5 the occupational background in two ways: taking the first occupation a (future) Member chose and the actual occupation the Member occupied when elected. Inevitably, these two types of graphs show substantial differences in view of the occupational career Members followed between the time-points. Thus Figure 5 shows the overwhelming importance of free professions as a starting point of careers in the first and, to a lesser extent, the second period. It also makes clear that in those same earlier periods later Members clearly moved toward positions in the judiciary and in various kinds of government office, long before election to Parliament. Close to one-half of Members in the first period had themselves had direct experience in government when elected; this figure remained above one-third for most of the period until the First World War. The graph masks the very real shift, however, which took place over the years within the "governmental" category. Whereas in the earlier two periods Members were either judges (see Graph B) or often occupied other prominent government offices, in the later periods not only did judges largely disappear, but also the erstwhile holders of independent government offices were supplemented or replaced by persons who had been officials in departments organized in normal hierarchical manner.[20]

In the latter two periods, experience in education became markedly more important, particularly as a starting point. Yet by far the most significant increase is among Members who at the time of their election occupied functions in social organizations (including, notably, party bureaucracies, different types of unions, and a variety of social welfare organizations); included in this category are also journalists, who tend to take a steady 7 percent of Parliament. The share of members grouped under the encompassing label of "industry, commerce, agriculture, etc.," remains a modest one throughout the period of study: 8 percent of the deputies had their occupation in this sector on election in the first period, 17 percent in the second period, 11 percent in the interwar period, and only 7.5 percent in the postwar period. If one probes the category of functionaries of different social organizations to see whether this group covers a compensatingly high figure of interest group representatives on behalf of industry, commerce, or agriculture, one finds very substantial shares for farmer, retailer, and worker interests but few representatives directly concerned with large-scale enterprise. The Netherlands may have been an old commercial nation which was to develop large-scale industry in the twenteith century. Yet Parliament has tended to mirror the realities of government, of the free professions and later of a host of social institutions and other interest group

FIGURE 5.
First Occupation and Occupation on Election of Deputies in Seven
Categories, 1848–1967 (in percent)*

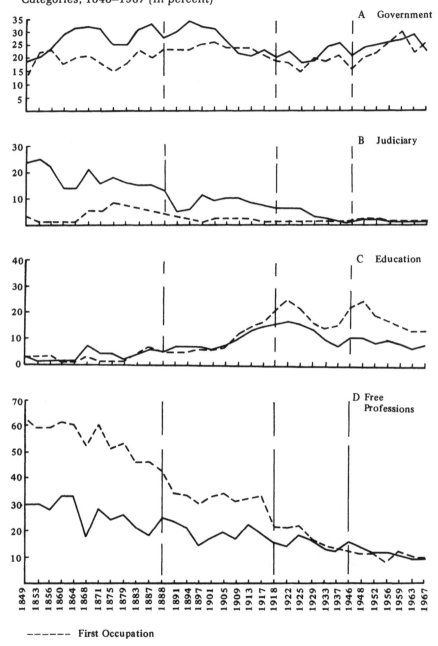

------ First Occupation

——— Occupation on Election

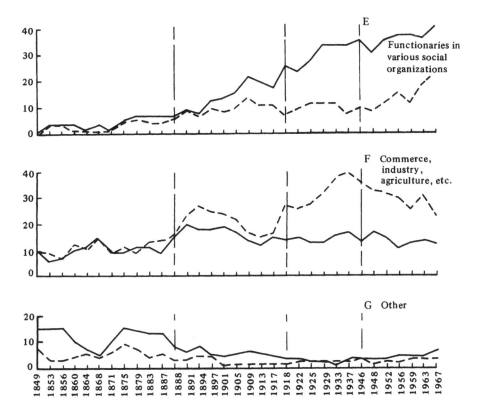

*The dotted lines represent first occupations of the Members, and the unbroken lines indicate their occupation on election.

organizations, much more directly than any type of large-scale business.

The graphs in Figure 5 and the preceding paragraphs only summarize developments for Parliament as a whole, without as yet doing justice to differences in individual political groupings. Such developments are not easy to portray, because they comprise not only differences among different groupings, but also changes within each of them, and all this over a long time period. Generally speaking, the old Conservatives and the earlier Protestants had a particularly large share of persons connected with government office; the older Liberals showed a wider spread and were relatively more open to representatives from early business. Both in Liberal and Catholic circles, free professions had been and remained highly prominent, with persons from industry and commerce taking a somewhat higher share than they did in other parties. Both Catholics and Socialists initially had only a low share of persons from governing milieux, reflecting a persistent historically determined underrepresentation of Catholics

FIGURE 6.
Percentage of Deputies by Different Kinds of Education, 1848–1967

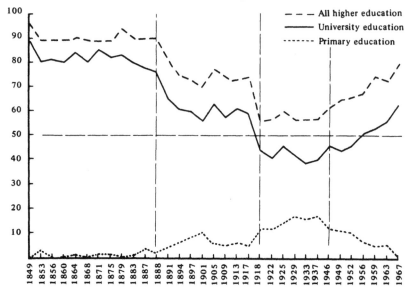

and a slow penetration of Socialists into government—a process which achieved a substantial momentum only in the period after World War II. Teachers were most strongly represented among Socialists and Catholics. All three larger subcultural groupings saw a large increase in the number of representatives of party bureaucrats and social organizations; such members long represented the majority of Socialist deputies and also came to form the dominant group in Catholic representation, which became very clearly reflective of the wide spread of social organizations within its subculture. In later years, the Liberals also saw an influx of organization men. More generally, toward the end of the period of the study the makeup of the different party groups had become increasingly similar, each party group showing a broader spread of experiences, but a preponderance of functionaries with experience either in government, interest groups, or other political and social organizations.

VII.   Educational Background: The Share of University-Trained Members

Figure 6 shows the proportion of Members of the Dutch Lower House who held an academic degree during the period under review. The pattern is a clear one. During the first, most elitist, period the percentage of university-trained personnel was very high indeed,

FIGURE 7.
Percentage of University-Trained Deputies, and Percentage Trained in
Law, 1848–1967

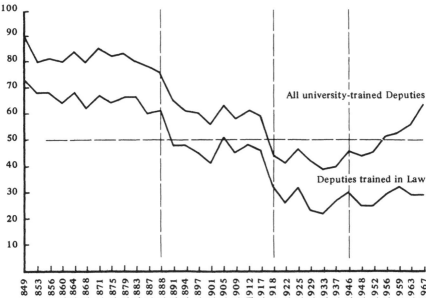

with close to 90 percent of the university-trained Members holding degrees in law. The proportion of university-trained Members declined substantially during the second period of growing party organization, reaching its lowest limit in the third period of full-blown social segmentation. In the last period, the number of academically trained Members increased again substantially, but with graduates from other disciplines than law making the real gains, as shown in Figure 7. Among these groups economists made the greatest jump. Scientists tended to form a fairly steady percentage of university-trained Members from an earlier period (ranging from five to ten members in the House as a whole). Theologians had some significance in the second and third periods, but they lost out rapidly in the postwar era. Men of letters, on the other hand, remained a very marginal group in the Dutch Parliament throughout the period.

To get a clearer view of the dominant group of lawyers among the Members, we have divided them, in Figure 8, into two groups:

1. Those who fulfilled a clear professional role at the time of their elections as either government lawyers (judges and prosecutors), lawyers in private practice, or professors in law faculties.

2. Persons with legal training employed in other roles (e.g., as civil servants, interest group representatives, and so on).

FIGURE 8.
Absolute Number of Professional Lawyers Contrasted with Other
Law-Trained Deputies, 1848–1959

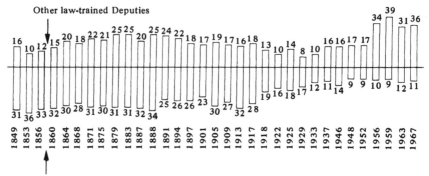

Other law-trained Deputies

Professional lawyers (in government,
teaching, or private practice)

As shown in Figure 8, the results indicate that professional law-yers dominated the first two periods, and were in rough balance with other law-trained categories in the third period; but they were re-duced to a minor share as compared to the second group in the last two decades.

VIII. Educational Background:
The Non-University-Trained Members

The relatively high level of educational background of Dutch Members of Parliament, as made apparent in the strong proportion of university-trained members, can be further substantiated by two other facts: first, the presence next to the formal university graduates of a constant share of about 10 to 20 percent of persons with other advanced post-secondary school training (this figure is even higher if teachers are also included in that category); and second, in reverse, a very low share of members with primary education only. (Both categories are also presented graphically in Figure 6.) The latter group was absent in the first period and remained low in the second pe-riod. Only in the interwar period and shortly after World War II did the percentage of members with primary education rise above 10 percent, to dwindle again rapidly in the last decade. These figures represent the very low share of Dutch Deputies who were manual workers, such members usually having risen, through union activity, into positions of substantial experience and responsibility during employment in factories and fields. That this number (though mod-est) was largest in the third period again illustrates the importance of the Verzuiling process in democratizing representation. Persons with a relatively modest education were brought onto the party list not only by the Socialists but also by the religious parties. Catholics and Protestants usually had at least half their members from non-university milieux in the interwar period. The share of non-academics among Socialist Deputies was, then, even higher, but any real differences between the Socialists and the religious parties tended to disappear after 1956, with all three groupings contributing to a new rise in university-trained representation from that time onward.

IX. Deputies and Their Religion

In the presentation of our data, we have left the religious background of Members of Parliament for last. In a political system in which parties formed on the basis of rival views on the relation between state and religion, this factor is obviously a major one. Yet this very fact causes variation to be mainly significant *among*, rather than *within*, the different parties. The religious makeup of the Lower House reflects, therefore, the very development of the party system over time, in all its complications of mobilization and representation.

The simplest way to understand the religious map of the Netherlands is to start from a division into four categories: Catholics, adherents of the Dutch Reformed Church, Protestant dissenters, and a non-Church group.[21] Of these four, the Dutch Reformed was much the largest, and initially also the most influential; in the two centuries of the Dutch Republic before 1795, offices were in principle reserved to its adherents. Yet ever since the Reformation Catholics remained a very large minority, which almost monopolized the (later-conquered) Southern provinces of Brabant, Limburg, and certain adjacent areas. But Catholics also represented a substantial share in both the cities and the countryside of the province of Holland. Protestant dissenters (the *Doopsgezinden,* or Mennonites, who in the Netherlands form a much less inbred and less orthodox community than in the U.S.; the Lutherans; and the Remonstrants; a seventeenth-century libertarian offshoot from the Dutch Reformed Church) were always very small in numbers yet intellectually influential. The non-Church group is the product of increasing secularization which in the twentieth century assumed massive proportions, particularly in the larger cities and the less fundamentalist Protestant areas of the West and the Northeast of the country.

It is easiest to dispose of the Protestant dissenters. We find a somewhat large number of Mennonites and a sprinkling of Lutherans, particularly in the earlier periods. Remonstrants were also represented generally with one or two members and showed a relatively high representation in the period after World War II. The Protestant dissenters as a group have tended to be over-represented in relation to the population in general, but less so when one compares the membership of Parliament with highly educated groups in the Netherlands. (In this context, it is worth noting that confessing Jews too, were represented early with one or two members; that number increased to three or four members at the time of most active Liberal mobilization in the 1890's and 1913 and was highest under the PR list system in the interwar period with a maximum of five members just before the outbreak of World War II. Protestant dissenters were found almost exclusively in the ranks of Liberals and Socialists, as was inevitably true for confessing Jews, though not for baptized ones.)[22]

For the larger groups of Dutch Reformed, Catholics, and non-Church members, we have plotted, in Figures 9A and 9B, graphs showing their share in the population as compared to their share in the membership of Parliament.

The easiest to interpret are the two graphs for the Catholics. They show the very sizable and rather steady share of the Catholics in the population, a portion which has moved between the narrow limits of 35 and 40 percent. The figures show a substantial but narrowing lag in Catholic representation before 1917. This reflects the unwillingness of Protestant voters to vote for Catholic representatives in mixed areas, Catholics therefore being in fact eligible only in districts where Catholic voters were in an absolute majority. Once PR was introduced, this discriminating factor was done away with. After 1917 the figure of Catholic Deputies remains proportionally still somewhat below that of Catholics in the general population. This appears to be so because not *all* nominal Catholics in fact voted for the Catholic party (even though in a comparative perspective Dutch Catholics did so to a very high degree) and also because the actual number of Catholics in the voting population over the age of twenty-five was substantially below that of the over twenty-five population as a whole. The highest number of Catholics in the Dutch Parliament was found in the immediate postwar period, when the Catholic party itself was at its zenith, and the Socialists consciously included Catholics on their party slate to indicate their deliberate wish to break through the older lines of separation. (In the 1970's Socialists no longer followed this policy, but the Liberals took over in that respect. By that time, Catholic cohesion had been shattered, however, with drastic consequences for the strength of Catholic deputies in Parliament.[23]

The two graphs for the non-Church group show a parallel upward trend. Abandonment of Church associations in Parliament outdistanced that of the population only in the periods after World War I and World War II, when some parties of the Left (including Communists) achieved a relatively large representation.

The most complex picture is that of the Dutch Reformed group. The Dutch Reformed Church was closer to being a national Church—if not in law, then in numbers and historical claim—than any other religious group. During the period of our investigation its share in the population dropped from 55 percent in 1849 to 23 percent at the

FIGURE 9A.
Religion of Deputies Compared with Population, 1848–1967 (in percent)*

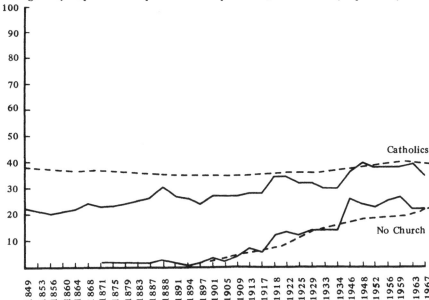

FIGURE 9B.

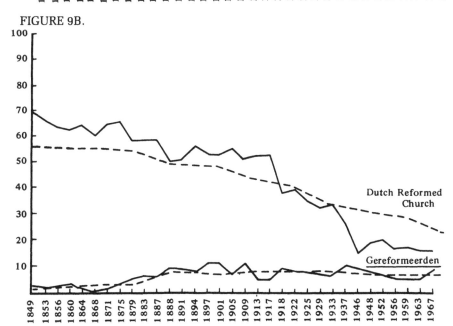

*The unbroken lines represent the religion of the Deputies, and the dotted lines represent the religion of the population as a whole.

census of 1970. This development is explained by a combination of three factors: a demographic one (consisting of a comparatively low birthrate and correspondingly high mortality of an aging sector of the population), the process of secularization (contributing largely to the great increase in persons—22 percent in 1970—no longer acknowledging Church membership), and a series of walkouts by fundamentalist believers. The most important of these took place in 1886, when the militant statesman and clergyman Abraham Kuyper, the founder of the Antirevolutionary Party in 1879, led a flock of fundamentalists out of the Dutch Reformed Church, to form the *Gereformeerde Kerken* in 1892 with a number of earlier secessionist groupings. The picture of Calvinist Protestantism in the Netherlands since than can be understood only if two facts are realized:

1. Not all members of the Dutch Reformed Church are fundamentalists, libertarian elements having been an important force since the beginning of the nineteenth century, if not earlier.

2. Fundamentalist Protestants are scattered among a number of churches, including several important strands within the Dutch Reformed Church, the 1892 *Gereformeerden* (which account for a steady 7 percent of the population), and a number of smaller Calvinist sects (some of them dating from the days of the Reformation, others being remnants of walkouts from the Dutch Reformed Church earlier in the nineteenth century, and yet others the product of splits from the *Gereformeerde Kerken* after 1892; these smaller sects account in *toto* for about 2 percent of the population).

Figure 9B shows clearly that the number of Dutch Reformed Members of Parliament was substantially higher than that of their percentage in population until the advent of proportional representation in 1917. This fact simply mirrors the bias against Catholic representation until that time, a bias which worked to the advantage of both Liberals and various Orthodox Protestant candidates at different times. In the same figure, we have drawn the proportion of the various *Gereformeerden* in both the population and in Parliament. Their parliamentary share was highest in 1901 and 1909, when the militant Antirevolutionaries spearheaded the drive of the various religious parties to carve out their own organized place in society, and again in 1937 when a strong Calvinist politician led his slate to victory, thus augmenting the share of Calvinist Deputies, paradoxically as a result also of many non-Calvinist votes. The sizable drop of Dutch Reformed Members below the group's proportional share of the population in the post-1918 era, particularly after 1946, is the reverse of the increase in the share of non-Church representatives. Both Liberals and Socialists have always appealed to Dutch Reformed voters, and there has always been a substantial number of Dutch Reformed Deputies on the slate of either party; yet their added number was not proportionate to that of Dutch Reformed voters for both parties.

Clearly, then, changes in the composition of the membership of the Dutch House rather closely followed developments in the population at large. The dominance of the Dutch Reformed Church in the early nineteenth century was, if anything, overreflected, with only small groups of Protestant dissenters and Catholic representation of little cohesion appearing next to it. Yet the broad nature of the Dutch Reformed Church made it anything but a distinct and cohesive force in politics. This Church in practice housed many latitudinarian elements, who in politics generally identified with Liberals and later also with Socialists rather than with explicitly religious parties. The very fact of practical permissiveness within the Church helped to stir Orthodox countermovements which disagreed among themselves on the value of retaining the "general" Church as an institution: whereas some Orthodox Protestants wished to reorganize the Dutch Reformed Church from within, others preferred a walkout. The Protestant subculture therefore came to include very different strands which were fragmented in doctrine, in party organization, and in Church membership. As we have added the various Protestant groupings together in this paper, such differences do not appear in our graphs—except for the characteristic group of the *Gereformeerden* who formed the backbone, but not the exclusive support, of the Antirevolutionary Party. A more detailed analysis would require a separate paper. Here we must satisfy ourselves with the conclusion that the Orthodox elements within the Dutch Reformed Church were represented in Parliament by a variety of parties but not in such large numbers as to compensate for the actual underrepresentation of Dutch Reformed members on the lists of Liberals and Socialists. The long-term trend of the Dutch Reformed in Parliament is therefore downward, even when compared with the Church's already large-scale decline in the population as a whole.

Catholics received increasing representation, initially through the geographic representation of voters in dominantly Catholic areas alone, but once PR was introduced, through a very high correlation of Catholic religion and voting. Toward the end of our 1848–1967 period, that correlation dropped dramatically, however, eventually leading to a decline in the number of Catholic Deputies who were not adequately replaced by the appearance of Catholics on the list of nonreligious parties. The difference was made up to some extent by Protestant dissenters, but above all by the non-Church group.

XI. Summary of Findings

We have investigated changes in the composition of the Dutch Lower House of Parliament on the basis of biographic data of all members who sat in the House between 1848 and 1967. We have divided that period into phases, first on the basis of changes in the number of eligible voters and the electoral system and later on the basis of the watershed of World War II, thus arriving at four distinct periods:

1. The period of responsible government on the basis of a highly limited franchise (1848–1888)

2. The period of franchise extension between 1888 and 1917, which saw an increased party organization and a sharper demarcation between a Right (consisting of a variety of Orthodox Protestant groupings and the Catholics) and a Left (composed of assorted Liberals who encountered a rapidly increasing competition from parliamentary Socialists)

3. The interwar period (1918–1940), which witnessed a stabilization of party forces and a rapidly increasing social segmentation (*Verzuiling*)

4. The period between 1945 and 1967, in which the proportionate strength of the different political families remained still relatively stable but became characterized by a much fuller integration of a widened Socialist movement in government and society.

One of our strongest findings has been the persistence long after 1848 of *milieux* which had been associated with government long before responsible government was introduced. This finding was substantiated by the continuing presence of sons of the nobility and the *Patriciaat*; by a very strong role fathers of members had already played in government, whether in an official or representative capacity; and by an overwhelming number of university-trained members (almost invariably lawyers, including a very large number of judges, holders of other independent offices, and persons with experience in the free professions). Study of the regional origin of Members in this period revealed a strong coincidence between place of birth and domicile, underlining the importance of traditional forms of geographic representation in national decision-making. Interestingly, deputies in the early period were overwhelmingly born in cities rather than in the countryside, and noticeably in provincial capitals.

Characteristic recruitment patterns of the first period persisted into the second period to some degree, but all indicators—e.g., the number of representatives and other families from the nobility and *Patriciaat*, the number of members whose fathers had already served in government, the role of judges and other holders of offices, the importance of the free professions as a recruiting ground, the percentage of Deputies who had gone to universities or had received other forms of higher education—pointed downward. These changes were partly the result of the increased representation of Orthodox Protestants and Catholics as well as the entry of Socialists into Parliament; but they also reflected clear shifts *within* the major movements, including the Liberals and the religious parties.

Using similar indicators, we found the third interwar period of 1918 to 1940 to be the period of greatest democratization. This pe-

riod saw the largest number of representatives from relatively modest milieux with primary or secondary education only; the largest
influx of persons originally trained as teachers (always a significant
group in upward social mobility); the virtual disappearance of judges;
a strong decline of the free professions; and a large increase of Members who entered after experience as functionaries in parties, interest
groups, and social institutions. One significant development in that
period was the considerable increase of members born in smaller
villages. The process of democratization would seem to have resulted in a diminution of the traditional hegemony of cities in Dutch
politics, as the tightening organization of religious groups resulted
notably in an increased integration of long-disadvantaged rural areas
in the political process.

During the last period, the level of academic preparation of Members went again sharply upward. But at the same time traditional
recruiting grounds like the free professions declined further, as did
judgeships. The sharpest rise was again in the number of persons
who had served in various political and social organizations. Also,
the number of persons who had previously served in government
increased again, and within that category the number of officials, as
against the traditional holders of government offices. The modern
Parliament became overwhelmingly an assembly of functionaries.

We may also summarize these findings not so much in sequential
terms as in terms of more general processes:

1. Ancient geographic differences in recruitment persisted as first
under a district system and then under proportional representation
parties, increasingly organized on nationwide bases. By place of birth
(although not by domicile) the Dutch parliamentary elite remained
roughly proportionate to the spread of population over the different
provinces. However, in a period of increasing urbanization, the share
of Deputies not born in cities went up significantly, a finding which
would seem to illustrate the belated integration of rural areas in a
polity which had been traditionally city dominated.

2. In the first decades after 1848 Dutch public life retained a strong
Protestant flavor, the Dutch Reformed Church being not only the
church of the majority of the population but also the one closely
associated with the traditional governing elite.[24] But the very place
of the Dutch Reformed Church became a strong bone of contention
as it was increasingly challenged from within, both by more latitudinarian and by more orthodox Calvinist elements, as the Catholics
became increasingly self-reliant, and as secularization eventually
demanded a heavier and heavier toll. As a result, the spread of members in religious association became greatly more diversified, with
the old Dutch Reformed Church ending up as the Church of only a
modest minority of members—and a very heterogeneous one at that.

3. Traditional representation was very heavily skewed toward tra-

ditional families reared in, or closely attached to, government. Such links were rapidly broken down once franchise extension and new forms of political and social mobilization brought many new circles into politics. The shift to new groups and new milieux can be traced in all political groupings, among older ones like the Orthodox Protestants and Liberals as well as among the Catholics and Socialists. But employment in government remained a substantial recruiting channel, albeit with a definite lag for the Catholics first, the Socialists later, both groups becoming integrated into government rather later than Liberals or Calvinists.

4. Among the groups with the least direct representation in Parliament, two stand out: the world of commerce and industry and that of manual labor. As compared to the other major recruiting grounds—government in all its forms, the free professions, the world of education, and that of party politics and social and cultural organizations—the world of the trading firm or the large factory is conspicuously low in parliamentary representation. For farmers, retailers, and workers this apparent lack was to a considerable extent compensated for by the rapid increase from the 1920's onward in the number of interest group functionaries. This was far less true for commerce and industry, who found only a modicum of direct representation through Liberals and Catholics.[25]

5. The period of recruitment from the most modest milieux (measured in terms of occupation of fathers, own occupation, and/or level of education) was not the most recent period but the period between the wars. To this not only the Socialists but also the Calvinists and Catholics contributed heavily. If one defines democratization in terms of spreading of recruitment to lower milieux and to the widest possible array of social groups, the period of its greatest impact was that of the heyday of Verzuiling.

6. Throughout the entire period the Netherlands Parliament had a very large percentage of members with a high degree of education. Only in the just-mentioned period of maximum Verzuiling did that share substantially decline, but the postwar world, and with it the Parliament of the Netherlands, saw a new surge in the number of persons with university degrees or other forms of higher education. One might argue that this trend reflects the result of growing levels of education in European society generally, as well as the inevitable requirement for expert knowledge in modern government. But the very high proportion of academics and related groups may well reflect also ancient habits of virtual representation in the Netherlands, as well as the disproportionately favorable political resources which academics enjoy in the world of modern politics.

7. Among all the groups contributing to parliamentary representation, that of the functionaries in social organizations grew fastest and became largest. This category, in fact, covers an array of organi-

zations including party bureaucracies, the media, interest group organizations, and welfare and cultural organizations. It could be tempting to describe developments as analyzed in this paper in terms of a shift from an elite-dominated regional pluralism toward that of a wide-ranging representation of functional organizations. Yet such a characterization meets with at least one paradox. In recent decades, Dutch society (like societies elsewhere in Western Europe) has indeed witnessed a massive growth of specialized social organizations. At one time, such organizations tended to be stimulated and mediated through the major parties of the general Verzuiling system. But they have now become so firmly rooted and have developed such close independent links with executive departments and among one another that neither party nor Parliament seems to be still a vital cog in their operation. At the same time, the job of a Deputy has become much more of a full-time profession which increasingly also lures self-starting politicians into the competition for nomination to Parliament. The very debate about the relation between what Rokkan once termed the "party-election channel" and the world of corporate pluralism[26] is now assuming an importance it did not have at the time when Verzuiling made for what then seemed a natural and inevitable integration of both circuits.

We gratefully acknowledge the data collection activities of many co-workers in the Parliamentary Documentation Centre at Leyden University and in particular the tireless efforts of Mrs. Ineke P. Secker. Much fuller data and analyses are presented in Joop Th. J. van den Berg, "De Herkomst van de Tweede Kamerleden in de Periode 1848–1967" (Ph.D. diss., University of Leyden, forthcoming).

Notes

1. See for Lijphart's analysis of Dutch political experience *The Politics of Accommodation: Pluralism and Democracy in the Netherlands* (Berkeley: University of California Press, 1968) and, for his more general typological writing, "Typologies of Democratic Systems," *Comparative Political Studies* 1 (1968), pp. 3–44; "Consociational Democracy," *World Politics* 21 (1969), pp. 207–25; and *Democracy in Plural Societies: A Comparative Exploration* (New Haven: Yale University Press, 1977).

2. Hans Daalder, "On Building Consociational Nations: The Cases of the Netherlands and Switzerland," *International Social Science Journal* 23 (1971), pp. 355–70; and Hans Daalder, "The Consociational Democracy Theme," *World Politics* 26 (1974), pp. 604–21.

3. Hans Daalder, "The Netherlands: Opposition in a Segmented Society," in *Political Oppositions in Western Democracies*, ed. Robert A. Dahl (New Haven: Yale University Press, pp. 188–236); and Hans Daalder, "Consociationalism, Centre and Periphery in the Netherlands," in *Mobilization, Centre-Periphery Structures and Nation-Building*, ed. Per Torsvik (Oslo: Universitetsforlaget, 1981), pp. 181–239.

4. Ian Lustick, "Stability in Deeply Divided Societies: Consociational-ism versus Control," *World Politics* 31 (1979), pp. 325–44; Ilja Scholten, "Does Consociationalism Exist? A Critique of the Dutch Experience," in *Electoral Participation* (London: Sage, 1981), pp. 329–54; Ronald A. Kieve, "Pillars of Sand: A Marxist Critique of Consociational Democracy in the Netherlands," *Comparative Politics* 13 (1981), pp. 313–37; and M. P. C. M. van Schendelen, "Verzuiling en Restauratie in de Nederlandse Politiek," *Beleid en Maatschappij* 5 (1978), pp. 42–54. For further references and a more general discussion, see Daalder, "Consociationalism, Centre and Periphery in the Netherlands."

5. Mattei Dogan and Maria Scheffer-van der Veen, "Le Personnel Min-isteriel Hollandais," *L'Annee Sociologique* 7 (1957), pp. 95–125. See also Nico Cramer, "De Herkomst van de Kabinetsleider," *Acta Politica* 2 (1969), pp. 220–33.

6. For studies of the historical background of particular Dutch par-liamentary periods, see Th. van Tijn, "The Party Structure of Holland and the Outer Provinces in the Nineteenth Century," in *Britain and the Neth-erlands: Metropolis, Dominion and Province* (The Hague: Nijhoff, 1971), pp. 176–207. E. H. Kossman, *The Low Countries, 1780–1940*, vols. 6 (Ox-ford: Clarendon Press, 1978); S. J. Fockema Andreae, "De Grootburgers 1848–1879," in *500 Jaren Staten-Generaal in de Nederlanden: Van Sta-tenvergadering tot Volksvertegenwoordiging* (Assen, the Netherlands: Van Gorcum, 1964), pp. 209–40; R. Reinsma, "De Invasie der Kerkelijken: De A. R. Kamerleden van 1897–1917," *Antirevolutionaire Staatkunde* 36 (1969), pp. 241–65. And for the same general subject, see above all D. H. Kuiper, *De Voormannen: Een Sociaal-Wetenschappelijke Studie over Ideologie, Konflikt en Kerngroepvorming binnen de Gereformeerde Wer-eld tussen 1820 en 1930* (Boom, the Netherlands: Meppel & Kok Kampen).

7. Hans Daalder and Sonja Hubee-Boonazzijer, "Sociale Herkomst en Politieke Recrutering van Nederlandse Kamerleden in 1968," *Acta Poli-tica* 5 (1969), pp. 292–333, 371–416; Jan Kooiman, *Over de Kamer Gespro-ken* (The Hague: Staatsuitgeverij, 1976); J. J. A. Thomassen, *Kiezers en Gekozenen in een Representatieve Democratie* (Alphen a/d Rijn: Samsom, 1976); M. P. C. M. van Schendelen, J. J. A. Thomassen, and H. Daudt, eds., *Leden van de Staten-Generaal: Kamerleden over de Werking van het Parlement* (The Hague: Vuga, 1981), particularly J. Th. J. van den Berg, "Herkomst, Ervaring en Toekomstperspectief van Kamerleden," pp. 21–72 in that collection.

8. For an example see Robert L. Morlan, *Gemeentepolitiek in Debat: Opvatting van Burgers en Bestuurders* (Alphen a/d Rijn: Samsom, 1974).

9. Samuel J. Eldersveld, Jan Kooiman, and Theo van der Tak, *Elite Images of Dutch Politics: Accommodation and Conflict* (Ann Arbor: Uni-versity of Michigan Press, 1981).

10. Bert P. Middel and Wijbrandt H. van Schuur, "Dutch Party Dele-gates: Background Characteristics, Attitudes toward the European Com-munity and toward Dutch Politics of Delegates from CDA, D'66, PvdA, and VVD," *Acta Politica* 16 (1981), pp. 241–63.

11. G. Gerding and B. de Jong, *De Politieke en Ambtelijke Top*, Rapport nr. 6, Commissie Hoofdstructuur Rijksdienst (The Hague: Staatsuitgeverij, 1981).

12. Stein Rokkan, "Dimensions of State Formation and Nation-Building: A Possible Paradign for Research on Variations with Europe," in *The Formation of National States in Western Europe*, ed. Charles Tilly (Princeton, N.J.: Princeton University Press, pp. 562–600).

13. For more details, see the later sections of Daalder, "Consociationalism, Centre and Periphery in the Netherlands."

14. The biographical archive contains material on many elite groups in Dutch society in addition to ministers and Members of Parliament; it is being extended backward into history by different groups of historians. The material is stored in coded as well as narrative form, so that both statistical analysis and textual reproduction are feasible. Nicola Cramer, has devised an intriguing computer package for the archive, which is now being tested further for use in the development of automated systems for the Dutch Parliament generally.

15. Kooiman, *Over de Kamer Gesproken*; Thomassen, *Kiezers en Gekozenen in in een Representatieve Democratie*; and van Schendelen, Thomassen, and Daudt, *Leden van de Staten-Generaal: Kamerleden over de Werking van het Parlement*.

16. Daalder, "Extreme Proportional Representation: The Dutch Experience," in *Adversary Politics and Electoral Reform*, ed. S. E. Finer (London: Anthony Wigram, 1975), pp. 223–48; Daalder, "Consociationalism, Centre and Periphery in the Netherlands"; J. Th. J. van den Berg, "De Evenredige Vertegenwoordiging in Nederland," *Tijdschrift voor Geschiedenis* 92 (1979), pp. 452–72; and C. B. Wels, "Stemmen en Kiezen 1795–1922," *Tijdschrift voor Geschiedenis* 92 (1979), pp. 313–32.

17. See also Daalder, "The Netherlands," and "Consociationalism, Centre and Periphery."

18. For the relevant groups, see van den Berg, "De Evenredige Vertegenwoordiging in Nederland."

19. F. van Heek and E. V. W. Vercruijsse, "De Nederlandse Beroepsprestige-stratificatie," in *Sociale Stijging in Nederland*, ed. F. van Heek (Leyden: Stenfert Kroese, 1958), pp. 11–48; J. J. M. van Tulder, *De Beroepsmobiliteit in Nederland van 1919 tot 1954* (Leyden: Stenfert Kroese, 1962); and P. Vinke, *De Maatschappelijke Plaats en Herkomst der Directeuren en Commissarissen van de Open en daarmee Vergelijkbare Naamloze Vennootschappen* (Leyden: Stenfert Kroese, 1961).

20. It should be realized that officials in the departments of the national government, when elected to Parliament, receive leaves of absence, while retaining their pay and normal annual salary increases minus the normal pay of a Deputy. This factor represented a substantial incentive as long as the parliamentary indemnity was modest, as indeed it was until 1968.

21. See for more details Daalder, "Consociationalism, Centre and Periphery in the Netherlands," pp. 204–14.

22. Hans Daalder, "Dutch Jews in a Segmented Society," *Acta Historiae Neerlandicae*, vol. 10 (The Hague: Nijhoff, 1978), pp. 175–94.

23. For fuller data, based on the 1979 survey among Lower House Members, see van den Berg, "Herkomst, Ervaring en Toekomstperspectief van Kamerleden."

24. Within the Dutch Reformed Church a small elite has traditionally

organized in the so-called *Eglise Vallone*. While this group had never more than 0.3 percent of the total population, the figure among nineteenth century Deputies rose occasionally to more than 10 percent.

25. We emphasize the word "direct" representation. Members who did not themselves have an immediate experience of trade or industry might well be drawn into contact with business through board memberships and the like. We have data on this in our files, but they are still too scattered to allow for a reliable quantitative assessment over time.

26. Stein Rokkan, "Norway: Numerical Democracy and Corporate Pluralism," in *Political Oppositions in Western Democracies*, ed. Robert A. Dahl (New Haven: Yale University Press, 1966), pp. 70–115; and Stein Rokkan, "Votes Count, Resources Decide," in *Makt og Motiv. Et Festskrift til Jens*, ed. Arup Seip (Oslo: Gyldendal, 1975), pp. 216–24.

Patterns and Consequences of Subcultural Integration of the Dutch Elite

Thomas R. Rochon

In all societies . . . two classes of people appear—a class that rules and a class that is ruled. The first class, always the less numerous, performs all political functions, monopolizes power and enjoys the advantages that power brings, whereas the second, the more numerous class, is directed and controlled by the first.[1]

With these words, Gaetano Mosca indicated the ubiquitous existence of a political elite. It is an elite, according to Mosca, which rules by virtue of being an organized minority, as well as by possession of other "qualities that give them a certain material, intellectual or even moral superiority."[2]

To Mosca, as well as to other elite theorists such as Michels and Pareto, the proposition that "elites matter" is a self-evident one, clearly set out as the starting point of their work. Some social scientists today would call that proposition into doubt, saying that elites merely reflect broader social cleavages in their patterns of conflict and decision making. Yet the translation of conflict behavior from cleavages to mass political culture to elite political culture need not always be automatic. In some cases, a divided society can still be governed by a cohesive elite. When that occurs, the claim that elites matter is clearly supported. Mosca points out that a society may be divided and nonetheless be ruled as though it were founded upon strong social unity.

This situation arises whenever the political formula, on which the ruling class in a given society bases its dominion, is not accessible to the lower classes, or [has] . . . not sunk deeply enough into the consciousness of the more populous and less well educated strata of society. The same thing occurs when there is any considerable difference between the customs, culture and habits of the ruling class and those of the governed classes.[3]

Mosca's examples of a social group to which the elite does not respond include the slaves in Rome and Athens and the casteless *harijans* in India. In confining himself to examples of exclusion from the political community, however, Mosca failed to anticipate the degree of independence from popular sentiment that even elites chosen on the basis of universal suffrage might attain. One such example of elite independence from the mass political will is the case of consociational democracy.

This article will focus on elite attitudes in the Netherlands, the cradle of consociational democracy. Its purpose is to examine elite attitudes toward their own roles, toward rival elites, and toward the political system as a whole in a country where elite domination of politics is a relatively obvious fact. If the central elements of elite theories are consciousness, coherence, and conspiracy,[4] then consociational democracy in the Netherlands meets the criteria rather well.

The concept of consociational democracy originated with Arend Lijphart in 1968; he has later described the "paradox" of the smooth operation of the Dutch political system despite the centrality of class and religion as social and political cleavages.[5] The Netherlands was, and still is to a great degree, characterized by highly institutionalized cleavages which segregate the population and limit cross-cleavage interaction. This separation of the population into isolated groups or subcultures extends beyond the political realm to all areas of social life. Discussing Dutch Catholicism, L. J. Rogier has noted

> the remarkable . . . constellation of an almost autarkic Catholic community, within whose boundaries one not only supports a political party, but also subscribes to a Catholic newspaper, a Catholic fashion magazine, a Catholic illustrated weekly, and a Catholic youth magazine. The children enjoy Catholic education from nursery school to the university, and it is in a Catholic context that one listens to the radio, goes on a trip, buys life insurance, and enjoys art, science, and sport. It is . . . a system which to the ultimate degree has raised isolation to a style of life, even to the basic principle of life.[6]

The system of organizational segregation is thorough enough that the Dutch use the image of "pillars" to describe the phenomenon. The pillars are a series of vertical organizational columns, each separate from the other. As a metaphor for the structure of Dutch society, they are both graphic and crucial to the pattern of political and social mobilization of the Dutch public.

The consociational democracy pattern posits elite behavior that is largely independent of these aspects of social segregation. That is not to say that the elites are not a part of the pillarized system. Lijphart's examination of the Dutch parliamentary elite shows that many of them are also members of the elite of allied social organizations. An example of this would be the Labor party member who is also a leader of one of the socialist trade unions. However, Lijphart remarks:

> Though the degree of overlap differs from bloc to bloc, it occurs only within the bloc. Intrabloc overlap is the rule and not a single instance of overlap between different blocs can be found: not one Protestant union leader represents the Labor Party in parliament, not one leader of the Catholic employers belongs in the Liberal party elite, and not one of the professors in parliament is connected with the "wrong" university.[7]

Although they share in the segmentation of the society, the elites nonetheless have attitudes which allow them to bridge the gaps between the subcultures. They are prepared to compromise in order to reach agreement on policy, thereby maintaining a stable democracy despite the severity of the social cleavages. As Hans Daalder put it,

> This would explain why the Netherlands can have party disputes that are almost theological in nature, and yet have sound administration, and why there can be such great disagreement over politics and yet, in some ways, alarmingly little over policy.[8]

It is clear that elites do matter in a consociational democracy, that they play a major role in moderating the political impact of social cleavages. It is an elite conspiracy with the presumably benign intent of keeping political conflict within safe limits. However, effective elite conspiracies appear to be rare in the empirical world. What we know of elite attitudes and behavior suggests that competition and rivalry, rather than cohesion and cooperation, are generally characteristic of relationships between elites of different parties.[9] For this reason, the type of elite attitudes described in the consociational democracy model should not be taken for granted as an inference from elite theories of politics. They are worth exploring.

Standing in the way of that exploration, however, is the fact that consociational democracy is an ideal type for which empirical approximations are becoming increasingly hard to find. Belgium, Canada, Colombia, and Lebanon are among the countries that have been described as consociational in recent years.[10] And in each of these cases, to varying degrees, it can be noted that elites are no longer able to contain political conflict as well as they once did. Even in the Netherlands, a charter member of the consociational club, both the segmented character of the mass public and the accommodationist attitudes of the Dutch elite have been changing rapidly in the last fifteen years. This fact was already apparent to Lijphart as he set down his description of Dutch consociationalism, and others have written on similar change in the Netherlands and elsewhere.[11]

At the mass level, the primary changes have been deconfessionalization, depillarization, and politicization.[12] All three of these changes strike at essential prerequisites of consociational democracy, but the most important of them has been deconfessionalization, or the secularization of society. In 1948, 91 percent of Dutch Catholics voted for the Catholic People's party (KVP). In 1963 this percentage had fallen somewhat but still held at 83. In 1967, only 67 percent of Catholics voted for the KVP, and in 1972 the percentage dipped to 38. Between the 1972 and 1977 elections, the KVP actually went out of business, federating with two Protestant parties to form a centrist Christian Democratic Appeal (CDA). The very fact that the merger could take place, of course, is further evidence for the decline of the relevance of the confessional cleavage in the Netherlands.

Partially in response to the secularization of the Dutch public, the political behavior of the Dutch elite has also changed. Politics has become more open, conflictual, and polarized.[13] There have been widespread demands for structural changes in the political system in the last two decades, including calls for direct election of the prime minister, the election of mayors, establishment of a district system for election to Parliament, and abolition of the monarchy. Seven new parties, most of them not tied to the established pillars, have gained parliamentary representation in the six general elections since 1959.

Politics in the Netherlands has thus been changing rapidly in the last fifteen years. Some of the changes at the mass level, such as the secularization of society, may make it easier rather than harder for elites to reach compromises between subcultures. Yet increasing demands for mass involvement in politics, coupled with the readiness on the part of a growing number of voters to abandon their subcultural affiliations, has increased the amount of politicization and competition between elites at the national level.

This fact, suggests that the place to study consociational attitudes in the Netherlands is at the local level, where politics is quieter, more elite-dominated, and run along lines strongly suggestive of the consociational mentality. For example, the institutions of local government and the behavior of local politicians put a great deal of stress on rule by a small elite in the College of B & W (the mayor and the aldermen), which is the local equivalent of a cabinet. Long-standing norms hold that parties should participate in the College of B & W in proportion to their strength in the City Council, and that the Council should generally defer to the legislative recommendations of the College.[14] Since elitist, consensual institutions and practices of local government have been less under fire than those of the national level of government, the result has been less change at local levels. In addition, the sheer inertia and continuity of political cultures would lead us to expect local elites to continue to display many of the attitudes associated with the politics of accommodation.

The study of local party elites reported here is part of a larger study of local activists in the parties, trade unions, and citizens' groups in three Dutch cities—Breda, Delft, and Ede. The cities were chosen for their roughly similar sizes and economic profiles, coupled with their diversity in terms of subcultural composition.[15] For present purposes it is important only to note that no significant attitudinal differences were found among party leaders in the three cities. Thus, generalizations to urban party activitists in the Netherlands as a whole are probably not unreasonable.

Consensus on the Rules of the Game

The cornerstone of the consociational model of elite behavior is common agreement on what Mosca would call the political formula,[16] what Lijphart calls the rules of the game. The rules of the game set criteria for decision making, for the conduct of politics, and for relations with other elite groups and with the mass public. Of course, unwritten norms of behavior are not unique to the Netherlands. There usually exists in a country an "elite political culture" which is more specialized than the mass political culture. Rules of the game are simply aspects of that elite political culture, and to suggest that the game is played according to a unified set of rules is simply to posit a homogeneous elite political culture.

For a number of reasons, it is not the purpose of this article to test the validity of the rules of the game that were proposed for the Netherlands by Lijphart. One reason is that Lijphart was referring to the national political elite; he made no claim that similar rules could be expected to apply to local elites. A more serious obstacle to a test of Lijphart's rules is the fact that the Dutch political scene has changed drastically in the last fifteen years. Rules that are no longer observed may well have guided elite behavior under the *ancien régime*.

Even so, Lijphart's rules of the game provide a standard that can serve as a basis for measuring the support by different segments of the local elite for the informal norms of consociational democracy. Since the rules all have to do with the methods and bases of political decision making, division on them is a good indicator of a lack of intra-elite consensus.

Table 1 offers a summary of Lijphart's seven rules of the game in elite political cultures. The table also includes the questions that were asked of the local activists in order to test their adherence to these rules.

Lijphart's first rule, that politics is a serious business, is not well suited to empirical test. Upon reflection, it is clear that politically involved people will nearly always think of politics as more than a game, in the Netherlands and elsewhere. But this does not mean that

TABLE 1.
Operationalization of Lijphart's Rules of the Game

Lijphart's Rules	Question Formulation
The business of politics (A serious means to a serious end)	No question asked
Agreement to disagree (Accept ideological differences)	Agree/Disagree: It is dangerous to come to a compromise with political opponents, because that commonly leads to betrayal of one's own group. Each Dutch government is formed by an alliance between parties. If a party joins a government, do you think that party should remain faithful to the *main points* of its program, or can it deviate from them?
Summit diplomacy (Government by the elite)	Agree/Disagree: The chosen leaders of a group must have the authority to make decisions or compromises without consulting their supporters.
Proportionality (In allocating values)	Once the opinions of all the involved people have been heard, do you think that the majority has the right to put its position through, or should there still be a compromise with the minority? There is some disagreement these days about the composition of the College of B & W. Some people think that a combination of parties which has a majority in the Council may claim all the aldermen's seats in order to carry out its program (a program college). Others feel that the College of B & W ought to reflect the entire composition of the City Council (a mirror college). Which kind do you prefer?
Depoliticization (To neutralize potentially divisive political disputes)	Do you think that the cabinet should handle matters primarily in a political way, or is it better to treat them as practical, nonpolitical questions?
Secrecy (To insulate decisions from the knowledge of the rank and file)	Agree/Disagree: It is often necessary that political decisions be made in secret.
Government's right to govern (A semi-separation of powers between Cabinet and Parliament)	Do you think that important decisions should be made primarily by the Cabinet, or should the Parliament have the most important say?

Lijphart's first rule is trivial; perhaps the Dutch elite takes politics more seriously than the elite of other countries.[17] The remaining six rules all proved to be amenable to some sort of operational formulation.[18] The rules on summit diplomacy, depoliticization, secrecy, and the government's right to govern can all be translated fairly literally into question form.

The remaining two rules of the game, agreement to disagree and proportionality, are more difficult to phrase in terms of viable survey questions. In both cases the abstract principle behind the rule is an attractive one. Hence, it would be easy for many respondents to profess agreement with the rule and yet be reluctant to apply the rule to their behavior. For this reason, both items were operationalized by an abstract statement of the rule as well as by a concrete example in which the respondent was asked to pick the most desirable course of action.

Actual levels of agreement with the six rules are reported by party in Table 2. In each case, the percentage given is the percentage that endorses the accommodationist side of the question. The most striking result shown in the table is that adherence to Lijphart's rules of the game is a minority stance. The eight indicators obtain an average of 48 percent agreement, and only three of the propositions receive majority support. One of them, the claim that to compromise with others does not involve treachery to one's own group, is surely only a minimal statement of readiness to compromise.

The second interesting result from Table 2 is the amount of variation between parties in their support for the rules of the game. In every indicator of support for the rules except one, the two leftist parties (the Labor party, or PvdA, and the Radical party, the PPR) are clearly more opposed to rules than the more conservative CDA and

TABLE 2.
Agreement on Rules of the Game*

	VVD	CDA	PvdA	PPR	All	Tau-b
Individual compromise	92	91	79	50	84	0.24
Party compromise	50	52	46	13	45	0.16
Let leaders lead	83	67	21	21	56	0.41
Compromise with minority	48	39	42	50	42	0.06
Mirror college best	100	97	21	17	75	0.56
Business-like cabinet best	63	48	00	13	38	0.28
Keep decisions secret	33	35	4	4	26	0.36
Give Cabinet most power	26	20	4	4	17	0.19
Average percent agreement	61.9	56.1	27.1	21.5	47.9	
N	24	94	24	24	166	

*VVD refers to the Liberal party, CDA to the Christian Democrats, PvdA to the Labor party, and PPR to the Radicals.

VVD. Only on the necessity of compromise with a minority faction is the variation between parties too small to produce a significant relationship.

In general, it is clear that Dutch politics today is a game that is played with at least two sets of rules, one for the Left and one for the Right. The set of rules suggested by Lijphart can no longer be considered a general formula by which the Dutch elite governs.[19] The changes in the intervening years have simply been too great. While even the Christian Democratic and Liberal activists are not 100 percent in favor of the rules of the game, their support is clearly much greater than that of the parties of the Left, which have evolved a new set of rules. Lijphart proposed, as the justification of the rules, that the Netherlands would be ungovernable without them; but it is clear that a "democratic critique," championed by the Left, is now encroaching upon that analysis.

Perceptions of Rival Parties

We have seen that local Dutch elites no longer subscribe to a single set of rules of the game. This surely means that the search for compromise is no longer as easy as it was in a time when there was agreement on fundamentals. However, it is possible, though more difficult, for men and women of goodwill to govern together without agreement on a set of procedures for making decisions. The catch is that they must be of goodwill toward each other, for elites who both disagree on basic principles and exhibit mutual hostility will certainly not behave in true consociational fashion. As Eric Nordlinger put it:

> A conflict may be "intense" even when the issue distance separating the conflict groups is relatively short and their goals are not incompatible. For conflict groups are often embroiled in "severe" conflicts because of deep-seated prejudices, long-standing jealousies, invidious beliefs, and emotionally-charged animosities which have little relationship to the distance and incompatibility of the issues themselves.[20]

Thus, we turn now to look at the nature of interparty perceptions among the Dutch local elite.

Figure 1 portrays by means of the thermometer scale the "sympathy" that the different groups have for each other. The rankings in the figure are anything but a surprise. They show that sympathy with a group depends almost entirely on its Left-Right position. Although the two overlap and present little conflict with each other, Left-Right position seems to be more important than subculture in determining one's sympathy for other groups. For example, Labor party activists feel considerably more sympathetic toward the Protestant Trade Union

FIGURE 1.
Sympathies of the Activists

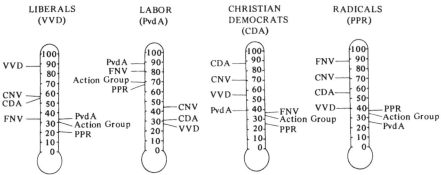

Federation than they do toward the Christian Democratic Appeal. Both are of the same pillar, but the union is more progressive than the party. Although both the Federation of Dutch Trade Unions (FNV) and the Radical party (PPR) contain sizable confessional elements, Christian Democratic activists give them low rankings, as we would expect on the basis of the gap between them on the Left-Right scale. More detailed breakdowns show that even the former Catholic party activists among the Christian Democrats place the Catholic Trade Union Federation (NKV) below the ideologically more moderate Protestant Trade Union Federation (CNV). Thus, relative placement on the Left-Right scale is more important than subcultural ties in determining the sympathies of the party activists.[21]

In order to get more detailed information on affect between subcultures, the activists were asked which of a list of characteristics could be applied to union members, action group activists, Socialists, Catholics, Dutch Reformed, and Reformed people.[22] Certainly in the Netherlands there has been a history of religious prejudice and animosity which, although it never achieved nearly the dimensions of, for example, the race problem in the United States, has still at times not been concealed very well.[23] Even today both Catholics and Protestants exhibit a readiness to characterize the two groups as having distinct personality types.[24] It is worth knowing, then, how much of a distinction the party activists make between different types of Dutchmen.

These questions produced a complex but fairly predictable set of responses. Overall, union members and action group activists were most often characterized as militant, Socialists as progressive, Dutch Reformed and Catholics as open-minded, and Reformed people as rigid. Of course, there are striking variations in these images, depending on which group an individual belongs to. But for our purposes, it is not necessary to present fully the personality profiles reported by the different party activists. It is sufficient to give an idea of how the images of specific groups are related forming a perceptual mapping of the traits of the different groups in society.

To do that, a factor analysis was done on the set of traits for each group mentioned. In each case, a single factor dominated the solution, explaining about 20 percent of the variance. An array of the factor score means by party yields results that strongly suggest that each factor taps positive or negative affect toward the group of people asked about. For example, the Labor party activists have a mean factor score of +.55 for "Socialists," while the CDA and Liberal activists have scores of −.48 and −.51 respectively. Similarly, the religious groups are evaluated very positively by the Christian Democratic activists, negatively by the Labor and Radical party activists, and in a neutral or mildly favorable light by the Liberal party activists. In sum, ideology and partisanship are the cause of negative evaluations of rival elites.

It is clear that local party elites in the Netherlands no longer have the accommodationist attitudes that might be expected of a consociational elite. The Left-Right spectrum dominates confessional or subcultural considerations in feelings of sympathy with various groups, suggesting that political conflict in the Netherlands has become unidimensional. The agreement on basic rules of the game that is so essential to the making of compromises is no longer present. Other analyses of the same interview materials make clear that local party elites also have more polarized issue preferences than the mass supporters of their parties.[25] When all these facts are put together, it is clear that local Dutch elites, far from having a moderating effect on political conflict, actually have attitudes that would tend to exacerbate conflict.

Correlates of Change in the Dutch Elite Political Culture

We have seen that local elites in the Netherlands do not conform to the consociational image of an accommodating leadership. The degree of subcultural integration of the Dutch elite and the consequences of varying levels of subcultural integration for attitudes related to consociational democracy remain to be explored.

Integration in a subculture is a result of encapsulation in a series of subculturally based organizations. In a perfectly segmented society, knowledge of which political party an individual supports should enable an observer to predict with great accuracy which trade union federation, professional organization, church, hobby club, and so on the person belongs to. It should also be possible to deduce what kind of school the person went to and where children of that individual are likely to be sent. It should be possible to guess which newspaper and which radio/television guide the person reads or subscribes to. Indeed, any one of these pieces of information is the key to all the others. Any one of them can serve as a way of summarizing a host of attitudes that given individuals hold about themselves and about society. In the extreme case of mutually exclusive subcultures, a survey of individuals in the society need ask only the question "Which group do you belong to?" in order to receive an implicit answer to every other imaginable question.

Of course, no society is really that simple. Certainly the Netherlands isn't. But there is in the Netherlands a great degree of subcultural segmentation. There remains today a variety of parallel social organizations, each serving the same function for a different clientele. And while the consociational model is of doubtful relevance for the present-day Netherlands, a great amount of change must still take place before the last vestiges of organizational segmentation will have disappeared. This point holds especially for the activists in the various subcultural organizations, including the parties. They are the ones who are most involved in the public life of their subcultures, and they can be expected to hold the subcultures' values most tenaciously.

Integration into a subculture, then, can be broken down into a number of component behaviors: organizational memberships, the use of subculturally aligned mass media, and patterns of friendships and personal interactions. Because these various aspects of subcultural integration are related to each other, and indeed must be related to each other by the very definition of a subculture, they can be combined into an overall index of subcultural integration. Table 3 provides the elements of such an index.

First, it should be noted that these elements of subcultural integration are, on the face of it, very diverse. When answers to a battery of attitudinal items in a survey are indexed, there is usually a clear link between the items, not only conceptually but also in their wording, subject matter, and place in the interview. If this similarity becomes apparent to the respondent, it may lead to response set, which in turn can inflate the intercorrelations of the index components. Such is not the case with this index. The items were scattered throughout the questionnaire and are mostly behavioral in nature (thus less liable to response set). They are, on the face of it, a diverse group of variables, linked only by their relevance to the concept of group integration.

Under these circumstances, the intercorrelations among the items in Table 3 are impressive confirmation that the concept of subculture is meaningful in the study of Dutch party activists. If membership in a party were motivated simply by concern for the goals of the group, then that membership would not be so clearly related to other organizational activities. The correlations in the table suggest that activism in a Dutch political party cannot be viewed as an isolated event, explainable only in terms of the structure of goals of the organization

TABLE 3.
The Index of Subcultural Integration*

Variable Socialization Factors	Scoring	Average Correlation with Other Variables	Correlation with Index
Join due to upbringing?	Yes = 2/No = 0	0.18	0.50
Father's party congruent?	Yes = 2/No = −2	0.20	0.66
Religion congruent?	Yes = 2/No = −2	0.17	0.55
Organizational Factors			
Congruent memberships	+1	0.26	0.60
Neutral memberships	0	0.12	−0.17
Noncongruent memberships	−1	0.21	−0.43
Congruent readerships	+1	0.25	0.54
Neutral readerships	0	0.13	−0.25
Noncongruent readerships	−1	0.23	−0.48

*Multiple mentions of organizations and readerships make the maximum Index score 29 points. Column 3 is the mean of the absolute values of the correlation of each element of the Index with each other element. Absolute values are used because some intercorrelations are expected to be negative—e.g., those between congruent and noncongruent memberships. All correlations run in the expected direction and are based on the non-party as well as party activists (N = 290).

itself, but must instead be seen in the context of a broader subcultural identification. In short, the table demonstrates that a reasonable basis exists for thinking of Dutch party activism in the context of commitment to a broader subculture.

What difference does it make whether parties are based on subcultural cleavages rather than on narrowly political criteria? Activism in a subculturally based party has a political and social significance that goes beyond adherence to a set of issue positions. Subculturally based activism is viewed as an integral part of an individual's life. The political realm is not separated from the personal. Seventy percent of the Christian Democratic and 50 percent of the Labor party activists said that their role in the party was a direct result of their upbringing. They were joined by only 21 percent of the Liberal party activists and 29 percent of the Radical party activists, two parties which did not build their own social subcultures. Ninety percent of the activists in the confessional parties have fathers who supported the same party, compared to less than 50 percent of the Liberals.

Does a tradition of support for a subcultural party, as opposed to being "first generation," mean that a person is likely to be less fully integrated into that subculture? Table 4 explores the question of whether upbringing makes a difference in current participation in

TABLE 4.
Relationship between Father's Party and Current Activity*

Father's Party Is	N	Congruent Broadcast Association	Noncongruent Broadcast Association	Congruent Voluntary Organizations	Noncongruent Voluntary Organizations	Congruent Print Media	Noncongruent Print Media
Congruent	123	0.76	0.05	1.02	0.13	2.45	0.46
Noncongruent	40	0.47	0.17	0.67	0.33	2.15	0.50
Eta²		0.05	0.03	0.03	0.03	0.01	0.00

*Entries are mean numbers of congruent or noncongruent memberships or readships per activist. For example, 0.76 means that when a father's party preference was congruent with the activist's own subculture, the activists had an average of 0.76 congruent broadcast association memberships.

subcultural affairs. The columns of the table display information on several aspects of subcultural integration: membership in broadcast associations, membership in voluntary organizations, and readership of newspapers, news magazines, and other political magazines. Although eta^2 never reaches above 0.05, all but the last two coefficients are significant at the 0.05 level, and each points in the same direction. Individuals raised in the same subculture in which they are now active are more likely to join congruent voluntary organizations and broadcast associations and are more likely to read congruent political materials than are individuals who have become active in a party outside the subculture they were raised in. Similarly, those who have stayed within the same subculture are less likely to have joined noncongruent associations or to read noncongruent materials than are those who have switched subcultures.

This finding suggests the important role of the subcultures in childhood socialization in the Netherlands. Even for individuals now active in subcultures different from those they were brought up in, that activity is not as likely to be part of a broader commitment to participation in the subculture. Perhaps "switchers" see their party activism as a discrete decision not related to identification with the subculture as a whole.

Subcultural commitment (or integration) is also associated with the level of activity in a party. Highly integrated activists are distinctive in a number of ways that go beyond organizational memberships and what they read. The correlations in Table 5 show that party activists who are more integated into their subcultures are also likely to be older and to have been members of the party longer. In addition, subculturally integrated activists generally hold more party of-

TABLE 5.
Correlates of Subcultural Integration*

Correlation of the ISI With	PPR	PvdA	CDA	VVD	All
Age	0.22	0.27	0.21	0.23	0.33
Years as member	−0.05	0.55	0.36	0.14	0.37
Number of functions	−0.04	0.20	0.22	0.31	0.14
Party work (in hours per week)	−0.25	−0.13	−0.10	0.14	−0.21
N	24	24	94	24	166

*Entries are the correlation of the ISI (described in Table 3) with the variables listed in each row. PPR refers to the Radical Party, PvdA to the Labor Party, CDA to the Christian Democrats, and VVD to the Liberals.

fices during the course of their careers in the party. This too is a result of their greater seniority.

The bottom line of the table presents the surprising information that activists who are more integrated into their party's subcultures work fewer hours per week for the party. This is due to the fact that younger activists are less integrated into subcultures yet are likely to devote more time to their party (the correlation between age and number of hours per week is -0.20). In addition, greater integration into the subculture may well mean that personal resources are spread out over a greater number of subcultural organizations, resulting in fewer hours given to the party.

Degree of subcultural integration thus has an ambiguous impact on the amount of activism in a political party. The findings suggest that young activists are less integrated into the party subcultures but are nonetheless likely to spend more time working for their parties. Although it cannot be proven with cross-sectional data, the most plausible explanation for this result is that there is a generational change in the nature of activism in Dutch politics. Among the younger local party elites, activism is not motivated by integration into one of the Dutch subcultures. For them, party loyalty is not as likely to be tied to a broader subcultural loyalty. This helps us understand the more open, competitive nature of the current Dutch party system. However, the question with which this article began is still unanswered: can we see the remains of a consociational attitude, of an autonomous elite political culture, among the local party elite?

Subcultural Integration and System Satisfaction

To understand the implications of consociational democracy for the attitudes of political elites, our attention must be focused on that portion of the local elite which is relatively highly integrated into a subculture. Given the fact that these activists are generally older, we are in a sense analyzing the historical remnant of what was once the dominant theme of the Dutch elite political culture.

One of the most remarkable aspects of consociational democracy is the fact that it requires of elites that they combine an active involvement in a full range of subcultural institutions with a strong commitment to the overarching political system that tries to mediate between those subcultures—this despite the fact that subcultural loyalties, particularly those based on such cleavages as language, ethnicity, and religion, are sometimes thought to be necessarily destructive of national loyalties. Such is the rationale behind campaigns against minority groups in states where nation building is considered to be the primary goal. To use the opinions of the party activists in the Netherlands is to pose an especially stringent test of this theory, since the sample contains those who are most involved in Dutch subcultural politics.

The Dutch activists were asked to report their satisfaction with policy, power, and cooperation in local politics. Their answers are reported in Table 6 in the form of relationships between satisfaction and subcultural integration. Higher levels of satisfaction are associated with higher levels of subcultural integration. Thus, subcultural integration appears to be compatible with high levels of system satisfaction.

These relationships are affected by the fact that the activists in some political parties are more likely to be integrated into a subculture than are others. And, of course, satisfaction with local politics varies strikingly by party. This is partly a matter of partisan control of the municipal government and partly related to the fact that the "democratic critique" of the consociational style of government comes primarily from the left part of the political spectrum. Table 7 shows this effect clearly, using a Democratic Critique Index.[26] Within each of the parties, activists who believe that the rules of the consociational game are wrong are more dissatisfied with national and local politics and even with their country and their city in general.

The Index of Subcultural Integration, on the other hand, has a more nuanced relationship with political satisfaction. For the two parties which formed the core of the pillarized, subcultural system of Dutch government, the Labor party and the (antecedents of) the Christian Democrats, higher subcultural integration implies greater satisfaction with the political system. This is precisely the attitude that is predicted by the consociational model of the Dutch elite. It shows that integration into a subculture and satisfaction with the political system as a whole are compatible with each other.

The Radical and Liberal parties, on the other hand, did not build subcultures which isolated their adherents from other sectors of so-

TABLE 6.
ISI and System Satisfaction*

Index of Subcultural Integration	Municipal Policy	Satisfaction With Distribution of Local Power	Local Political Cooperation
Low	3.9	3.3	4.0
2	3.8	3.4	3.1
3	4.6	4.4	4.0
High	5.1	4.8	4.2
Eta²	0.13	0.16	0.07
N	165	162	164

*Satisfaction items are scored from one (very dissatisfied) to seven (very satisfied). All three eta²'s are significant at the 0.01 level.

TABLE 7.
System Satisfaction, Subcultural Integration, and
Consociational Attitudes

Mean Satisfaction With	Radicals ISI	Radicals DCI	Labor ISI	Labor DCI	Christian Democrats ISI	Christian Democrats DCI	Liberals ISI	Liberals DCI
General items*	−0.08	−0.25	0.89	−0.54	0.26	0.09	−0.19	−0.50
National politics*	−0.06	−0.43	0.77	0.03	0.21	−0.40	−0.20	−0.42
Local politics*	−0.39	−0.37	0.92	−0.26	0.38	−0.08	−0.47	−0.67
N	24		24		94		24	

*Entries are mean differences in satisfaction between those scoring low and those scoring high on the Subcultural Integration and Democratic Critique Indexes within each party. Positive numbers indicate that those scoring higher on the Index are more satisfied; negative numbers mean that they are less satisfied. "General Items" refers to questions about life as a whole and the Netherlands and the local city in general. "National Politics" is the mean satisfaction with policy, democracy, social justice, economic equality, and the distribution of power at the national level. "Local Politics" is the mean of items referring to policy, power, and cooperation at the local level.

ciety.[27] In fact the Radical party, formed in 1968, never participated in the consociational form of government; and it explicitly rejects the idea of a pillarized society. Yet because pillarized forms of social organization do exist in the Netherlands, the Liberal and Radical parties cannot help but make associational and media choices that are interpretable in the context of the subcultures.[28] In these two parties, higher subcultural integration is associated with less satisfaction with the political system, particularly at the local level.

Considering the basis of operation of the Dutch politicial system, in which the established pillars are given every opportunity to deploy themselves fully throughout society, there need be no incompatibility between loyalty to the subculture and loyalty to the nation as a whole. Assuming that each group wants a full share of the society's wealth, power, and other values, but that no group desires to establish hegemony, it is possible for a responsive state to satisfy different groups. This is particularly so of the parties that participate in these arrangements.

In an extremely interesting analysis that makes use of both economic and sociological approaches, Olson has shown that "a society will, other things being equal, be more likely to cohere if people are socialized to have diverse wants with respect to private goods and similar wants with respect to public goods."[29] Olson reasons that differences in taste on individually consumed goods foster cooperative behavior, since all parties will benefit from trade among themselves. To this we might add that diversity in tastes for private goods lessens competition for those goods. If I like brightly colored cloth-

ing, my enjoyment of that good is not at all lessened by your preference for more muted colors. And I'm more likely to find the bright
colors in the store as well.

Collective goods, on the other hand, cannot be varied to suit individual tastes. We must all consume the same amount of defense and
the same constitutional guarantees of free speech. Thus, different
tastes with regard to collective goods are destructive of social cohesion.

The effects of a consociational form of government on producing
system satisfaction under conditions of diverse demands for collective goods can be interpreted in this light. Normally, it would be
expected that conflicts over level of support for religious institutions
or over laws that increase the economic and political power of the
working class would put stress on social unity. The consociational
system, however, privatizes these collective goods by creating parallel social systems. People who want Catholic education get Catholic education. Those who prefer Protestant or secular education are
provided with goods to suit their taste. Thus, the problem of conflicting demands for public goods is defused by meeting all demands on
an equal basis.

In principle, this system of accommodation could be adapted to
meet any set of noncompatible demands for collective goods, except
for those in the realm of defense and foreign policy, where the state
must by definition remain a unitary actor, or in the realm of the rules
for decision making. As we saw in Table 2, it is in the latter sphere
that consensus has broken down, provoking a crisis in which Dutch
consociationalism could no longer meet the variety of demands placed
upon it.

Conclusions

This paper has been concerned with the extent of subcultural integration among local party activists and with their adherence to the
norms associated with consociational democracy. The root of this
concern is the desire to learn more about the relevance of political
parties for the structuring of political conflict and, in particular,
whether consociational attitudes are able to reconcile the tension
between subcultural and system loyalty.

We have seen evidence of both change and continuity in the adherence of Dutch political activists to the various subcultures. The
degree of change can be seen in the lack of agreement on the consociational rules of the game and in the negative images that local party
elites have of rival parties. Lijphart hypothesized that agreement on
such rules was fundamental to the ability of the Dutch political elite
to hold the fragmented society together. But those rules are no longer
at the core of a common elite political culture, and the younger
activists are particularly likely to subscribe to what has been called

the "Democratic Critique" of the consociational form of government. At the same time, the subcultures are still relevant in Dutch society. Nearly all of the activists are more likely to join organizations and to read newspapers that are affiliated with their own subculture than they are to support rival or even neutral institutions. The subcultures still play a role in structuring activism in the parties and other political and social organizations. And, most importantly in terms of verifying one of the central theses of the consociational model, integration into a subculture is perfectly compatible with high system satisfaction among the local activists in the parties which formed the consociational system. Loyalty to the part does not detract from loyalty to the whole. We can still see the remains of what was once an elite political culture autonomous from social forces in the country it governed.

Notes

1. Gaetano Mosca, The Ruling Class, trans. H. D. Kahn (New York: McGraw-Hill, 1939), p. 50.

2. Ibid., p. 53.

3. Ibid., pp. 106–7.

4. James A. Meisel, The Myth of the Ruling Class (Ann Arbor: University of Michigan Press, 1962), p. 4.

5. Arend Lijphart, "Consociational Democracy," World Politics 21 (January 1969), pp. 207–25; and Lijphart, The Politics of Accommodation, 2d ed. (Berkeley: University of California Press, 1975).

6. L. J. Rogier's remarks are quoted here as they appear in Jacob P. Kruijt and Walter Goddijn, "Verzuiling en ontzuiling als sociologisch proces," in Drift en koers: een halve eeuw sociale verandering in Nederland, ed. A. N. J. den Hallander et al. (Assen, the Netherlands: Van Gorcum, 1972), p. 229.

7. Lijphart, The Politics of Accommodation, p. 68. (Emphasis in the original.)

8. Hans Daalder, "Parties and Politics in the Netherlands," Political Studies 3 (July 1974): p. 16.

9. Robert D. Putnam, The Beliefs of Politicians (New Haven: Yale University Press, 1973); and John D. May, "Opinion Structure of Political Parties: The Special Law of Curvilinear Disparity," Political Studies 21 (June 1973), pp. 135–51.

10. Particularly relevant studies of these countries are as follows. On Belgium, Lucien Huyse, Passiviteit, passificatie, en verzuiling in de Belgische politiek (Antwerp: Standaard Wetenschappelijke Uitgeverij, 1970); on Canada, Robert Presthus, Elite Accommodation in Canadian Politics (Cambridge: At the University Press, 1973); on Colombia, R. Albert Berry and Ronald Hellman, The Politics of Compromise: Coalition Government in Colombia (New Brunswick, N.J.: Transaction Books, 1980); and on Lebanon, Michael W. Suleiman, Political Parties in Lebanon (Ithaca, N.Y.: Cornell University Press.

11. Joop van den Berg and H. A. A. Molleman most clearly state the changes (Crisis in de Nederlandse politiek [Alphen a/d Rijn: Samsom,

1974). See also Arend Lijphart, "Kentering in de Nederlandse politiek," *Acta Politica* 4 (April 1969), pp. 231–47; and, for time series data on the decreasing subcultural segmentation in support for the Dutch parties, see Joseph J. Houska, "The Organizational Connection: Elites, Masses, and Elections in Austria and the Netherlande" (Ph.D. diss., Yale University). The sources and consequences of deconfessionalization for the Dutch party system are further discussed in Warren E. Miller and Philip C. Stouthard, "Confessional Attachment and Electoral Behavior in the Netherlands," *European Journal of Political Research* 3 (September 1975), pp. 219–58. Herman Bakvis, *Catholic Power in the Netherlands* (Toronto: McGill-Queen's University Press, 1981) contains a particularly detailed account of the decline of the Catholic People's party.

12. Thomas R. Rochon, "Local Elites and the Structure of Political Conflict: Parties, Unions, and Action Groups in the Netherlands" (Ph.D. diss., University of Michigan, 1980), pp. 19–29.

13. See discussions by Hans Daalder, "The Consociational Democracy Theme," *World Politics* 26 (July 1974), pp. 604–21; and Samuel J. Eldersveld, Jan Kooiman, and Theo van der Tak, *Elite Images of Dutch Politics* (Ann Arbor: University of Michigan Press, 1981).

14. Robert L. Morlan, *Gemeentepolitiek in debat* (Alphen a/d Rijn: Samsom, 1974); and Rochon, "Local Elites and the Structure of Political Conflict," pp. 30–35.

15. The three cities—Breda, Delft, and Ede—range in size from just under 120,000 to just over 80,000. More importantly, Breda is in the southern, predominantly Catholic part of the country; Ede is in the highly Protestant central section; and the balance between Catholic, Protestant, and secular elements in Delft is almost exactly even, closely reflecting the balance in the country as a whole.

The terms "local elites" and "local activists" will be used interchangeably in this paper, defined as "all office holders in the local parties." This includes, then, aldermen from the College of B & W, City Council members, officials in the local party organization, and some former officials who still regularly attend meetings. With one exception, random samples of eight activists in each party in the three cities were drawn from this grouping of party activists. In one case, the local party secretary selected respondents, using a non-random basis. The overall response rate among the party activists was 93 percent.

16. Mosca, *The Ruling Class*, pp. 70–71.

17. Just how seriously politics is taken by the Dutch elite is indicated by the rest of the rules. As Lijphart put it, "All rules discussed so far [rules 1 through 6] are closely related to the first rule or axiom that politics is a serious business. The seventh rule is a direct deduction from this axiom" (*The Politics of Accommodation*, p. 134).

18. Guido Dierickx gives a less comprehensive formulation of Lijphart's rules in terms of survey questions. Dierickx's questions, posed to Members of Parliament in Belgium, focus exclusively on readiness to compromise and the need for secrecy ("Ideological Opposition and Consociational Attitudes in the Belgian Parliament," *Legislative Studies Quarterly* 3 [February 1978], pp. 133–60).

19. Although the respondents in this study are active only at the local level, an examination of national party platforms and statements makes

clear that official policies in the various parties are divided along the same lines.

20. Eric A. Nordlinger, *Conflict Regulation in Divided Societies* (Boston: Harvard Center for International Affairs, Occasional Papers No. 29, January 1972), p. 8.

21. The dominance of the Left-Right or the socioeconomic cleavage may be generally true of elite politics. Arend Lijphart finds that socioeconomic class is far more important than religion in coalition formation, even in countries where religion is more important for mass voting behavior ("Changing Ideological Dimensions of Cabinet Formation" [Paper delivered at the meetings of the American Political Science Association, September 1981]). Lee E. Dutter finds a pattern of inter-bloc sympathies among the Dutch mass public in which religion plays a greater role than is found here among the party activists ("The Netherlands as a Plural Society," *Comparative Political Studies* 10 [January 1978], pp. 555–88).

22. The characteristics suggested were (in their adjectival forms) progressiveness, rigidity, hypocrisy, militancy, trustworthiness, narrowmindedness, tolerance, superficiality, authoritarianism, democracy, and irresponsibility. For each of the groups mentioned, respondents could say which characteristics generally applied, or failed to do so. These traits are similar to those posed to a sample of Dutch adults in 1966, with reference to the religious groups only. At that time, the answers showed an even more differentiated view of the various religions than was found here. L. H. L. Zeegers, G. Dekker, and J. W. M. Peeters have written of the 1966 study (*God in Nederland* [Amsterdam: Van Ditmar, 1967]).

23. For discussions, see Walter Goddijn, *Katholieke minderheid en Protestantse dominant* (Assen: Van Gorcum, 1957); and Jacob P. Kruijt, "Rooms Katholieken en Protestanten in Nederland," *Sociologisch Bulletin* 1 (Spring 1948), pp. 3–29.

24. Northern Protestants told me in the course of my study to expect southern Catholics to be happier, more carefree, and to miss more appointments than they themselves would do because the southern Catholics were less responsible than their northern Protestant countrymen. In the south, the same images are used, expressed in terms that suggest, however, that the Calvinists have the problem of being too serious and somber. Jacob P. Kruijt reported much the same image use (but as virtual gospel) in "Mentaliteitsverschillen in ons volk in verband met godsdienstige verschillen," *Mensch en Maatschappij* 19 (January–February 1943), pp. 1–28. And it was my own experience, by the way, that the southern Catholics *did* miss more appointments.

25. Rochon, "Local Elites and the Structure of Political Conflict," chap. 7.

26. The Democratic Critique Index is an additive index that incorporates dissent from the consociational rules of the game (see Table 1) and several items related to desired changes in the constitutional order. The potential changes in political institutions included in the Index are direct election of the prime minister, election of MPs by district, the formation of party coalitions before elections, abolition of the monarchy, and the popular election of mayors. For details on construction of the Index, see Rochon, "Local Elites and the Structure of Political Conflict," pp. 145–47.

27. The Liberals (though not the Radicals) have a negative mean score on the Index of Subcultural Integration. That means that they are slightly

more likely to join noncongruent organizations, or read noncongruent newspapers, than to remain in their secular subculture.

28. There is an analogy here with race in the United States, which has a greater significance as a cultural phenomenon than as a biological or genetic one (Duane Lockard, "Race Policy," in *Handbook of Political Science*, vol. 6, ed. Fred Greenstein and Nelson Polsby [Reading, Mass.: Addison-Wesley, 1975], pp. 245–48). "Racism, far from being the simple delusion of a bigoted and ignorant minority, is a set of beliefs whose structure arises from the deepest levels in our lives—from the fabric of assumptions we make about the world, ourselves, others, and from the patterns of our fundamental social activities" (Joel Kovel, *White Racism: A Psychohistory* [New York: Pantheon Books, 1970], p. 3). Thus, just as Americans cannot help having a conscious reaction to skin color (be it malevolent, neutral, or benign), so too is it part of the psychology of being Dutch that one is conscious of the pillars, and in particular of the religious groupings.

29. Mancur Olson, "The Relationship between Economics and the Other Social Sciences," in *Politics and the Social Sciences*, ed. S. M. Lipset (New York: Oxford University Press, 1969), p. 151.

Mosca and Moscow: Elite Recruitment in the Soviet Union

Bohdan Harasymiw

"Complete immobility in a human society is an artificial thing, whereas continuous change in ideas, sentiments and customs, which cannot help having its repercussions upon political organization, is natural."[1] These words, penned before the beginning of this century by Gaetano Mosca, seem to serve as the touchstone of many a present-day study and much of the common perception of the problem of political leadership in the Soviet Union. Today in Moscow there is, as one scholar puts it, a "superstability of personnel" among the topmost political elite which cannot help but be severely disrupted by the incumbents' eventual demise. "The gates of the dam have been closed for very long," Seweryn Bialer writes, "and there must be a great deal of pent-up frustration and impatience among the younger members of the elite, a frustration which is mitigated to a large extent by the hopes of advancement which they associate with the expected Brezhnev departure and the passing of the old generation."[2] Change, most of us believe, following Mosca, "is natural"; is lack of change, then, a sign of stability, or of its opposite—instability?

Stability, change, and decay within political systems as well as their ruling classes were processes of major concern to Mosca. There is, he believed, a natural tendency for social change to be transmitted through recruitment, to affect the composition of the ruling class as well as at the same time its stability and the security of its position. "Ruling classes," he wrote, "decline inevitably when they cease to find scope for the capacities through which they rose to power, when they can no longer render the social services which they once rendered, or when the talents and services they render lose in importance in the social environment in which they live."[3] In modern social science terminology we should attribute such decline to a loss of capability, function, and status. But the incumbent political elite is not powerless in the face of its inevitable challenge.[4] In the conflict between officeholders and officeseekers,[5] only when the latter over-whelm the former does a revolution—a displacement of the ruling class, as Mosca called the elite—occur.[6] Otherwise, the rulers may transform themselves by absorbing their challengers. "Nations die," Mosca warned, "when their ruling classes are incapable of reorgan-izing in such a way as to meet the needs of changing times by draw-ing from the lower and deeper strata of society new elements that serve to give them new blood and new life."[7] As he put it, "there is only one way to avoid the death of a state . . . that . . . is to provide for a slow but continuous modification of ruling classes, . . . assimi-lation by them of new elements or moral cohesion that will gradually supplant the old."[8] This "molecular rejuvenation,"[9] then, is Mosca's prescription for meeting the challenge of change, for avoiding an aristocracy's decay (and along with it that of the entire political order), and for ensuring stability.

Needless to say, Mosca has left us no pat theory of elite circulation. The latter term was not even coined by him, but by Pareto. Mosca did, however, leave behind several fundamental assumptions about the distribution of power in society, the importance of which to contemporary social science has only recently been discovered. These go beyond such pedestrian questions as the existence and nature of the political elite, its power base, and its means of maintaining itself in power.[10] They include the very general idea of locating the con-cept "political elite" (today's widely agreed upon equivalent of "rul-ing class") within "powerful explanatory theories" in order to enhance both its meaning and utility.[11] Second, as Alan Zuckerman points out, "Mosca and Pareto . . . shared the view that it is theoretically useful and empirically correct to presume a political stratification of society: most are not involved in political life. It makes sense, there-fore, to develop hypotheses using the variable characteristics of the political activists, those who compete for the control of authoritative decisions."[12] Mosca also implies that rulers are drawn from social classes,[13] but the question of interest to him is not, as we know, the "linear" process of recruitment. It is rather the relationship, the "cir-culation," as we have come to call it, between incumbents and aspi-rants, a term which suggests a "more realistic dynamic" than do current elite studies with their foci on attitudes and representation.[14] He reminds us, in brief, that the rise and fall of elites is a *social* phenomenon.

Today's Soviet Union lends itself well to an exploration of the circulation of the elite. Here is an industrialized country undergoing steady change in social structure, with one central system of politi-cal recruitment and great stability of personnel at the topmost level of the political elite. Can it be said that the recruitment system is indeed a transmitter of social change, and is the Soviet political elite in fact being rejuvenated? What response to social change is appar-ent on the part of either the Soviet leadership or the recruitment

FIGURE 1.
A Model of Political and Elite Recruitment

	Stage: Personnel	THE RECRUITMENT PROCESS				
"Pushing" Factors or Forces		Initial Recruitment "Eligibles"	Recruitment "Activists"	Selection "Political Elite"	Promotion "Power Elite"	"Pulling" Factors or Forces
Individual	Motivation (personality, ambition)					Patronage (sponsorship, connections, friendship)
Social	Occupational role Status					Political role Selectors' preferences
Institutional	Organizational affiliation					Structure of political opportunities

system as a whole? Is there a circulation of the elite in the Soviet Union, and is the political recruitment system as stable as the composition of the top leaders under Brezhnev appears? Such questions are the focus of this paper.

In elite studies the concern is generally more with the composition of the elite and less with the process of recruitment. In the present study I wish to reverse that emphasis. Following numerous suggestions gleaned from the elite studies literature, a rudimentary theoretical framework for this purpose can be constructed as an analytical aid similar to that presented in Figure 1.[15] In it, the process of recruitment is broken down into several stages, the recruits at each of them being given a distinct designation suggestive of their differing degrees of involvement in politics. At the first stage, initial recruitment, a pool of eligibles is drawn from the adult population. Out of these eligibles, in turn, are drawn the activists, those with a part-time involvement in politics. Full-time politicians, members of the political elite, are selected from among activists. Within the political elite we may speak of promotion, eventually into the power elite. A comparison of the proportions of personnel drawn from each preceding stage of political involvement—as opposed to being co-opted altogether from outside this system—would provide a measure of the permeability of political recruitment in the given society.[16]

The framework presented in Figure 1 also suggests that recruitment, as well as being a multi-staged process, must be analyzed on the three levels conventionally employed in sociological analysis: personal, social, and institutional (structural). Within each of these sets of factors, furthermore, a distinction may be made through the successive stages between the attributes of the candidates which push them along and the requirements set by the selectors which pull the candidates. Recruitment and selection will depend on the strengths as well as on the coincidence of these various factors. Such attributes as personal amibiton, social status, and organizational affiliation, for example, will be rewarded with success only if they coincide with or are at least not diametrically opposed to the requirements (preferences) of the selectors in terms of the three levels—personal, social, and institutional. A full-scale theory of political recruitment would state the relationship between the three levels and between the push and pull factors, this should be one of the objectives of further research.

To operationalize this framework is probably simpler in the Soviet context than in many others. We know that there is one central political institution, the Communist Party of the Soviet Union (CPSU), and that its involvement in political and elite recruitment is predominant. The analysis of that latter process, therefore, may be carried out in terms of the framework by equating our previously formulated stages of recruitment with a corresponding number of discrete stages of involvement in the activities of the CPSU (see Figure 2). Thus initial recruitment may be taken to mean the induction of members of the labor force into the probationary stage of candidate member of the CPSU. Candidate members become eligible for full membership after a year's service. Full members of the Party may be considered the pool of eligibles from among whom are recruited the activists. In the Soviet case, the latter may be treated as equivalent to the similarly named party activists (collectively designated as the *aktiv*). They constitute the source of persons selected into the political elite, equivalent for practical purposes with the Party's patronage list, the *nomenklatura*. Promotion beyond this into the power elite may be equated to inscription into the highest-level *nomenklatura*, that handled by the Party's Central Committee in Moscow. The study of Soviet political recruitment is further simplified by the availability of data. Although studies of current holders of elite positions (e.g., Politburo or Central Committee members, or *obkom* secretaries) have utilized data on individuals, systematic and representative samples of categories of personnel corresponding to the above framework which would permit study of the *recruitment process*, are unavailable and unlikely to become otherwise. This means that examination of the role of personality and of personal relationships (notwithstanding the interest shown by scholars in the topic of patron-client relations in the USSR) in political recruitment in the Soviet context is for the time being closed so far as chances of contributing to reliable knowledge of the subject are concerned. So, indeed, is virtually any attempt at individual-level analysis, not only in the area of personality but also in the social and organizational areas as well, excepting perhaps via biographies of the famous, whose lives are reasonably documented. There are, however, aggregate data; not, unfortunately, in terms of personality types or of institutional affiliations antecedent to Communist party membership, but in terms of the social composition of, on the one hand, the Soviet population and labor force and, on the other, the several categories of involvement in the CPSU, from candidate member to full-time party politician (*nomenklaturnyi rabotnik*). These aggregate data, arranged in accordance with the analytical framework proposed earlier, are utilized in this paper to reveal, in admittedly incomplete but nevertheless theoretically significant fashion, the process of political recruitment in the Soviet Union today—theoretically significant because the social aggregates on which we have data are the closest obtainable indicators of social classes and thus of their role in the Soviet political elite's recruitment and its circulation.

This paper focuses on a generally stable period of time in the history of the political system and makes certain assumptions (hy-

FIGURE 2.
Proposed Operationalization of the Model of Political and Elite Recruitment in USSR Context

Initial recruitment	"Eligibles"	"Activists"	"Political Elite"	"Power Elite"
Admission of candidate members of CPSU	Full and candidate members of CPSU	The party *aktiv*, specifically: elected committee members, primary party organization secretaries	Personnel enrolled in the party patronage list, the *nomenklatura*	Personnel listed in CPSU Central Committee *nomenklatura*

potheses) about the operation of the recruitment process. The time period chosen is the post-Stalin era, characterized by the absence of war and purges and by relatively abundant information on the composition of the party as well as fairly regular censuses of the population (for comparative purposes). The principal assumption of the study is that, as in other industrial societies, categories of the population characterized by higher social status will tend to be over-represented in political roles, the more so with increased importance of the role.[17] If the push effect of social status were the only factor active, in other words, we should see clearly what Putnam has called the law of increasing disproportion[18] at work. Naturally, the pull of selectors' preferences and the tendency toward bureaucratization common in all modern organizations will have some influence on which social status categories actually get recruited. These pulling influences will likely be more evident in the later rather than the early stages of political recruitment. Will these push and pull forces be working in tandem or in opposition? In the Soviet case, the latter is more likely. We know that the recruitment system in the USSR is highly structured and relatively impermeable. We also know that selectors often attempt to replicate themselves and that bureaucracy tends to overtake political processes.[19] Add to this the fact that the Soviet Union is an industrial society characterized by a changing social structure with relatively high mobility, and the chances are very good that in political recruitment the social status of a group of aspirants will sooner or later be at odds with the preferences of the selectors. This paper seeks to discover what trends there have been in the transmission of social change through the various stages of political recruitment in the post-Stalin USSR. If social change is not, as expected, being transmitted through the recruitment system, then where are the nodes at which aspirants for elite positions are apparently, in Zartman's language, bunching up?[20] What is the social composition of these aspirants, do they have the rudimentary characteristics of social classes, and are they liable to challenge the incumbents? Is the Soviet Union an example of controlled change in the composition of the political elite (controlled, that is, by the incumbents)? Is controlled change possible? Is the recruitment system in the USSR, then, really as stable as the apparent permanence of its gerontocracy suggests?

Initial Recruitment of Eligibles

Before examining the actual composition of candidates recruited into the Communist party under Khrushchev and Brezhnev, it will be necessary to note certain features of party recruitment policy during these two regimes. Both the overall growth rate of the CPSU and the leaders' expressed preferences in favor of certain social categories have implications for political opportunities. Briefly, Khrushchev's policy emphasized the induction into the party of blue-collar workers and of farmers (both those on the state farms as well as the collective farm peasants or *kolkhozniki*), but apparently encouraged unlimited growth of the organization's membership.[21] Brezhnev, on the other hand, has drastically reduced the party's growth rate to the point where the proportion of Communists in the Soviet adult population is likely to remain stable at just under 10 percent (rather than increasing from 5 to 9 percent, as happened between 1956 and 1970). In absolute numbers, of course, this pool of eligibles aspiring to further political recruitment will steadily become larger; if frustration is to be avoided, elite opportunities will have to be increased. Since policy is opposed to the latter, and since a sharp decline in party growth rate is very likely on Brezhnev's departure (as with both Stalin and Khrushchev), then frustration probably will be unavoidable—for potential and actual eligibles alike.

Brezhnev's policy is also clearer than was Khrushchev's on the desirable social composition of party recruits. It emphasizes that the CPSU is a proletarian party; first priority in choosing candidates must be assigned to "the best" representatives of the blue-collar working class, principally from industry, construction, and transportation.[22] Second priority goes to *kolkhozniki*, except that here, too, selectors are directed to give preference to the more highly skilled, the "leading trades," as they are called (e.g., tractor drivers, machinery and combine operators, and livestock workers, as opposed to milkmaids and laborers).[23] Members of the intelligentsia and other white-collar "employees" (*sluzhashchie*) are given third place. Once again, however, the preference is for those with higher levels of education (and therefore status) such as scientists, engineers and technicians, people employed in the cultural field, and "other specialists of the national economy" (a phrase that means in fact persons with higher or secondary specialized education).[24] According to the Brezhnev party recruitment policy, therefore, the CPSU is to be a mirror (a rose-tinted one, unblemished by the presence of unworthy, "accidental people" [*sluchainye liudi*]) of Soviet society.[25] The aim is to select into the party's ranks "the best of the best," as party literature so often reiterates, persons judged superior by their peers and whose work is crucial to the task of building Communism as defined by the CPSU.

How does the actual composition of party recruits compare with these preferences? Let us look at two classifications, social position and occupation. "Social position" is the Soviet term for one's social origin and is reported in only three categories—worker, collective farm peasant (*kolkhoznik*) and (white-collar) "employee." Very unsatisfactory from an analytical point of view, it is reported in both party as well as census statistics and does give an approximation of the coincidence between social status and selectors' preferences in the recruitment of party candidates. Generally, the rank order of the three social position categories is: "employees," workers, and, finally, peasants. From the mid-1950's to the mid-1970's, the percentage of workers in the annual intake of party candidates does show an increase; correspondingly, the percentages of the other two classes drop. In this sense, the party leaders' preference for persons of worker origin seems to have won out over the latter's social status disadvantage vis-á-vis the white-collar class. At the same time, another way to assess this advantage is by comparing percentages of "worker" recruits with the percentage of "workers" by social origin in the labor force. Such a comparison, for nine of the fifteen constituent union republics of the USSR, yields the following results: large discrepancies in the representation of the three classes are diminishing; but, with one exception, workers are not as well represented among party recruits according to the latest data as are white-collar "employees."[26] "Workers," in other words, are not generally over-represented among party candidates as compared to their share of the labor force, which itself is, of course, changing ("workers" have more children than do "employees"). In this sense, party recruitment policy can be said to have had only a limited impact on the actual composition of recruits.

Indeed, the primary determinant of recruitment, for "workers" and "employees" alike, seems to be education (and hence status) rather than the leaders' preferences. Larger proportions of these two categories are drawn into the party in those republics where the same categories of the labor force are better educated.[27] Ostensibly, therefore, the higher-status class of "employees" appears over time to have lost ground to the lower-status "workers." But this is only true in terms of their respective shares of the annual intake of party recruits. In actuality, the regional variations in these percentages and in the representation ratios are very closely associated with the source groups' levels of education, which suggests that the push of status rather than the pull of selectors' preferences continues to determine initial recruitment into the CPSU, at least in terms of "social position" (i.e., origin).

Occupation provides a more accurate measure of social status than does origin (at any rate, as the Soviets report the latter), and it gives a rather more interesting picture of party recruitment. In the post-Stalin period, as indicated in Table 1, workers have steadily increased their proportion of the annual intake of recruits into the party, peasants and bureaucrats have decreased, and what may loosely be termed the intelligentsia has held its own. In the meantime, of course, the composition of the labor force has altered, with the percentages occupied by manual (blue-collar) workers and intelligent-

TABLE 1.

Candidate Admissions to CPSU by Types of Occupations, Selected
Years, 1952–1976 (in Percent)*

	1952– 1955	1956– 1961	1962– 1965	1966– 1970	1971– 1975	1976
1. Manual workers	28.3	41.1	44.7	52.0	57.6	58.6
2. Collective farm peasants	15.8	22.0	15.0	13.4	11.3	10.6
3. Technical intelligentsia (Engineers and technicians, agricultural specialists, scientists, teachers, physicians, and "other specialists of the national economy"	26.4	23.3	28.2	26.4	24.5	25.1
4. Personnel employed in administration	25.6	12.5	11.1	7.5	5.2	4.3
5. Students	3.9	1.1	1.0	0.7	1.4	1.4

*Source: "KPSS v tsifrakh: (K 60-i godovishchine Velikoi Oktiabr'skoi sotsiatisti-cheskoi revoliutsii)," Partiinaia zhizn' 21 (1977), p. 25.

sia increasing, the percentage of collective farmers decreasing greatly,
and that of bureaucrats and other white-collar employees remaining
steady. When compared to the labor force, therefore, the representation of these four major occupational categories among party candidates, as shown in Table 2, reveals that after two decades of supposedly

TABLE 2.

Representation Ratios for Candidate Admissions to CPSU, by Types
of Occupations, 1956–1976*

	Manual Workers	Collective Farmers	Technical and Scientific Intelligentsia	Functionaries and Other Employees
1956–1961	0.76	0.85	1.97	1.73
1966–1970	0.87	0.87	1.57	1.04
1971	0.95	0.80	1.26	
1972	0.96	0.82	1.20	
1971–1975	0.96	0.82	1.19	
1976	0.97	0.86	1.36	0.59

*Sources: "KPSS v tsifrakh," Partiinaia zhizn' 14 (1973), p. 13; ibid., 10 (1976), p.
14; ibid., no. 21 (1977), p. 25; Narkhoz SSSR 1967, pp. 492 and 648; ibid., 1972,
pp. 407, 504, and 510; ibid., 1975, pp. 441, 532, and 539; and ibid., za 60 let (1977),
pp. 376, 463, 466, and 475. Students excluded.

affirmative action on their behalf, workers and peasants remained under-represented, while the technical intelligentsia retained its over-representation (though to a lesser extent). When social class is defined occupationally, therefore, some positive results of the policy of "proletarianizing" the party are evident over time in the growing percentage of worker candidates. From the point of view of the four broad occupational categories in the labor force on which data are available, however, one's chances of recruitment into the CPSU are still markedly better as a member of the higher status intelligentsia than any other group.

The Eligibles and Their Attributes

Recruitment into the circle of eligibles in the Soviet context should, strictly speaking, be studied by looking at the admission of candidates into full membership of the CPSU. This is not possible, because such data are not available in a comprehensive form; nor is it really necessary since no fewer than nineteen out of every twenty candidates are regularly promoted to full party membership status. Thus, even if the data were available, the candidate-to-full member stage may be considered as not of any great analytical interest or importance. The pool of eligibles, therefore, for purposes of this study is equivalent to the combined candidate plus full membership of the party.[28] Thus defined, the pool of those eligible for recruitment into part- and full-time political roles is a dynamic aggregate, its composition only partially determined by the makeup of the incoming cohorts of candidate members. Its composition is also determined by whatever changes party members themselves undergo; they cannot change their sex, nationality, or social origin (as these features are affected directly by recruitment), but they can and do change place of residence, education, and occupation. The study of the composition of recruits into the party is not, therefore, entirely synonymous with that of party members; nor is studying the composition of party members the same thing as recruitment.[29] In order to appreciate the degree to which change is transmitted through the recruitment system, it is necessary to compare the dynamics of party membership with the dynamics of Soviet society.

There has been a steady transformation of the CPSU since Stalin's day in terms of its members' social position (origin). This change is in favor of "workers" at the expense of peasants and "employees," but it seems recently to be losing momentum. Compared to the class composition of the Soviet population, "employees and others" still had the best chances of belonging to the party, this in spite of two decades' efforts by the leaders to "proletarianize" that organization. These efforts may be counterproductive (see Table 3). The fastest-growing category of the population in the period from 1959 through

TABLE 3.
Average Annual Rates of Growth of Social Origin Categories in
Population and Communist Party, USSR, 1939–1977 (in Percent)

	Workers	Peasants	Employees and Others	Total
		Soviet Population		
1939–1979	+ 2.3	− 1.9	+ 0.9	+ 0.5
1959–1970	+ 2.6	− 2.5	+ 3.0	+ 1.3
1970–1979				+ 0.9
		CPSU Members		
1947–1957	+ 1.6	+ 1.7	+ 2.7	+ 2.2
1957–1967	+ 7.3	+ 4.6	+ 4.3	+ 5.4
1967–1977	+ 3.3	+ 0.7	+ 2.0	+ 2.3

Sources: "KPSS v tsifrakh," Partiinaia zhizn' 21 (1977), p. 28; Narkhoz SSSR 1972,
pp. 16 and 42; Itogi 1970, Vol. 5, pp. 8–9; and Naselenie SSSR 1979, p. 4 (full
citation in n. 32).

1970 was "employees and others"; in the 1967–1977 decade within
the CPSU, on the other hand, it was "workers." It seems likely that
in the very near future there will be increasing pressure for entry
into the party from the white-collar social origin category on grounds
not only of status but also of numbers.

Although adequate data do not exist on the types of occupations
in which Communists are engaged, there is some information on the
sectoral employment of party members which indicates a developing gap between the objectives of recruitment policy under Brezhnev
and the actual composition of the CPSU. One of these objectives is
enhanced representation of Communists in the leading sectors of the
economy (industry, construction, and transportation). The results do
not clearly indicate success.[30] In the twenty years leading to 1977,
the percentage of Communists in industry and construction rose, but
in transport and communications it fell; in the former case it just
managed to keep pace with the corresponding figure for the labor
force, while in the latter it failed. It failed also in three other sectors,
a fact that may be of some significance. These are sectors which have
large contingents of women employed in them and which are noto-
rious for being generally of lower status; this decreasing representation among party members may be indicative of a trend on the part
of Communists to gravitate into the higher status sectors of employment much more easily than does the non-party labor force. This
tendency for sectoral representation in the party to diverge rather
than to converge may have been accelerated by Brezhnev's policy of
reducing the annual growth rate of the CPSU. By comparing the best-
and the least-represented sectors as indicative of the equity of sec-

toral representation, we find that its value was 15 in 1956 through
1958 (7.7 ÷ 0.5), 6.6 in 1971, and nearly 10 in 1977. It seems,
therefore, that one of the costs of suppressing the party's physical
growth has been increased inequity in sectoral representation; and
among those sectors paying this penalty are two if not three of definitely lower relative status. This is a curious way to go about making
the CPSU more proletarian, unless, of course, that term is redefined
to include only industrial workers.

Even in the industrial sector of the economy, however, the percentage of Communists registered no increase between 1965 and
1977, despite Brezhnev's policy emphasizing party representation in
this sector (see Table 4). Ironically, this and other sectors of "material
production," favored over the "non-productive" half of the economy
as a source of recruits, show (with the exception of construction)
growth under Khrushchev and stagnation, generally speaking, under

TABLE 4.
Communist Party Saturation of Sectors of the Civilian Economy,
USSR, 1956, 1965, and 1977 (in Percent)

	1956	1965	1977
1. Administration	66.7	63.4	48.1
2. Industry	9.2	11.3	11.2
3. Science, health, education, culture, and art	9.2	12.3	10.5
4. Agriculture	3.2	8.1	10.2
a. State farms	4.4	9.6	10.2
b. Collective farms	2.4	7.0	9.4
c. Other	9.8	18.2	18.2
5. Transportation	10.2	11.4	9.9
6. Construction	4.7	8.1	9.8
7. Communications	10.7	10.9	9.2
8. Trade, etc.	8.5	8.0	7.7
9. All others	2.8	6.7	3.7
10. All sectors	6.8	10.6	10.7
Absolute Numbers (estimated in thousands)			
a. CPSU (civilian employment)	5,815	10,175	12,964
b. Labor force	85,437	95,544	120,993

Sources: "KPSS v tsifrakh," Partiinaia zhizn' 10 (1965), p. 14, and ibid., 10 (1976),
p. 17; Partiinoe stroitel'stvo (Moscow: Izdatel'stvo politicheskoi literatury, 1970),
pp. 360 and 370; Partiinoe stroitel'stvo, 3d ed. (Moscow: Izdatel'stvo politicheskoi
literatury, 1973), pp. 377 and 389; Partiinoe stroitel'stvo, 5th ed. (Moscow:
Izdatel'stvo politicheskoi literatury, 1978), pp. 329, 360, and 371; Narkhoz SSSR
1959, pp. 583–84 and 588–89; ibid., 1960, p. 473; ibid., 1965, pp. 436, 555, and
558–59; ibid., 1922–1972, pp. 283, 343, and 346–47; and ibid., 1978, pp. 287, 363,
and 366.

Brezhnev. Thus holding the lid on recruitment as Brezhnev has done means keeping at a steady level the percentage of party members, in particular in the decisive economic sectors. This seems incongruent with the intentions of the leader's policies.

Further evidence that the attributes of the eligibles in the Soviet Union are keeping pace neither with Brezhnev's recruitment priorities nor with change in social structure is presented in Table 5. By comparison with growth rates in the labor force, the number of Communists in all but two sectors grew faster under Khrushchev. Under Brezhnev, meanwhile, tne number of Communists grew at a slower rate in six additional sectors, including industry, transportation, and communications. If these trends continue, the party contingent in the leading sectors of the economy will continue to fall, the party's representativeness will be seriously impaired, and pressure for entry into the CPSU from the most rapidly-growing sectors of the economy may develop.

For such pressure to develop, however, there would have to be a significant status inconsistency between the excluded and the included categories; and such an inconsistency is already evident. It is apparent in the divergent directions in the annual rates of growth of the number of persons with higher education in the CPSU as compared with the Soviet population (see Table 6). Since Khrushchev's time, the former has been decelerating; the latter, accelerating. By 1977, the corresponding category of party members was dropping behind that of the population by better than 3 percent per annum. As this process continues, it will narrow the gap in terms of education between party and society and will in all likelihood increase the clamor for entry into the party's ranks of a cohort far better educated than any before.[31]

A larger discrepancy has affected the secondary education category; its growth rate has fallen more than has the higher education group in the party between the 1960's and 1970's. Meanwhile, the corresponding portion of the population is growing at an accelerating rate.[32] Data on specialists according to their specialties and levels of education indicate that, in 1967–1977, of those with higher education only physicians and economists experienced a lower average annual growth rate in the party than in the labor force; of those with secondary education, all except technicians did so.[33] The latter thus appear to be the beneficiaries of the process of recruitment and intra-party occupational mobility; the others with specialized secondary education—agricultural specialists, medical personnel, teachers, and others—the losers. As the composition of the party itself changes (with members upgrading their education, for example, or being moved into administrative positions), it becomes, under conditions of restricted membership growth such as prevail under Brezhnev, an increasingly distorted mirror of Soviet society, a less rather than more proletarian body.

TABLE 5.
Average Annual Rates of Growth of Communist Party and Labor
Force by Sector of the Economy, 1956–1965 and 1965–1977
(in Percent)

	1956–1965			1965–1977		
	Commu-nist Party	Labor Force	Difference	Commu-nist Party	Labor Force	Difference
Administration	+0.0	+0.9	−0.9	+1.5	+3.8	−2.4
Industry	+7.0	+4.5	+2.5	+2.1	+2.1	−0.1
Construction	+15.2	+8.3	+6.9	+5.1	+3.3	+1.7
Transportation	+5.0	+3.7	+1.3	+1.1	+2.4	−1.2
Communications	+5.6	+5.5	+0.2	+2.4	+3.7	−1.3
Agriculture	+6.2	−4.3	+10.5	+1.3	−0.6	+1.9
Sovkhozy	+22.7	+12.5	+10.1	+2.1	+1.5	+0.5
Kolkhozy	+5.0	−6.8	+11.7	+0.5	−2.0	+2.5
Other	−8.6	+10.3	−18.8	+3.3	+3.3	−0.0
Science, health, education, culture, art	+9.7	+6.2	+3.5	+2.1	+3.4	−1.3
Trade	+4.4	+5.1	+0.8	+3.4	+3.6	−0.2
Others	+11.4	+1.4	+10.0	−0.4	+4.6	−5.0
Total	+6.4	+1.3	+5.2	+1.9	+2.0	−0.1

Sources: As in Table 4.

TABLE 6.
Average Annual Rates of Growth of Numbers of Persons with
Higher Education in CPSU and in USSR Population, 1957–1977
(in Percent)

	1 In CPSU	2 In USSR population		Approximate Difference (Column 1 − Column 2)
1957–1961	9.0			
1961–1967	9.4	1959–1970	7.4	+1.4
1967–1971	7.7			
1971–1973	6.7			
1973–1976	5.9	1970–1976	6.3	−0.1
1976–1977	5.3		8.7	−3.4
		1977–1979	8.9	

Sources: "KPSS v tsifrakh," Partiinaia zhizn' 14 (1973), pp. 10 and 16; ibid., 10 (1976), p. 15; ibid., 21 (1977), p. 29; Itogi 1970, vol. 3, p. 358; Narkhoz SSSR 1974, p. 19; and Naselenie SSSR 1979, p. 19.

The Activists

If social status appears to overwhelm the selectors' preferences in the recruitment and composition of the eligibles in Soviet politics, this cannot be said of the "active stratum." Here party members of higher social status (as judged by occupation) are not assured of better representation than Communists of lower status. What sorts of people, then, can count on being pulled up into the ranks of the activists?

One of the most readily accessible sources of data on political activists in the Soviet Union, though it is incomplete, is that on the makeup of primary party organization secretaries and elected primary and middle level party committees. By no means a full inventory of part-time politicians, these positions nonetheless constitute the source of an overwhelming majority of selections into full-time political work and are therefore a convenient and reasonably valid measure.

Social position (origin) is not reported on these party activists; occupation is. This, of course, reduces the possibilities for comparison with earlier stages of recruitment, but it must be accepted as an unavoidable constraint. The data do, however, answer some of our major questions.

Generally, as reported in statistics covering part of the 1970's, manual workers and collective farm peasants have been well represented on party committees by comparison with their share in the CPSU as a whole (see Table 7), and their representation showed a steady increase over the given period of time. Considering their earlier-noted, rather modest representation in the party itself (as compared to that of the labor force), as well as their lower social status compared to white-collar personnel, this must be interpreted as an effective piece of affirmative action on behalf of these blue-collar workers and peasants. Further data going back to 1961 (not shown here) indicate clearly that this practice of favoring workers and peasants as committee members began in the late 1960's; that is, under Brezhnev.[34] Furthermore, they also show that this benefit was secured for them not at the expense either of party/Soviet bureaucrats or enterprise managers (all of them already, in terms of this study, members of the political elite) but rather of technical specialists and personnel in science, education, health, and culture. The latter are precisely the categories we should have expected to be propelled into the activist ranks from the eligibles. But such has not, apparently, been the case. The law of increasing disproportion, to borrow Putnam's phrase again, under which persons of higher status become more over-represented in the upper levels of the political stratification system, stops operating in the Soviet Union for higher status occu-

TABLE 7.
Workers and Peasants (by Occupation) in the CPSU and among
Communist Party Activists, USSR, Selected Years

	1971	1972	1975–1976	1977
1. In CPSU (percent)	30.7	31.3	30.7	31.4
2. In elected posts and committees (percent)				
a. *Obkomy, kraikomy,* union republic CCs, and auditing commissions	27.8	29.3	30.2	30.2
b. *Raikomy, gorkomy, okruzhkomy,* and auditing commissions	35.9	38.9	41.1	41.1
i. Bureaux of above	12.6	12.6	13.4	13.4
c. PPO committees, bureaux, secretaries, and deputy secretaries	30.7	33.3	33.0	32.8
d. Shop committees, bureaux, secretaries, and deputy secretaries	40.6	43.8	43.0	43.1
3. Representation ratios (2 ÷ 1)				
a. *Obkomy, kraikomy,* UR CCs	0.91	0.94	0.98	0.96
b. *Raikomy, gorkomy*	1.17	1.24	1.34	1.31
i. Bureaux	0.40	0.40	0.44	0.42
c. PPO	1.00	1.06	1.07	1.04
d. Shop	1.32	1.40	1.40	1.37

Sources: "KPSS v tsifrakh," *Partiinaia zhizn'* 14 (1973), p. 16, ibid., 10 (1976), pp. 15 and 17; ibid., 21 (1977), pp. 28, 34, and 39; *Partiinoe stroitel'stvo*, 3d ed., pp. 69, 125, and 377; and ibid., 5th ed., pp. 70 and 117.

pational categories on the doorsteps of Communist Party committee rooms.

One respect in which the "law of increasing disproportion" does operate under Brezhnev as it did under Khrushchev is in regard to education, higher (post-secondary) education in particular. The further removed from the ranks of eligibles the activist (committee member) is, the more likely he or she will be to have a higher education. This is easily seen in the data presented in Table 8, although these merely dichotomize the intermediate level committees. The apparently natural progression of percentage of committeemen with higher education hand in hand with administrative level is more clearly evident in the finer gradations offered by the statistics on several republic Communist parties.[35] By the mid-1970's, approximately 80 percent of republic Central Committee members, and about one-half of *gorkom* and *raikom* members, had higher education, compared to one-fifth to one-quarter of rank and file Communists. Also more evident in the republic data is the progressive narrowing

TABLE 8.

Higher Education among Communists and Elected Party Committee
Members, USSR, 1971 and 1976 (in Percent)

| | All Communists | Elected Members of | |
		Raikomy, gorkomy, okruzhkomy	Obkomy, kraikomy, Republic CCs
1971	19.6	44.9	68.3
1976	24.3	49.9	69.3

Sources: "KPSS v tsifrakh," Partiinaia zhizn' 10 (1976), pp. 15 and 21; and V. I. Strukov, KPSS: Nagliadnoe posobie po partiinomu stroitel'stvu (Moscow: Politizdat, 1969), p. 86.

of the gap over time between these latter multitudes and the more select committeemen in terms of education. This is true everywhere except at the lowest level, that of rural raikom. Higher status in terms of occupation may not be a determinant in the selection of political activists, but education certainly is.

This curious twist to the Brezhnev policy of "proletarianizing" the party (and its activist core, too, apparently) has been evident among primary party organization secretaries as well. The prevalence of higher education has not only increased among them but has accelerated at a faster rate than among rank and file party members, as shown in Table 9. In fact, the secretaries were more representative of ordinary members on this particular indicator of education in the bad old inegalitarian days of Stalin than they have been under Brezhnev. Higher education was a more powerful determinant of this particular activist role in the 1970's than it had been in the 1950's. This points to a possibly increasing degree of difficulty for an eligible in making the transition to activist in the Soviet Union: perhaps the stage of greatest frustration has advanced since Stalin's time from the threshold of the former (eligible) to that of the latter (activist).

TABLE 9.
Higher Education among Primary Party Organization Secretaries
and CPSU Membership, USSR, Selected Years

	1947	1957	1967	1977
1. Secretaries (in percent)	8.8	12.5	30.1	49.7
2. CPSU members (in percent)	7.5	11.6	16.5	25.1
3. Ratios (1 ÷ 2)	1.17	1.08	1.82	1.98

Source: "KPSS v tsifrakh," Partiinaia zhizn' 21 (1977), pp. 29 and 40.

Choosing the Soviet Political Elite

According to the party literature, one of the major requirements for selection into the political elite (the CPSU's patronage list or *nomenklatura*) is worker or peasant background, either practical or social. This theme has lasted from the 1920's, when the Soviet party and state apparatuses were first being staffed, right through to the present day.[36] No accurate or comprehensive figures are given, however, for the contingent of workers and peasants actually in *nomenklatura* positions or in the intake cohort of a given year. Whether this type of background is truly a determinant of selection or whether the statements to this effect are merely lip service to the myth of proletarian rule is hard to judge. It may be the latter, for in a number of instances when the percentage of former workers and peasants among party, government, and economic executives is compared with the corresponding category in the party or labor force, it is always less, sometimes by as much as one-half.[37] For the time being, the answer to this question remains obscure.

Whatever the advantages of social and occupational background may be, there is little doubt about the importance of education and of in-house training (the latter especially so for party *apparatchiki*). A person selected for a *nomenklatura* position will usually already have a higher or specialized secondary education or will acquire it in the course of initial assignments. This includes, of course, personnel of blue-collar worker background.[38] From the limited data available (fragmentary figures for four republics covering the period 1953–1976, but not presented here),[39] we may surmise that: (1) higher education is very definitely a determinant of selection into the political elite; (2) the percentage of personnel with higher education varies directly with the administrative level or importance of the given *nomenklatura;* and (3) the gap in higher education separating party members from *nomenklatura* personnel is gradually narrowing over time, just as is that between party members and the labor force. Assuming that Uzbekistan is reasonably typical in this regard, it would appear to be easier for a party activist to become a *nomenklaturnyi rabotnik* than for a rank and file party member to become an activist. If this is true generally in the USSR, it emphasizes the crucial importance of recruitment into the activist role for eventual selection into the political elite.

By way of summing up, a comparison of growth rates of (presumed) *nomenklatura* personnel with party activists and members (Tables 10 and 11) gives some idea of relative overall opportunities between stages of political recruitment and across time. The data, of course, are incomplete, but some general trends are discernible and may not be significantly affected by this incompleteness. In the 1960's (Table 10), there were considerable variations in the average annual

TABLE 10.
Census Civilian Occupational Categories Presumed to be in CPSU
Nomenklatura, USSR, 1959 and 1970

	1959	1970	Average annual growth rate (in percent)
Leaders of organs of state administration and their structural subdivisions	246,534	210,824	−1.4
Leaders of all-union to oblast' level institutions	51,151	52,276	+0.2
Leaders of raion and city level institutions	90,890	70,314	−2.4
Chairman and secretaries of village and settlement Soviet executive committees	104,493	88,234	−1.5
Leaders of party, Komsomol, trade union, and other mass organizations and their subdivisions	145,597	194,960	+2.7
Leaders of all-Union to oblast' level organizations	25,912	24,571	−0.5
Leaders of raion and city level organizations	61,728	74,934	+1.8
Leaders of primary organizations	57,957	95,455	+4.6
Leaders of enterprises (in industry, construction, agriculture, forestry, transportation and communications)	1,694,832	1,977,545	+1.4
Enterprise directors	283,346	300,843	+5.5
Department and sector heads	135,005	392,599	+10.2
Shop and section heads	321,593	581,893	+5.5
Captains of vessels	61,449	82,396	+2.7
State farm directors	8,835	25,571	+10.1
Heads of units within state farms	42,228	53,967	+2.3
Collective farm chairmen	102,768	50,518	−6.7

TABLE 10. (cont.)

	1959	1970	Average annual growth rate (in percent)
Heads of collective farm units	143,097	82,381	−5.1
Brigade leaders	596,511	407,377	−3.5
Chief engineers and specialists	134,650	282,299	+7.0
Chief surgeons and hospital directors	39,176	59,794	+3.9
Directors of scientific and educational establishments	303,172	633,278	+6.9
Directors of scientific establishments	188,276	455,625	+8.4
Directors of educational establishments	114,896	177,653	+4.0
Directors (and others) of publishing enterprises	30,375	39,262	+2.4
Total	2,594,336	3,397,962	+2.5
All "mental workers"	19,345,096	31,445,358	+4.5
All "physical workers"	79,785,116	83,758,718	+0.4
Entire labor force	99,130,212	115,204,076	+1.4

Source: Itogi 1970, vol. 6, pp. 14–23.

TABLE 11.
Average Annual Growth Rates of Communist Party Activists and
Members, and of Labor Force, USSR, 1961–1977 (in Percent)

	1961–1971	1967–1971	1971–1977
1. Activists			
Union republic CC, obkom, and kraikom members	→+2.5	+3.0	+1.0
Okruzhkom, gorkom, and raikom members		+2.8	+1.0
PPO committee and bureau members and secretaries	→+5.1		+1.7
Shop committee and bureau members and secretaries			+5.5
All activists		+4.8	+3.3
2. CPSU members	+4.5	+3.2	+1.8
3. Labor force	+1.4	+1.8	+1.8
	(1959–1970)		(1970–1979)

Sources: "KPSS v tsifrakh," Partiinaia zhizn' 1 (1962), p. 53; ibid., 19 (1967), p. 19;
ibid., 21 (1977), p. 39; Itogi 1970, vol. 6, p. 14; and Naselenie SSSR 1979, p. 31.

growth rates of the various occupational categories assumed to be in the nomenklatura. The greatest increases were experienced by chief engineers and specialists, as well as by directors of scientific establishments. Agricultural and governmental officials, by contrast, underwent a contraction in numbers. The difference between the extremes was a quite considerable ten percentage points. Undoubtedly, opportunities are not uniform within the nomenklatura system, either between administrative levels or economic sectors. Generally, however, the growth rate of nomenklatura positions in the 1959–1970 period was behind the white-collar ("mental workers") occupations as a whole. This indicates a relative difficulty for persons moving to the former from the latter.

The intervening stages of recruitment separate the white-collar employee (or any employed person) from a position in the political elite. Their rates of growth for the 1960's and 1970's are presented in Table 11. This shows quite clearly, to the extent that these rates of growth may be taken as a measure of opportunity, that in the 1960's it was quite easy for a member of the labor force to become a party member (eligible), and easy as well for the latter to become an activist; however, it was more difficult to advance into the elite. In the 1970's, it was still easiest for an eligible to become an activist, more difficult to acquire party membership, and probably also difficult to be selected into the elite. This slackening in the numerical growth of opportunities for eligibles to become activists under Brezhnev, coupled with the reduced turnover among nomenklatura personnel, indicates a very severe restriction of chances for advancement into the political elite. This restriction will undoubtedly be lifted (if only temporarily) in the post-Brezhnev succession. But whether it will redress the apparent imbalance between the numerical growth of opportunities for elite positions in science, industry, and technology, on the one hand, and the earlier noted under-representation of members of the scientific and technical intelligentsia among party activists, on the other, is a moot point. In the meantime, the resultant growing resentment of the nomenklatura system, and calls for its abandonment such as have been made by Andrei Sakharov,[40] can be expected to mount. An open conflict over the elite recruitment system between the incumbent political elite and its challengers—the technical intelligentsia—requires only the organization of the latter into a self-conscious class.

Conclusion

Has there, over the past thirty years, indeed been a circulation of elites within the Soviet political system? Or is this too short a period of time in which to observe a transition of sufficiently significant scope? In other words, does the analysis presented here show the

Soviet recruitment system between 1950 and 1980 as being adaptable to societal change or impervious to it?

As the route to a position in the political elite of the USSR generally leads through the ranks of the Communist party, this study first examined recruitment of candidate members of the CPSU. It found that Brezhnev's efforts to induct a larger proportion of manual workers into the party have, in gross terms, been successful. Yet among the workers so recruited, it is nevertheless those with higher wages and those from the more prestigious occupational sectors of the economy which predominate. Among collective farm peasants, it is also the better skilled who are preferred. Thus the policy of "proletarianizing" the party, as put into effect under Brezhnev, means disproportionately good chances of recruitment of workers and peasants of higher status. Social status has not been displaced as a motor of political mobility, and persons of white-collar occupations are not likely to go unrepresented among the cohorts of party candidates in the foreseeable future. Education, a very reliable indicator of status, remains a very strong determinant of initial recruitment into the CPSU.

Brezhnev's "proletarianizing" policy of recruitment has been accompanied by a sharp reduction in the year-to-year growth rate of the party. The consequence for the latter as a body (the pool of eligibles) has been a paradoxical one. Since recruited members of the party experience mobility, and since for the most part this mobility is in an upward direction, the effect of restricting enrollment has been to produce, on the whole, a less, rather than more, proletarian party. Furthermore, holding the lid on party growth has led to a marked under-representation of the decisive sectors of the economy, science included, in the ranks of the CPSU. Nor is the development of a number of sectors of employment among party members keeping pace with that of the labor force. The result has been a great imbalance in the representation of occupations in the CPSU as compared to the labor force, particularly for those in the latter which are growing most rapidly. This is one important respect in which recruitment is not adapting to change, and a readjustment must sooner or later take place.

The "proletarianization" and slow-growth policy for the CPSU has also had an evident effect in the realm of education. Growth of the category of party members with higher education has noticeably decelerated under Brezhnev, particularly in relation to the same category in the labor force. This produces another imbalance, and more persons with a high education are liable to be clamoring for entry into the CPSU in the 1980's. Mobility will serve to aggravate the situation. The clamor for entry is liable to be even greater, therefore, among those with specialized secondary education. In the 1970's, it was evidently the medical personnel and teachers who were net

losers in the recruitment game among those with secondary education, while technicians were the winners. Depending on how important these losers regarded representation in the CPSU to be, they
might demand a redress of the balance.

In the next stage of recruitment, that of activists, an effective policy of affirmative action on behalf of workers and peasants has op-
erated under Brezhnev. The losers at this stage are evidently the
technical intelligentsia, unless they are co-opted directly into the
elite, thus bypassing this role. Such appeared to be the case in
the 1960's.[41] In the 1970's, however, according to Seweryn Bialer,
the practice of co-optation has declined.[42] The longer-term trend,
therefore, may be the exclusion of the intelligentsia (occupationally
defined, not by education) from activist roles which lead into the
political elite.

The present situation thus is one in which political recruits and
potential elites are, in William Zartman's phrase, bunched up. The
most likely impulse for unclogging this state of affairs, and thus
indeed inducing circulation (in the sense of movement), would be
the succession to Brezhnev. It can be expected that with his demise,
the rate of recruitment into the party will slacken further than had
been the case in the late 1970's. At the same time, there is likely to
be a rapid turnover of elite personnel. This will have a number of
effects, making certain categories of people happy, others frustrated.
The rapid turnover will be a boon to those at that point who are
already among the activists and eligibles, for their promotions to
elite positions will be swift. But it will not initially make a great
change in the composition of the political elite. For one thing, the
educational gap separating activists from the elite is already relatively narrow. For another, it is Brezhnev's proletarians who people
the activist roles. Unless his successors prefer co-optation of members of the technical intelligentsia directly into political elite roles,
the newcomers to the latter are likely to remain as noticeably blue
collar as the present incumbents. The unhappy ones will be the
eligibles and non-Communist members of the labor force, who will
see themselves as entitled to but deprived of access to the activist
and eligible roles. It is likely that these politically deprived groups
will exert pressure for the opening up of opportunities in the party
or for the establishment of new opportunity structures outside the
CPSU.

Notes

1. Gaetano Mosca, The Ruling Class: Elementi di scienza politica, ed.
and rev., with an introduction by Arthur Livingstone, trans. Hannah D.
Kahn (New York: McGraw-Hill, 1939), pp. 461–62.
2. Seweryn Bialer, Stalin's Successors: Leadership, Stability, and Change
in the Soviet Union (Cambridge: At the University Press, 1980), p. 95.
3. Mosca, The Ruling Class, pp. 65–66.

4. Geraint Parry, *Political Elites* (London: George Allen and Unwin, 1969), p. 59; and I. William Zartman, "The Study of Elite Circulation: Who's on First and What's He Doing There? Review Article," *Comparative Politics* 6 (April 1974), 487.

5. Zartman, "The Study of Elite Circulation," p. 487; and Suzanne Keller, *Beyond the Ruling Class: Strategic Elites in Modern Society* (New York: Random House, 1963), p. 11.

6. Mosca, p. 425; and Parry, pp. 58–59.

7. Mosca, p. 460.

8. Ibid., p. 462.

9. Parry, *Political Elites*, p. 59.

10. This is the essence of the summary of Mosca's contribution to political science given in James A. Bill and Robert L. Hardgrave, *Comparative Politics: The Quest for Theory* (Columbus, Ohio: Charles E. Merrill, 1973), pp. 156–57.

11. Alan Zuckerman, "The Concept 'Political Elite': Lessons from Mosca and Pareto," *Journal of Politics* 39 (1977), pp. 335–42.

12. Ibid., p. 342. For a discussion of political stratification, see Robert D. Putnam, *The Comparative Study of Political Elites* (Englewood Cliffs, N.J.: Prentice-Hall, 1976), pp. 8–15.

13. Mosca, *The Ruling Class*, pp. 65–66, 390–91, and 460.

14. Zartman, "Study of Elite Circulation," p. 487.

15. The source of the figure, as well as of the generalizations in this and the next two paragraphs is Bohdan Harasymiw, "A Framework for the Analysis of Soviet Political and Elite Recruitment" (Paper presented at the Fifty-third Annual Meeting of the Canadian Political Science Association, Halifax, Nova Scotia, 27 May 1981).

16. On the concept of permeability, see Putnam, *The Comparative Study of Political Elites*, pp. 47–49.

17. Ibid., pp. 21–26.

18. Ibid., pp. 33–36.

19. Ibid., p. 57; and Joseph LaPalombara, *Politics within Nations* (Englewood Cliffs, N.J.: Prentice-Hall, 1974), pp. 488, 547.

20. Zartman, "Toward a Theory of Elite Circulation," in *Elites in the Middle East*, ed. I. William Zartman (New York: Praeger, 1980), p. 95.

21. "Part I: Party Membership," in U.S. Central Intelligence Agency, *The CPSU Under Brezhnev: Research Aid* (15 April 1976), pp. 1–3.

22. P. Neshcheretnii, "Chlenstvo v partii, povyshenie zvaniia kommunista," *Partiinaia zhizn'* 4 (1980), pp. 22–23; I. Iudin, "Sotsial'naia baza rosta i kurepleniia sostava KPSS," ibid., 11 (1978), pp. 30–31; "Individual'nyi otbor v partiiu i rabota s molodymi kommunistami," ibid., 19 (1978), p. 55; T. Usubaliev, "Leninskoi partii—dostoinoe popolnenie," *Kommunist* 9 (1980), pp. 27–28; and the Central Committee decree of 28 September 1976, "O rabote partiinykh organizatsii Kirgizii po priemu v partiiu i vospitaniiu kandidatov v chleny KPSS," in *Spravochnik partiinogo rabotnika*, Vypusk 17 (Moscow: Politizdat, 1977), p. 359.

23. Neshcheretnii, "Chlenstvo v partii, povyshenie zvaniia kommunista," p. 23; and Iudin, "Sotsial'naia baza rosta i ukrepleniia sostava KPSS," p. 32.

24. Neshchevetnii, "Chlenstvo v partii, povyshenie zvaniia kommunista," p. 23.

290 DOES WHO GOVERNS MATTER?

25. Iudin, *Sotsial'naia baza rosta KPSS* (Moscow: Izdatel'stvo politicheskoi literatury, 1973), pp. 271–73. The phrase "sluchainye liudi" appeared in "O rabote partiinykh organizatsii Kirgizii po priemu v partiiu i vospitaniiu kandidatov v chleny KPSS," p. 358.

26. The data are not reproduced here, but they are available from the author.

27. Educational levels are given in *Itogi Vsesoiuznoi perepisi naseleniia 1970 goda*, 7 vols. (Moscow: "Statistika," 1972–1974), vol. 5: *Raspredelenie naseleniia SSSR, soiuznykh i avtonomnykh respublik, kraev i oblastei po obshchestvennym gruppam, istochnikam sredstv sushchestvovaniia i otrasliam narodnogo khoziaistva* (1973), pp. 66–85 (cited hereafter as *Itogi 1970*).

28. On 1 July 1977 there were in the CPSU 15,545,097 full and 658,349 candidate members, for a grand total of 16,203,446 ("KPSS v tsifrakh," *Partiinaia zhizn'* 21 [1977], p. 21).

29. Yet countless works by Sovietologists have treated analysis of the characteristics of party membership as in fact the study of recruitment. One such recent effort is Mary McAuley, "Party Recruitment and the Nationalities in the USSR: A Study in Centre-Republican Relationships," *British Journal of Political Science* 10 (October 1980), pp. 461–87.

30. These data, though not shown here, are available from the author.

31. Jerry F. Hough and Merle Fainsod, *How the Soviet Union Is Governed* (Cambridge, Mass., and London: Harvard University Press, 1979), p. 347.

32. "KPSS v tsifrakh" (1977), pp. 29–30; *Narodnoe khoziaistvo SSR v 1970* (Moscow: "Statistika," 1971), pp. 23–24 (cited hereafter as *Narkhoz SSSR [year]*); and *Naselenie SSSR: Po dannym Vsesoiuznoi perepisi naseleniia 1979 goda* (Moscow: Izdatel'stvo politicheskoi literatury, 1980), p. 19 (cited hereafter as *Naselenie SSSR 1979*).

33. *Narkhoz SSSR 1968*, p. 559; *Narkhoz SSSR 1977*, p. 393; and "KPSS v tsifrakh" (1977), p. 30.

34. "KPSS v tsifrakh," *Partiinaia zhizn'*, no. 1 (1962), pp. 48, 50, and 53; ibid., 10 (1965), pp. 11, 14, and 17; ibid., no. 19 (1967), pp. 13,17, and 19; ibid., 14 (1973), pp. 16 and 24; ibid. 10 (1976), pp. 15, 17, and 21; *Partiinoe stroitel'stvo*, 3d ed. (Moscow: Izdatel'stvo politicheskoi literatury, 1973), pp. 69, 111, and 377; and V. I. Strukov, comp., *KPSS: Nagliadnoe posobie po partiinomu stroitel'stvu* (Moscow: Politizdat, 1969), pp. 11, 69, and 107.

35. *Kommunisticheskaia partiia Belorussii v tsifrakh, 1918–1978* (Minsk: "Belarus'," 1978); *Kompartiia Kazakhstana za 50 let (1921–1971 gg.): Rost i regulirovanie sostava partiinoi organizatsii respubliki* (Alma-Ata: Izdatel'stvo "Kazakhstan," 1972); *Komunistychna partiia Ukrainy: Naochnyi posibnyk z partiinoho budivnytstva* (Kiev: Politvydav Ukrainy, 1972); *Kommunisticheskaia partiia Turkestana i Uzbekistana v tsifrakh (Sbornik statisticheskikh materialov), 1918–1967 gg.* (Tashkent: Izdatel'stvo "Uzbekistan," 1968); and "Kompartiia Uzbekistana v tsifrakh," *Partiinaia zhizn'* (Tashkent) 9 (1976), pp. 10–22.

36. For an account of the promotion of workers to positions of responsibility in governmental administration in the interwar years, see *Rabochii klass v upravlenii gosudarstvom (1926–1937 gg.)* (Moscow: Izdatal'stvo "Mysl'," 1968). In the aftermath of World War II, for example, the Latvian

HARASYMIW 291

party Central Committee is reported to have given first priority in promoting people to leading positions (i.e., in the *nomenklatura*) to "urban workers and the rural poor who had displayed their devotion to the Communist Party by their participation in the armed struggle against the Hitlerites and their lackeys, and in the building of socialism following the liberation of Latvia from the German fascist invaders." O. K. Rozhdestvenskii, "Deiatel'nost' Kommunisticheskoi partii Latvii po podboru, rasstanovke i vospitaniiu rukovodiashchikh sovetskikh i khoziaistvennykh kadrov (1945–1958 gg.)" (Précis of a dissertation presented for a degree of Candidate of Historical Sciences, Riga, 1971), p. 9. For more recent illustrations of this same emphasis on workers and peasants, see the sources cited in the following note.
    37. See, for instance, B. Krasnikov, "I doverie, i trebovatel'nost'," *Partiinaia zhizn'* (Tashkent) 8 (1972), pp. 47–48; S. V. Kozlov, "Kadry partii i gosudarstva," in *Pod leninskim znamenem sotsialisti-cheskogo internatsionalizma* (Baku: Azerbaidzhanskoe gosudarstvennoe izdatel-stvo, 1972), p. 96; N. A. Veselov, *Partiinyi kontrol' v rabote s kadrami* (Moscow: Izdatel'stvo politicheskoi literatury, 1975), p. 9; Sh. R. Rashidov, "O dal'neishem sovershenstvovanii raboty s kadrami v svete reshenii XXIV s"ezda KPSS," *Partiinaia zhizn'* (Tashkent) 3 (1973), p. 38; A. K. Zitmanis, "O praktike raboty Rizhskoi gorodskoi partiinoi organizatsii po podboru, rasstanovke i vospitaniiu rukovodiashchikh kadrov," in *Reshaiushchee zveno partiinogo rukovodstva: Iz opyta Rizhskoi gorodskoi partiinoi organizatsii po podboru, rasstanovke i vospitaniiu kadrov* (Riga: Izdatel'stvo "Liesma," 1973), p. 32; T. Kasymzhanov, "Rekomenduetsia na dolzhnost'," *Partiinaia zhizn' Kazakhstana* 7 (1975), p. 24; and Ermolovich, "Rekomenduetsia iz rezerva," ibid. 1 (1978), p. 14.
    38. K. Golovko, *Rabotu s kadrami-na uroven' trebovanii XXIV s"ezda KPSS* (Kiev: Izdatel'stvo politicheskoi literatury, 1973), pp. 22–23; and A. Chepel', "Bol'she vnimaniia kadram srednego zvena," *Partiinaia zhizn'* 9 (1977), p. 46.
    39. *Ocherki istorii Kommunisticheskoi partii Moldavii*, 2d. ed. (Kishinev: "Kartia Moldoveniaske," 1968), p. 403; *Rost i organizatsionnoe ukreplenie Kommunisticheskoi partii Moldavii, 1924–1974: Sbornik dokumentov i materialov*, ed. N. K. Bibileishvili et al. (Kishinev: Izdatel'stvo "Shtiintsa," 1976), pp. 236, 343, and 349; *Kommunist Moldavii* 2 (1962), p. 11; 8 (1965), p. 35; 10 (1966), p. 13; and 2 (1976), p. 60; M. M. Matviichuk, *Orhanizators'ka robota partii u promyslovosti Ukrainy (1952–1958 rr.)* (Kiev: Vydavnytstvo Kyivs'koho universytetu, 1966), pp. 30, 45; *Rost i regulirovanie sostava Kommunisticheskoi partii Kirgizii (1918–1962 gg.): sbornik dokumentov i materialov* (Frunze: Kirgizskoe knizhnoe izdatel'stvo, 1963), pp. 224, 231, and 255; I. Rakhmankulov, "Iz opyta organizatsii politicheskoi in ekonomicheskoi ucheby rukovodiashchikh kadrov," in *Ideinaia zakalka rukovodiashchikh kadrov* (Tashkent: Izdatel'stvo "Uzbekistan," 1974), p. 17; "Kompartiia Uzbekistana v tsifrakh," *Partiinaia zhizn'* (Tashkent) 9 (1974), p. 45; "Kompartiia Uzbekistana v tsifrakh," ibid., 9 (1976), p. 13.
    40. Andrei D. Sakharov, *Sakharov Speaks*, ed. Harrison Salisbury (London: Collins and Harvill Press, 1974), pp. 145–46.
    41. Frederic J. Fleron, "Co-optation as a Mechanism of Adaptation to Change," *Polity* 2 (1969), pp. 190–94; and his "Toward a Reconceptuali-

zation of Political Change in the Soviet Union: The Political Leadership System," *Comparative Politics* 1 (1969), pp. 228–44; and, again by Fleron, "System Attributes and Career Attributes: The Soviet Political Leadership System, 1952 to 1965," in Carl Beck, Frederic J. Fleron, Milton Lodge, Derek J. Waller, William A. Welsh, and M. George Zaninovich, *Comparative Communist Political Leadership*, (New York: David McKay, 1973), pp. 66–77.

42. *Stalin's Successors*, pp. 117–20.

Lightning Source UK Ltd.
Milton Keynes UK
UKHW040029300919
350631UK00012B/56/P

9 780875 805290